VINCENT
Gold Portfolio
1945-1980

Compiled by
R.M.Clarke

ISBN 1 85520 3863

BROOKLANDS BOOKS LTD.
P.O. BOX 146, COBHAM,
SURREY, KT11 1LG. UK

A -VINBGP

Brooklands Books

MOTORING

BROOKLANDS ROAD TEST SERIES

Abarth Gold Portfolio 1950-1971
AC Ace & Aceca 1953-1983
Alfa Romeo Giulietta Gold Portfolio 1954-1965
Alfa Romeo Giulia Coupés 1963-1976
Alfa Romeo Giulia Coupés Gold Port. 1963-1976
Alfa Romeo Spider 1966-1990
Alfa Romeo Spider Gold Portfolio 1966-1991
Alfa Romeo Alfasud 1972-1984
Alfa Romeo Alfetta Gold Portfolio 1972-1987
Alfa Romeo Alfetta GTV6 1980-1986
Allard Gold Portfolio 1937-1959
Alvis Gold Portfolio 1919-1967
AMX & Javelin Muscle Portfolio 1968-1974
Armstrong Siddeley Gold Portfolio 1945-1960
Aston Martin Gold Portfolio 1948-1971
Aston Martin Gold Portfolio 1972-1985
Aston Martin Gold Portfolio 1985-1995
Audi Quattro Gold Portfolio 1980-1991
Austin A30 & A35 1951-1962
Austin Healey 100 & 100/6 Gold Port. 1952-1959
Austin Healey 3000 Gold Portfolio 1959-1967
Austin Healey Sprite Gold Portfolio 1958-1971
Barracuda Muscle Portfolio 1964-1974
BMW 1600 Collection No.1 1966-1981
BMW 2002 Gold Portfolio 1968-1976
BMW 316, 318, 320 (4 cyl.) Gold Port. 1975-1990
BMW 320, 323, 325 (6 cyl.) Gold Port. 1977-1990
BMW M Series Performance Portfolio 1976-1993
BMW 5 Series Gold Portfolio 1981-1987
BMW 6 Series Gold Portfolio 1976-1989
Bricklin Gold Portfolio 1974-1975
Bristol Cars Gold Portfolio 1946-1992
Buick Automobiles 1947-1960
Buick Muscle Cars 1965-1970
Cadillac Allanté 1986-1993
Cadillac Automobiles 1949-1959
Cadillac Automobiles 1960-1969
Caprice 1965-1976 ☆ Limited Edition
Charger Muscle Portfolio 1966-1974
Checker ☆ Limited Edition
Chevrolet 1955-1957
Impala & SS Muscle Portfolio 1958-1972
Chevrolet Corvair 1959-1969
Chevy II & Nova SS Muscle Portfolio 1962-1974
Chevy El Camino & SS 1959-1987
Chevelle & SS Muscle Portfolio 1964-1972
Chevrolet Muscle Cars 1966-1971
Chevy Blazer 1969-1981
Chevrolet Corvette Gold Portfolio 1953-1962
Chevrolet Corvette Sting Ray Gold Port. 1963-1967
Chevrolet Corvette Gold Portfolio 1968-1977
High Performance Corvettes 1983-1989
Camaro Muscle Portfolio 1967-1973
Chevrolet Camaro & Z28 1973-1981
High Performance Camaros 1982-1988
Chrysler 300 Gold Portfolio 1955-1970
Chrysler Valiant 1960-1962
Citroen Traction Avant Gold Portfolio 1934-1957
Citroen 2CV Gold Portfolio 1948-1989
Citroen DS & ID 1955-1975
Citroen DS & ID Gold Portfolio 1955-1975
Citroen SM 1970-1975
Cobras & Replicas 1962-1983
Shelby Cobra Gold Portfolio 1962-1969
Cobras & Cobra Replicas Gold Portfolio 1962-1989
Cunningham Automobiles 1951-1955
Daimler SP250 Sports & V-8 250 Saloon Gold P. 1959-1969
Datsun Roadsters 1962-1971
Datsun 240Z 1970-1973
Datsun 280Z & ZX 1975-1983
DeLorean Gold Portfolio 1977-1995
Dodge Muscle Cars 1967-1970
Dodge Viper on the Road
Edsel 1957-1960 ☆ Limited Edition
ERA Gold Portfolio 1934-1994
Excalibur Collection No.1 1952-1981
Facel Vega 1954-1964
Ferrari 1947-1957 ☆ Limited Edition
Ferrari 1958-1963 ☆ Limited Edition
Ferrari Dino 1965-1974
Ferrari Dino 308 & Mondial Gold Portfolio1974-1985
Ferrari 328 • 348 • Mondial Gold Portfolio 1986-1994
Fiat 500 Gold Portfolio 1936-1972
Fiat 600 & 850 Gold Portfolio 1955-1972
Fiat Pininfarina 124 & 2000 Spider 1968-1985
Fiat X1/9 Gold Portfolio1973-1989
Fiat Abarth Performance Portfolio 1972-1987
Ford Consul, Zephyr, Zodiac Mk.I & II 1950-1962
Ford Zephyr, Zodiac, Executive, Mk.III & Mk.IV 1962-1971
Ford Cortina 1600E & GT 1967-1970
High Performance Capris Gold Portfolio 1969-1987
Capri Muscle Portfolio 1974-1987
High Performance Fiestas 1979-1991
High Performance Escorts Mk.I 1968-1974
High Performance Escorts Mk.II 1975-1980
High Performance Escorts 1980-1985
High Performance Escorts 1985-1990
High Performance Sierras & Merkurs
Gold Portfolio 1983-1990
Ford Automobiles 1949-1959
Ford Fairlane 1955-1970
Ford Ranchero 1957-1959
Ford Thunderbird 1955-1957
Ford Thunderbird 1958-1963
Ford GT40 Gold Portfolio 1964-1987
Ford Bronco 1966-1977
Ford Bronco 1978-1988
Goggomobil ☆ Limited Edition
Holden 1948-1962
Honda CRX 1983-1987
Imperial 1955-1970 ☆ Limited Edition
International Scout Gold Portfolio 1961-1980
Isetta Gold Portfolio 1953-1964
Iso & Bizzarrini Gold Portfolio 1962-1974
Kaiser • Frazer 1946-1955 ☆ Limited Edition
Jaguar and SS Gold Portfolio 1931-1951
Jaguar XK120, 140, 150 Gold Port. 1948-1960
Jaguar Mk.VII, VIII, IX, X, 420 Gold Port. 1950-1970
Jaguar Mk.1 & Mk.2 Gold Portfolio 1959-1969
Jaguar E-Type Gold Portfolio 1961-1971
Jaguar E-Type V-12 1971-1975
Jaguar S-Type & 420 ☆ Limited Edition
Jaguar XJ12, XJ5.3, V12 Gold Portfolio 1972-1990
Jaguar XJ6 Series I & II Gold Portfolio 1968-1979
Jaguar XJ6 Series III Perf. Portfolio 1979-1986
Jaguar XJ6 Gold Portfolio 1986-1994
Jaguar XJS Gold Portfolio 1975-1988
Jaguar XJS Gold Portfolio 1988-1995
Jeep CJ5 & CJ6 1960-1976
Jeep CJ5 & CJ7 1976-1986
Jensen Interceptor Gold Portfolio 1966-1986
Jensen Healey 1972-1976
Lagonda Gold Portfolio 1919-1964
Lancia Aurelia & Flaminia Gold Portfolio 1950-1970
Lancia Fulvia Gold Portfolio 1963-1976
Lancia Beta Gold Portfolio 1972-1984
Lancia Delta Gold Portfolio 1979-1994
Lancia Stratos 1972-1985
Land Rover Series I 1948-1958
Land Rover Series II & IIa 1958-1971
Land Rover Series III 1971-1985
Land Rover 90 110 Defender Gold Portfolio 1983-1994
Land Rover Discovery 1989-1994
Land Rover Story Part One 1948-1971
Lincoln Gold Portfolio 1949-1960
Lincoln Continental 1961-1969
Lincoln Continental 1969-1976
Lotus Sports Racers Gold Portfolio 1953-1965
Lotus Seven Gold Portfolio 1957-1974
Lotus Caterham Seven Gold Portfolio 1974-1995
Lotus Elan Gold Portfolio 1962-1974
Lotus Elan Collection No. 2 1963-1972
Lotus Elan & SE 1989-1992
Lotus Europa Gold Portfolio 1966-1975
Lotus Elite & Eclat 1974-1982
Lotus Turbo Esprit 1980-1986
Maserati 1965-1970
Matra 1965-1983 ☆ Limited Edition
Mazda Miata MX-5 Performance Portfolio 1989-1996
Mazda RX-7 Gold Portfolio 1978-1991
Mercedes 190 & 300 SL 1954-1963
Mercedes G Wagen 1981-1994
Mercedes S & 600 1965-1972
Mercedes S Class 1972-1979
Mercedes 230 • 250 • 280SL Gold Portfolio 1963-1971
Mercedes SLs & SLCs Gold Portfolio 1971-1989
Mercedes SLs Performance Portfolio 1989-1994
Mercury Muscle Cars 1966-1971
Messerschmitt Gold Portfolio 1954-1964
MG Gold Portfolio 1929-1939
MG TA & TC Gold Portfolio 1936-1949
MG TD & TF Gold Portfolio 1949-1955
MGA & Twin Cam Gold Portfolio 1955-1962
MG Midget Gold Portfolio 1961-1979
MGB Roadsters 1962-1980
MGB MGC & V8 Gold Portfolio 1962-1980
MGB GT 1965-1980
MGC & MGB GT V8 ☆ Limited Edition
MG Y-Type & Magnette ZA/ZB ☆ Limited Edition
Mini Gold Portfolio 1959-1969
Mini Gold Portfolio 1969-1980
Mini Gold Portfolio 1981-1997
High Performance Minis Gold Portfolio 1960-1973
Mini Cooper Gold Portfolio 1961-1971
Mini Moke Gold Portfolio 1964-1994
Morgan Three-Wheeler Gold Portfolio 1910-1952
Morgan Plus 4 & Four 4 Gold Portfolio 1936-1967
Morgan Cars 1960-1970
Morgan Cars Gold Portfolio 1968-1989
Morris Minor Collection No. 1 1948-1980
Shelby Mustang Muscle Portfolio 1965-1970
High Performance Mustang IIs 1974-1978
High Performance Mustangs 1982-1988
Nash & Nash-Healey 1949-1957 ☆ Limited Edition
Nash-Austin Metropolitan Gold Portfolio 1954-1962
Oldsmobile Automobiles 1955-1963
Oldsmobile Toronado 1966-1978
Opel GT Gold Portfolio 1968-1973
Opel Manta 1970-1975 ☆ Limited Edition
Packard Gold Portfolio 1946-1958
Pantera Gold Portfolio 1970-1989
Panther Gold Portfolio 1972-1990
Pontiac Tempest & GTO 1961-1965
Firebird & Trans-Am Muscle Portfolio 1973-1981
High Performance Firebirds 1982-1988
Pontiac Fiero 1984-1988
Porsche 356 Gold Portfolio 1953-1965
Porsche 911 1965-1969
Porsche 911 1970-1972
Porsche 911 1973-1977
Porsche 911 SC & Turbo Gold Portfolio 1978-1983
Porsche 911 Carrera & Turbo Gold Port. 1984-1989
Porsche 924 Gold Portfolio 1975-1988
Porsche 928 Performance Portfolio 1977-1994
Porsche 944 Gold Portfolio 1981-1991
Range Rover Gold Portfolio 1970-1985
Range Rover Gold Portfolio 1986-1995
Reliant Scimitar 1964-1986
Renault Alpine Gold Portfolio 1958-1994
Riley Gold Portfolio 1924-1939
Rolls Royce Silver Cloud & Bentley 'S' Series
Gold Portfolio 1955-1965
Rolls Royce Silver Shadow Gold Port. 1965-1980
Rolls Royce & Bentley Gold Port. 1980-1989
Rover P4 1949-1959
Rover P4 1955-1964
Rover 3 & 3.5 Litre Gold Portfolio 1958-1973
Rover 2000 & 2200 1963-1977
Rover 3500 & Vitesse 1976-1986
Saab Sonett Collection No.1 1966-1974
Saab Turbo 1976-1983
Studebaker Gold Portfolio 1947-1966
Studebaker Hawks & Larks 1956-1963
Avanti 1962-1990
Sunbeam Tiger & Alpine Gold Portfolio 1959-1967
Triumph Dolomite Sprint ☆ Limited Edition
Triumph TR2 & TR3 Gold Portfolio 1952-1961
Triumph TR4, TR5, TR250 1961-1968
Triumph TR6 Gold Portfolio 1969-1976
Triumph TR7 & TR8 Gold Portfolio 1975-1982
Triumph Herald 1959-1971
Triumph Vitesse 1962-1971
Triumph Spitfire Gold Portfolio 1962-1980
Triumph 2000, 2.5, 2500 1963-1977
Triumph GT6 Gold Portfolio 1966-1974
Triumph Stag Gold Portfolio 1970-1977
TVR Gold Portfolio 1959-1986
TVR Performance Portfolio 1986-1994
VW Beetle Gold Portfolio 1935-1967
VW Beetle Gold Portfolio 1968-1991
VW Beetle Collection No.1 1970-1982
VW Karmann Ghia 1955-1982
VW Bus, Camper, Van 1954-1967
VW Bus, Camper, Van 1968-1979
VW Bus, Camper, Van 1979-1989
VW Scirocco 1974-1981
VW Golf GTI 1976-1986
Volvo PV444 & PV544 1945-1965
Volvo Amazon-120 Gold Portfolio 1956-1970
Volvo 1800 Gold Portfolio 1960-1973
Volvo 140 & 160 Series Gold Portfolio 1966-1975
Westfield ☆ Limited Edition

Forty Years of Selling Volvo

BROOKLANDS ROAD & TRACK SERIES

Road & Track on Alfa Romeo 1964-1970
Road & Track on Alfa Romeo 1971-1976
Road & Track on Aston Martin 1962-1990
R & T on Auburn Cord and Duesenburg 1952-84
Road & Track on Audi & Auto Union 1952-1980
Road & Track on Audi & Auto Union 1980-1986
Road & Track on Austin Healey 1953-1970
Road & Track on BMW Cars 1966-1974
Road & Track on BMW Cars 1975-1978
Road & Track on BMW Cars 1979-1983
R & T on Cobra, Shelby & Ford GT40 1962-1992
Road & Track on Corvette 1953-1967
Road & Track on Corvette 1968-1982
Road & Track on Corvette 1982-1986
Road & Track on Corvette 1986-1990
Road & Track on Ferrari 1975-1981
Road & Track on Ferrari 1981-1984
Road & Track on Ferrari 1984-1988
Road & Track on Fiat Sports Cars 1968-1987
Road & Track on Jaguar 1950-1960
Road & Track on Jaguar 1961-1968
Road & Track on Jaguar 1968-1974
Road & Track on Jaguar 1974-1982
Road & Track on Jaguar 1983-1989
Road & Track on Lamborghini 1964-1985
Road & Track on Lotus 1972-1981
Road & Track on Maserati 1975-1983
R & T on Mazda RX-7 & MX-5 Miata 1986-1991
Road & Track on Mercedes 1952-1962
Road & Track on Mercedes 1963-1970
Road & Track on Mercedes 1971-1979
Road & Track on Mercedes 1980-1987
Road & Track on MG Sports Cars 1949-1961
Road & Track on MG Sports Cars 1962-1980
Road & Track on Mustang 1964-1977
R & T on Nissan 300-ZX & Turbo 1984-1989
Road & Track on Pontiac 1960-1983
Road & Track on Porsche 1951-1967
Road & Track on Porsche 1968-1971
Road & Track on Porsche 1972-1975
Road & Track on Porsche 1975-1978
Road & Track on Porsche 1985-1988
R & T on Rolls Royce & Bentley 1950-1965
R & T on Rolls Royce & Bentley 1966-1984
Road & Track on Saab 1972-1992
R & T on Toyota Sports & GT Cars 1966-1984
R & T on Triumph Sports Cars 1953-1967
R & T on Triumph Sports Cars 1967-1974
R & T on Triumph Sports Cars 1974-1982
Road & Track on Volkswagen 1951-1968
Road & Track on Volkswagen 1968-1978
Road & Track on Volkswagen 1978-1985
Road & Track on Volvo 1957-1974
Road & Track on Volvo 1977-1994
R & T - Henry Manney at Large & Abroad
R & T - Peter Egan's "Side Glances"
R & T - Peter Egan "At Large"

BROOKLANDS CAR AND DRIVER SERIES

Car and Driver on BMW 1955-1977
Car and Driver on BMW 1977-1985
C and D on Cobra, Shelby & Ford GT40 1963-84
Car and Driver on Corvette 1978-1982
Car and Driver on Corvette 1983-1988
C and D on Datsun Z 1600 & 2000 1966-1984
Car and Driver on Ferrari 1955-1962
Car and Driver on Ferrari 1963-1975
Car and Driver on Ferrari 1976-1983
Car and Driver on Mopar 1956-1967
Car and Driver on Mopar 1968-1975
Car and Driver on Mustang 1964-1972
Car and Driver on Pontiac 1961-1975
Car and Driver on Porsche 1955-1962
Car and Driver on Porsche 1963-1970
Car and Driver on Porsche 1970-1976
Car and Driver on Porsche 1977-1981
Car and Driver on Porsche 1982-1986
Car and Driver on Saab 1956-1985
Car and Driver on Volvo 1955-1986

BROOKLANDS PRACTICAL CLASSICS SERIES

PC on Austin A40 Restoration
PC on Land Rover Restoration
PC on Metalworking in Restoration
PC on Midget/Sprite Restoration
PC on MGB Restoration
PC on Sunbeam Rapier Restoration
PC on Triumph Herald/Vitesse
PC on Spitfire Restoration
PC on 1930s Car Restoration

BROOKLANDS HOT ROD 'MUSCLECAR & HI-PO ENGINES' SERIES

Chevy 265 & 283
Chevy 302 & 327
Chevy 348 & 409
Chevy 350 & 400
Chevy 396 & 427
Chevy 454 thru 512
Chrysler Hemi
Chrysler 273, 318, 340 & 360
Chrysler 361, 383, 400, 413, 426, 440
Ford 289, 302, Boss 302 & 351W
Ford 351C & Boss 351
Ford Big Block

BROOKLANDS RESTORATION SERIES

Auto Restoration Tips & Techniques
Basic Bodywork Tips & Techniques
Camaro Restoration Tips & Techniques
Chevrolet High Performance Tips & Techniques
Chevy Engine Swapping Tips & Techniques
Chevy-GMC Pickup Repair
Chrysler Engine Swapping Tips & Techniques
Engine Swapping Tips & Techniques
Ford Pickup Repair
Land Rover Restoration Tips & Techniques
MG 'T' Series Restoration Guide
MGA Restoration Guide
Mustang Restoration Tips & Techniques

MOTORCYCLING

BROOKLANDS ROAD TEST SERIES

AJS & Matchless Gold Portfolio 1945-1966
BSA Twins A7 & A10 Gold Portfolio 1946-1962
BSA Twins A50 & A65 Gold Portfolio 1962-1973
BMW Motorcycles Gold Portfolio 1950-1971
BMW Motorcycles Gold Portfolio 1971-1976
Ducati Gold Portfolio 1960-1974
Ducati Gold Portfolio 1974-1978
Ducati Gold Portfolio 1978-1982
Laverda Gold Portfolio 1967-1977
Moto Guzzi Gold Portfolio 1949-1973
Norton Commando Gold Portfolio 1968-1977
Triumph Bonneville Gold Portfolio 1959-1983
Vincent Gold Portfolio 1945-1980

BROOKLANDS CYCLE WORLD SERIES

Cycle World on BMW 1974-1980
Cycle World on BMW 1981-1986
Cycle World on Ducati 1982-1991
Cycle World on Harley-Davidson 1962-1968
Cycle World on Harley-Davidson 1978-1983
Cycle World on Harley-Davidson 1983-1987
Cycle World on Harley-Davidson 1987-1990
Cycle World on Harley-Davidson 1990-1992
Cycle World on Honda 1962-1967
Cycle World on Honda 1968-1971
Cycle World on Honda 1971-1974
Cycle World on Husqvarna 1966-1976
Cycle World on Husqvarna 1977-1984
Cycle World on Kawasaki 1966-1971
Cycle World on Kawasaki Off-Road Bikes 1972-1979
Cycle World on Kawasaki Street Bikes 1972-1976
Cycle World on Norton 1962-1971
Cycle World on Suzuki 1962-1970
Cycle World on Suzuki Off-Road Bikes 1971-1976
Cycle World on Suzuki Street Bikes 1971-1976
Cycle World on Triumph 1967-1972
Cycle World on Yamaha 1962-1969
Cycle World on Yamaha Off-Road Bikes 1970-1974
Cycle World on Yamaha Street Bikes 1970-1974

MILITARY

BROOKLANDS MILITARY VEHICLES SERIES

Allied Military Vehicles No.2 1941-1946
Complete WW2 Military Jeep Manual
Dodge Military Vehicles No.1 1940-1945
Hail To The Jeep
Military & Civilian Amphibians 1940-1990
Off Road Jeeps: Civ. & Mil. 1944-1971
US Military Vehicles 1941-1945
US Army Military Vehicles WW2-TM9-2800
VW Kubelwagen Military Portfolio 1940-1990
WW 2 Jeep Military Portfolio 1941-1945

RACING

Le Mans - The Jaguar Years - 1949-1957
Le Mans - The Ferrari Years - 1958-1965
Le Mans - The Ford & Matra Years - 1966-1974
Le Mans - The Porsche Years - 1975-1982

CONTENTS

ACKNOWLEDGEMENTS

Many years ago, we at Brooklands Books set ourselves the task of making available road tests and articles on transport subjects which are no longer easy to find. Our original publications covered motor cars, but demand led us to expand into motorcycles as well and we plan to publish many more books like this one.

These books rely on the help and cooperation of the owners of the material that make up these anthologies. In this case we are indebted to the owners of the following publications for allowing us to reprint their copyright stories - *Bike, The Biker, Classic Bike, Cycle, Cycle World, Motor Cycle, Motor Cycling, Motorcyclist, Motorcycle Illustrated, Motorcycle Mechanics, Motorcycle Sport* and *Superbike.*

Our thanks also go firstly to Bob Culver who at short notice photographed his beautiful Vincent Black Shadow which can be seen on our back cover (see notice on page 115) and also to John Wilding of the Vincent Owners Club (see notice on page 64) who also generously came to our assistance. Finally, once again our thanks go to Frank Westworth of Classic Bike Guide who saved the day by supplying our front cover photograph.

R.M. Clarke

The bikes which bore Phil Vincent's name reflected his ambition to manufacture the best bikes in the world, and arguably there was a time when he did just that. The 998cc vee-twin Series B Rapide which was introduced immediately after the 1939-1945 war was capable of 110 mph, a speed which made it a real superbike of its time, and the Black Shadow which was based on it was tested to 122 mph.

The Rapide had always been a vee-twin, but the post-war model had its engine as an integral part of the frame. That engine was all-new, with a bigger angle between the cylinders than its pre-war counterpart, and in tuned form (using many of the modifications seen on George Brown's 1947 record-breaking machine) it powered the magnificent Black Shadow. In essence, the Black Shadow was still a Rapide, but the baked-on black finish of its engine fins and crankcase, plus the rather ostentatious 150 mph speedometer, made it a most distinctive and desirable bike.

Series B models gave way to Series C types in 1951 as the latter brought a number of valuable modifications. However, the Vincents remained too expensive to sell in large numbers, and Phil Vincent needed volume sales to keep his company afloat. He had tried to increase sales by introducing a 499cc single called the Comet in 1948, but this model failed to capture the larger market he wanted despite sporting successes in the hands of George Brown and John Surtees. Unable to finance the development of a completely new bike, he announced the Series D models in 1954, which looked different because of the plastic panels which enclosed their frames. Underneath, the Black Knight (which replaced the Rapide) and Black Prince (which replaced the Black Shadow) were simply improved and updated versions of the old Vincents, though. Unfortunately, they never sold in the hoped-for quantities, and the Vincent company folded in 1956.

However, the Vincent legacy is one which continues to attract enthusiasts, including increasing numbers of those who were not even born when the last of these machines was built. For them, and for those old enough to remember - and maybe even to have owned a Vincent as an everyday machine - the articles in this book will make fascinating reading.

James Taylor

A 400lb. 998 c.c. Big Twin!

Vincent-H.R.D.s to Concentrate on the Famous "Rapide" Post-war—a Neater, Cobbier and Still More Thrilling Edition of It

This was the pre-war Vincent-H.R.D. " Rapide." The post-war model is to be lighter, much neater and have unit construction and a shorter wheelbase

FOR some time it has been known that Vincent-H.R.D.s intend to produce the "Rapide," their thrilling 998 c.c. roadster, after the war—to do so in a lighter and still more exhilarating form. What will surprise many, however, is that immediately the war is over they will be concentrating on this model. In their opinion, this 998 c.c. big-twin constitutes such a huge advance over their 500 c.c. singles that the singles will no longer be listed. Moreover, the evidence, they say, is that there will be such a world-wide demand for the Rapide that they will have no surplus production capacity for singles.

While the machine will, of course, be founded on the pre-war model it will have many important differences. First and, perhaps, foremost, light alloys are to be used to an extent never approached on pre-war standard motor cycles. The weight of the complete 998 c.c. fully equipped big-twin, it is stated, will be around the 400 lb. mark and may come out a little less. Secondly, the machine is to be as cobby a big-twin as has ever been marketed, for the wheelbase is being reduced to only 56 in., which is that of the pre-war T.T. "Replica" model—the T.T. 500 c.c. single.

Triplex Primary Chain

A further big change is that the machine will employ unit construction of the engine and gear box. The latter is of Vincent-H.R.D. design and manufacture. It is of four-speed type with ball bearings throughout. Primary drive is by a triplex roller chain. Previously the Rapide had a duplex primary chain. A new type of clutch, specially designed, like the gear box, to take the mighty

torque of the semi-o.h.c. twin, will be fitted.

So far as the reciprocating parts of the engine are concerned these will be similar to pre-war. The valve gear will be on the same principle, with its high camshafts—semi-o.h.c.—and two guides per valve, but much cleaned up and, it is said, should prove 100 per cent. oil-tight. Freedom from oil leaks is to be made a feature of the whole machine. Incidentally, all oil pipes, other than the two to the oil tank—the feed and the return pipes—are being eliminated. The oil pump, it will be gathered from this, will no longer be mounted on the timing cover, but built-in, although readily removable.

Same Springing Arrangements

The works state that they are quite satisfied with the steering and handling of the Rapide in the past and do not know how a long-action front fork would function on a machine of the Rapide's speed capabilities. They propose, therefore, keeping to the parallel-ruler-type front forks they used before the war. The spring frame, too, will be of the well-known Vincent-H.R.D. hinged type. There will, generally speaking, be the same "Duo" brakes—two brakes per wheel—and the same frame. Almost needless to state, the quickly detachable wheels, removal of which involves the use of no tools, are being retained. "Nitor," it may be recalled, once timed the removal of a Vincent-H.R.D. rear wheel by stop-watch; it took less than 45 seconds.

What the works have endeavoured to do over the new Rapide is to redesign *ab initio* those things owners or they

themselves did not like about the old model. The result, apart from major changes already touched upon, is a large number of new detail features. Some of these, it is stated, are of such a nature that publication at this date might give too much away. Separate magnetos and dynamos are to be employed with the latter of at least 50-watt output. Still wider use is to be made of stainless steel. It was employed for tanks, brake rods and other fittings pre-war and is now to be used instead of chromium plating wherever possible.

It will be recalled that the machine, in addition to its remarkable steering, road-holding and braking, was notable in the past for its combination of great power and speed with good traffic manners.

There was nothing of the high-compression monster about it, for it had only the compression ratio of 6.5 to 1, that of the "Meteor," their most "touring" five-hundred in the range. For after the war there is still to be this Jekyll and Hyde behaviour, but, with the new exceptionally high power/weight ratio and the shorter wheelbase, a still more thrilling performance.

Future Prospects ?

What of those Vincent-H.R.D. patents published in our issue of November 18th, 1943, under the title "A Trend of Thought"? All that can be said at this juncture is that the factory has very high hopes, but their full realisation in the form of a new super, entirely different motor cycle is in the future—necessarily, as everything must be tried and proved to the factory's satisfaction in the distant future.

Vincent-H.R.D. Design— A Thrilling New

A Thousand c.c. Mount with the Size and Weight of a Five = hundred : Numerous Interesting Constructional Features and Clever, Well = thought = out Detail Design

VINCENT-H.R.D.s are concentrating upon one model — the famous "Rapide." As a result of this policy and of their now magnificent production facilities, it is anticipated that the price of the 998 c.c. big-twin will show only a very small increase over the £145 of 1939, though in this country plus, of course, Purchase Tax. And this is in spite of the new and greatly improved specification. The whole conception is new, and the machine almost bristles with fresh features and "riders' points."

The aim in the new model is to provide a big-twin "thousand" which has outstanding speed and acceleration and first-class road manners coupled with the weight, the wheelbase and the ease of handling of a super five-hundred. It is when the eye roams from the combined engine and gear box to the wheels that full realisation begins to dawn that here is a cobby, extraordinarily compact machine which in every direction, other than its larger engine and its greater performance, *is* a five-hundred.

With the new design the wheelbase is 3in. shorter than on the old Rapide. It has been reduced to 56in., which is the same as on the Vincent-H.R.D. 500 c.c. T.T. machines. The weight has also been reduced. It is anticipated that this will be 400 to 405 lb.—again very much that of a five-hundred.

Engine Forms a " Tie "

As with every Vincent-H.R.D. that has been produced, there is pivot-action rear springing. The construction of the machine is, however, very different from the past. At first glance it may appear to be on standard lines. Then it is noticed that there is no front down tube—indeed, that there are remarkably few tubes. That robust, clean-looking engine-gear unit provides the link between the "backbone" of the machine, the top member, and the rear chainstays. With the so-called diamond frame the engine forms the tie between the front-down tube and the seat tube—does so automatically ; in the new Rapide, by ingenious design, full use is made of the opportunity the 50-degree twin proffers. As with diamond-frame machines the crankcase forms a tie, but this is a wide, extremely rigid engine-cum-gear unit designed specially, while as for the link between the top frame member and the bottom half of the unit, this comprises not the widely set cylinder holding-down studs as such, but studs within these studs. In other words, there are tubular studs for cylinder and cylinder-head holding-down purposes and, running down the axis of these are solid studs, approximately $\frac{3}{8}$in. diameter, to carry the frame loads. Each of the two types of stud has its own thread in the crankcase, and the two are thus independent of each other.

Construction of the top member is unusual and, as regards dimensions and strength, reminiscent of a lorry chassis.

A Thousand c.c. Mount with the Size and Weight of a Five = hundred : Numerous Interesting Constructional Features and Clever, Well = thought = out Detail Design

Running backwards from the forged steering-head lug, and riveted to it, is a six-pint oil tank which is a deep " ∩ " in cross-section. This is some $3\frac{1}{4}$in. wide and has a mean height of about 5in. Over this fits the $3\frac{3}{4}$-gallon stainless-steel fuel tank, which narrows towards the rear for riding comfort and is of semi-pistol grip type. The width at the rider's knees, incidentally, is approximately 11in. An interesting feature is that there is an air space between the oil and fuel tanks amounting to about $1\frac{1}{2}$ sq. in. on each side so that air can pass along the sides of the former tank, which by its design has a very large surface area.

As in the past, enclosed coil springs link the rear of the top member with the seat stays. The pivoted chainstays follow standard Vincent-H.R.D. practice, but, as on the earlier layout, the Skefko taper-roller bearings are carried in the chain-

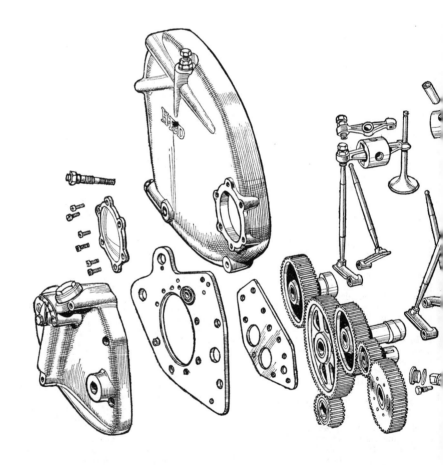

A special drawing revealing the detail construction of the new Rapide engine and the manner in which the parts go together. The ingenious valve gear is worthy of particularly close examination.

Big-twin Rapide

stay members. These bearings are of the same size and type as those for the front and rear wheels. Friction dampers are incorporated at the bottom of the rear members of the special Feridax Dualseat, which has the nose, rear and the front of the rear seat picked out in maroon to match the panels on the stainless-steel tank. It is a very special Dualseat with the tyre inflator running lengthwise in it and completely hidden and a tool-tray under the front portion. This tray pulls out like a drawer and has a felt inlay to provide a rattleproof housing for each of the tools. The question of the tool-kit is being investigated; it is hoped to be able to accommodate in addition a repair outfit, spare plugs and replacement lamp bulbs.

The front forks are of link- or girder-type, but redesigned with the object of providing forks which will operate efficiently over thousands of miles without attention, even lubrication. They have Nitralloy spindles working in porous bronze, oil-impregnated bushes. Side-thrust washers at the top links are also of this oil-retaining bronze. An anti-rattle mounting in the form of a compressed rubber bushing is provided for the knob

A Thrilling New Big-twin Rapide—

of the steering damper, which can therefore be left right "off" without any clatter occurring. Another improvement is a Bakelite knob for adjusting the friction dampers incorporated in the bottom links.

So much for the frame and front forks. The wheels are : Front, WM 1-20 rim fitted with a 3.00-20 ribbed tyre; rear, WM 3-19, with a 3.50-19 studded tyre. The aim has been to provide a front rim that is light for road-holding and a rear one which is sturdy and fully equal to high-speed sidecar work. While the foregoing is the standard specification, there

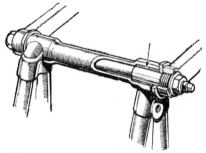

Oil-impregnated porous-bronze bushes and side-thrust washers are used in the new front forks

is room for 4.50-18 tyres both front and rear. Vincent-H.R.D.s want to fit stainless steel rims, but the difficulties are to get them and at what is construed a reasonable price. The alternative is chromium-plated rims. A single security bolt is being fitted front and rear and the wheels are being balanced on racing-car lines—by bolts and lead washers.

Both wheels have their twin brakes—"Duo" brakes—one each side, and are of the Vincent-H.R.D. really quick to detach type, which does not involve the use of tools. The hubs are now aluminium die-castings. The brakes, incidentally, are 7in. in diameter, with ⅞in. wide linings. A feature of the rear-wheel assembly is that the final driving chain, thanks to the tommy arrangement for the rearwheel spindle and hand-operated stainless-steel chain adjusters, which are of the self-locking "click" type, is also ad-

justable without the employment of tools.

Other features are : Racing-type duralumin mudguards—front, 4½in. wide and rear, 5in.; duralumin-strip front mudguard stays (touring guards will also be available, but the design has not yet been finalised); the almost straight, widely eulogised handlebars, but with Vincent-H.R.D. controls; speedometer head mounted on the front forks with a straight drive contained within a steel tube; 8in. diameter head lamp; air-control levers mounted just beneath the front of the tank so that there are short cables, the handlebars remain clean and there is general neatness; throttle cables arranged to come from the front of the tank and into the handlebar; a control wire to each carburettor so that should by any chance one nipple pull out it would be possible to carry on, using only one cylinder; a low-lift rear stand—approximately 2in. lift—with the rear mudguard hinged just behind the lifting handle at tyre level; a very wide hinge is fitted to give the mudguard lateral rigidity. On the handlebars are three control levers—clutch, front brake and exhaust-valves lifter—a built-in horn push that is an inch or more in diameter for ease of operation, and two

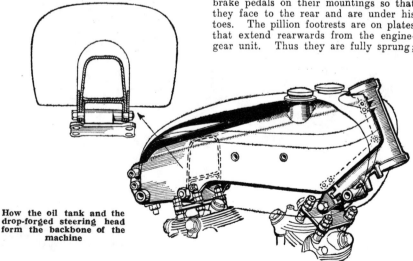

How the oil tank and the drop-forged steering head form the backbone of the machine

twist-grips. One of these last, of course, controls the throttles of the two carburettors; the other, which has a powerful spring-controlled click-over action, operates the dipswitch.

Considerable thought has been expended upon securing a riding position that is truly adjustable. The footrests are mounted on long hangers with taper fixings at the top and a series of holes near the bottom, which, the shank of the kick-starter pedal being inside the hanger and the exhaust system being of the low-level type, means that the footrests can be set in any position that might conceivably be desired. The footrest on the kick-starter pedal side—the kick-starter can be fitted on either side—is provided with a folding pad and it is proposed to fit a simple automatic arrangement whereby on the kick-starter pedal being depressed the pad flies out of the way, to be pressed down again when the engine has started.

Both the brake pedal and the foot gear change pedal are carried on the forgings that form the footrest hangers, so the pedals remain in the same relative position to the footrests. If a rider wishes to adopt a racing position he can use the pillion footrests and reverse the gear and brake pedals on their mountings so that they face to the rear and are under his toes. The pillion footrests are on plates that extend rearwards from the engine-gear unit. Thus they are fully sprung;

they are also fully adjustable, since there are three holes available and, in addition, they can be swivelled.

The kick-starter pedal, with its curved shank or arm, is unusual. It is designed to give first-class leverage, the start of the effective stroke being at approximately the 10 o'clock position and the end at roughly 8 o'clock. It is of folding type, and both it and the gear pedal will probably be of stainless steel.

alloy—silicon alloy for low expansion. The cylinder liners, which have a lip at the top and are, therefore, definitely held apart from the shrunk fit, project into the crankcase for approximately half their length.

"Silchrome" inlet valves and austenitic-steel exhaust valves are employed. The ports of the latter are $1\frac{7}{16}$ in. diameter, and of the former the diameter is $1\frac{11}{16}$ in.; the ports can be opened up very considerably if desired. Amal carburettors, with ver-

is by a $\frac{3}{8}$ in. pitch triplex chain, which is provided with an adjustable spring-blade tensioner on the lower run. The gear box, which is lubricated separately from the engine, is a Vincent-H.R.D. product and of racing-type design, with alternate dogs cut back approximately $\frac{1}{16}$ in. for ease of engagement. It is of

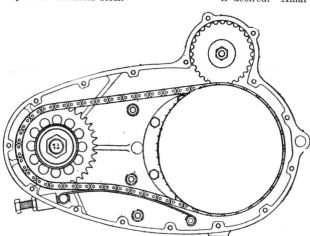

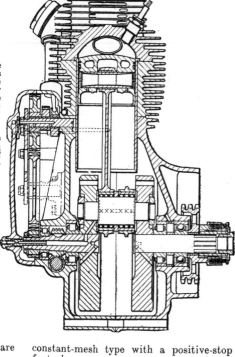

(Left) An adjustable spring blade forms the tensioner for the triplex primary chain. Note the manner in which the 50-watt dynamo is driven

(Right) A works drawing showing the arrangement of the main and big-end bearings

Naturally the 998 c.c. engine—84 × 90 mm.—is based on the highly successful Rapide of the past. It has only a moderate compression ratio (6.8 to 1), and is designed to provide high power with docility, long life and freedom from the need of frequent decarbonisation. The output, it is stated, is over 45 b.h.p. at 5,300, and the makers quote the speeds on petrol of 73 to 80 octane of 110 m.p.h. in top gear (3.6 to 1), 95-98 in third (4.3), 80-83 in second (5.6) and over 60 in bottom (9.6).

The engine is of the high-camshaft or "semi-o.h.c. camshaft" type with total enclosure of the valve gear. There are twin camshafts, one for each cylinder, with a large idler pinion between the engine-shaft and camshaft pinions. An idler pinion is also employed in the drive to the (B.T.-H. or Lucas) automatic advance-and-retard magneto; this incorporates a rotary release valve to release the crankcase pressure and ensure a clean engine. An aluminium outer steady plate is provided for the timing gear.

Rear Cylinder Offset

Both cylinders have their exhaust ports to the front, and the rear one is offset $1\frac{1}{4}$ in., thus permitting a direct air blast. The connecting rods are set side by side on a $1\frac{9}{16}$ in. diameter crankpin and are each mounted on 135 3 mm. diameter, 5 mm. long, uncaged rollers. The mainshafts are 1in. in diameter, pressed into the flywheels and have on the driving side one large roller bearing and one large ball bearing, and on the other two roller bearings, one large and one small. The connecting-rods are of nickel-chrome steel of about 65 tons/sq. in.

Heat-treated R.R.53 B light alloy is used for the cylinder heads which have shrunk-in valve seats, austenitic-iron inlets and aluminium-bronze exhausts. The finned cylinder jackets are also of light

tical mixing chambers and $1\frac{1}{16}$ in. bore are fitted.

Design of the valve gear, with its total enclosure and not even a rocker shaft hole through which oil can seep, is highly ingenious. As usual in Vincent-H.R.D. engines, the valves have twin guides, but now, for reasons of neatness and because at the r.p.m. involved there is little, if anything, to lose, the springs are of the coil-type instead of hairpin. Tappet adjustment is effected by removing the large die-cast hexagonal caps. By undoing the tappet adjuster the valve can, if he desires, pull both the push-rod and the valve rocker out of the tappet-adjuster hole. Stainless-steel push-rod tubes are fitted. Incidentally, the oil feed to the rockers is taken from the return from the oil pump — rotary-cum-reciprocating plunger type—to the oil tank, so that the oil is warm and flows readily. All oil is pumped straight through a felt filter of over 50 sq. in. total area mounted in a housing cast in the crankcase and removable for cleaning by undoing one cap on the near side; draining the oil tank beforehand is not required.

Pistons are "Specialloid," each with two $\frac{1}{16}$ in.-wide pressure rings and an $\frac{1}{8}$ in. scraper. The dynamo is of 50-watt output with the voltage-control unit mounted alongside. Plug covers are being standardised.

Drive from the engine to the gear box

constant-mesh type with a positive-stop foot change.

Other points are : A 6in. ground clearance, a saddle height of approximately $28\frac{1}{2}$ in. with the rider seated, and a choice of 10 or 12 rear chain wheels, with 46 T. standard and others—the rear wheel will accept one each side and can be changed round in the fork ends—available as extras to all who want them. The clutch? A new clutch of self-energising type, a clutch that has the advantage of excellent heat-dissipation properties, has been designed.

Delivery of Rapides should start about March, and may be earlier. At the present time probably 20 per cent. of the parts for the first 300 Rapides are ready. In the case of some parts, where material is readily available, sufficient for the first 500 have been made.

RELEASING DONINGTON

TO urge the early release of Donington, the famous pre-war racing venue—this was the object of a deputation which saw the Under-Secretary of State for War, Lord Nathan, last week. The deputation was sponsored by the R.A.C. Lord Nathan said he was anxious to ascertain whether it was possible for the track at Donington to be used for racing while other portions of the Park could still be utilised for storing W.D. vehicles.

Off-side view of the new 998 c.c. o.h.v. "Rapide," which shows to advantage the manner in which the unit-construction engine performs the joint functions of power plant and frame member.

SHOULD you be overtaken in the near future by the latest Vincent-H.R.D. "Rapide" undergoing tests you may be excused if you put it down as a well-preserved example of say, 1939 vintage. Provided its passing is not too swift you will instinctively spot the girder forks, the familiar glint of the maroon-panelled stainless steel tank, the hefty big-twin power unit and the dual brakes. That much will be observed by any discerning motorcyclist in the twinkling of an eye.

But if, a little farther down the road, you come across the tester making some notes and you stop for a look-see you will quickly realize just how deceptive a fleeting glance can be! One new feature after another will attract your attention until you will begin to wonder how a machine which has been so drastically redesigned can yet retain such a close resemblance to its distinguished forebears.

Problems Answered

The facts are that this new version of the "Rapide" represents the answers to a series of problems the Stevenage experts set out to solve in their search for an ideal, and the solution has been found in a design which is as unconventional as it is well thought out.

Briefly, it was postulated that the wheelbase and general handling characteristics must equal those of a T.T. model of half the capacity; that overall weight be reduced to the minimum; that exposed face joints should be relieved of loads likely to encourage oil leaks; that plated or enamelled parts liable to rust attack be dispensed with wherever possible; that "outside plumbing" and "bits and pieces" accessories be conspicuous by their absence; and that the riding position—with all vital controls—be readily adjustable for touring or racing without

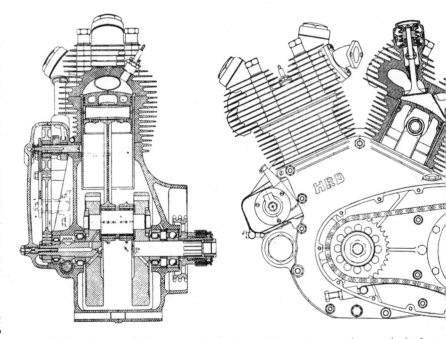

(Left) Cross-section of the power unit, showing triplex engine sprocket, method of mou the flywheel assembly on four well-spaced bearings, worm-driven oil pump, outrigger pla timing gears and massive proportions of the crankcase. (Right) Drive side of power showing horizontal magneto mounting, hexagon cap giving access to filter element, ext adjustment for chain tensioner and method of driving separate dynamo by central of the triplex chain.

the need for any additional parts.

The key to the majority of these designers' dilemmas is to be found in the massive o.h.v. 998 c.c. (84 mm. by 90 mm.) 50-degree twin-cylinder engine with its unit-construction four-speed gearbox. Instead of being supported in a tubular structure it reverses the normal practice by itself forming the "frame centre," thus dispensing with the usual front down tube and saddle tube. Indeed, there are but two frame members in the accepted sense—the

swinging stays carrying the rear wheel and the beam supporting the headlug. Thus is a 56-in. wheelbase achieved and many pounds of unwelcome weight removed.

The exceptionally deep and wide crankcase unit forms a box-girder of enormous strength, more than able to cope with the dual functions of frame member and power transmission. The flywheel assembly, with 1-in. diameter mainshafts, is carried on caged ball and roller bearings on the drive side and

t-H.R.D. "Rapide"

two widely spaced caged roller bearings on the timing side. The nickel-chrome connecting rods run side by side on a $1\frac{9}{16}$-in. crankpin, each big-end housing three rows of 3 mm. by 5 mm. rollers. Each Specialloid light-alloy piston carries two compression rings and one scraper ring, with a circlip-retained floating gudgeon pin.

The alloy cylinder barrels with shrunk-in cast iron liners are spigoted deeply into the case and these, together with the R.R.53b aluminium-alloy heads fitted with valve-seat inserts, are held in position by long sleeve bolts through which pass the 60-ton tensile bolts connecting the crankcase to the front and rear of the top frame member. This ingenious system of concentric bolts enables normal expansion to take place, whilst no frame loads are transmitted to the cylinders.

The Timing Gear

The timing wheels run on stationary shafts supported by an outrigger plate, the panel cover joint thus being relieved of all loads. An engine-speed timed rotary breather valve is incorporated in the idler wheel which meshes with the front camwheel and magneto drive pinion, the oil mist being carried to the rear chain by a suitable pipe.

Flat-faced cam followers operate the pushrods, which are housed in stainless steel tubular covers. A worm on the mainshaft drives a horizontal reciprocating and rotary plunger pump which circulates oil from the six-pint tank at the rate of 20 gallons per hour. The lubricant is forced from the pump through a star-shaped detachable felt filter boasting no fewer than 50 sq. ins. area, and thence by drilled passages to the big-ends and camshafts, with additional leads to the rear of each cylinder. The feed for the o.h.v. rocker gear is taken off the scavenge pump lead to the tank, thus dispensing with the need for minute oilways, the flow being controlled by a valve which raises the pressure in the pipeline to a few ounces above atmospheric.

The Vincent-H.R.D. system of double valve guides is retained, the top light-alloy guide forming the lower abutment for the duplex concentric valve springs. Each fork-ended rocker is housed in a slotted cylindrical member located in its tunnel by an extension of the banjo bolt through which the oil is fed, the outer end of the tunnel being closed by a large screwed cap. This clever system makes removal of the rockers extremely easy and relieves the appropriate external face joints of all load, whilst providing "full turn of the spanner" accessibility to valve clearance adjustment on the rocker arms.

Twin Carburetters

Two vertical $1\frac{1}{16}$-in. Amal needle-jet-type carburetters supply the mixture, whilst the twin, forward-facing $1\frac{3}{8}$-in. exhaust pipes blend into a common pipe leading to a large cylindrical silencer incorporating a special baffle. This system saves weight, and experiments have proved that the resultant noise abatement is more efficacious than when separate silencers are fitted. It is of interest to note that all port dimensions and similar factors controlling the breathing of the power unit are identical with those of the 1939 design—proof of past success—and with a 6.8 to 1 compression ratio the engine develops 45 b.h.p., although deliberately restricted to provide maximum flexibility and a pleasant all-

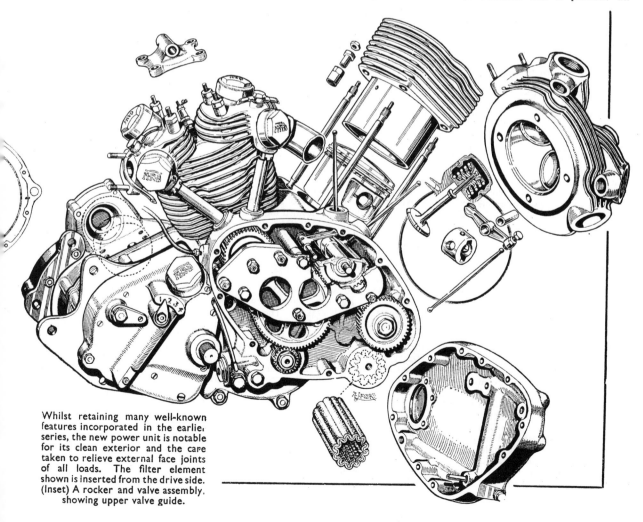

Whilst retaining many well-known features incorporated in the earlier series, the new power unit is notable for its clean exterior and the care taken to relieve external face joints of all loads. The filter element shown is inserted from the drive side. (Inset) A rocker and valve assembly, showing upper valve guide.

round performance. There is no difficulty, however, in obtaining nearly double this figure for racing purposes.

The exceptionally massive gears, with the main and layshafts lying in one horizontal plane and running on large ball bearings, are designed to transmit 100 b.h.p.—a margin of strength which will be obvious to the reader. Movement of the positive-stop operating pedal is transmitted by a shaft and bevel gear to a horizontal camplate and each alternate dog on the pinions is relieved to ensure an easy change.

There is no face joint on the off side of the box, access to the gear assembly being obtained through a spigoted, dowelled and bolted-on cover plate situated behind the clutch—yet another instance of the care taken to eradicate sources of oil leakage. There is an external gear indicator and an inspection cap for clutch cable adjustment. The clutch, of the self-servo type, with special provision for heat dissipation, cannot at present be described in detail,

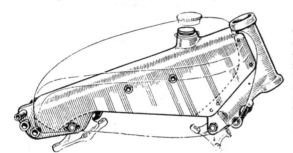

as certain patents are pending. The gear ratios are 3.6, 4.3, 5.6 and 9.6 to 1.

The three-lobe face-cam type mainshaft shock absorber transmits the primary drive by a $\frac{3}{8}$-in. triplex chain provided with an external adjustment for the spring blade tensioner. The outer runs of this chain drive the duplex clutch sprocket, the dynamo sprocket meshing with the central run. This system enables the special 50-watt output dynamo to be removed readily without disturbing the drive. Transmission to the rear wheel is by an adequately guarded $\frac{5}{8}$-in. by $\frac{3}{8}$-in. chain with finger adjustment for tension.

Anticipated performance is over 110 m.p.h. in top, 100 m.p.h. in third, 82 m.p.h. in second and 60 m.p.h. in bottom, with exceptional acceleration throughout the range. Fuel consumption naturally depends upon a number of factors, primarily the mood of the rider, but is anticipated to be between 50 m.p.g. and 70 m.p.g. at very fast touring speeds.

As will be seen in the illustration, the top frame member is a deep " ∩ "-shaped steel pressing, with a " floor " welded in to form a box section, riveted to the steel drop-forged head lug and tapering in depth towards the rear. A downward extension of the head lug is attached to a bracket held to the front cylinder head by the four forward long crankcase bolts already mentioned; a similar bracket on the rear cylinder is attached to the after-end of the beam by a bolt fitted in slotted holes to provide for the thermal expansion of the engine.

The " floor " converts the beam member into a six-pint oil tank and the support for the 3$\frac{3}{4}$-gallon stainless steel fuel container, an air gap of $\frac{1}{4}$-in. between the two receptacles allowing for the passage of cooling air over all surfaces of the lubricant container.

The manufacturers believe that for such strains as those imposed by high-speed sidecar work—a purpose for which such a powerful machine is likely to be used—the girder-type fork is to be preferred to existing designs of the telescopic variety; thus their well-proven pattern is retained. The shackles run on Nitralloy steel spindles and are equipped with self-lubricating bushes. The shock absorbers are now fitted with a plastic handwheel, while the steering damper incorporates an anti-rattle device.

The rear springing system, which has proved completely successful over a long period of years, remains unaltered. The pivot bearing for the swinging chain stays is mounted between massive plates bolted to the rear flanks of the

The top frame member which combines the functions of oil tank and support for the fuel tank. Note method of attachment to the power unit to allow for expansion. The dotted line indicates the contour of the oil reservoir.

gearbox casting, the whole forming a very rigid structure. The saddle stays terminate in two parallel telescopic spring boxes attached to the rear of the beam top frame member. The one-piece saddle-cum-pillion seat is supported at the rear on short stays provided with adjustable friction dampers, an assembly identical with that used on Vincent-H.R.D. machines ridden in the T.T. races.

Another detail typical of the thought given to avoiding excrescences is the provision of a drawer-type tool container, complete with felt-lined moulded slots for each tool, beneath the forward half of the saddle. Similarly, the tyre inflator disappears up a tunnel formed in the length of the seat!

The light-alloy wheel hubs run on 1$\frac{5}{16}$-in. Skefco taper roller bearings and incorporate the well-known Vincent-H.R.D. 7-in. by $\frac{7}{8}$-in. balanced and compensating dual brakes. The rear hub has been modified to provide a wider spoke base (for sidecar work) and the chain line is now such that an over-size tyre up to 4.50-in. can be fitted if required. For a small extra charge the hub can be equipped with a sprocket on each side; as the wheel is reversible, the overall gear ratios can be changed by this means in four minutes without the aid of tools, tommy-bar spindle nuts and a spring-loaded torque arm making this possible.

Standard equipment consists of a 26-in. by 3.00-in. (W.M.1 by 20-in. rim) ribbed tyre on the front wheel and a 26-in. by 3.50-in. (W.M.2 by 19-in. rim) studded rear tyre. The ground

clearance is 6 ins., the overall movement of the spring frame 5$\frac{1}{2}$ ins. and the unladen saddle height 30 ins.

The sports type mudguards illustrated are in light alloy, but the option will be given on a heavier touring type. An ingenious front stand (not illustrated) attached to the front of the crankcase acts as a prop on either side at will, whilst a low-lift rear stand and a hinged portion to the mudguard provide for back wheel removal.

The long high-tensile steel footrest hangers have a really excellent range of vertical and horizontal adjustment. As the hangers carry the brake and gear change pedals these vital controls always remain in the same relative position to the feet. When converting the machine from the touring to the racing position these control pedals are reversible so that the rider may use the pillion rests for high-speed work. This is but another example of well-planned designing, to which should be added the fact that the kick-starter can be fitted to either side of the machine at will, a matter of great convenience for overseas buyers in those countries where sidecars are " worn " on the off side.

Rust Defied

The effort made to eliminate enamelled or plated steel parts has been very thorough. Wherever nuts, operating rods and the like cannot be fabricated in stainless steel they are cadmium plated and light alloys are used at many points usually subject to rust attack. Indeed, with the exception of the chromium-plated exhaust system and the few frame parts, there is little on the machine likely to suffer from the ravages of exposure.

In production form handlebar controls will be cleaned up considerably. Two light-alloy straight-pull twist-grips will operate throttle and dipper switch respectively and into one will be built the horn button, whilst cables will be concealed so far as is possible.

Standard equipment includes a 120 m.p.h. speedometer (calibrated in kilometres at option), pillion footrests, electric horn, and lighting set with 8-in. head lamp incorporating the switch-gear. The battery is mounted in a special container directly above the pivotal point of the rear chain stays, where it obtains maximum protection from vibration.

The makers can be proud of the fact that they have produced a 1,000 c.c. big twin with an outstanding performance and luxury equipment at an overall weight of 405 lb. The design shows evidence at many points of the ingenuity and thought directed to the production of an ideal specification equally suitable for touring or sports use. Deliveries are expected to commence in March, although it is understood that a considerable percentage of the 1946 output has already been earmarked for overseas distribution. It is the intention of the Vincent-H.R.D. Co., Ltd., Stevenage, Herts, to concentrate on this model, the price of which, we are advised, will come as a pleasant surprise to many when announced in the near future.

The 500 c.c. Rotary Valve Cross

THIS series is intended primarily for owners, actual and potential, of pre-war machines. In view, however, of the undoubtable interest that is maintained in rotary valves—as evidenced at the I.A.E. meetings and club discussions—it has been decided to recall our road test of a very unconventional motor-cycle indeed, albeit one that cannot be bought. It is the 500 c.c. Cross-engined Vincent H.R.D., which was in our hands in the spring of 1937.

A linerless aluminium cylinder barrel was a principal feature of the engine (as with all Cross products), the Y-alloy piston being prevented from touching the cylinder walls by means of a special hardened, deep-section ring at the top and a series of guide rings, made from high-tensile, square-section alloy steel wire, down the skirt of the piston.

Thus, there was no piston slap; and, incidentally, the compression ratio was 10½ to 1.

Immediately above the combustion chamber was the rotary valve, chain driven from the engine shaft. This valve was divided diagonally so that, as it rotated, connection was made alternately with the inlet port on the near side and the exhaust port on the off side. A point on which the designer, Mr. R. C. Cross, had spent a great deal of time was the lubrication of the valve. Although the amount of oil in circulation was unusually large, not a drop penetrated to the combustion chamber; the flow of lubricant to the valve varied in direct proportion to the engine speed, a form of throttle-controlled oiling being used.

The valve housing was split, the upper half being hinged to the cylinder and also tied to the crankcase. The cylinder was mounted on an adjustable spring so that it floated; thus, expansion of the valve under heat was compensated for and only sufficient pressure was exerted upon the valve for it to maintain its contact with the sealing port-edge lip. As the pressure in the cylinder rose, it endeavoured to press the valve away from the port but always the valve was given a little more pressure to seal

the port than the gas could exert upon it to press it away.

This same system has been used on later engines, except that, the required strength having been determined, the spring incorporated in the cylinder mounting has been tucked away out of sight. So great is the reliability of the prototype model, however, that it has run throughout the war period, and is still running, without alteration.

Performance.—Side-valve flexibility with super-tuned o.h.v. acceleration and maximum speed was the keynote of the Cross engine—and the one tested was just a hack, experimental, touring-type job. It had not been carefully balanced; it had been taken down only once during 15 months of a strenuous life, and that six months prior to our test. Even the plug was 15 months old.

The acceleration was phenomenal. As the graph shows, it needed only 28.5 secs. to reach, from a standing start, the flat-out speed of 87 m.p.h., at which the engine was revolving at the rate of

6,300 r.p.m. The maxima in third and second, respectively, were 73 m.p.h. (6,600 r.p.m., reached in 17.5 secs.) and 61 m.p.h. (7,400 r.p.m., in 11.5 secs.). The "standing quarter" was covered at an average of 53.4 m.p.h., 80 m.p.h. being exceeded at the end of the measured straight; and the "flying quarter" was traversed at 85.88 m.p.h.

Whilst the minimum non-snatch speed in top gear was 18 m.p.h., it was easily possible to trickle along in the same ratio at a fast walking pace, provided, of course, one ignored the protests of the transmission. Perhaps, however, an even greater demonstration of flexibility was made on Southstoke, a 1-in-4 hill near Bath, which is approached along a narrow lane and which has a sharp hairpin bend at the top. This was climbed repeatedly in top—even "two-up," although, then, a very little clutch-slip was necessary to negotiate the hairpin. Never was there a sign of pinking, or of any fuss at all except from the chains, which were never intended for such "thumpy" treatment, anyway.

On the open road 75 m.p.h. was a natural cruising speed, at which the engine never seemed to tire or "dry up." Naturally, there was no mechanical clatter; the only sound was a faint whir

from the rotary valve. And Mr. Cross's own design of absorption silencer attended efficiently to the exhaust. Consequently, the machine was in all ways a delightful one to ride.

Handling.—We cannot conclude this review without reference to the Vincent H.R.D. spring frame in which the motor was fitted. The machine could be steered to a hair at all speeds, indifferent surfaces did not affect the ease of control in the slightest, and the well-known Duo brakes pulled the model up from 30 m.p.h. in 29 ft. on the damp Brooklands concrete. The tester wrote at the time: " . . . a revelation in motorcycles

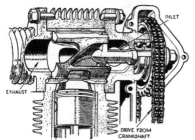

On the left is the experimental 500 c.c. Cross engine in its Vincent H.R.D. frame; the excellence of its performance is evident from the graph below. Above is a sectioned drawing of a 250 c.c. Cross valve and head; although there are several detail differences between this and the design tested, the principle of the rotary valve is clearly shown.

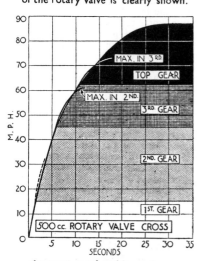

. . . the most comfortable we have ever ridden on the (Brooklands) Track."

Consumption and Starting.—Fuel consumption averaged 56 m.p.g., that of oil being 1,250 m.p.g. Starting was always of the first-kick variety, it being necessary only to flood the carburetter and ease the motor over compression once or, perhaps, twice.

Summary.—Whether Cross motors will feature in any post-war design, we do not know. We can say, however, that development has been quietly going on at Bath, even during the war years. If, therefore, you read in some future specification the words "500 c.c. Rotary-valve Cross Engine"—or 350 c.c., or 250 c.c.—you may rest assured that the description is of a well-tried product.

latter offering anchorage for a pillion rider's feet, although set just a shade too far forward in view of the potential acceleration of the machine.

A point of criticism on the 1939 "Rapide" concerned the clutch, which on occasion, was prone to slip, following the abuse

Accent on acceleration. What happe[...] when Charles Markham snapped o[...] the throttle during a timed stand[...] start test. Note that he is using [...] auxiliary pillion‑cum‑racing footre[...]

THE 998 c.[...]
o.h.v. SERIES "[...]
VINCEN[...]

OUTSTANDING example of post-war enterprise and ingenuity in design—phenomenal in performance to a degree whereat its creators proudly claim it to be "The World's Fastest Standard Motorcycle"—such is the Series "B" Vincent-H.R.D. "Rapide."

It cannot be denied that the prospect of road-testing a machine possessing so many remarkable features in performance and layout brought with it a deep sense of curiosity. The pre-war "Rapide" had proved to be no sluggard, with a maximum of just on 110 m.p.h., and the handling brought no complaints. Would this redesigned model, with its unique engine-gearbox unit forming a foundation for the mounting of the combined pressed-steel backbone and forged steering head, offer an even better ride? Absence of the conventional front down tube, and the consequent ability to house the big-twin unit within a wheelbase proportionate to 500 c.c. practice, sounded interesting on paper, but what happened on fast, bumpy curves?

With these and many other pertinent queries in mind, a production model was recently put through its paces—and very handsome paces they proved to be! Enthusiastic road-burners, studying the usual report sheet and acceleration graph with times and figures recorded, will be interested to know that a 9-stone girl experienced no difficulty in starting the machine—thanks to a kick-starter crank of sufficient length and leverage to allow one prod to "spin" the motor. The initial period of test was carried out under extremely cold-weather conditions, yet the correct drill never failed to bring response at the second attempt, even if the machine had been idle for some few days.

Provided that both air levers (mounted on a common control) were fully closed, that the merest depression of both carburetter ticklers was not exceeded and that the large valve lifter control was sensibly employed, there were no worries on the score of starting up. Once in action, the air levers could be opened to the half-way position, and left for a brief spell during the initial warming-up period, whilst the unit settled down to a most reliable and gentlemanly tick-over. If anything was calculated to dispel illusions concerning speed at the expense of good manners and flexibility, it was this comforting ability to shut the grip with assurance that a certain tick-over would result.

However, long periods of traffic riding showed that, although it required no juggling of taps to "slow march" down to 16-18 m.p.h. in top gear, the front plug objected to the procedure as a habit, and "spitting back" occurred.

Just to emphasize the dual personality of the "Rapide," it should be mentioned that the particular machine under review was handed over to J. T. Peake, who took it through the London-Land's End Trial to gain a premier award!

A first reaction, upon sampling the riding position, is to conclude that the short bars may cause low-speed "weaving," yet it was always possible to ride down to a mere 3 m.p.h. in a dead-straight line without conscious effort. The tester—5 ft. 4 ins. in height and scaling but 10 stone—experienced no difficulty in threading a casual path through the traffic and tramlines of London and Birmingham. With the Feridax Dualseat offering generous accommodation, and footrests set exactly as individual fancy dictated, a nicely braced feeling resulted. And here it should be noted that, although the footrest hangers are effective through an unusually wide arc, the brake pedal stays with the near-side rest, thus dispensing with time-wasting and fiddlesome adjustment. Both normal and "scrapping rests" are hinged, the

A nearside close-up which shows many interesting features. Note tommybar rear spindle, finger chain adjuster, pillion-seat friction damper, brake pedal hinged on forward footrest, dynamo drive inspection disc and magneto cover.

consequent on racing changes. With the entirely new centrifugal servo type, however, almost unlimited deliberate slipping may be indulged in without any loss of positive grip when the servo shoes are home. Moreover, the lever can be operated by a single finger.

The clutch originally fitted to the test machine was, however, fierce on the "take-up," and a replacement was substituted from stock, which proved much sweeter in action. As the accompanying illustrations show, the newly designed clutch is contained complete in its own housing.

Mechanical noise from the twin cylinders was evident at low speeds, but was certainly not offensive to the ear, and

as the speed rose it tended to quieten appreciably. Meriting high praise is the fact that the exhaust was completely inaudible to the rider at any speed unless the head was turned in a deliberate attempt to catch the muffled burble. In setting up high averages over long cross-country journeys this feature played no mean part by enabling the rider to travel and arrive without objectionable advertisement.

Nicety in navigation. So compact is the 1,000 c.c. "Rapide" that it can be handled with the ease of any good machine of half the cubic capacity.

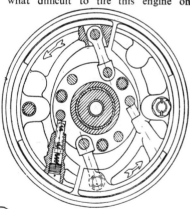

(Right) Housed beneath the special Feridax Dualseat is a sliding tool tray. (Below) Excellent road-holding and exceptionally powerful brakes encourage really fast travel.

H.R.D. "RAPIDE"

The physical comfort offered was excellent—aided by the already well-known Vincent-H.R.D. system of rear springing (via swinging rear chain-stays), which provided generous deflection over the most prominent manhole covers. Steering was positive and safe at all speeds, whilst the damper on the girder-type forks was ignored at anything below 90 m.p.h. Above this gait it was set to "just biting," merely as a precautionary measure and not because it seemed necessary. "Hands-off" riding, whilst never to be recommended on modern roads with the ever-present uncertainty of potholes and erratic drivers, was achieved without worry, while the Vincent's speedometer denoted 85-90 m.p.h.!

Vibration was virtually non-existent throughout the whole range of revolutions. The close pitch finning of the deeply spigoted alloy barrels, with their

cast-iron liners, combined with a crankcase assembly able to cope with double the standard b.h.p. figure, immediately suggests enormous rigidity capable of withstanding continuous high power output without sacrifice of reliability. With a compression ratio measuring no more than 6.8 to 1, this 50-degree twin unit should possess the attribute of trouble-free mileage unaffected by maintained high speeds. When it is remembered that a cruising speed of 55 m.p.h. in top gear means no more than revolutions in the neighbourhood of 2,500, it can be realized that it would be somewhat difficult to tire this engine on

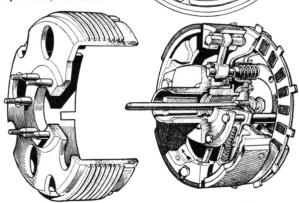

(Right) Component parts of the new clutch. As the pilot friction plate takes up the drive the servo clutch shoes are expanded within the sprocket drum, their grip increasing with the torque. The sectioned drawing above shows that both shoes are of the leading type. Note the centralizing springs.

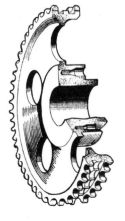

BRIEF SPECIFICATION 998 c.c. VINCENT-H.R.D. "RAPIDE" SERIES "B."

Engine: 50-degree twin-cylinder o.h.v.; 84 mm. bore by 90 mm. stroke—998 c.c.; compression ratio 6.8 to 1; crankshaft carried on roller and ball bearings on drive side and roller on timing side with outrigger roller journal; nickel-chrome connecting rods mounted on triple-row needle-roller big-end bearings; alloy cylinder barrels with shrunk-in cast-iron liners; alloy heads; high camshaft; short push-rod all-enclosed valve gear; dry-sump lubrication by reciprocating and rotary plunger pump with pressure feed to valve gear; two Amal carburetters; forward-mounted, gear-driven magneto.

Transmission: Unit-construction four-speed, foot-operated gearbox with gear indicator; ratios 3.5, 4.2, 5.5 and 9.1 to 1; self-servo operated clutch; ⅜-in. triplex primary chain with externally adjusted spring-blade tensioner; polished aluminium oilbath chaincase; rear chain, ⅝ in. by ⅜ in. roller with finger adjuster.

Frame: Engine comprises frame basis; pressed-steel top member, bolted to cylinder heads, containing 6-pint oil tank and supports fuel tank; pivot type, triangulated suspension at rear with adjustable shock-absorbers and enclosed springs, front forks, girder pattern with central compression spring and shock dampers.

Wheels: 26-in. by 3.00-in. front tyre and 26-in. by 3.50 studded rear tyre fitted on polished rims; hubs of light alloy with Skefko taper-roller bearings; brakes, Vincent-H.R.D. dual type, balanced and compensated, 7-in. dia. by ⅞ in.; both wheels quickly detachable with tommy-bar spindle nuts; mudguards of polished duralumin; propstand each side and rear stand.

Fuel tank: 3¾ gals. stainless steel; rubber kneegrips.

Dimensions: Wheelbase, 56 ins.; overall length, 85½ ins., overall width, 25½ ins. saddle height, 30 ins. (unladen), ground clearance, 5½ ins. weight, 455 lb.

Finish: Small parts cadmium plated; exhaust pipes, silencer, wheels, etc., chromium plated; tank, black, with gold lettering and lining; frame members, black enamel.

Equipment: Miller 6 v. 50 w. separate dynamo, driven from primary chain; 8-in. head lamp; electric horn; 120 m.p.h. Smith speedometer with internal front-wheel gearing; pillion footrests; Feridax Dualseat.

Price: £235 plus £63 4s. P.T.

Extra: Double sprocket rear hub, price £2 7s. 6d.

Makers: The Vincent-H.R.D. Co., Ltd., Stevenage, Herts.

British roads. Despite the 998 c.c.s, and because of the high gearing, it was possible to cover nearly 60 miles to the gallon under favourable conditions of flat country and little traffic, provided that the cruising speed was kept below 65-70 m.p.h.

Beyond the legal restrictions of "built-up" areas, in the matter of full sporting performance, it would require a very expensive four-wheeler to retain a glimpse of the "Rapide's" rear plate. Under conditions of clear road the acceleration was terrific, and normal gear-change speeds were: Bottom to second, 30 m.p.h.; second to third, 65 m.p.h.; and into top at just on 80 m.p.h. Care was necessary on wet roads if wheelspin was to be avoided, and even on the second to third change it was possible to detect a slight squirm if the throttle was banged open following the change of ratio.

Fast open bends could be tackled with a definite intention to stay on a chosen line, and no ordinary bump could throw either wheel off course. Unless the speedometer was watched it was very easy to enter sharp bends far too quickly, because of the utter absence of fuss. Fortunately, the machine is exceptionally well found in the matter of brakes, and the fourfold power exerted by the duo-stoppers on front and rear wheels provides an ample measure of security. With 45 very effective b.h.p. available within the confines of a 56-in. wheelbase, and a weight, with fuel, in the region of 450 lb., smooth braking becomes an absolute essential.

The gear change was a shade heavy, and unless the "cog-shifting" was neatly timed there was a discernible "clonk" as the new gear went home. If gear changes were made at high revs. this criticism ceased to apply.

Many fast miles over roads pitted with new and unexpected frost-produced potholes showed a need for keeping the fork dampers on the tight side, otherwise unpleasant bottoming occurred, but other than this nothing but praise could be applied to the front suspension.

Fast night riding became a pleasure with the powerful Miller 50-watt dynamo supplying an 8-in. head lamp possessed of an exceptionally penetrating beam. Objects 200 yds. ahead could be distinguished with the main "pencil" light, but up to speeds of 50 m.p.h. the dipped light provided a plentiful spread of illumination.

Close watch was kept for possible oil leaks, but nothing more than a vague mist appeared on the rear inlet push-rod tube, following a 200-mile journey in warm weather, with the "sitting upright" maximum of 97 m.p.h. used when favourable road conditions permitted. With acceleration from the 60 m.p.h. figure to this touring maximum available within 20 seconds, high averages became a matter-of-course business on long journeys.

Accessibility is excellent, thanks to the many practical features embodied, and a glance at the tommy-bar wheel nuts, in conjunction with the generously proportioned thumb bolts, lends ready credence to the fact that a timed adjustment of the rear chain occupied exactly 35 seconds without the use of spanners. Beneath the Dualseat slides the instantly available tool-tray, with a set of good-quality spanners quickly available.

The general finish and appearance of the machine are good. Polished surfaces on the huge timing case, magneto cover, dynamo-drive cover-plate and oil-bath casing make for quick and easy cleaning, whilst the ebony and gold-lined tank finish is quietly impressive.

TESTER'S ROAD REPORT

MODEL 998 c.c. VINCENT H.R.D. RAPIDE SERIES B

Maximum Speeds in:—

			Time from Standing Start
Top Gear (Ratio 3.5 to 1)	112 m.p.h. = 5179 r.p.m.	44 secs.
Third Gear (Ratio 4.2 to 1)	101 m.p.h. = 5579 r.p.m.	24⅘ secs.
Second Gear (Ratio 5.5 to 1)	83 m.p.h. = 5971 r.p.m.	14⅘ secs.

Speeds over measured Quarter Mile:—

Flying Start 108.5 m.p.h. Standing Start 62.1 m.p.h.

Braking Figures On DAMP TARRED ROAD **Surface, from 30 m.p.h.:—**

Both Brakes 27 ft. Front Brake 32 ft. Rear Brake 59 ft.

Fuel Consumption:— 49 M.P.G.

Oil Consumption:— 1550 m.p.g.

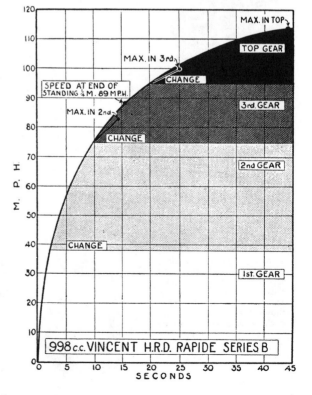

998 c.c. VINCENT H.R.D. RAPIDE SERIES B

And Very Nice, Too!

A Test Run on the Prototype "Series B" Vincent-H.R.D. Rapide Described by **Graham Walker**

long, snaky line alternately up and down the kerb running alongside an arterial road. Despite the fact that the kerb was attacked at a narrow angle of some 30 degrees, there was no effect whatsoever on the steering, the engine maintained its even beat, and there were no signs of protest—not even from the passenger!

EVER since my advance description of the new 998 c.c. "Series B" Vincent-H.R.D. Rapide appeared in our December 6, 1945, issue I have been bombarded with letters from enthusiasts from as far away as America, Canada, Australia, South Africa, and, it seems, most of the places in between!

All the writers have clamoured for further details and the majority have suggested what they would give for a ride on one.

"How does it handle, and what'll it do?"

"When do you expect deliveries to commence? I've got one on order."

"Is it *really* as compact as it looks in the pictures, and what about accessibility?"

These are typical examples of the questions asked, but the one that tickled me most was: "Is the 'boneless wonder' frame a success?"

This, of course, was a reference to the very novel construction which dispenses with the front down tube and seat tube, the massive engine-gearbox unit forming the foundation on which is mounted the combined pressed-steel oil tank-cum-backbone and forged steering head, also the swinging rear chain stays of the well-proven rear-springing system developed by the Stevenage people.

Well, chaps, at last I can answer some of the questions, as I recently had the very good fortune to ride the production pilot model quite a few miles over nicely assorted country. From this fact you will gather that deliveries will shortly be on the way, and let me add that whatever my various correspondents offered for a gallop on the model would be well worth while!

The new design is really delightful. Of many impressions, perhaps the most vivid is the compactness of the machine. On the previous Sunday I lapped the Cadwell Park circuit on G. Brown's record-holding 500 c.c. single-cylinder model; the new big twin is, quite literally, exactly similar with regard to its main dimensions; furthermore, it steers just as well, and that is saying a very great deal.

The prototype had done very few miles, having, in fact, only been assembled the previous day, thus, no attempt was made to give it the gun; that oppor-

(Above) Aptly nicknamed the "Little Big Twin," the new Rapide is a masterpiece of compactness. On production models a prop stand will be fitted to the forward extension of the engine plates.

(Right) The proportions of the new model can be gauged by this picture of six-foot Graham Walker in the saddle with Phil Irving on the pillion.

tunity will, I hope, come later on, when the engine is fully run-in. Suffice to say that one has only to tweak the grip more than an eighth of an inch to realize what the urge will be like when that happy day arrives. There is something peculiarly satisfying about a model which lifts its headlug appreciably when the throttle is opened suddenly!

At the other end of the scale the flexibility is truly outstanding; at less than 20 m.p.h. in top gear (and with Phil Irving on the pillion portion of the combined seat) the model was ridden in a

The general handling is exactly like that of the 500 c.c. job, despite the fact that the weight is temporarily around 425 pounds, due to the enforced use of steel for several parts which, in production, will be fabricated in light alloy. It has, in fact, been due to the difficulty in obtaining correct forgings that the pilot model was not ready for test several weeks ago.

The servo-type clutch which increases its grip with increase of load is extraordinarily light in operation;

Continued on page 21

Despite its novel frame construction, the Rapide combines an orthodox appearance with its imposing lines. Among many ingenious features are brake and gear-change pedals which remain in constant relation to the adjustable footrests.

The 998 c.c

A Connoisseur's Machine with a Co

FEW machines have ever aroused so much interest as the Series B "Rapide" Vincent-H.R.D. There is a number of reasons for the near-excitement with which this model is discussed in motor cycle circles; it is an entirely new post-war model; it is unconventional in design in that, among other features, the massive vee-twin engine forms part of the frame; it gives a high-speed performance to which movie superlatives might well apply;

The massive vee-twin engine itself forms part of the frame. The result is extraordinary compactness and a 56in wheelbase

it is designed and manufactured by enthusiasts with an unassailable belief in the rightness of their project.

But it needs to be appreciated that much of the interest is purely academic. The machine was conceived, and emerges, as a product primarily suitable for the experienced motor cyclist who is a connoisseur—the man who knows the uses of this remarkable motor cycle and who at the same time knows how to use it. On this "initiated" basis the road test was conducted and this report is given.

It is next to impossible to get acquainted with the new "Rapide" without recalling the pre-war edition. In its capacity for eating up miles and for clocking three figures, no matter what its tune, the old model achieved widespread fame in spite of a few shortcomings such as heavy low-speed steering, a clutch and gear box that were overstressed by the tremendous torque of the engine, inaccessibility, and an oil- and petrol-pipe layout that gave rise to the affectionate expression "a plumber's nightmare." The measure of criticism that these points aroused was usually in inverse proportion to the enthusiasm of the owner, but in any case, the points do not arise with the new model.

Light and Accurate Steering

It is true that in the second or so between the time the wheels turn and the time the neat rider has his feet on the rests a very slight steering roll is felt; but beyond that point the steering is light yet of hair-line accuracy. The new gear box in unit with the engine is so massive as to be virtually indestructible, and the self-servo clutch is designed to increase its gripping power as the torque increases. On accessibility and cleanliness in design the new unit is well up to modern standards, bearing in mind that it is a vee-twin equipped with two carburettors.

How far the designers have justified the machine's nickname, "little big-twin," is apparent immediately one is astride the special Dualseat. The wheelbase of 56in is

about average for a five-hundred, tank width is comfortable, and there is no heaviness in the feel of the machine. It can be manœuvred manually and kick-started without undue exertion.

The kick-starter crank is a long, curved arm giving immense leverage. It does not spin the engine, yet is fully effective. Part of the test was carried out during the abnormal freeze-up, and even under those conditions two or three long, swinging kicks gave a certain start providing one knew the wrinkles of flooding the carburettors—the front more than the rear—and the throttle setting. With a warm engine it was more usual to obtain a first-kick start than otherwise. And when the engine was warm the tick-over was clock-like and reliable.

Mechanically the engine is quiet apart from rocker-gear clatter, audible till the rush of wind past the ears takes its place. Exhaust silencing is commendably effective at all speeds and under all conditions of acceleration. Control layout is conventional, but the riding position is not. Vincents retain the narrow, flat and almost straight handlebars which give a precision and endearing "tautness" to handling. The Dualseat is highish and, coupled with the widely adjustable footrests, results in the rider's being poised over the machine rather than "in" it, as with a "sit-up-and-beg" riding position. The feeling of full command that results is, of course, admirably suited to high-speed travelling and, in the case of the "Rapide," has no disadvantages when trickling along in town.

Riding postures are always a matter of individual taste, but there is little doubt that few riders would want to make radical alterations on this Vincent-H.R.D. The Dualseat, which is attached at the rear to the unsprung

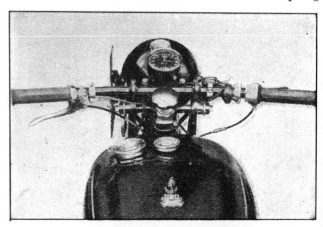

Almost straight handlebars have been a feature of Vincent-H.R.D.s for many years. The riding position of the Series B is first class

/INCENT-H.R.D. RAPIDE

ormance and Many Appealing Features

forks, is commendably free from sway, but with this arrangement is inclined to seem hard on a long run.

The rear footrests and the Dualseat serve a twin function. Used normally there is excellent accommodation for a pillion passenger, with a measure of comfort better than the general run of pillion equipment. Alternatively, the rear seat and footrests may be used by the solo rider when occasionally wishing to reduce windage—they were used to obtain the maximum speed figures during this test. For racing purposes, when the rear position would be used most of the time, both the rear brake pedal and the gear-change pedal may be reversed to bring them under the toes. All footrests and the kick-starter pedal fold, a feature appreciated when there is a minimum of space for parking or garaging.

Of remarkable lightness in operation—the handlebar lever is easily raised by the little finger—the self-servo clutch takes up the drive smoothly, but so quickly that it leaves no margin for the slightest ham-fistedness. The drive is either engaged or disengaged during a very short movement of the lever, and with a 9.4 to 1 bottom gear traffic work, at first, required more than usual concentration. The engine is very tractable and would pull away without harshness at tick-over speeds.

Gear changing from bottom to second and vice versa has to be done slowly if quietness is to be achieved, and for the other ratios a lazy pedal movement is better than slickness. Particularly between the two higher ratios, it seemed advantageous not to use the clutch. Some difficulty with second and third gears jumping out of mesh was remedied by the fitting of a stronger selector spring.

When built-up areas have been left behind the "Rapide" comes into its own. It may be asserted with confidence that there has never before been a production model with so much to commend it as a road-burner's dream. From 40 m.p.h. up to the maximum of over 100

Information Panel

998 c.c. Vincent-H.R.D. Rapide

SPECIFICATION

TYPE : Vincent-H.R.D. Series B "Rapide."

ENGINE : 998 c.c. (84 x 90 mm) vee-twin, high camshaft O.H.V., in unit with gear box. Fully enclosed valve gear. Dry-sump lubrication.

CARBURETTORS : Amal ; twist-grip throttle control and twin handlebar-mounted air levers.

GEAR BOX : Vincent-H.R.D. with positive-stop foot control. Bottom, 9.4 to 1. Second, 5.5 to 1. Third, 4.2 to 1. Top, 3.5 to 1.

CLUTCH : Self-servo Vincent-H.R.D.

TRANSMISSION : Chain. Primary 3/8in. triple. Secondary 5/8 x 3/8in.

IGNITION : Lucas magneto, auto-advance.

LIGHTING : Miller dynamo ; 8in head lamp ; stoplight.

DYNAMO OUTPUT : 50 watts.

FUEL CAPACITY : Over 3½ gal.

OIL CAPACITY : 6 pints.

TYRE SIZE : Front 3.00 x 20in Avon ribbed ; Rear 3.50 x 19in Avon studded.

BRAKES : Twin on each wheel ; drums 7in diameter x 7/8in wide.

SUSPENSION : Single-spring girder forks, with porous-bronze bushes ; pivot-action rear springing.

WHEELBASE : 56in.

GROUND CLEARANCE : 5in unladen.

SADDLE : Special Feridax Dualseat.

WEIGHT : 476lb (with 2½ gallons of fuel and fully equipped.)

PRICE : £231 plus Purchase Tax (in Britain)—£293 7s. 5d. Speedometer extra £4, plus £1 1s 8d Purchase Tax.

MAKERS : The Vincent-H.R.D. Co., Ltd., Stevenage, Herts.

PERFORMANCE DATA

MAXIMUM SPEED : First : 56 m.p.h.
Second : 86 m.p.h.
Third : 98 m.p.h.
Top : Not obtained.

ACCELERATION :

	10-30 m.p.h.	20-40 m.p.h.	30-50 m.p.h.
Bottom	2⅗ secs	2⅖ secs	2⅘ secs
Second	—	3⅖ secs	3⅕ secs
Third	—	4⅘ secs	4⅕ secs

Speed at end of quarter-mile from rest : 86 m.p.h.

Time to cover standing quarter mile : 15⅖ secs.

PETROL CONSUMPTION : At 40 m.p.h., 67 m.p.g. At 50 m.p.h., 64 m.p.g. At 60 m.p.h., 62 m.p.g.

BRAKING from 30 m.p.h. to rest 26ft (surface : dry tar macadam).

TURNING CIRCLE : 17ft diameter.

MINIMUM NON-SNATCH SPEED : 17 m.p.h. in top gear.

WEIGHT PER C.C. ; 0.47lb per c.c.

R.P.M. IN TOP GEAR at 30 m.p.h. : 1,371.

m.p.h. there is thrilling performance available at a twist of the grip. This is achieved by a high power/weight ratio and an engine, with lowish compression ratio and "easy" valve timing, pulling high gears. In consequence, the performance is available in top gear, it being unnecessary to use third and second unless the limit of acceleration is required.

Throughout the speed range there is no vibration. The engine churns out its power with unusual smoothness and, at all times—even at maximum speed—feels to be working easily and "solidly."

It seems to be the natural order of things to cruise at speeds between 80 and 85 m.p.h. Then the engine speed is under 4,000 r.p.m. in top gear and, unless there is an adverse wind, the throttle is not much more than half open. If, then, the grip is given a tweak to full bore, the "Rapide" responds quite definitely.

Excellent Brakes

It may sound unreal to quote such high cruising speeds. But rapid road work is the type of riding for which the Vincent-H.R.D. is designed. Steering and road-holding are absolutely first class. The machine is rock steady and holds its line on the straights and in curves in a manner that is uncanny.

Each wheel has compensated dual brakes. Front-wheel braking is outstanding and light pressure on the standard-length handlebar lever will squeal the tyre unmercifully. Rear brake leverage is, by design, at a minimum to avoid the danger of a locked wheel at high speed; very heavy pressure is required and the reduction in leverage, it is suggested, has been overdone. But the fact remains that, used together and with the front brakes taking nearly all the load, the figures achieved were considerably better than average.

Performance figures on the previous page tell their own story. They show that, in spite of (or because of) its large capacity, the machine is reasonably economical on petrol. When cruising at higher than average speeds—and that is as might be expected—there is but a small difference in the figures achieved at 40 m.p.h. and 60 m.p.h. Mean maximum speeds are given for first, second and third gears,

Without tools the tail of the mudguard can be clamped up as shown and the rear wheel removed; neither are tools required for chain adjustment. However, the tool kit is stowed in a readily accessible tray under the Dualseat.

but it was not possible to find a private road with a suitable run-in to achieve a mean two-way maximum speed in top gear. It can be taken, however, that in top gear the "Rapide" will exceed 100 m.p.h. without difficulty—in fact, flash readings of 105 to 107 were twice recorded and, in circumstances that were favourable, 114 m.p.h. was reached.

Though the big engine and high gearing of the machine suggest easy, loping, fussless mile-eating there is searing acceleration available if required. Standing-start getaways against the watch provide a memorable thrill and leave a black line of burnt rubber on the road surface. Perhaps more telling than the speed at the end of a quarter-mile given in the table is the time to cover that distance from a standing start—15⅔s was the two-direction mean of six runs. This type of riding is punishment to the clutch, bearing in mind the 9.4 to 1 bottom gear; the latest clutch, however, stood up well even to a whole series of standing starts.

The Vincent-H.R.D. has innumerable "rider's points." There is a 50-watt Miller dynamo which keeps the battery adequately charged though the machine may be used mainly for town work at tick-over speeds. The machine under test was fitted with a 24-watt main bulb in the 8in head lamp which provided a really good, wide beam of white intensity; as soon as supplies are available a larger-capacity bulb will be used, when the lighting should be in a class by itself.

Both wheels have detachable spindles with integral tommy bars. For setting chain tension there are hand-operated "click"-type adjusters and the job can be done without tools; further, no tools are necessary for wheel removal.

The Vincent-H.R.D. Series B "Rapide" is a machine in a class by itself; a dream machine for the rider who is competent to handle its colossal performance; a machine that will continue to be talked about wherever motor cyclists forgather.

At its best when travelling at very high speeds; the rider can adopt a crouched riding position by using the pillion footrests and the back of the Dualseat. If required, the gear change pedal and the brake pedal can be reversed to bring them near the rear footrests

The "Black Shadow" Assumes Substance

Details of a Sports Addition to the Vincent-H.R.D. Big-Twin Programme

The "first off" of the new "Black Shadows" from the Stevenage factory. Lighting equipment and a streamlined back to the speedometer will be features of the production model, listed at £300 plus purchase tax.

THAT notoriously ignorant fellow, the man in the street, might very well think that 112 m.p.h. from a standard production motorcycle is speed enough for everyone . . . but apparently it is not, and the Vincent-H.R.D. company have just proved the point to their own satisfaction. As the makers of the "world's fastest standard motorcycle" they should be in a position to assess the world demand for speed machinery, and quite some time ago they decided that a sports edition of the now famous Series B "Rapide" would fill what might be called a long-felt want.

Experimentation with a "pepped-up" Series B began last year and the outcome was seen at the "Bemsee" Dunholme meeting when George Brown finished the 100-mile Senior race in second berth at 85.40 m.p.h. on the prototype. The production model was announced to the trade a short while ago and already the entire output of approximately 20 a month has been booked up for three months to come. As some 75 per cent. of these machines are for export to all parts of the globe, it seems fairly conclusive that this old planet still breeds men who must have "just that bit more."

A Marked Appearance

As was stated in "Motor Cycling," January 1, when we made the first announcement concerning it, this newcomer differs principally from the standard model in internal details and it was because they wanted to give it a distinguishing, characteristic appearance of its own that the makers decided on a novel "colour" scheme. To achieve this, the cylinder barrels and heads and the crankcase are anodized black, with the fin tips left polished, while the chain and magneto covers are stove-enamelled in shining ebony. Thus comes a new addition to motorcycle nomenclature—the "Black Shadow."

A quick glance over the imposing machine reveals other changes from standard, apart from the finish. For example, all four brake drums are of cast iron with cooling ribbing and they are operated by heavyweight Bowdenex cables. Then there is the 5-in. diameter speedometer, calibrated to 150 m.p.h. or 250 k.p.h., mounted on a special bracket for easy reading at speed. In production the back of the instrument will have a streamlined cover—our photograph does not show it.

Changes from standard practice which are not external include the following:—the connecting rods and rockers are highly polished, while high-compression pistons give a ratio of 7.3 to 1, with higher ratios available if desired. Lapped-side, high-pressure piston rings are used and the inlet and exhaust ports are individually polished and blended to streamline shape. In the induction ports bronze adaptors are fitted to carry the bigger carburetters—1⅛-in. bores as against the normal 1 1/16-in.

Triple valve springs replace the standard double coils and ignition efficiency is enhanced by the employment of a laboratory-tested magneto.

Alterations to the transmission incorporate a lightened clutch shoe carrier, a lighter cam-plate for the gear-shift mechanism and a rearrangement of the intermediate ratios giving 2.07 to 1 reduction on bottom gear, that is a 7.25 to 1 gear with a 46-tooth rear sprocket.

In addition to the ribbed drums the braking efficiency is still further increased by the use of Ferodo MR41 linings.

In other respects the "Black Shadow" embodies the numerous refinements which have made the Series B such an outstanding machine, and it is being listed complete with lighting, speedometer, pillion equipment and the "under-the-saddle" tool kit at £300 plus £81 purchase tax. The makers, the Vincent-H.R.D. Co., Ltd., of Stevenage, Herts, expect to deliver the first batch by the end of March.

And Very Nice, Too !—
Continued from page 17
incidentally, this is now housed in a separate compartment external to the oilbath primary chaincase. Another point which impressed me immensely was the ease of starting; on practically any machine nowadays I find this difficult, due to a gammy ankle, but the "Little Big Twin" can be prodded into action with what I can best describe as the first *depression* of the pedal as distinct from a lusty, swinging kick.

Since the original description a short external lever on the gear-selector shaft enables "neutral" to be found immediately and such is the freedom of the gear assembly and the excellent design of the dogs that it is possible to change from third to top, and vice versa, without so much as touching the clutch or easing the throttle.

Mechanical noise was conspicuous by its absence and the exhaust note was pleasantly subdued whilst somehow subtly indicating potent power. Great pains have been taken throughout the design to eliminate sources of oil leaks. Admittedly, the mileage covered has been insufficient to provide positive proof on this point, but a diligent search all over the engine-gear unit revealed only two "weeps"—one from a temporary jury-rigged exhaust lifter fitting, the other from an insufficiently tightened gland nut on a pushrod tube.

With the aid of a few tools housed in the cunning under-the-saddle sliding tray Phil demonstrated the accessibility of the valve clearance adjustments, easy detachability of battery and dynamo, and the fact that the two vertical carburetters can be got out without contortions. One by one I went over with him the points enumerated in my original description. Yes, there can be no doubt about it, all the aims of the designers have been achieved.

This is truly a motorcycle conceived and built by motorcyclists who know the answers for motorcyclists who have asked the questions.

Forgotten to mention the two-on-each-hub Duo brakes? No, I haven't! Like the front forks, they are one of the features which are not new because it has been found impossible to improve them.

By now you will probably have gathered that I was *very* impressed with the Series B. If so, that is precisely what I intended, because I am. Sorry I can't answer that "What'll it do?" question yet, but it won't be long . . . !

"Black Shadow" Model with a Maximum Speed of 125 m.p.h.

WHEN the remarkable high-speed performance of the Vincent-H.R.D. Series B "Rapide" is called to mind, it may seem unreal that a faster model should be made available. But it is a fact that right from the drawing-board stage of the "Rapide" the designers had in mind producing faster editions of this unorthodox 998 c.c. high-camshaft vee-twin.

Now that production of the basic model has settled down to a steady flow, it is possible to introduce the first of the variants. It is called the "Black Shadow"; and, in keeping with its sombre yet misleading name, the new model has a black finish for the cylinder heads, cylinders, crankcase and crankcase covers. The aim has been to provide a machine with an even more lively performance than the 110 m.p.h. "Rapide," while retaining the low-speed characteristics of the latter. In other words, the "Black Shadow" is not a super-sports machine which achieves top-end brake horse-power at the cost of easy starting, tractability and mechanical quietness. As a short run on one of the new models proved, these commendable features have not been sacrificed to obtain the added liveliness and about 15 m.p.h. higher maximum speed.

Never Stressed

What may be construed as a paradox in the last observation can be readily explained by reference to the "Rapide." This model gives a thrilling performance yet is never highly stressed. The compression ratio is but 6.45 to 1 (as usually assembled with a $\frac{1}{32}$in compression plate), the valve lift and valve timing are "easy," and the intake bore of $1\frac{1}{8}$in does not allow the engine to reach its power peak. High power/weight ratio (less than $\frac{1}{2}$lb per c.c. is a guide) and high gearing give the model easy, loping speed. At 90 m.p.h., with the standard top gear ratio of 3.5 to 1, engine revolutions are about 4,100. Compare this with a high-geared five-hundred such as the pre-war Vincent-H.R.D. Comet; the r.p m. at 90 m.p.h. would be well over

5,200; or nearly 5,900 with the 5 to 1 top gear common to many present-day 500 c.c. machines.

Hence the increased b.h.p. "permitted" the Black Shadow engine has been accomplished largely by providing better breathing and a slightly higher compression ratio. The choke diameter of the carburettors is $1\frac{1}{8}$in and the inlet ports have bronze adaptors of that diameter. These modifications mean some 18 per cent increased breathing capacity. The compression ratio is 7.3 to 1 (achieved by pistons with higher crowns than those fitted to the standard model), which, it wih be noted, is not unduly high and is entirely suitable for Pool fuel.

Streamlined Parts

These changes are by no means the whole story, but they are fundamentally responsible for giving the additional engine revolutions to provide a 125 m.p.h. maximum. At that speed the r.p.m. are but 5,800! To obtain the best possible gas flow, inlet and exhaust ports are blended to streamline shape and are highly polished. And to ensure that at the higher r.p.m. the valves follow accurately the cam contours, the valve-spring pressure is increased by about 10 per cent by the addition of a third spring inside the standard two helical springs to each valve.

With the object of eliminating any surface scratches which might precipitate a fracture under extreme stresses, the connecting-rods and valve rockers are fully polished. Another difference, so far as the engine is concerned, is the use of lapped-side high-pressure piston rings.

There are three modifications in the gear box. First of all, the bottom ratio is 7.25 to 1, assuming the usual 46-tooth rear wheel sprocket is used. This ratio compares with 9.0 to 1 used on the stan-

dard "Rapide." Other ratios—5.5, 4.2 and 3.5 to 1—remain the same, the advantage of the higher bottom gear for the "Black Shadow" being that the relatively big jump from bottom to second with the standard gearing is avoided. Second alteration is a drilled and thus lightened shoe carrier in the self-servo clutch; and third is a similarly lightened selector cam plate. The last two modifications are aimed at facilitating rapid gear changing. Lightening the shoe carrier reduces clutch inertia—a great

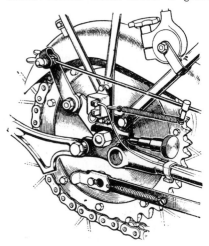

No tools are necessary for wheel removal or chain adjustment. Both wheels have detachable spindles with the integral tommy-bars on the nearside

advantage at high engine speeds. In the same way a reduction in the weight of the cam plate ensures that inertia does not cause a gear to be "passed" during ultra-rapid changes.

Magnetos on "Black Shadow" engines are specially selected and laboratory-tested. Braking under the most arduous conditions is improved by the use of ribbed one-piece cast-iron brake drums on both wheels, by Ferodo MR41 linings noted for their non-fading characteristics, and by the use of Bowdenex cable for front-brake operation.

The high maximum speed of the "Black Shadow" has made a special speedometer necessary. This is a Smith's instrument with a 5in dial calibrated up to 150 m.p.h. It is mounted on the fork girder bridge piece and can be read with a minimum of distraction from the road ahead.

Larger-bore carburettors and a slightly higher compression ratio have endowed the engine with increased b.h.p.

VINCENT-H.R.D.

As intimated earlier, the new model is distinctive in its sober appearance. The light-alloy cylinders and heads are anodized black except at the fin tips, which are virgin alloy polished. Black stove enamel is used on the crankcase and covers. It is probable, though not finally decided, that the light-alloy mudguards will also be finished in black enamel.

Numerous improvements have been incorporated in the standard "Rapide" model during the past year, and these are, of course, common to the new model. Most noticeable from an external examination are the light-alloy water excluders riveted to the front brake plates—these excluders, incidentally, may be readily fitted to brakes in service before the change. Other alterations which are quickly noticed are the additional rear mudguard stays and an improved stoplight switch.

A three-quarter view of the new model. A special 5-in dial speedometer calibrated up to 150 m.p.h. is fitted

Six-spring Clutch

Six springs are now used in the clutch. The clutch was originally designed for six springs, but three were found to give sufficient pressure for all purposes. The result was amazingly light operation—so light indeed that careful control when engaging the clutch was none too easy. With the full complement of springs, operation is still light, while smooth engagement is more readily achieved. Other modifications are a strengthened gear selector pawl spring, and a kick-starter return spring which keeps the pedal crank hard against its stop, which has also been redesigned.

A slight tendency for oil to drain down the inlet-valve guide of the front cylinder has been eliminated by the provision of two grooves in the inlet rocker bush. Another detail change is the fitting of Champion N8 plugs, which are of a softer type than the NA8 used in earlier engines. These two changes have rectified slight cold-starting difficulties experienced occasionally.

The flip on a "Black Shadow" model, referred to earlier, was a stimulating experience. The machine had covered only 94 miles and had to be treated gently—that meant no cruising above 90 m.p.h.! To get a valid comparison, a standard "Rapide," almost equally new (speedometer reading 48 miles), was taken out immediately afterwards. As anticipated, the "Black Shadow" was livelier above 60 m.p.h.—indeed, if the throttle was tweaked open at that speed in top gear, one had to grip the handlebars very firmly to avoid being jerked along the Dualseat. The speedometer needle travelled round relentlessly and in an estimated 14 seconds was passing the 110 mark. Solicitude for the newly born engine meant that the throttle had to be rolled back smartly, but the impression was gained that the claimed maximum speed could have been reached without difficulty. As with all Vincent-H.R.D.s, the high-speed handling was absolutely first-class and there was no vibration.

Perhaps of greater interest was the low-speed performance. The 7.25 to 1 bottom gear seemed to be no disadvantage either when getting away or in the midday traffic of two Hertfordshire towns. Nor was it by any means difficult to handle the throttle so that there was no pinking. In fact, the only time that pinking was heard was when accelerating hard from 60 m.p.h. in the tests mentioned in the last paragraph. First-kick starting was easy, and idling was slow and regular—both excellent characteristics were as good with the new model as with the standard "Rapide." In short, both models seemed as near identical as makes no difference until speeds above 60 or 70 m.p.h. were reached—then the "Black Shadow" came into its own.

Standard equipment on the "Black Shadow" includes electric lighting, horn, stop-light, speedometer, licence holder, and full pillion equipment. The price is £300 plus, in Great Britain, £81 Purchase Tax. The machine can be supplied without lighting equipment, when a price adjustment is made. Makers are The Vincent-H.R.D. Co., Ltd., Stevenage, Herts.

Details of the self-servo clutch. The single-plate pilot clutch brings into operation the shoes which increase their pressure on the drum as the loading increases

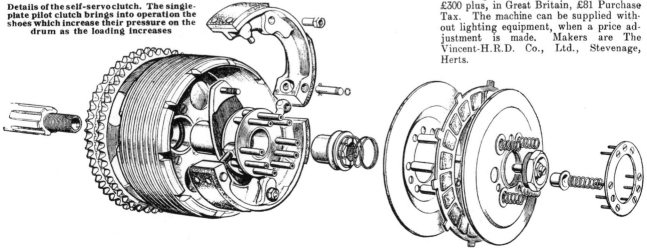

MORE THAN

A Hard-riding Pressman Finds His
Fast Motorcycling Reformed by the
"Black Shadow" Vincent-H.R.

(Left to right), Tom Henn, Editor, "Radio Times" and keen rider, Cyril Quantrill, Chas. Markham and S.-E. Centre speedman Angus Herbert survey the "Black Shadow" standing on the T.T. Course.

DO you remember the song and dance I created last year on account of having covered a measured quarter-mile in a shortage of time which equalled 112 m.p.h.? "Fastest standard machine in the world"—I quoted and sat back with a complacent air completely belied by a readiness to mention my "fastest-ever" performance whenever the Tall Stories Dept. forgathered to exchange incredible yarns accompanied by pop-eyed wonder.

It was a Vincent-H.R.D. Series B "Rapide" that enabled me to claim intimate knowledge of the blurred landscape existing above 110 m.p.h.—and it was its creators, those same supermen of Stevenage, who robbed my boast of its headline attraction by producing a *sports* edition based upon that touring tornado. This variation on a thousand-c.c. theme would be known as the "Black Shadow" and would possess a maximum in the region of 125 "per"—such was the gist of early Press notices. At which stage I ceased to marvel at my own previous daring dice and proceeded to lie doggo! Then, in mid-May, a brief note arrived which concluded, ". . . in the Island will be a 'Black Shadow' for your transport and road test to follow. . . ."

* * *

BY now, the highly individual specification which distinguishes a modern 998 c.c. Vincent-H.R.D. has been closely studied and keenly discussed by every bunch of roadburners the world over. The panel overleaf deals briefly with general details and measurements of this extraordinarily successful 50-degree twin with its high camshaft, short push-rod unit which produces such prodigious b.h.p., so let us dwell for a moment on the differences which make the "Shadow" faster than the previous fastest big multi.

Type 289 Amal carburetters of $1\frac{3}{8}$-in. bore replace the more modest $1\frac{1}{16}$-in. Type G instruments of the "Rapide" —with bronze adaptors to suit. Pistons with "a bump" raise compression ratio from 6.8 to 7.3 to 1; ports, rockers and connecting rods are highly polished and triple-valve springs replace the duplex pattern. Bottom gear becomes 7.25 in place of 9.1, whilst the gear cam-plate and clutch shoe carrier are drilled as an aid to swift "cog-shifting."

Markham has his education completed ". . . with full knowledge of how it feels to hit the atmosphere at two miles per minute . . ."

Navigator's bridge. The short handlebars, with their nicely placed controls, are features of the "Black Shadow." Note the dual carburetter air levers, the 5-in. 150-m.p.h. trip speedometer and the oil filler projecting through the fuel tank.

WO MILES A MINUTE!

By CHARLES MARKHAM

Ribbed cast-iron brake drums in place of steel and Ferodo MR 41 linings to replace MZ offer reassuring anchorage on a new high level, of which more anon.

All engine components are specially selected for accuracy and fit in assembly, the Lucas magneto is laboratory tested and cylinder heads, barrels, crankcase and covers are "Pylumin" treated for paint adherence before receiving a stove-enamelling in lustrous black. The Miller electrical equipment features a 7-in. head lamp (in place of the "Rapide's" 8-in.) and a 50-watt output dynamo of 3-in. diameter—this latter size will eventually replace the 3½-in. pattern at present standardized on the "Rapide." Finally, there is a Smiths speedometer of noble 5-in. diameter and most impressive 150-m.p.h. calibration!

It was Graham Walker himself who introduced me to the "Black Shadow"—with some typically candid comment

(Below) Weighing only 457 lb., the "Black Shadow" can be laid over in full confidence when cornering fast and steers to perfection.

"Pin-up" for any motor-cyclist! The sleek compactness of the machine (below) makes an attractive picture.

anent our respective proportions. I found it somewhat of a strain to ride nonchalantly when permanently confronted by a "clock" with such ambitious figuring, and if you had seen the eager crowds which collected wherever the "Shadow" was parked in the Island you would have realized that modern manhood has renounced Betty Grable as "essential to lasting happiness." So impressive are the zestful proportions of this latest space-pulverizer that my fellow North-countryman and B.B.C. favourite—Wilfred Pickles—was tempted to accompany me for a brief trip. And he thought "it were reet grand," too!

Following the convincing demonstration of Vincent-H.R.D. handling produced by the 1948 Senior Clubman's race, it would be superfluous for me to add any remarks on this score. Early last year, in my report on the "Rapide," I wrote that "fast open bends could be tackled with a definite intention to stay on a chosen line . . ." and there is little need to add to the compliment in view of recent events. Once accustomed to the short bars a tendency towards "wander" at low speeds becomes minimized, but is always evident on initial getaway. Above walking speed there is no suggestion of conscious effort in piloting this 450-odd lb. of beautifully contrived metal exactly as required.

It took me a couple of days to get the starting drill fully organized, but here I should interject that when I took over, the machine had covered over 2,000 miles of gruelling test work. With two new plugs fitted (Champion NA.8 type) the method from cold was: close both air levers, gently flood near-side carburetter, place right hand over intake of off-side carburetter and give three priming kicks of the well-proportioned starter crank. With the grip turned an infinitesimal amount a first-kick response could then be assured. "Hot" commencing required no special knack, but if the machine had been parked on its near-side prop for a short period it was found that the off-side carburetter tended to flood through the jet orifice, with a consequent spot of bother due to rich mixture.

The combination of a clutch somewhat "sudden" in action and a bottom gear ratio of 7.25 to 1 provided some startling getaways until I began to acquire the "feel" of things, but a little traffic-driving very quickly brought mastery. Two fingers are sufficient to control this ingenious self-servo clutch, which deals capably with all manner of abuse. Despite the need for generous revs. to obtain a smooth take-off in bottom gear it was possible to slow-march in top gear at 18 m.p.h. and to accelerate away in this 3.5 ratio from 22 m.p.h. Too much of this "plonking" technique did not suit the front plug, however, and is

BRIEF SPECIFICATION OF THE 998 c.c. VINCENT-H.R.D. "BLACK SHADOW"

Engine: 50-degree twin-cylinder o.h.v.; 84 mm. bore by 90 mm. stroke=998 c.c.; compression ratio, 7.3 to 1; crankshaft carried on roller and ball bearings on drive side and roller on timing side with outrigger roller journal; nickel-chrome connecting rods mounted on triple-row needle-roller big-end bearings; alloy cylinder barrels with shrunk-in cast-iron liners; alloy heads; high camshaft; short push-rod all-enclosed valve gear; triple valve springs; polished ports, rockers and connecting rods; dry-sump lubrication by reciprocating and rotary plunger pump with pressure feed to valve gear; separate type 289 Amal carburetters, 1⅛-in. bore with bronze adaptors; forward-mounted, gear-driven Lucas magneto—laboratory tested; all engine components specially selected on assembly for accuracy and fit.

Transmission: Unit construction four-speed foot-operated gearbox with gear indicator; ratios 3.5, 4.2, 5.5 and 7.25 to 1; self-servo operated clutch; ⅜-in. triplex primary chain with externally adjusted spring-blade tensioner; aluminium oil-bath chaincase; rear chain, ⅝-in. by ⅜-in. roller with finger adjustment; gear cam plate and clutch shoe carrier drilled to facilitate high-speed gear changing.

Frame: Engine unit comprises frame basis; pressed-steel top member containing 6-pint oil tank bolted to cylinder heads and supporting fuel tank; pivot-type triangulated suspension at rear with adjustable shock absorbers and enclosed springs; front forks, girder pattern, with central compression spring and shock dampers.

Wheels: 26-in by 3.00-in. front tyre ribbed and 26-in. by 3.50-in. rear studded pattern; hubs of light alloy with Skefko taper-roller bearings; brakes, Vincent-H.R.D. dual type balanced and compensated, 7-in. diameter by ⅞-in.; ribbed cast-iron drums with Ferodo MR 41 linings; both wheels quickly detachable with tommy-bar spindle nuts; mudguards of polished duralumin; spring-up prop stands each side and rear stand with tommy-bar fixing.

Fuel tank: 3¾ gallons capacity stainless steel

Dimensions: Wheelbase, 56 ins.; overall length, 85½ ins.; overall width, 25½ ins.; saddle height, 30 ins. (unladen), ground clearance 5½ ins.; weight, 457 lb. (dry).

Finish: Small parts cadmium plated; exhaust pipes, silencer, wheels, etc., chromium plated; tank, black, with gold lettering and lining; frame members, black enamel; heads, barrels, crankcase and covers treated by "Pylumin" process (for paint adherence) and enamelled black.

Equipment: Miller 6-v. 50-w. separate dynamo (3-in.), driven from primary chain; 7-in. head lamp and rear lamp incorporating stoplight; electric horn; special 150 m.p.h. Smiths speedometer with 5-in. dial, internal front wheel gearing; Feridax Dualseat incorporating tool tray; pillion footrests.

Price: £300 plus £81 P.T.

Extra: Double sprocket rear hub, price £2 7s. 6d. plus P.T.

Makers: The Vincent-H.R.D. Co. Ltd., Stevenage, Herts.

a practice neither desirable nor necessary because all intermediate ratios are inaudible in use.

The question of gear changing brings two points of criticism—a tendency to "drift" out of gear on the over-run and a certain difficulty in engaging third at anything above 65 m.p.h. in second.

To state a definite cruising speed on the open road is well-nigh impossible, as the margin is set only by road conditions and the rider's capabilities. From a standstill to 100 m.p.h. acceleration is constant and colossal—there can be no other description—and in the course of a 362 miles-in-the-day test run I recorded an average I dare not print. A non-stop 270 miles, except for very brief refuelling, was easily accomplished between lunch and tea—I never dine before 7 p.m.!

Such performance as this would be impossible or highly dangerous without a measure of braking capable of coping with two-miles-a-minute velocity. Take a peep at the test sheet and note that from 30 m.p.h. in top gear it is possible to stop in *22 ft. 6 ins.!* That I finished up seated on the filler-cap is hardly surprising—although it occasioned much mirth from two amazed witnesses. If there is anything more decided than the power of the "Shadow's" front and rear duo-braking I'm not sure that I want to experience it.

High-speed touring did not prove so hard on fuel as I anticipated, a state of affairs not difficult to understand when it is remembered that 60 m.p.h. in top gear means a mere whiff of throttle and no more than 2,700 r.p.m. On long-distance runs the tank would barely accept three gallons after 178 miles of mixed going and 75-80 m.p.h. cruising with the wind astern. This easy and effortless travel brought a lively problem concerning other road users who frequently misjudged the "Shadow's" rate of approach, due to the lack of noise and fuss. There was hardly more than a smooth burble from the exhaust, and although the valve gear could be detected at work it never reached annoying cadence.

Vibration was not apparent at any engine speed, the most that was felt being a faint tremor at peak revolutions in second gear. Pinking was evident and clearly audible if liberties were taken with the throttle, and if *real* acceleration were required from speeds as low as 50 m.p.h. it was kinder and more pleasant to employ the 4.2-to-1 third gear.

No doubt smooth power output is contributed to largely by the impressive rigidity of the engine unit with its deeply spigoted cylinder barrels and sturdy crankcase dimensions—a power plant which guarantees speed plus long-term reliability. Which reminds me to apologize to the makers for having worn a "flat" on the clutch cover due to a certain heartiness in "laying 'er over" in the course of high-speed cornering!

Full marks are hereby awarded to such features as adjustable spring-frame damping, exceptional range of footrest adjustment (and the rear brake pedal follows suit), the Feridax Dualseat with sliding tool-tray, tommy-bar wheel fixing and the means to adjust the rear chain without use of spanners, two prop-stands in addition to a stout rear stand, hand-adjustable brakes, ditto fork damper, steering which never required the damper at all, an indicator-cum-hand control for setting the "cogs" to neutral or as required, and a stout pair of hinged scrapping or pillion rests. In short, a machine designed and built by riders for those who ride hard, far and fast.

And now, with full knowledge of how it feels to hit the atmosphere at two miles per minute, I go to compose a new song-and-dance routine. . .

MOTOR CYCLING

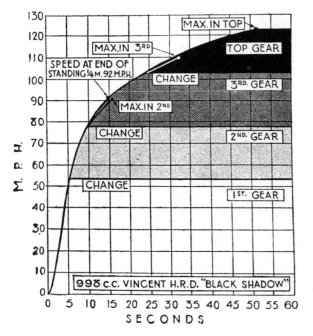

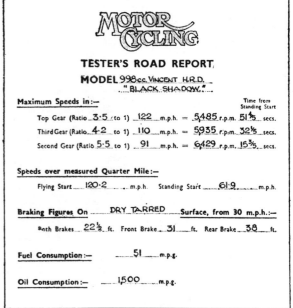

TESTER'S ROAD REPORT

MODEL 998 c.c. VINCENT H.R.D. "BLACK SHADOW."

Maximum Speeds in:— Time from Standing Start

Top Gear (Ratio 3·5 to 1) 122 m.p.h. = 5,485 r.p.m. 51⅘ secs.

Third Gear (Ratio 4·2 to 1) 110 m.p.h. = 5,935 r.p.m. 32⅕ secs.

Second Gear (Ratio 5·5 to 1) 91 m.p.h. = 6,429 r.p.m. 15⅗ secs.

Speeds over measured Quarter Mile:—

Flying Start 120·2 m.p.h. Standing Start 61·9 m.p.h.

Braking Figures On DRY TARRED **Surface, from 30 m.p.h.:—**

Both Brakes 22½ ft. Front Brake 31 ft. Rear Brake 38 ft.

Fuel Consumption:— 51 m.p.g.

Oil Consumption:— 1,500 m.p.g.

VINCENT-H.R.D.

Stand 10 : Girdraulic Fork Acclaimed: Popular Rapides

TEN sleek Vincent-H.R.D.s—no wonder Stand 10 was a Mecca for enthusiasts from all over the country! Of the seven models in the range, it was impossible to choose one that was the most interesting; but the majority voted the 998 c.c. Rapide the popular favourite. Since its inception as one of the first true post-war designs, the Rapide, with its powerful 998 c.c. engine and comparatively light weight, has established itself as undoubtedly the world's fastest standard machine. Now, its dark sister, the Black Shadow, is even faster!

In order to keep fully in step with the phenomenal performance of the big-twins, the new Girdraulic front fork has been designed. What impressed those visiting the stand who tried the fork were its soft easy action both on compression and rebound, and the massive proportions of the light-alloy fork blades.

A point that emphasizes the ingenuity behind the design is that should the machine be wanted for sidecar work, the fork trail can be altered merely by turning the eccentric top mounting for the spring units through 180 deg.

The single-cylinder models are very much "half a Rapide." The Comet in particular embodies the majority of the well-known luxury features of the make: the new fork, Feridax Dualseat, spring-frame, 50-watt dynamo, and four brakes. The rear brake pedal, incidentally, can

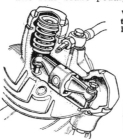

Valve operation on the latest models

be adjusted for both height and length without interfering with the brake adjustment.

Also on the stand was a sectioned Rapide engine. Enthusiasts crowding round praised the clever method of valve operation. There was also a speedway engine which has what is basically a pre-war Comet crankcase and timing gear, and a Rapide cylinder and head. As with most speedway engines, this one has total-loss lubrication and a clearly functional appearance.

Above: Designed for speeds of 140 m.p.h. and more, the 1,000 c.c. Black Lightning has already gained the American maximum speed record

Left: a new single-cylinder engine and the new Vincent-H.R.D. front fork are fitted to the 499 c.c. Comet

General Specifications.—Lucas magnetos; Miller lighting; Amal carburettors; Vincent-H.R.D. gear box with positive-stop foot change. Comet and Meteor have Burman four-speed gear boxes with positive-stop foot change. Avon tyres (Black Lightning, 3.00×21 in front, 3.50×20 rear; all others, 3.00×20 in front, 3.50×19 in rear). Fuel capacity, 3¾g; oil, 6pt. Dry-sump lubrication.

Prices.—Series B Meteor, £195 (plus, in Britain, £52 13s tax); Series B Rapide, £250 (£67 10s); Series B Black Shadow, £300 (£81 0s); Series C Comet, £215 (£58 1s); Series C Rapide, £265 (£71 11s); Series C Black Shadow, £315 (£85 1s); Series C Black Lightning, £400 (£108 0s). Vincent-H.R.D. Co., Ltd, Stevenage, Herts.

998 c.c. Vincent-H.R.D

An Ultra-high Performance Mount for
holding and a Cruis

MERE mention of the name "Black Shadow" is enough to speed the pulse. Since the machine's introduction last year as a super-sports brother to the already famous Rapide, the sombrely finished "Shadow" has achieved wide distinction. It is a connoisseur's machine: one with speed and acceleration far greater than those of any other standard motor cycle; and it is a motor cycle with unique and ingenious features which make it one of the outstanding designs of all time.

So far as the standards of engine performance, handling and braking are concerned—the chief features which can make or mar an otherwise perfect mount—the mighty Black Shadow must

Every line of the 998 c.c. vee-twin Black Shadow is suggestive of powerful urge. Cruising speed is anything up to 100 m.p.h.!

be awarded 99 out of 100 marks; 99 because nothing, it is said, is perfect

The machine has all the performance at the top end of the scale of a Senior T.T. mount. At the opposite end of the range, notwithstanding the combination of a 3.5 to 1 gear ratio, 7.3 to 1 compression ratio and pool quality fuel, it will "chuff" happily in top at 29-30 m.p.h. Indeed, in top gear without fuss, and with the throttle turned the merest fraction off its closed stop, it will surmount average gradients at 30 m.p.h.

In Britain the machine's cruising speed is not only limited by road conditions, it is severely restricted. It is difficult for the average rider in this country to visualize a route on which the

Black Shadow could be driven for any length of time at its limit or near limit. During the test runs speeds of 85-90 m.p.h. were commonplace; 100 m.p.h. was held on brief stretches and, occasionally, the needle of the special 150 m.p.h. Smith's speedometer would indicate 110. No airfield or stretch of road could be found which would allow absolute maximum speed to be obtained in two directions, against the watch. Flash readings in two directions of 118 and 114 were obtained, and in neither case had the machine attained its maximum. Acceleration from 100 m.p.h., though not vivid, was markedly good.

The compression ratio of the test model, as has been remarked, was 7.3 to 1. This is the standard ratio but models for the home market and low-octane fuel are generally fitted with compression plates which reduce the ratio to 6.5 to 1. The greater part of the test was carried out on "pool," though petrol-benzole was used when the attempts were made to obtain the maximum speed figures.

Steering and road-holding were fully in keeping with the exceptionally high engine performance. A soft yet positive movement is provided by the massively proportioned Girdraulic fork. There is a "tautness" and solid feeling about the steering which engenders confidence no matter what the speed and almost irrespective of the condition of the road surface. Corners and bends can be taken stylishly and safely at ultra-high speeds. There was no chopping, no "sawing"; not one of the faults which are sometimes apparent on high-speed machines. Bottoming and consequent clashing of the front fork were, however, experienced once or twice. Low-speed steering was reather heavy.

Any grumble the critics may have had with regard to the Vincent rear suspension has been met by the fitting of the hydraulic damper between the spring plunger units. So efficient is the rear springing now, that never once was the rider bumped off the Dualseat or forced to poise on the rests. Even at speeds around the 100 m.p.h. mark, only the absence of road shocks gave indication that there was any form of rear-springing, such was the smoothness and lateral rigidity.

Straight-ahead steering was in a class by itself. The model could be steered hands off at 15 m.p.h. with engine barely pulling or just as easily at 95 to 100 m.p.h. The steering damper was required only at speeds over 115 m.p.h.

Used in unison, the four brakes (two per wheel) provided immense stopping power. Light pressure of two fingers on the front-brake lever was sufficient to provide all the braking the front wheel would permit. One of the front brakes, incidentally, squealed when in use. The leverage provided at the rear brake is small, and the brake operation was heavy.

The compact engine-gear unit remained exceptionally clean throughout the 700-mile test. Only a faint smear of oil and slight discoloration of the front exhaust pipe close to the port indicated that the model had been ridden at all

Black Shadow

nnoisseur : Magnificent Steering and Road-
:ed of Up to 100 m.p.h.

Engine starting from cold was found difficult at first. Cold starting was certain, however, provided that only the front carburettor was flooded and the throttle control was closed. When the engine was hot, there was no difficulty.

After a cold or warm start the engine would immediately settle down to a true chuff-chuff tickover. Throughout the course of the test the tickover remained slow, certain and one-hundred per cent reliable. No matter how hard the previous miles had been, the twistgrip could always be rolled back against its closed stop with a positive assurance that a consistent tickover would result.

The engine was only tolerably quiet mechanically. At idling speeds, there was a fair amount of clatter, particularly from the valve gear. But so far as the rider was concerned all mechanical noise disappeared at anything over 40 m.p.h. All that remained audible was the pleasant low-toned burble of the exhaust and the sound of the wind in the rider's ears.

Bottom gear on the Black Shadow is 7.25 to 1. Starting away from rest can seem at first to require a certain amount of skill in handling the throttle and clutch. The servo-assisted clutch had a tendency to bite quickly as it began to engage.

Extreme lateral rigidity is a feature of the massively - proportioned Girdraulic fork. The trail can be altered for sidecar work in a few minutes

The Riding Position

The riding position for the 5ft 7in rider who carried out the greater part of the test proved to be first-class. The saddle height is 31in which is comfortable for the majority of riders. The footrests are sufficiently high to allow the rider complete peace of mind when the machine is heeled over to the limit, and were sufficiently low to provide a comfortable position for the 5ft 7in rider's legs.

Now famous, the 25½in from tip to tip, almost straight, Vincent-H.R.D. handlebar provides a most comfortable wrist angle and a straight-arm posture. All controls are widely adjustable—the gear pedal and brake pedal for both height and length. Both these controls, incidentally, move with the footrests when the latter are adjusted.

The gear change was instantaneous but slightly heavy in operation. Snap gear changes could be made as rapidly as the controls could be operated. The clutch freed perfectly throughout the test and bottom gear could be noiselessly selected when the machine was at standstill with the engine idling. However, because of the pressure required to raise the pedal it was sometimes necessary to select neutral by means of the hand lever on the side of the gear box, and also to engage bottom gear by hand.

In the 700 miles of the road test the tools were never required. In spite of the high speeds there was no apparent sign of stress. Primary and rear chains remained properly adjusted. There was very slight discolouring of the front exhaust pipe close to the port and a smear of oil from the base of one of the push rod tubes on the rear cylinder. The ammeter showed a charge at 30 m.p.h. in top gear when all the lights were switched on and the road illumination was better than average. An excellent tool-kit is provided and carried in a special tray under the Feridax Dualseat.

There are many ingenious features of the Vincent-H.R.D. which brand it as a luxury mount built by highly skilled engineers who at the same time are knowledgeable motor cycle enthusiasts. The Black Shadow finish is distinctive, obviously durable and very smart; and only a minor reason why the " Shadow " attracts a crowd of interested passers-by wherever it is seen !

Information Panel

SPECIFICATION

ENGINE : 998 c.c. (84 x 90 mm) vee-twin high camshaft o.h.v. with gear box in unit. Fully enclosed valve gear. Dry-sump lubrication : tank capacity, 6 pints. Four main bearings. Roller-bearing big-ends. Specialloid pistons. Cast-iron liners shrunk into aluminium-alloy cylinder barrels. Aluminium-alloy cylinder heads.

CARBURETTORS : Amal : twistgrip throttle control and twin handlebar-mounted air levers.

TRANSMISSION : Vincent-H.R.D. 4-speed gear box with positive-stop foot control. Gear ratios ; Top, 3.5 to 1. Second, 5.5 to 1. Bottom, 7.25 to 1. Servo-assisted clutch. Primary chain, ⅜in pitch triplex, enclosed in aluminium-alloy case. Secondary chain, ⅝ x ⅜in with guard over top run, R.p.m. at 30 m.p.h. in top gear ; 1,392 approx.

IGNITION AND LIGHTING : Lucas magneto with auto-advance. Miller dynamo : 7in head lamp : stoplight. Dynamo output, 50 watts.

FUEL CAPACITY : 3¾ gallons.

TYRES : Front, 3.00 x 20in. Avon ribbed : rear, 3.50 x 19 Avon studded.

BRAKES : Twin on each wheel : drums 7in diameter x ⅞in wide.

SUSPENSION : Girdraulic front fork with twin helical compression springs and hydraulic damping ; link action ; pivot-action rear springing hydraulically damped.

WHEELBASE : 56in. Ground-clearance, 5in unladen.

SADDLE : Feridax Dualseat. Unladen height, 31in.

WEIGHT : 476 lb fully equipped and with approximately ¾ gallon of fuel.

PRICE : £315 plus purchase tax (in Britain only) £85 1s. Price includes Smith's speedometer.

ROAD TAX : £3 15s a year (£1 0s 8d a quarter). Half rate if used only on standard ration.

DESCRIPTION : *The Motor Cycle* dated February 19th, 1948.

PERFORMANCE DATA

MEAN MAXIMUM SPEED : Bottom : 68 m.p.h.
Second : 87 m.p.h.
Third : 110 m.p.h.
Top : Not obtained.

ACCELERATION :

	10-30 m.p.h.	20-40 m.p.h.	30-50 m.p.h.
Bottom	2.4 secs	2.8 secs	3 secs
Second	3.6 secs	4.2 secs	3.4 secs
Third	—	5.8 secs	4.8 secs
Top	—	—	7.6 secs

Speed at end of quarter-mile from rest : 96 m.p.h.
Time to cover standing quarter-mile : 14.2 secs.

PETROL CONSUMPTION : At 30 m.p.h., 96 m.p.g. At 40 m.p.h., 91.2 m.p.g. At 50 m.p.h., 86.4 m.p.g. At 60 m.p.h., 70 m.p.g.

BRAKING : From 30 m.p.h. to rest, 26ft 6in (surface, coarse, dry chipping).

TURNING CIRCLE : 14 ft.

MINIMUM NON-SNATCH SPEED : 21 m.p.h. in top gear.

WEIGHT PER C.C. : 0.48 lb.

499 c.c. Vincent

High-performance Single With Magnificent Roadhold

ABOUT two years ago Vincents added single-cylinder models to their range of famous vee-twins. This fact in itself called for no special comment since there were Vincent singles and twins in pre-war years, but there was an unusual aspect in the policy announced at the end of 1948. The new singles comprise a very high proportion of the components employed for the twins; indeed, it might almost be said that the singles are twins modified as necessary.

It is to be expected, therefore, that many of the outstanding characteristics of the larger machines are retained with the

Most of the distinctive features of the Vincent twins are retained with the Comet

singles. Frame and Girdraulic fork of the Series C Comet are, as near as can be, identical with those of the Series C twins, the handling of which is of that high order which has earned praise from experienced riders throughout the world.

At very low speeds there is a slight heaviness in the steering—a steering-head roll that might be thought to be caused by damper friction—but this sensation is lost as soon as the speed is above 10 m.p.h. and, in any event, is unnoticed when the rider has had a few hours' experience with the machine. Apart from this minor fault, the steering is superbly precise and light.

The link-type fork gives about five inches of movement at the wheel spindle and its action is soft yet entirely free from flutter. At the one extreme, small surface ripples are efficiently absorbed and, at the other extreme, even the worst of shocks, such as sunken roadside drains purposely taken at speed, are minimized to only a minor movement felt at the handlebar.

A feeling of tautness and rigidity is provided by the frame of the Comet. The rear wheel, controlled by the twin spring cylinders and the separate hydraulic unit, maintains contact with the road in a leech-like fashion, but so effective is the hydraulic damper that, as with the front fork, there is never any suggestion of excessive reaction or patter. Front and rear suspension characteristics harmonize in an exemplary manner and result in steering and roadholding which is not only a sheer delight, especially at high speeds, but which also makes the maximum mechanical contribution to safety.

At all times there is a pleasing rigidity about the handling which gives a precision that means so much when the machine is cornering.

As with all Vincent models, the rider sits high on the comfortable, Dunlopillo-filled, Feridax Dualseat with the layout of the footrests and the narrow, almost straight handlebar such that he is over the machine in a slightly crouching position. This riding position plays an important part in inspiring confident, fast travel for which Vincents are renowned. The model under test was particularly stable and handled as well as the best on slippery surfaces.

The Comet is an uncompromising, high-speed, sporting single with the disadvantages and advantages of that type of machine. Standard compression ratio of 6.8 to 1 means that on pool petrol the rider has to be gentle-handed with the twistgrip if pinking is to be avoided, and the top gear ratio of 4.64 to 1 is too high for the utmost in maximum speed to be achieved except in very favourable circumstances. Under average driving conditions the engine repays for skilled handling of the throttle and frequent gear changing.

For the purposes of experiment, 50/50 petrol/benzole fuel was tried. The change in the behaviour of the engine was marked, with pinking eliminated, acceleration slightly improved, and power delivery made smoother. The major part of the road mileage and the performance figures were, however, completed on straight pool fuel.

High gearing gives a soothing, easy sensation to high-speed riding. At 60 m.p.h. in top gear, for example, engine revolutions are only about 3,600 a minute; the machine is free from vibration, the engine has the feeling of running at no more than a fast tickover, and the throttle twistgrip is only about a quarter open. The engine is, in fact, a lusty slogger with a remarkably powerful punch that means tireless travel—high performance at relatively low revs. It seemed impossible to over-drive the engine, which

Light-alloys are extensively employed. The gear box is a four-speed Burman

Enclosed by the light-alloy cover in front of the crankcase is the magneto with auto-advance. The separate Miller dynamo has a rated output of 50 watts

under all conditions of usage during the test remained noticeably cool. As a corollary, the engine maintains its tune for very long periods and, it might confidently be supposed, would give long service before replacements would be necessary.

As mentioned earlier, the machine is singularly free from engine vibration; there is a remote feel about the power unit, which seems to be working lazily and easily. Power delivery through the transmission is slightly harsh unless engine r.p.m. is higher than about 2,000, and it was thought that a manual ignition control, knowledgeably used, would provide smoother low-speed pulling. A certain amount of valve clatter can be heard, although other common sources of noise such as the piston, the primary drive, and the indirect gear ratios were commendably quiet. The exhaust note was dull-toned, but staccato, and considered to be too raucous for town use, especially if hard acceleration was used.

Starting required a fairly lusty swing on the pedal and then a first-time response was usual if the engine was hot. Under cold-starting conditions, a flooded carburettor and a closed air slide, together with a fractionally open throttle (as for a hot engine) gave the same quick start. The engine attained a working temperature quickly and would then idle slowly and reliably, as it would also on being throttled-down after long-distance, hard riding.

Unlike the twin-cylinder models, the single-cylinder Comet has a Burman gear box and clutch. Average handlebar lever pressure was required to disengage the clutch, which freed cleanly and quickly so that bottom-gear engagement with the machine stationary and the engine ticking over could be made noiselessly. Take-up of the drive by the clutch was sweet and progressive, with just the right amount of lever movement for easy control.

The positive-stop gear-change mechanism was decisive in movement and pleasurable to use; neutral could be selected from either bottom or second gears very readily. Upward gear changes were accomplished neatly and quietly provided there was just a suggestion of pause in pedal movement before engagement of the higher ratio; clean downward changes could be made as smartly as the controls could be operated.

The Vincent has two inter-connected brakes for each wheel. On the machine tested, the front wheel brakes were strikingly efficient—light to operate and powerful, and progressive in action. Rear-wheel brakes were most effective, but required slightly heavy pedal pressure—this heavy pressure is the result of the small leverage provided intentionally in the design as a precaution against inadvertent locking of the rear wheel. As the figures show, the Comet can be stopped from 30 m.p.h. in the unusually short distance of 26ft; more than this, the pleasure of using the silky deceleration of the front brakes is enhanced by a fork which does not deflect markedly under braking.

Driving light provided by the Miller equipment with a rated 50-watt output dynamo was very good and the deflection of beam of the off-focus filament sufficient to prevent dazzle of on-coming motorists. During the test, the bulb-holder in the tail light fractured and a battery lead short-circuited. The speedometer registered approximately six per cent fast throughout the range. Two prop-stands are fitted, one on each side; they are sturdy and hold the machine safely, provided the front wheel is turned in the direction of lean.

Finish of the Comet is stoved black enamel for tank, frame, fork blades and chain guard, with light-alloy mudguards and chromium plate for handlebar, controls, wheelrims and exhaust system.

Information Panel

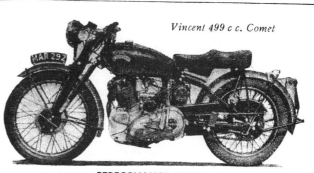

Vincent 499 c.c. Comet

SPECIFICATION

ENGINE : 499 c.c. (84 x 90 mm) single-cylinder high camshaft, overhead valves. Light-alloy cylinder head with integral rocker housings ; light-alloy cylinder barrel with shrunk-in cast-iron liner. Dry-sump lubrication ; 6 pt. oil-tank. Four main bearings. Compression ratio, 6.8 to 1.

CARBURETTOR : Amal, two-lever, 1⅛in choke ; twistgrip throttle control.

TRANSMISSION : Burman four-speed gear box with positive-stop foot control. Gear ratios : Bottom, 12.4 to 1. Second, 8.17 to 1. Third, 5.94 to 1. Top, 4.64 to 1. Multi-plate clutch. Primary chain ½ x ⁵⁄₁₆in, in oil-bath case. Secondary chain ⅝ x ¼in, with guard over top run. R.p.m. at 30 m.p.h. in top gear, approximately 1,800.

IGNITION AND LIGHTING : Lucas magneto with automatic advance. Miller dynamo. 7in head lamp ; stop-light.

FUEL CAPACITY : 3¾ gallons.

TYRES : Avon. 3.00 x 20in ribbed, front ; 3.50 x 19in studded, rear.

SUSPENSION : Girdraulic front fork with twin helical compression springs and hydraulic damping ; link action. Pivot-action rear-springing hydraulically damped.

BRAKES : Twin on each wheel ; 7 x ⅞in front and rear.

WHEELBASE : 56in. Ground clearance 6in, unladen.

SADDLE : Feridax Dualseat. Unladen height, 31in.

WEIGHT : 413 lb, with approximately one gallon of fuel.

TURNING CIRCLE : 15ft.

PRICE : £190, plus Purchase Tax, £51 6s.

ROAD TAX : £3 15s a year ; £1 0s 8d a quarter.

MAKERS : Vincent H.R.D. Co., Ltd., Stevenage, Herts.

PERFORMANCE DATA

MEAN MAXIMUM SPEED : Bottom : 38 m.p.h.
Second : 63 m.p.h.
Third : 78 m.p.h.
Top : 84 m.p.h.

MEAN ACCELERATION :

	10-30 m.p.h.	20-40 m.p.h.	30-50 m.p.h
Bottom	3.0 secs		
Second	—	3.8 secs	4.2 secs
Third	—	7.2 secs	6 0 secs
Top	—	—	8.4 secs

Mean speed at end of quarter mile from rest : 71 m.p.h.
Mean time to cover standing quarter mile : 13.2 secs. *

PETROL CONSUMPTION : At 30 m.p.h., 122 m.p.g. At 40 m.p.h., 104 m.p.g. At 50 m.p.g. 79 m.p.g. At 60 m.p.h. 55 m.p.g.

BRAKING : From 30 m.p.h. to rest, 26ft (surface, dry tar macadam).

MINIMUM NON-SNATCH SPEED : 22 m.p.h. in top gear.

WEIGHT PER C.C. : 0.83 lb.

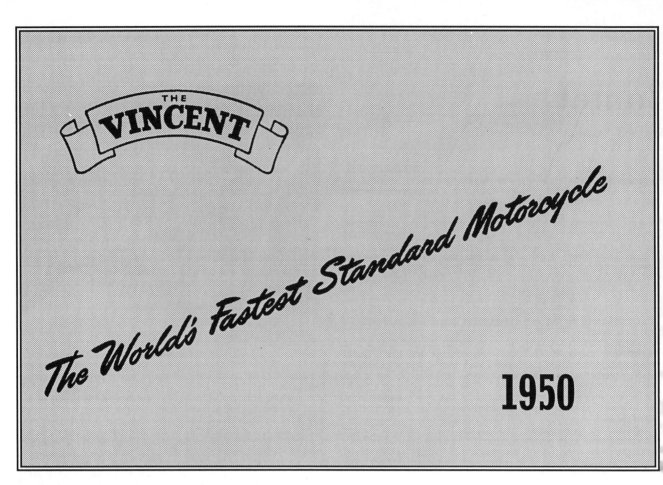

THE VINCENT

The World's Fastest Standard Motorcycle

1950

Introduction

With the announcement of our 1950 programme, we complete our twenty-first year as motor cycle manufacturers. During these years we have always concentrated exclusively on the highest quality enthusiast type machines, built always to the highest " Specialist " standards.

The range of performance we offer is so brilliantly outstanding above all others that it is still difficult to comprehend and to believe. Yet this performance has been fully proved in many countries against the cold, unrelenting logic of the time keepers' electric timing, notably in the establishment of a new U.S. National Maximum Speed Record at Bonneville Salt Flats at the remarkable speed of 150.313 m.p.h., with a privately owned production model Black Lightning just as delivered from the works, on September 13th, 1948, and the further establishment of two World Sidecar Records for the Standing Start Mile and Kilometre, at 94 and 83.5 m.p.h. respectively, the same week, on a similar machine, in Belgium. The world's best acceleration.

These figures prove that our new Black Lightning Racing Rapide is far and away the fastest production model ever offered to the public. The two sidecar records referred to were captured from two very special racing models that were successfully designed and built for the purpose of breaking the World's Maximum speed record. That an unsupercharged production model should better the figures of the two fastest and most redoubtable special racing machines ever built, gives a true indication of the brilliant design, superb materials and careful workmanship that are built into every machine that we make.

For the really hard, fast rider, especially those who revel in covering great distances at consistently high cruising speeds, we provide the wonderful Black Shadow Sports Model, a machine whose extreme silence and tractability completely belie its tempestuous performance. A maximum speed in the neighbourhood of 125 m.p.h. in touring trim gives it a performance above all but a select few of the most specialised racing machines.

Taking another big step down the performance scale we reach the extremely silent and docile standard Rapide, which is deliberately tamed to a mere 110 m.p.h. maximum in order to endow it fully with the many charming attributes that the tourist demands of his favourite mount. Nevertheless even this amazing tractable, fussless and reliable machine is still faster than any other standard motor cycle in the world (except the Black Lightning and Black Shadow), as proved very convincingly at scores of events in nearly every country, but most notably at Rosamond Dry Lakes, California, on several occasions.

Greatly increased production facilities have enabled us at last to re-introduce the ever popular Comet and Meteor models, in response to persistent demands from the thousands of enthusiasts who regard these trim and efficient 500 c.c. singles as the apple of their eye. Naturally we have taken the opportunity completely to modernize these machines and to adopt, where possible, the features that have proved so astoundingly successful on the Series B Rapides, so riders with experience of the pre-war models will find that the latest versions retain all their endearing qualities with the addition of many others. The Comet with 90 to 95 m.p.h. maximum and the Meteor with its 80 to 85 m.p.h. will hold their own satisfactorily with the general run of 500 c.c. o.h.v. models with the added advantage of far superior steering, cornering, roadholding, braking and comfort. The great majority of the parts of these new singles are identical and interchangeable with those of the astounding Rapides, so we leave it to you the reader to estimate the safety factor, which ensures reliability and long life !

Remembering the thousand upon thousand times that we have answered NO to the oft repeated question as to whether we intended to fit Telescopic Forks, it is with considerable relief that we disclose our own thoughts on the front fork question. Perhaps we shall now be left in peace ! The new Girdraulic fork is the result of several years' applied thought by our technicians, who insist on complete lateral rigidity and freedom from twist in all connecting members between the two wheels. The Girdraulic provides considerably more travel than the usual girder fork ; it provides the maximum travel that our designers will permit, for perfect high speed handling. It is hydraulically damped and has hydraulic limit stops to prevent metallic " bottoming," in both directions. Yet it has only one damper, and that is easily detachable for servicing and when detached *leaves the machine still rideable* ! The Girdraulic possesses abnormal lateral rigidity which makes it specially good for sidecar work of the toughest nature, and the fact that its trail and spring strength can be adjusted to suit sidecar or solo in a few minutes is another unique advantage typical of the all-round brilliance of Vincent design.

The New "Girdraulic" Fork

British Registered Trade Mark No. 675,834.

Staunch believers always in the necessity of preserving absolute rigidity against all forms of lateral whip or twist in all components connecting the two wheels of a motor cycle, if perfect handling is to be expected at high speeds, we refused to join the general post-war stampede into new fork designs—we wanted time to consider all possible methods, weigh the pros and cons and strike the best balance—always with firm insistence on *lateral rigidity* for perfect steering and cornering.

As makers of *standard* models capable of 150 m.p.h., we have to exercise great care in fork design.

Fortunately we started with the considerable advantage of far greater experience in motor cycle springing, for we are the *only* well known makers *who have never built a rigid frame.*

During the last twenty-one years we have perfected our fully triangulated and completely whip-free spring frame and we did not intend to throw away this great advantage by using a parallel membered front fork, depending largely on the wheel spindle for any rigidity.

We therefore decided to retain the well proved girder principle for its inherent rigidity. We obtained a new high level in rigidity-weight ratio by using forged light alloy blades of tapered oval section and preserved the maximum of this rigidity by using one-piece forged links. The new fork is at least twice as rigid as the earlier tubular design.

The long soft action so popular in these days has been provided by mounting very long springs in telescopic cases between the bottom of the crown lug and the fork ends, but we

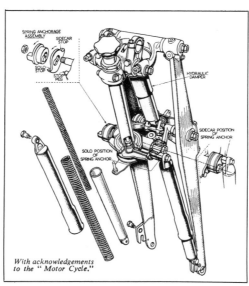

With acknowledgements to the "Motor Cycle."

have kept this action within the limits demanded by safety at high speeds. An ingenious eccentric action provides a variation of spring loading and fork trail to suit solo or sidecar use ; this adjustment can be made in a few minutes without using any extra or different parts.

The other great improvement of modern fork design is also provided in the form of a two-way hydraulic shock-absorber, with hydraulic limit stops in both directions to eliminate metallic " bottoming," but with these important differences, vital differences to the thousands who live great distances from the factory or the dealer :—

1. The shock-absorber can be detached easily.

2. It weighs less than two pounds and is only eight inches long, so it can be sent by parcel post.

3. The machine can be ridden at reasonable speeds without the shock-absorber.

Now that simplifies service, doesn't it ?

To ensure long life and freedom from attention, large diameter ground high tensile steel spindles are used in conjunction with oil retaining bronze brushes. No oiling is required.

Girdraulic Forks have now been in the hands of the public for well over a year and have given extremely reliable service. They have been used most successfully for breaking world and national speed records and for arduous racing and trials work. They have received the highest praise, alike from expert riders, the press and the public. We have no hesitation in saying that the Girdraulic is the finest motor cycle fork ever made.

SERIES " C " COMET MODEL

Specification

The current range of our models incorporates six distinctive engine types, of widely varying performance to suit many kinds of rider, yet through rational and advanced design the great majority of the components of these engines are identical and interchangeable. This ensures economy of manufacture and greatly simplifies the provision of an adequate and world-wide spares service.

The six engine types consist of three 500 c.c. (30·50 cu. in.) singles and three 1,000 c.c. (61 cu. in.) Vee twins—the singles, the Meteor touring, Comet sports and Grey Flash racing—the twins, the Rapide touring, the Black Shadow sports and the Black Lightning racing engines.

Dealing first with those parts which are common to all engines—

THE CYLINDER HEAD AND VALVE GEAR.—Aluminium " Y " Alloy aircraft specification heat treated casting, inclined o.h. valves with twin valve guides. Inlet valve 1·8 in. dia. (46 m.m.) silchrome steel, exhaust valve 1·67 in. dia. (42·5 m.m.) of DTD 49B steel, valve seats shrunk in, inlet seat austenitic cast iron, exhaust seat aluminium bronze. Entirely enclosed and lubricated o.h. rockers of straight rigid design, forged from K.E. 805 steel and running in duralumin bearings. The rockers operate against a hardened contact collar placed on valve stem between upper and lower guides. Very accessible tappet adjustment. Totally enclosed and lubricated duplex helical valve springs. These springs are seated on the top of the cool upper valve guide which in turn is separated by a large air space from the top of the hot exhaust port, on which the springs are seated in conventional design engines. All exhaust ports face forwards, are liberally finned and are positioned so as to receive the best cooling airstream. Due to the clever and unusual positioning of our separate rocker boxes, we have been able to provide liberal finning and to ensure absolutely free circulation of air over the whole cylinder head, thus enabling consistent high speeds to be maintained for longer periods in the hottest climates without engine fatigue or distress.

PISTON AND CYLINDER. —Aluminium alloy piston with two Wellworthy pressure rings and one scraper, $\frac{7}{8}$ in. dia. (22 m.m.) rigid taper-bored gudgeon pin fully floating retained by circlips. These pistons are available to give a wide range of compression ratios but maintaining a constant relationship in the positioning of the rings relative to the gudgeon pin height. Meteor and Standard Rapide engines are normally supplied 7·3 to 1, but in countries where the standard fuel is of a low octane rating these ratios are normally reduced by fitting lower compression pistons and/or compression plates. Ratios on the Grey Flash and Black Lightning are supplied to the customer's requirements. The cylinder bore is 84 m.m. and the piston stroke 90 m.m., giving the single a capacity of 499 c.c. and the twin 998 c.c.

The cylinder barrel consists of a detachable high grade cast iron liner shrunk into a finned aluminium cylinder jacket.

CONNECTING ROD AND BIG END ASSEMBLY.—Forged connecting rods of 65 ton nickel chrome steel (75-80 tons on Grey Flash and Black Lightning), polished finish on Black Shadow and Black Lightning models. Big end liners of EN31 carbon chrome steel, hardened, ground and honed for super finish. Three rows of 3 m.m. dia. × 5 m.m. long rollers in each connecting rod's big end, separated and guided by hardened, ground and lapped rings between each row of rollers. Crank pin 1$\frac{9}{16}$ in. dia. (37·7 m.m.) EN36 casehardened nickel chrome steel ; the only difference between the single and twin crankpins lies in their lengths. Drilled oilways in pin, flywheel and mainshaft ensure a copious supply of cooling lubricant to the big end.

TIMING GEAR.—A separate camshaft is provided for each cylinder mounted very high in the timing case with push rods only 6 in. (152 m.m.) long, which operate within stainless steel push rod tubes. A mechanical rotary breather valve is provided, but the design differs in detail between the singles and the twins, as does also in some respects that of the exhaust valve lifter mechanism. On all models the Lucas magneto is gear driven from the timing gear through

SERIES " C " METEOR MODEL

34

Specification *Continued*

a Lucas automatic advance and retard unit (except the Grey Flash and Black Lightning which have manual control). On the 500 c.c. models only, the Miller 50 watt dynamo is also gear driven from the timing gear train.

LUBRICATION.—Dry sump system. A large double acting rotary plunger pump, worm driven from the timing side mainshaft, draws oil from a six-pint (3·4 litre) oil tank, through a gauze filter and a large bore pipe, pumps it through a very large, 54 sq. in. full flow Tecalemit fabric filter, and hence direct to the big end assembly, camshaft bearings and the rear of the cylinder walls. Return oil is scraped from the fly-wheels and pumped back to the tank. By-pass jets from return pipe to the tank lubricate the valve gear.

CRANKCASE MAIN BEARINGS.—Four large diameter main bearings are provided, two to each mainshaft, well separated to provide a rigid support, ensuring vibrationless running and long life. Three of these are roller bearings and the fourth is a ball bearing for endwise location of the crankshaft.

Turning now to the specialised components—

CRANKCASE. GENERAL.—Cast in DTD424 aircraft specification aluminium alloy. Massively ribbed and of substantial section to provide a rigid base on which to build the engine, thus eliminating vibration and loss of power and wear through deformation. A housing for the large oil filter is cast integral with the timing side case. Very massive anchorage bosses are provided for the cylinder head bolts. For additional rigidity the cylinder liner extension below the jacket is spigotted in to the massive upper throat of the crankcase. The oil pump is housed in an accurately bored cylinder formed in the lower part of the timing case and feeds the oil direct through a drilled passage into the filter housing.

1,000 c.c. MODEL.—The upper faces of the paired cases are machined to accept two cylinders at 50° in Vee formation, the rear cylinder being offset 1¼ in. towards the timing gear for improved cooling. The timing case is shaped and machined to accept the camshafts for both cylinders and their appropriate operating gear. This model having a unit construction gearbox, the gearbox housing and the inner half of the oilbath for the primary chain, are cast integral with the crankcase.

500 c.c. MODEL.—This differs in having provision for only one cylinder inclined forward at 25°, and for one set of timing gear. These castings do not incorporate either oilbath or gearbox housing as these units are separate on the 500 c.c. models.

FLYWHEEL ASSEMBLY. GENERAL.—Forged in 40 ton carbon steel, machined all over and jig drilled for consistent balance. (Polished on Grey Flash and Black Lightning). Nickel chrome steel mainshafts, drive side splined to accept 3-lobe engine shock absorber sprocket carried on a separate hardened splined sleeve. Timing side carries oil pump drive worm and half time pinion. Mainshafts are a tight pressed fit in flywheels, and the outside diameter and one raised face flange on each flywheel are subsequently ground off the mainshaft centres to bring them exactly true to the shafts themselves. These ground locations are then used to position the flywheels for the boring and facing of the crankpin holes ; thus ensuring an astonishing and completely unusual degree of accuracy in the true running of the completed flywheel assembly. This in turn assures a very long life for the main bearings and a remarkable smoothness of running. Both mainshafts and both ends of the crankpin are an accurate and parallel fit in the flywheels, thus obviating the well-known disadvantages of taper fits.

1,000 c.c. MODEL.—These flywheels are specially machined and balanced to suit the characteristics of the Vee twin engine.

500 c.c. MODEL.—The necessary alterations are made to the machining and balance to suit the single cylinder model.

SERIES "C" GREY FLASH

TRANSMISSION. RAPIDE MODELS.—Gearbox. Unit construction with the engine, four speeds, constant mesh, of our own design and made throughout in our factory. The shafts are very rigid and supported by large diameter ball bearings. All gears are of casehardened nickel chrome, EN36 steel and are notable for their silent running. The end cover is of circular design and spigots accurately into the case, thus relieving the studs of all transmission stresses. Accessible oil filler with dip-stick. The external gear indicator lever can be used to select neutral or change by hand. The foot-change mechanism and kick-starter are mounted in a separate, easily detachable cover. The kick-starter can be mounted on the left hand side of the machine, at an extra charge, when a right-hand sidecar is fitted. The starter crank is of special design giving great leverage and fitted with a folding footpiece.

The whole primary transmission is contained in an oilbath case cast integral with the crankcase and gearbox, with a detachable aluminium cover.

The gearbox is driven by a Triplex $\frac{3}{8}$ in. pitch Renold chain the tension of which is controlled by our special design stiff leaf spring tensioner.

An accessible external screw varies the curvature of the spring, and hence the chain adjustment. The engine sprocket, of 35 teeth, drives a 56 tooth clutch sprocket. The engine shaft shock absorber is of the 3-lobe cam type with 36 light coil springs which endow it with a remarkably smooth and supple action. The cam slides on a separate hardened and splined sleeve, so that in the event of wear after a long period the sleeve alone, which is very easily detachable, need be replaced. In normal design it is necessary to dismantle the whole engine and replace the mainshaft.

The clutch is of our own special patented design, and manufacture, and is contained in a separate oiltight housing in the chaincase cover. A normal single plate clutch provides the expanding pressure to work a pair of shoes in a nickel chrome alloy cast iron ribbed drum. Although incredibly light in operation, this clutch will transmit tremendous torque. Great care has been taken, by the provision of special oil seals, to prevent the entry of any lubricant into the clutch. A separate cover permits ready access to the clutch.

The final drive sprocket has 21 teeth but 22 teeth sprockets are available for providing extra high gear ratios for racing. The rear chain is Renold $\frac{5}{8}$ in. $\times \frac{3}{8}$ in. and the chain line is sufficiently wide to permit the fitting of large tyres. Final drive is changed by altering the rear wheel sprocket, which has 46 teeth as standard for solo use. Where desired a second sprocket can be fitted to the other brake drum and ratios quickly changed by reversing the wheel. Adjustment of the chain tension may be effected in less than one minute without tools by using the unique finger adjustment provided.

Standard Rapide gearbox reduction ratios are 1, 1·19, 1·61 and 2·6 to 1, giving with the standard sprockets overall ratios of 3·5, 4·2, 5·6 and 9·1 to 1.

Black Shadow and Black Lightning ratios are the same except that bottom gear is raised to 2·07 (7·2 to 1), and the dogs on the latter model have much more backlash to ease gear changing.

500 c.c. MODELS.—A separate 4-speed Burman gearbox and clutch are fitted, driven by a $\frac{1}{2}$ in. $\times \frac{5}{16}$ in. Renold chain in an oilbath. The shock absorber is of the same design, and all details of the final drive (except that the gearbox sprocket has 18 teeth and the chain is on the opposite side of the machine) are the same as for the Rapides. Standard gear ratios are 4·64, 5·94, 8·17 and 12·4 to 1. The Grey Flash is fitted with a 4-speed Albion gearbox.

IGNITION.—Gear-driven Lucas flange-mounted magneto with automatic advance ; protected by polished aluminium cowl. On Grey Flash and Black Lightning we fit a special manually controlled Lucas Racing Magneto.

LIGHTING SET.—Special Miller 6-volt 50 watt voltage controlled, separate dynamo. On Standard Rapides and Black Shadows this is driven from the primary chain and the sprocket is very easily detachable. On 500 c.c. models it is gear driven from the timing case. Stop light is coupled to the brakes. Very accessible 13 a.h. Exide battery fully sprung. Lucas Altette horn. No lighting on Black Lightning.

CARBURETTORS.—Standard Rapides and Black Shadows are fitted with two vertical Amal touring carburettors of $1\frac{1}{16}$ in. (27 m.m.) and $1\frac{1}{8}$ in. (29 m.m.) dia. chokes respectively. Air filters can be supplied as extras. Grey Flash and Black Lightning models are fitted with racing Amal carburettors of the type most suitable for the customer's requirements. Simple adjusters for synchronizing are provided, together with separate air levers on the handlebar. Meteor and Comet models are fitted with a single Amal standard type carburettor of $1\frac{1}{16}$ in. (27 m.m.) and $1\frac{1}{8}$ in. (29 m.m.) choke respectively.

SERIES " C " RAPIDE MODEL

FRAME.—On the modern Vincent this important item of the specification has almost disappeared ! What is even more remarkable is that it has become stronger, neater, lighter and more attractive in appearance by the act of its near disappearance !

It now consists of an exceptionally strong head lug which bolts to a forged steel bracket on the front cylinder head. A strong triangulated oil tank of six pints capacity stays it against a similar lug on the rear cylinder head (or in the case of the singles, against the cast aluminium rear seat stay).

The only other important frame members are the rigid triangulated rear forks of our usual design and the plates which secure this fork to the rear end of the engine unit.

The rear springing provides a long soft action of about 6 in. travel, controlled by our new hydraulic damper as used on the Girdraulic fork. There is only one bearing in our springing system and that runs on large Timken taper roller bearings ; hence its 100 per cent. reliability. Our patented system of seat support by swinging links enables a pillion passenger to be carried without alteration to the rear spring strength.

All necessary sidecar attachment points are provided.

BRAKES.—For sixteen years all Vincent models have been fitted as standard with FOUR powerful 7 in. dia. (178 m.m.) × ⅞ in. (22 m.m.) wide internal expanding brakes. This policy has proved so successful and popular that it is naturally continued, this year with the great improvement of high duty nickel-chrome alloy cast iron drums.

The spreading of the braking stresses over four brakes, and the resulting perfect balance of forces provides our machines with controllability and safety far beyond the standards that are normally considered first class. A recent Motor Cycling test of a " Comet " gave a stopping distance of 21 ft. from 30 m.p.h., 30 ft. is the usually accepted figure for 100 per cent. braking efficiency ! Overheating of our brakes is virtually unknown because of their large cooling area, adjustment is rarely required, the life of the linings is quite abnormal. This saves money for you on repairs as well as increasing your safety.

No matter how heavily you may apply the brakes the reactions are always balanced on both sides of the frame and forks. Consequently, the wheels maintain perfect alignment and there is no tendency to skid, a most valuable feature on slippery roads, or on racing circuits. On " Grey Flash," " Black Shadow " and " Black Lightning " models the drums are deeply finned for cooling and rigidity. On the " Grey Flash " and " Black Lightning " cast magnesium brake plates are used, with duplex airscoops on the front brakes.

WHEELS.—The wheels run on very large diameter Timken taper roller bearings which usually outlast the machine. These bearings are mounted on a ground hollow spindle of ¾ in. dia. and in a diecast aluminium alloy hub.

The wheels are detachable in less than a minute without using any tools, and the rear wheel may be mounted either way round in the machine if two sprockets of different sizes are fitted for speedy changing of gear ratios. The brake drums may be removed without disturbing the spokes.

On 1,000 c.c. models both wheels are fitted with one security bolt and two balance weights. On the " Grey Flash " and " Black Lightning " models when used solo Aluminium Alloy Racing Rims are fitted as standard; on the other machines Dunlop chromium plated steel rims, with black centres lined in red, are used. The heavy gauge spokes are cadmium plated.

TYRES.—Our usual standard tyres on all models except the " Grey Flash " and " Black Lightning " are Avon Supreme studded 19 in. × 3·50 in. rear and Avon Speedster ribbed 20 in. × 3·00 in. front. In cases where extra heavy duty is anticipated, or the roads are very rough, we can supply without extra charge Avon Supreme studded 18 in. × 4·00 in. rear and Avon Speedster ribbed 19 in. × 3·50 in. Standard equipment on " Grey Flash " and " Black Lightning " with sidecar is as above, but for solo usage we supply special racing Avon tyres with rayon casings and treads developed by our engineers and racing riders in conjunction with the Avon India Rubber Company's technicians. These tyres are 20 in. × 3·50 in. on the rear and 21 in. × 3·00 in. on the front wheels, with, of course, special racing inner tubes.

SEAT.—Specially designed by co-operation between our engineers and Messrs. Feridax Ltd. Great trouble has been taken to ensure that this exclusive Feridax Dual Seat of moulded Dunlopillo shall provide the maximum comfort for both rider and passenger. Rear end sprung by our

SERIES " C " RAPIDE TOURING MODEL

patented method, British Patent No. 424644. The very neat tool tray slides out of sight under this seat.

PETROL TANK.—Very handsome pressed steel design, bonderized, enamelled black and hand lined with real gold leaf. Capacity 3¾ Imperial gallons, 4 American gallons (17 litres). Dropped rear end prevents water or dirt reaching tap outlet. Twin petrol taps, one for reserve. Quick-action filler cap.

PETROL AND OIL PIPES.—Brazed joints with flexible hose insertions to prevent fracture. ⅜ in. (7 m.m.) bore oil feed pipe to ensure easy flow in Arctic weather.

OIL TANK.—Forms part of frame. Very strong design. Capacity six pints —(3·4 litres). Outlet union automatically shuts off oil when feed pipe is detached.

MUDGUARDS.—Special light alloy, highly polished. Enamelled tubular steel stays. Rear guard hinged for easy wheel removal. Alternative heavy steel valanced type (as shown in illustration of Series C Rapide) with black enamelled finish may be supplied without extra charge.

STANDS.—Rear tubular stand. Twin prop stands, one either side, can also be swung down together to form front stand. Prop stands are not fitted to the Meteor model or the Black Lightning, but may be supplied on the former at an extra charge.

EXHAUST SYSTEM.—On Standard Rapides and Black Shadows two 1⅝ in. (41·5 m.m.) dia. steel exhaust pipes join and run direct into silencer. On Grey Flash and Black Lightning special separate straight through pipes are supplied. Comets and Meteors have the usual single exhaust pipe. All pipes are secured to the heads by finned nuts, and the systems as a whole are heavily chromium plated on a copper and nickel base.

FOOTRESTS.—Provide a very wide range of adjustment and folding pillion footrests, which are fully sprung and can be used for a racing riding position, are fitted as standard equipment to all models except Grey Flash and Black Lightning.

HANDLEBARS.—The famous narrow straight Vincent bars which have been praised so highly by the technical experts. They give a remarkably comfortable riding position. Can be adjusted for wrist angle. Control

levers of racing pattern are also adjustable. Sprint bars are available on Black Lightning model. Upswept " cowhorn " bars optional without extra charge.

FINISH.—All enamelled parts are bonderized and finished in Pinchin Johnson's best cycle stoving enamel. Bright parts are mostly polished stainless steel or aluminium ; others are chromium or cadmium plated. On Black Shadow and Black Lightning models the power units are Pyluminised and most distinctively enamelled glossy black. Grey Flash models have a distinctive silver grey finish.

SPEEDOMETER.—Smith's " Chronometric " with total and trip recorder and internal illuminator is fitted as standard to all models. The Black Lightning has a very special 180 m.p.h., or 280 k.p.h., 3 in. (76 m.m.) dial instrument which matches the 8,000 r.p.m. tachometer which is also standard on this model. The Black Shadow has a magnificent 5 in. dial 150 m.p.h., or 250 k.p.h., instrument mounted in a clearly visible position on the top of the fork girder. The remaining models have 3 in. dial 120 m.p.h., or 180 k.p.h., speedometers. All speedometers are driven from inside the front brake drum for great accuracy.

EQUIPMENT.—Includes tyre inflator, a complete set of high quality tools, grease-gun and tyre levers.

GROUND CLEARANCE.—6 inches (150 m.m.).

WHEELBASE.—56 inches (1,420 m.m.).

WIDTH OVER HANDLEBARS.—25½ inches (650 m.m.).

TURNING CIRCLE AT TYRES.—Under 16 feet (5 metres) dia. of circle.

LENGTH OVERALL.—85½ inches (2,175 m.m.).

SHIPPING DIMENSIONS.—Assembled complete in closed case—handlebars detached.

Length	...	...	...	7 ft. 3½ in. — 2,220 m.m.
Width	...	...	...	1 ft. 9 in. — 500 m.m.
Height	...	...	...	3 ft. 6½ in. — 1,080 m.m.

Approximate Gross weight Standard Rapide and Black Shadow 6 cwts. (305 kilos.). Other Models 5½ cwts. (280 kilos.).

SERIES " C " BLACK SHADOW MODEL

Specification *Continued*

PERFORMANCE CHARACTERISTICS

Characteristic	Black Lightning	Black Shadow	Standard Rapide	Comet	Meteor	Units of measurement
Power to Weight Ratio	480	280	222	150	130	Brake-horse power per ton
Dry Weight	380 / 172	458 / 207	455 / 206	390 / 176	380 / 172	Pounds / Kilogrammes
Petrol Consumption	— / — / —	55 to 65 / 50 to 60 / 5 to 6	55 to 65 / 50 to 60 / 5 to 6	75 to 80 / 70 to 75 / 4 to 5	75 to 80 / 70 to 75 / 4 to 5	Miles per Imp. Gall. / ,, Amer. ,, / Litres per 100 kilos.
Oil Consumption	— / —	1,500 / 500	1,500 / 500	2,000 / 650	2,000 / 650	Miles per gallon / Kilos per litre
Cruising Speed	—	100 / 160	85 / 136	65 / 104	60 / 96	Miles per hour / Kilos. ,,
Maximum Speed	150+ / 240+	125 / 200	110 / 175	90 to 95 / 144 to 152	80 to 85 / 128 to 136	Miles per hour / Kilos. ,,

Characteristic	Black Lightning	Black Shadow	Standard Rapide	Comet	Meteor	Units of measurement
Minimum Speed in top gear	—	18 / 29	18 / 29	19 / 31	19 / 31	Miles per hour / Kilos. ,,
Maximum Safe Speeds in Indirect Gears.	According to Gearing	110 / 85 / 65 — 175 / 136 / 104	96 / 80 / 50 — 154 / 127 / 80	77 / 55 / 38 — 123 / 88 / 60	70 / 50 / 34 — 112 / 80 / 55	3rd / 2nd / 1st } miles per hour — 3rd / 2nd / 1st } kilos. per hour
Acceleration through gears as recorded in "Motor Cycling" Road Tests	Not yet tested	3½ secs. / 6½ ,, / 10 ,, / 21 ,, / 31 ,, / 44 ,,	1½ secs. / 6 ,, / 12 ,, / 24 ,, / 35 ,, / —	3 secs. / 9½ ,, / 21 ,, / — / — / —	Not yet tested	0–30 miles per hour / 0–48 kilos. ,, / 0–60 miles / 0–96 kilos. ,, / 0–80 miles / 0–128 kilos. ,, / 0–100 miles / 0–160 kilos. ,, / 0–110 miles / 0–175 kilos. ,, / 0–120 miles / 0–192 kilos. ,,

SPORTS SINGLE SEATER SIDECAR.

While the design of this sidecar is upon definite sporting lines, the passenger's comfort has in no wise been sacrificed. Ample body room has been provided and a specially designed screen, together with an efficient, fully disappearing hood, add to the passenger's comfort, whilst ensuring perfect weather protection.

Extremely good luggage accommodation is provided, the external locker door being complete with a Yale lock and keys.

This model can be supplied with either left or right-hand mounting thus being complementary to all Rapide models which have, of course, full provision for mounting the sidecar on either side of the machine, while the kick-start mechanism can be fitted to the left-hand side for a small extra charge.

The standard finish is in black and silver. Passenger grab rail supplied extra.

SERIES "C" BLACK LIGHTNING MODEL

Racing Models

The many racing successes of Vincent Motor cycles give an unusually accurate indication of the performance, reliability and perfect handling qualities of the standard road models which the average owner prefers.

In recent years it has unfortunately become more and more the general practice for racing models to be specially designed machines that bear but little resemblance to the road models, thus drifting away from the good old practice prevalent until about eighteen years ago, when the racers were but tuned editions of the standard sports models, with a few experimental improvements which were later adopted as standard if successful. It was on this basis that racing made its major contributions to improving the breed, and the ordinary rider received immediate benefit from the lessons learned.

All Vincent motor cycles are designed in the first place to be absolutely reliable first class road models, with a sparkling performance, crisp precise handling and wonderful braking. We feel that the ordinary rider requires and deserves these qualities just as much as the racing man and we can see no reason why he should not have them.

It is therefore not surprising to find that our racing models have only minor differences from the touring and sports machines, in fact the majority of the parts are identical. When a Vincent machine breaks a record or wins a race it is proving the excellence of the standard model that you can buy and ride yourself.

Due to our policy of using the finest materials available, and due also to the sound principles of design employed, they possess such an inbuilt stamina and efficiency, together with such perfect steering, braking and other handling qualities, that they have proved themselves the masters of specially built racing machines in scores of races and record attempts.

The following speed records are held by standard Black Lightning models—very, very truly " The World's Fastest Standard Motorcycle."

SIDECAR WORLD RECORDS, 1,000 c.c. CLASS.

1 Kilometer Standing Start 83·5 m.p.h.			
1 Mile	,,	,, 94 m.p.h.	Rider - Rene Milhoux.
5 Kilometers Flying	,,	126 m.p.h.	
5 Miles	,,	,, 106 m.p.h.	

SOLO NATIONAL RECORDS.

AMERICA.

1 Mile Flying Start at 150·313 m.p.h.	Rollie Free.

AUSTRALIA.

1 Mile Flying Start at 139·8 m.p.h.	Les Warton.
½ Mile Standing Start at 88·7 m.p.h.	,, ,,
¼ ,, ,, ,, ,, 68·1 m.p.h.	,, ,,

SOUTH AFRICA.

1 Kilometer Flying Start at 136·4 m.p.h.	Vic Procter.
1 Mile Flying Start at 136·2 m.p.h.	,, ,,
1 Kilometer Standing Start at 88·9 m.p.h. ,,	,,
1 Mile ,, ,, ,, 101·8 m.p.h. ,,	,,

Continued below

SIDECAR NATIONAL RECORDS.

AUSTRALIA.

1 Mile Flying Start at 122·5 m.p.h.	Les Warton.
½ ,, Standing ,, at 77·1 m.p.h.	,, ,,
¼ ,, ,, ,, at 61·0 m.p.h.	,, ,,

BELGIUM.

1 Kilometer Flying Start 128·8 m.p.h.	Rene Milhoux.

Even our standard touring Rapide model comes into the record holding picture. One of these machines holds the Canadian Solo Speed Record at 114·1 m.p.h.   Rider - Mr. E. Stidolph.

All these outstanding successes have been achieved on standard machines the same as you can buy. What is probably more important is that over 90 per cent. of their components are standard parts identical to those used in the standard road models.

The road racing successes achieved by our machines in the last 3½ years are far too numerous to attempt to list them. We may mention however that in Argentina, Australia, Brazil, Cuba and Great Britain our machines have been particularly successful, winning scores of important events on standard models.

In Argentina five standard touring model " Rapides " finished first, second, third, fourth, and fifth at record speed in the unlimited class of the famous Rafaela XII hours Road Race run over dusty earth roads in semi-tropical heat. The winner averaged over 76 m.p.h. for 12 hours on a touring machine that he bought secondhand the previous week, and on which no preparatory work was carried out before the Race !

In Australia, Mr. Tony McAlpine riding a standard sports " Black Shadow " won every Senior Class Race in Victoria during 1949 !

In Brazil, eighteen consecutive entries in important events produced eighteen victories !

As mentioned the " Grey Flash " and " Black Lightning " are essentially the same as the " Comet " and " Black Shadow," the general design being similar and the great majority of the parts interchangeable with the road models.

In the general specifications on earlier pages we have described the details in which the racing models are modified in order to make them perfectly suited to the more specialised nature of their use.

Briefly the cam contours, pistons and carburettors are modified and all highly stressed parts are mirror polished to prevent fatigue fractures of the metal. The ports are enlarged and streamlined, closer ratios are fitted to the gearbox, and a special straight through exhaust is fitted, carefully designed to suit the characteristics of the engine.

The wheels and brakes are improved in respect of their cooling qualities to enable them to operate without over-heating after the longest periods of heavy braking from very high speeds. Rigid magnesium alloy brake plates carry the aluminium shoes, and the front pair are fitted with large airscoops to permit free circulation of cooling air through the interior of the brakes. Massive finned brake drums further aid cooling. For solo machines aluminium alloy or high tensile steel rims can be fitted, but we strongly recommend the steel rims for sidecar racing.

Aluminium alloy mudguards to F.I.C.M. racing regulations are fitted. Every racing model is assembled with great care, ridden gently for over 100 miles, and when freed up is tested on a track against the watch.

Vincent in the World Press

AUSTRALIA

" Australian Motor Sports," December, 1949 : Naturally, with such performance available over the counter to the general public, road-holding and brakes must be above reproach, and no research has been spared to ensure that this is the case. Every part of the machine shows evidence of careful thought in its design, and only the finest of materials and workmanship have gone into its manufacture. Since Vincents were first marketed, 21 years ago this year, they have never had a rigid frame, and their whip-free spring frame has been brought near to perfection during that time ; for the last fifteen years, four powerful brakes have been fitted to all their machines ; and a post-war development is the Girdraulic front fork, which combines the lateral rigidity of the girder type with the soft suspension and good road-holding of the plunger type. A not unnatural outcome of this policy of excellence is that almost every rider who has had anything to do with a Vincent finds himself unsatisfied with other machines, however fine their reputation.

BELGIUM

" Les Sports," Dec. 5th, 1946 : A sensational motor cycle ! Under this title one of our colleagues announced recently the appearance of the H.R.D. " Rapide " Series " B." This H.R.D. is in fact the first entirely new model which has made its appearance on the motor cycle market and it is truly sensational in more than a title. Let us recall that the H.R.D. concern holds a reputation in English motor cycling similar to that of Rolls-Royce for cars . . . . The " Rapide " Series " B," a motor cycle to a unique formula, is truly the ideal Roadster. It equals in performance a fast racing 500, but possesses over and above this all the advantages of a touring machine : kick-starter, lights and use of commercial petrol. Furthermore, it is a true two-seater machine with two seats of comfort unequalled to date.

FRANCE

" What seems particularly remarkable to us is that in spite of their terrific speed the Vincent-H.R.D.'s, even the ' Black Shadow,' are extremely flexible machines, easy to start, smooth to ride, not in the least capricious, needing the minimum of care for maintenance, usable for continuous service and admirably adaptable for long distance touring.... There are with us, as throughout the world, sportsmen who are prepared to make considerable financial sacrifice in exchange for all the joys that can be given by a truly exceptional machine which combines harmoniously the qualities of a touring motor cycle and those of a racer, flexible like the one, fast like the other."

3rd September, 1948. " *Moto Revue*," *Paris.*

Twenty, and even ten, years ago the very idea of delivering to the public a machine capable of and exceeding 200 k.p.h. would not only have seemed impossible, but folly, on account of the danger of riding on open roads at such speeds, and the skill required for handling a motor turning out more than 40 b.h.p.

But now, progress has given us such a combination of safety in road holding and brakes that the problem can be solved.

Obviously Vincent-H.R.D. have marketed a model for which the slogan could be " Safety at 200 k.p.h." . . . .

The " Black Shadow " is no racing machine. We could class it in the super sport touring category for, with its engine tuned for ordinary petrol, gearbox with kick-starter, lighting equipment, electric horn, silent performance which avoids attracting the disagreeable interest of passers-by . . . and the police, there is nothing which indicates a machine for competition except the many horses inside the all-black engine.

What seems most strange on such a powerful model is the flexibility of the engine, the pick up from low speeds without pinking, the possibility of following a slow vehicle without slipping the clutch, the sweetness of the acceleration if one opens the throttle progressively without noticing the slightest flat spot in the carburation, and this should re-assure the " Black Shadow " enthusiasts who could have doubts as to the suitability for town work.

Our stopwatches are in position and I take off again. First up to 70, second to 100, third to 130 and I engage top. At once one has the impression of formidable power for the twist grip is hardly half open. Having enough run up I turn and take the direction back. I turn easily in bottom where the road is wide without touching the clutch. With the tip of my boots I swing down the rear foot rests which will serve me in adopting a flat riding position ; I slide away from the bars, squat on the rear of the dual seat and go through the gears. In this position the road holding is perfect and the rider need not wrestle against any unpleasant or dangerous reactions. All the same, it is difficult to realise the speed in spite of the rate at which the landscape rolls by.

I am now flat out and the speed begins to settle down. The speedometer registers 190, then the needle reaches the figure 200, passes it nicely.

I am anxious to know the result ; *206 say my colleagues.

So the speedometer is accurate and I am certain that I have passed the magic figure on two wheels.

But the stability of the Vincent-H.R.D. is such that it is a performance within the capabilities of any motor cyclist who is accustomed to some speed.

* 128 m.p.h.

7th January, 1949. " *Moto Revue*," *Paris.*

GREAT BRITAIN

Few machines have ever aroused so much interest as the Series " B " " Rapide " Vincent-H.R.D. There is a number of reasons for the near-excitement with which this model is discussed in motor cycle circles ; it is an entirely new post-war model; it is unconventional in design in that, among other features, the massive Vee-twin engine forms part of the frame ; it gives a high-speed performance to which movie superlatives might well apply ; it is designed and manufactured by enthusiasts with an unassailable belief in the rightness of their project.

How far the designers have justified the machine's nickname, " little big-twin," is apparent immediately one is astride the special Dualseat. The wheelbase of 56 in. is about average for a 500, tank width is comfortable, and there

Continued below

is no heaviness in the feel of the machine. It can be manoeuvred manually and kick-started without undue exertion.

Vincents retain the narrow, flat and almost straight handlebars which give a precision and endearing " tautness " to handling . . . .

. . . . The engine is very tractable and would pull away without harshness at tick-over speeds.

. . . . It may be asserted with confidence that there has never before been a production model with so much to commend it as a road-burner's dream. From 40 m.p.h. up to the maximum of over 100 m.p.h. there is a thrilling performance available at a twist of the grip. This is achieved by a high power/weight ratio and an engine, with lowish compression ratio and " easy " valve timing, pulling high gears. In consequence, the performance is available in top gear, it being unnecessary to use third and second unless the limit of acceleration is required. Throughout the speed range there is no vibration . . . .

Steering and road-holding are absolutely first class. The machine is rock steady and holds its line on the straights and in curves in a manner that is uncanny.

Though the big engine and high gearing of the machine suggest easy, loping, fussless mile-eating there is searing acceleration available if required. Standing start getaways against the watch provide a memorable thrill and leave a black line of burnt rubber on the road surface . . . .

The Vincent-H.R.D. Series " B " " Rapide " is a machine in a class by itself; a dream machine for the rider who is competent to handle its colossal performance ; a machine that will continue to be talked about wherever motor cyclists foregather.

29th May, 1947. " *The Motor Cycle.*"

Outstanding example of post-war enterprise and ingenuity in design—phenomenal in performance to a degree whereat its creators proudly claim it to be " The World's Fastest Standard Motor Cycle "—such is the Series " B " Vincent-H.R.D. " Rapide."

. . . . If anything was calculated to dispel illusions concerning speed at the expense of good manners and flexibility, it was this comforting ability to shut the grip with assurance that a certain tick-over would result . . . .

. . . . Meriting high praise is the fact that the exhaust was completely inaudible to the rider at any speed unless the head was turned in a deliberate attempt to catch the muffled burble . . . .

. . . . The physical comfort offered was excellent—aided by the already well-known Vincent-H.R.D. system of rear springing (via swinging rear chain-stays), which provided generous deflection over the most prominent manhole covers. Steering was positive and safe at all speeds . . . .

. . . . " Hands off " riding, whilst never to be recommended on modern roads with the ever present uncertainty of potholes and erratic drivers, was achieved without worry, while the Vincent's speedometer denoted 85–90 m.p.h. !

Vibration was virtually non-existent throughout the whole range of revolutions . . . .

. . . . Despite the 998 c.c.s., and because of the high gearing, it was possible to cover nearly 60 miles to the gallon under favourable conditions of flat country and little traffic, provided that the cruising speed was kept below 65–70 m.p.h.

Fast open bends could be tackled with a definite intention to stay on a chosen line, and no ordinary bump could throw either wheel off course. Unless the speedometer was watched it was very easy to enter sharp bends far too quickly, because of the utter absence of fuss. Fortunately, the machine is exceptionally well found in the matter of brakes, and the fourfold power exerted by the duo-stoppers on front and rear wheel provides an ample measure of security . . . .

Accessibility is excellent, thanks to the many practical features embodied, and a glance at the tommy-bar wheel nuts, in conjunction with the generously proportioned thumb bolts, lends ready credence to the fact that a timed adjustment of the rear chain occupied exactly 35 seconds without the use of spanners.

29th May, 1947. " *Motor Cycling.*"

. . . . There's not much noise, plenty of sports " 500 " register more than double the phon distribution of this mile-eater. Close up the gasworks, here's the roundabout—a gentle squeeze on the front brake lever—and three seconds later we go all red and feel daft. Trouble is that we have to open up again to reach the turning point, having discovered that duo-braking is substantially more than sales talk!

Heel over, open up gently and sit back—whoops ! We pull into the straight again with a vicious power slide and shut back smartly ! Try again as we point up the straight . . . . that's better. An impassive needle quotes " 45 " in bottom cog and we open up hard—" Gunga Din " just seems to gather himself and all of an instant later our grip on the bars becomes a feverish grab ! 60–65—whoosh—that's second ; hang on hard, here comes third with a mere gesture on the clutch lever. Was there ever such acceleration ? We wonder, as the needle sweeps rapidly beyond 85–90–95 whilst senses are temporarily numbed by a hurricane of wind pressure. 103 m.p.h. says the clock—" Blimey " says we, and make a manful decision to try top gear some other time.

Winding, leafy country roads came and went with incredible ease—no need to take risks on the bends, for with such terrific acceleration on tap an average well above the round " fifty " becomes a practical possibility. Over the Pennines via Holme Moss, lonely and windswept in the grey light of an autumn afternoon, we surged with a cruising speed which many a " 500 " would be pleased to claim as maximum . . . .

13th November, 1947. " *Motor Cycling.*"

Here one has, as you well know, a motor cycle of exceptional speed, a motor cycle capable of 100 PLUS. Yet it is not a high-compression rip-snorter. High power has been achieved with the moderate compression ratio of 6.8—1 by a clever design, which includes excellent breathing. With the power output available, and particularly the type of power, one has a machine which pulls a very high gear and yet is sufficiently docile for meandering through city traffic. I went out one day with two of the Staff who previously had had no experience with the latest " Rapide." Once out on a nice straight stretch free from side-turnings I handed over the machine with the idea that each should have a flip on it, later to put in more extensive mileage. Rider No. 1 went down the road, turned round and shot back at something between 85 and 90. Rider No. 2 returned at over 95. That I feel, gives a good idea of the confidence this remarkable motor cycle bestows.

Continued

The steering and braking of the H.R.D. are, as regards standard road machines, just about in classes of their own. For all its speed it has inbuilt safety that is outstanding . . .

1st January, 1948. " *The Motor Cycle.*"

To state a definite cruising speed on the open road is well-nigh impossible, as the margin is set only by road conditions and the rider's capabilities. From a standstill to 100 m.p.h. acceleration is constant and colossal—there can be no other description—and in the course of a 362 miles-in-the-day test run I recorded an average I dare not print.

Such performance as this would be impossible or highly dangerous without a measure of braking capable of coping with two-miles-a-minute velocity. Take a peep at the test sheet and note that from 30 m.p.h. in top gear it is possible to stop in 22 ft. 6 ins. ! . . . .

High-speed touring did not prove so hard on fuel as I anticipated, a state of affairs not difficult to understand when it is remembered that 60 m.p.h. in top gear means a mere whiff of throttle and no more than 2,700 r.p.m. On long-distance runs the tank would barely accept three gallons after 178 miles of mixed going and 75–80 m.p.h. cruising with the wind astern. This easy and effortless travel brought a lively problem concerning other road users who frequently misjudged the " Shadow's " rate of approach, due to the lack of noise and fuss . . . .

In short, a machine designed and built by riders for those who ride hard, far and fast.

15th July, 1948. " *Motor Cycling.*"

. . . . Since its inception as one of the first true post-war designs, the " Rapide," with its powerful 998 c.c. engine and comparatively light weight, has established itself as undoubtedly the world's fastest standard machine. Now, its dark sister, the " Black Shadow," is even faster !

In order to keep fully in step with the phenomenal performance of the big-twins, the new Girdraulic front fork has been designed. What impressed those visiting the stand who tried the fork were its soft easy action both on compression and rebound, and the massive proportions of the light-alloy fork blades.

25th November, 1948. " *The Motor Cycle* " (*London Show Report*).

Let us pass on to another thousand, the Vincent-H.R.D. This is a very different type of machine from the four-cylinder job we have been discussing ; it has been described as " rorty and naughty." There is a great deal to be said for a 1,000 c.c. Vee-twin pulling a gear ratio of $3\frac{1}{2}$ to 1. There is an easy, loping gait, and the way this machine gathers itself together under one when one takes a fistful of grip is great. Here, if ever there was one, is a man's motor cycle, and it is a machine which is essentially masculine in both outline and behaviour.

I was delighted with the flexibility of the machine—the way one trickles along in top gear in 30 m.p.h. limits—and, of course, in the outstandingly good power output and braking . . . .

. . . . What I will say here and now is that if you want a thrilling, zestful mount that is unique in performance of the variety that should have a capital " P," the " Rapide " provides the answer—and a very good answer, too.

6th January, 1949. " *The Motor Cycle.*"

" Mere mention of the name ' Black Shadow ' is enough to speed the pulse. Since the machine's introduction last year as a super-sports brother to the already famous ' Rapide,' the sombrely finished ' Shadow ' has achieved wide distinction. It is a connoisseur's machine ; one with speed and acceleration far greater than those of any other standard motor cycle ; and it is a motor cycle with unique and ingenious features which make it one of the outstanding designs of all time.

So far as the standards of engine performance, handling and braking are concerned—the chief features which can make or mar an otherwise perfect mount—the mighty ' Black Shadow ' must be awarded 99 out of 100 marks 99 because nothing, it is said, is perfect.

The machine has all the performance at the top end of the scale of a Senior T.T. mount. At the opposite end of the range, notwithstanding the combination of a 3·5 to 1 gear ratio, 7·3 to 1 compression ratio and pool quality fuel, it will ' chuff ' happily in top at 29–30 m.p.h. Indeed, in top gear without fuss, and with the throttle turned the merest fraction off its closed stop, it will surmount average gradients at 30 m.p.h. . . . .

. . . . During the test runs speeds of 85–90 m.p.h. were commonplace 100 m.p.h. was held on brief stretches and, occasionally, the needle of the special 150 m.p.h. Smith's speedometer would indicate 110. No airfield or stretch of road could be found which would allow absolute maximum speed to be obtained in two directions, against the watch. Flash readings in two directions of 118 and 114 were obtained, and in neither case had the machine attained its maximum . . . .

. . . . Steering and road-holding were fully in keeping with the exceptionally high engine performance. A soft yet positive movement is provided by the massively proportioned ' Girdraulic ' Fork. There is a ' tautness ' and solid feeling about the steering which engenders confidence no matter what the speed and almost irrespective of the condition of the road surface. Corners and bends can be taken stylishly and safely at ultra-high speeds. There was no chopping no ' sawing ' ; not one of the faults which are sometimes apparent on high speed machines . . . .

. . . . So efficient is the rear springing now, that never once was the rider bumped off the Dualseat or forced to poise on the rests. Even at speeds around the 100 m.p.h. mark, only the absence of road shocks gave indication that there was any form of rear-springing, such was the smoothness and lateral rigidity. Straight-ahead steering was in a class by itself. The model could be steered hands off at 15 m.p.h. with engine barely pulling or just as easily at 95 to 100 m.p.h. The steering damper was required only at speeds over 115 m.p.h. Used in unison, the four brakes (two per wheel) provided immense stopping power. Light pressure of two fingers on the front-brake lever was sufficient to provide all the braking the front wheel would permit . . . .

. . . . In the 700 miles of the road test the tools were never required. In spite of the high speeds there was no apparent sign of stress . . . .

. . . . There are many ingenious features of the Vincent-H.R.D. which brand

Continued below

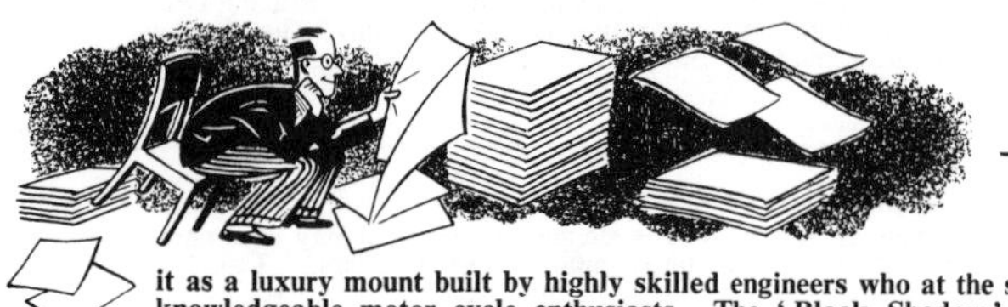

it as a luxury mount built by highly skilled engineers who at the same time are knowledgeable motor cycle enthusiasts. The ' Black Shadow ' finish is distinctive, obviously durable and very smart ; and only a minor reason why the ' Shadow ' attracts a crowd of interested passers-by wherever it is seen ! "

11th August, 1949. " *Motor Cycle.*"

" A small 250 c.c. side-valve machine with coil ignition could not have provided easier starting from cold or hot in any weather, than did the ' Comet ' recently road tested . . . . the faster the machine was ridden, the better became the steering. The stability on indifferent and greasy road surfaces gave the rider full confidence and no excessive caution was needed to negotiate treacherous tram lines and wet wood blocks . . . .

. . . . The rear suspension ironed out road bumps in a most satisfactory fashion and both front and rear wheels adhered firmly to the road in all circumstances. Confirming the manufacturers' claim, the ' Girdraulic ' forks held the front wheel steadily on any line chosen without a trace of waver and it would appear that the performance characteristics of the forks improve as the speed rises. Variations in road surface and even rain did not appear to affect the way in which the ' Comet ' could be ridden. It could be heeled over with the sure knowledge that nothing untoward would happen and on several occasions weaved its way through a series of bends without, apparently, any assistance from the rider . . . .

. . . . At no engine speed was any vibration apparent, the revs. rising with a smoothness reminiscent of a dynamo . . . .

. . . . Test panel brake figures verge on the incredible, but give factual evidence of something almost beyond even journalistic capabilities of description. Alone, the front brake provided a figure that is very satisfactory for any machine using both stoppers together . . . . On one occasion, when travelling on the ' Comet ' at a steady 70 m.p.h. a lorry, without warning, pulled straight across the road. Anticipating considerable difficulty in stopping, both brakes went hard on, only to be released again when the Vincent came down to walking pace some 50 or 60 yards from the offending vehicle ! Such large drum areas increase the periods between adjustment, and in over 600 miles the front brake required only two turns of the adjuster knob."

26th January, 1950. " *Motor Cycling.*"

SOUTH AFRICA

. . . . It is impossible, without indulging in hyperbole to describe these fabulous " mile-eaters." Suffice to say that they have obviously been constructed regardless of cost, to procure the highest degree possible of efficiency and craftsmanship.

On being taken for a short run, I was warned to hold on while the owner took a large handful of grip. We swooped up to 60 m.p.h. in one breathtaking rush (actual cold testimony of a stop watch shows that it takes eight seconds to reach that speed from a standstill), and then pulled up in what seemed to be a few lengths as the four brakes (two per wheel) took hold. Afterwards the owner modestly explained that he did not exceed 60 m.p.h. because the makers do not recommend it while the machine is being run in !

16th November, 1948. " *Eastern Province Herald,*" *South Africa.*

NEW ZEALAND

The " Rapide " models are, as is well known, capable of most astounding speeds in their standard form as sold, ranging from 110 m.p.h. in the case of the Standard " Rapide," through 125 m.p.h. with the " Black Shadows," up to as high as 150 m.p.h. with the new " Black Lightning " Racer. No road vehicle of any type has ever been offered for sale before in the world capable of such amazing performances.

20th December, 1948. " *New Zealand Motor Cyclist.*"

RHODESIA

The acceleration is terrific, and with it all is the quietness and lack of fuss which only a large engine can produce. Combined with this whirlwind performance are the most super brakes to enable the best use to be made of this performance. Two brakes per wheel are fitted, and even when applied hard at speeds higher than most people travel in a lifetime, they produce no juddering or jarring, no wavering or deviations from the intended course ; its just as if a giant hand takes charge, smoothly bringing the m.p.h. down to an easily managed figure in less time than it takes to think about it. I understand the Police figure for 100 per cent. braking efficiency is to stop from 30 m.p.h. in 30 feet. From the same speed the Vincent stops in 23 feet. . . . .

Open road work on the big Vincent is like giving a donkey strawberries. The effortlessness with which it swings around the corners is more reminiscent of a good 250 than a lusty 1,000 c.c. job, and one soon enters into the spirit of this beefiest of machines. Mile-eating is its business. The engine seems to call for more and more work to do, and the hardest of hard riders could scarcely tire this motor. The frame and forks perform their jobs so inconspicuously as to be perfect, while these super brakes form the background to this exhilarating mile-eating cruise, always ready to do more than their job. Truly a magnificent machine.

All those little things, plus the big things, go to complete an article built for a connoisseur—a connoisseur who intends to get there quickly in safety. Altogether a very beautiful device.

November, 1948. " *Road and Air,*" *Rhodesia.*

U.S.A.

. . . . The Vincent-H.R.D. Company whose Standard " Rapide " is certainly living up to advertised claims of 110 m.p.h. plus, when tuned only according to " Standard " specifications. Under the quite generous tuning alterations permitted by Class " C " ruling the " Rapide " certainly could be relied upon to do much better ; and we predict that one of these days some one will scrap up the shekels needed to finance an A.M.A.-sanctioned Dry Lakes Trials for Class " C " and possibly a Class " A " " Rapide," and then watch the American records go smash.

In the meantime, let me assure you that the Vincent-H.R.D. Standard " Rapide " is very, very Rapide indeed, and we, in all sincerity do believe them to be the " World's Fastest Standard Motor Cycle."

August, 1948. " *Motorcyclist,*" *Los Angeles, U.S.A.*

Vincent

Series C Singles and Twins: Models for the Road and Racing

ALL Vincent resources are now concentrated on Series C models. The range comprises three 998 c.c. vee-twins and two 499 c.c. singles although one of the singles, the Grey Flash, is listed in three forms—for racing, for road use or with equipment suitable for both purposes. However, owing to pressure of orders for other models in the range, Grey Flash models are temporarily withdrawn.

Engines are of advanced design in which extensive use is made of light-alloys and, in the case of the twins, the gear box is in

solid, forged pinion, and piston clearances have been slightly reduced. Oil flow to the rockers is now controlled by a metering device and the oil feeds to the rockers have clearing wires fitted to prevent clogging.

The pivot-action rear fork is controlled by springs in telescopic cylinders mounted beneath the nose of the Dualseat; between the spring cylinders is an hydraulic damper. The Girdraulic front fork has forged light-alloy blades of tapered, oval section with forged links to the steering-stem lugs. On each side, between the crown lug and the

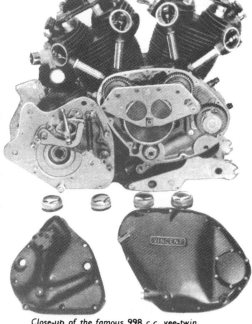

A picture of the 499 c.c. single-cylinder unit which shows how the engine forms part of the frame

Close-up of the famous 998 c.c. vee-twin. Extensive use is made of light-alloys, and the gear box is built in unit

Potent performer—the Series C Rapide 998 c.c. twin

Single-cylinder 499 c.c. Vincent Comet

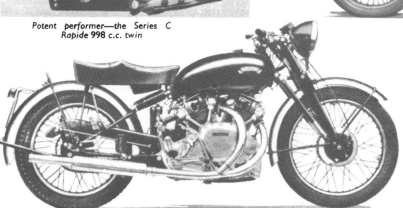

unit. A most unusual feature is that the engine forms part of the frame.

Latest engine modifications are aimed at obtaining quieter running. A large bronze idler wheel in the timing gear which tended to "ring" has been replaced by a

fork ends is a telescopic case enclosing two springs, and a two-way hydraulic damper is mounted between the top steering-stem lug and the lower link member. The combination of the Vincent frame and the Girdraulic fork endow both twin- and single-

cylinder models with outstanding steering and road-holding qualities.

Vincents have always been noteworthy for many features that appeal to experienced riders. Among these are twin brakes on both wheels; a wide range of adjustment for the footrests with the rear-brake pedal mounted in such a manner that its position can be altered to suit the footrest setting chosen; and quickly detachable wheels that can be removed without using tools.

General Specification.—Lucas and B.T.-H. magnetos; Miller lighting; Amal carburettors; Vincent four-speed gear box with positive-stop foot-change on twins, Burman on the Comet, Albion on the Grey Flash; Avon tyres: Comet, Meteor, Rapide and Black Shadow, 3.00 x 20in front and 3.50 x 19in rear; Grey Flash and Black Lightning, 3.00 x 21in front and 3.50 x 20in rear; tank capacities: fuel 3¾ gal, oil 6 pt.

Prices.—998 c.c. Black Lightning twin, £395 (in Gt. Britain, with P.T., £501 13s); 998 c.c. Black Shadow twin, £296 (£375 18s 5d); 998 c.c. Rapide twin, £255 (£323 17s); 499 c.c. Comet single, £190 (£241 6s); 499 c.c. Grey Flash single, racing, £260 (£330 4s); 499 c.c. Grey Flash, road equipment, £275 (£349 5s); 499 c.c. Grey Flash, dual equipment, £285 (£361 19s). Vincent H.R.D. Co. Ltd., Stevenage, Herts.

---

998 c.c. Vincent Rapide

An Enthralling, High-performance Big-twin

SPEEDS in excess of 80 m.p.h. are apt to be talked of glibly. Yet if the truth be admitted, the number of riders who have, in fact, bettered 80 m.p.h. are without doubt in the minority—and for many of those who have, it has been a once- or twice-only experience. So far as the vast majority of sidecar men are concerned, 80 m.p.h. is probably at least 10 m.p.h. faster than anything within their ken. The exceptions, racing men and freak conditions aside, are only those who have sampled the o.h.v big-twin type outfit exemplified by the modern Vincent, the Rapide edition of which, wedded to a sidecar, will

Hydraulically damped rear-springing is fitted to the Vincent Rapide

cruise effortlessly and without fuss at "eighty" and indeed exceed that gait in third gear.

High, tireless cruising speed was certainly not the sole attribute, or even the most likeable one, of the outfit under test. It was described by Vincents as a "semi-sporting outfit"—a standard Series C Rapide with a Swallow Jet 80 sidecar. On first acquaintance it appeared to be just that: semi-sporting—with a lusty, smooth and vibrationless performance at low speeds, and starting as effortless as that of the most docile tourer.

From idling speeds right up the engine speed scale, the pick-up was clean-cut and brisk, and acceleration such that, in this

respect, the outfit had few equals on the road—whether they were two-wheelers or four. The big-twin's power meant that wheel-spin was easily set up in first or second gears. It was such, too, that it sent the blood coursing quickly through the arteries and engendered an enthusiastic feeling of thrilled anticipation.

In view of the inordinately high gearing of the outfit—bottom gear was 10.66 to 1 and second as high as 6.35 to 1—the darting acceleration comes rather as a surprise. But the fact is that the mighty Vincent engine has characteristics which make it ideally suited for pulling high gear ratios. Though it is true that the road speed had to be as high as 6 or 7 m.p.h. before the clutch could be fully engaged, unless transmission snatch was to be experienced, there was no lack of power at engine speeds so low that the firing strokes could almost be counted. The combination of high gearing and a large-capacity engine spells effortlessness at high speeds and the avoidance of rapid wear and tear on engine and transmission. At 60 m.p.h. the engine is turning over at only 3,240 r.p.m.

During the normal course of the test, on which over 1,000 miles were covered, the tools were never once required. Later, when the performance figures were being taken and the engine grossly over-revved, the valve collars moved up on the valve stems. This trouble was rectified at the Works and gave no sign of recurring when the figures were obtained finally.

Speeds in the 80 m.p.h. region were used with the outfit whenever practicable—the engine turning over with no more fuss than at 50 m.p.h. Indeed, when the mood was one of seeking real sport, the engine was quite often driven as near flat-out as maybe. It was commonplace, for instance, to run the outfit up to 75 m.p.h. before engaging top gear. Yet, the rear chain was only once adjusted—no tools are necessary to do this—and no other form of adjustment whatever was necessary. No oil leaks manifested themselves. The slow and reliable tickover persisted no matter how severe the treatment of the engine had been.

Naturally, an imperative requirement of a sidecar outfit in this class is that the fork possesses a high degree of lateral rigidity. In this respect the massive Girdraulic fork earned full marks. Corners and bends could be entered with a zest approaching abandon, the driver at all times confident that any chosen line could be effortlessly held. The handling was such that only the slightest trace of damper was required at speeds over 35 m.p.h. Below that speed, considerably more damping was necessary to curb the tendency of the front wheel to wobble. The Girdraulic fork has numerous novel features, one of them being the ease with which it may be altered to provide solo or sidecar trial. For sidecar work, steering was delightfully light at high speeds. At low speeds it was naturally heavier, but never unduly so.

Contributing to the excellent handling of the outfit, the Vincent riding position is one that causes the driver to sit well over the machine, in a straight-arm posture, body leaning slightly forward and with the feet well back. It is a

The Vincent power unit is of most advanced design. Light-alloy components are extensively employed

nd Sidecar

oisseur's Features

The Swallow Jet 80 sidecar has elegant, sporting lines Suspension is by means of rubber bushes

position which afforded excellent control at high or low speeds. Both the standard Vincent handlebar—the famous short, almost straight bar—and the touring one which has a rather more orthodox bend were tried. In each case there was ample leverage, though it was felt that, for sidecar work, slightly greater angle of the grips in relation to the machine's lateral axis would have been preferred.

All controls are fully adjustable and may be perfectly positioned for ease of operation. The Servo-assisted clutch was remarkably light to use—so light, indeed, that the pressure of one finger was sufficient—and it required very little travel. The front brakes, too, were light in operation. In contrast, the twistgrip proved "heavy," and inordinately heavy pressure was required at the rear brake pedal in order to obtain maximum braking efficiency. Once the four brakes—there are two per wheel—had bedded down, they came well up to the recognized Vincent standard—which means, of course, that they were in keeping with the outfit's colossal performance.

Gear Changing

Even in these enlightened times, many an otherwise excellent machine is condemned because of its having a poor gear change. With the Vincent there was no question of this. A slight pause was necessary—because of the rather wide jump in ratios—when changing between first and second gears, but all other changes could be made quite effortlessly, and just as rapidly as the controls could be moved. The gear pedal is pleasantly short, well positioned and it has a brief travel. The only criticism that could be levelled at the gear box was that the change was

rather heavy. None of the indirect ratios was more than just audible.

The driving beam from the 7in Miller head lamp was adequate for speeds up to 50 m.p.h. under average night conditions. Surprisingly good protection from water and road filth was provided by the polished light-alloy mudguards. In its position under the Feridax Dualseat, the tool tray was easily accessible, but rather too small to accommodate a full list of tools, with spare plugs, bulbs, and a puncture repair outfit.

What of the Swallow Jet 80 sidecar? There is probably no sports sidecar with cleaner lines in production in the world today. The chassis was fitted with an excellent four-point attachment and proved completely rigid. Average comfort was provided by the rubber suspension. For Britain's capricious climate the windscreen was rather too small; the height inside when the hood was raised was, for all but passengers of smaller than average stature, rather inadequate. Finish of the outfit was black, chromium and silver.

Information Panel

SPECIFICATION

ENGINE: 998 c.c. (84 x 90 mm) vee-twin high-camshaft o.h.v., with gear box in unit. Fully enclosed valve-gear. Dry-sump lubrication: tank capacity 6 pints. Four main bearings. Roller-bearing big-ends. Specialloid pistons. Cast-iron liners shrunk into aluminium-alloy cylinder barrels. Aluminium-alloy cylinder heads.

CARBURETTORS: Amal: Twistgrip throttle control and twin handle-bar-mounted air levers.

IGNITION AND LIGHTING: Lucas magneto with auto-advance. Miller dynamo: 7in head lamp: stoplight. Dynamo output, 50 watts.

TRANSMISSION: Vincent four-speed gear box with positive-stop foot control. Gear ratios: Top, 4.1 to 1. Third, 4.88 to 1. Second, 6.35 to 1. Bottom, 10.66. Alternative ratios (available by reversing rear wheel): Top, 3.96 to 1. Third, 4.71 to 1. Second, 6.14 to 1. Bottom, 10.30 to 1. Servo-assisted clutch. Primary chain, in triplex, enclosed in aluminium-alloy oil-bath case. Secondary chain, ⅝ x ⅜in with guard over top run. R.p.m. at 30 m.p.h. in top gear (with higher ratios), 1,620.

FUEL CAPACITY: 3½ gallons.

TYRES: Front, 3.00 x 20in. Avon ribbed, rear 3.50 x 19in Avon studded.

BRAKES: Twin on each wheel; drums 7in diameter x ⅞in wide.

SUSPENSION: Girdraulic link-action front fork with twin helical compression springs and hydraulic damping; pivot-action rear-springing hydraulically damped.

WHEELBASE: 56in. Ground clearance, 5in unladen.

SEAT: Feridax Dualseat. Unladen height, 31in.

WEIGHT: 728lb, fully equipped and with one gallon of fuel and oil-tank full.

PRICE: Machine only, £255, plus (in Great Britain only), £68 17s. P.T.

ROAD TAX: £5 a year; £1 7s 6d a quarter.

DESCRIPTION: *The Motor Cycle*, 31 August, 1950.

MAKERS: The Vincent H.R.D. Co., Ltd., Stevenage, Herts.

SIDECAR

MODEL: Swallow Jet 80.

CHASSIS: Swallow "Silk" tubular chassis with forward pivot mounting for body at front and torsion arms on bonded rubber bushes at rear. Wheel is also carried on rubber-bushed mounting.

BODY: All-steel welded construction with no doors. Length is 82in; width, 25½in; distance from squab to nose, 42½in; height inside with hood raised, 30in. Locker dimensions are 24in long x 19½in wide x 15in deep. Black twill hood.

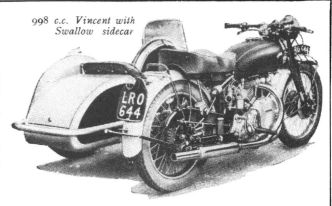

998 c.c. Vincent with Swallow sidecar

PRICE: £70 13s 2d (complete) plus (in Great Britain only), £18 16s 10d P.T. **MAKERS:** Swallow Coachbuilding Co. (1935), Ltd., The Airport, Walsall, Staffs.

PERFORMANCE DATA

MEAN MAXIMUM SPEED: Bottom: 45 m.p.h.
Second: 72 m.p.h.
Third : 81 m.p.h.
Top: 88 m.p.h.

ACCELERATION:		10-30 m.p.h.	20-40 m.p.h.	30-50 m.p.h.
Bottom	...	2.8 secs	3 secs	—
Second	...	—	4 secs	4 secs
Third	...	—	6.2 secs	5.6 secs
Top	...	—	10 secs	7.6 secs

Speed at end of quarter mile from rest: 77 m.p.h.
Time to cover standing quarter-mile: 16.8 secs.

PETROL CONSUMPTION: At 30 m.p.h., 75 m.p.g. At 40 m.p.h. 64 m.p.g. At 50 m.p.h., 54 m.p.g. At 60 m.p.h., 46 m.p.g.

BRAKING: From 30 m.p.h. to rest, 36ft 6in (surface, wet tar-macadam).

TURNING CIRCLE: 16ft.

MINIMUM NON-SNATCH SPEED: 20 m.p.h. in top gear.

WEIGHT PER C.C.: 0.73lb.

THE 998 c

VINCEN

child-adult "Sherwood" saloon, mounted on the standard "Safety" chassis, was specified to be hitched to a touring "Rapide," with deep-section mudguards and "fat" tyres (3.50 ins. by 19 ins. front and 4.00 ins. by 18 ins. rear).

The outfit has been "on the strength" for six months now, during which time it has covered some 4,000 miles, and—unless calamity intervenes in the form of a telephone call from Stevenage demanding its return—the "barouche," as it has come to be known, will be out again next week-end, on a duty trip or taking a "free" member of the staff and his family on a pleasure run.

Being no newcomer to the market, the "Rapide" needs only a brief description. Its massive 998 c.c. power-unit is nowadays the only British example of what is often described as "the side-carrist's ideal"—an o.h.v. vee-twin "thousand." Its high-camshaft, short-

WHAT is a reasonable cruising speed for a two-seater sidecar outfit? Fifty? Fifty-five, perhaps? Even a mile a minute if an over-500 c.c. motor is providing the power? Or what?

One Sunday evening, last November, Cyril Quantrill walked into the "local"—back from covering some trial. "Most unusual," said Bernal Osborne, "you're early!" "On the new Vinc.," said Quantrill. "Oh," said Osborne. "Goes well," said Quantrill, "really good . . . know what? . . ." "No," said Osborne. "Holds '75' with the family aboard." "Straight?" "Straight!" "Strewth" . . . and Bernal took such a gulp of his bitter that he nearly choked.

Two years ago Quantrill shocked a lot of purist speed men by hitching a "Rapide" to a two-seater "chair" in order to combine a holiday *en famille* on the Continent with the urgent business of covering two "classic" race meetings in one week, and in the process became a Vincent fan.

At the time, almost everyone seemed to regard this high-performance big twin as essentially a solo mount, but the general motorcycling public has now decided that it is also an ideal machine for heavy-duty sidecar work. There are to be seen nowadays a succession of "Rapides," speeding town-dwelling families to the seaside.

"Motor Cycling" decided to test a Vincent in sidecar trim and—because Blacknell Sidecars, Ltd., of Nottingham. have produced a range of chassis and bodies particularly adapted for use with a machine, such as the Vincent, with swinging arm rear suspension—a

A connoisseur's combination! The Series C Vincent "Rapide" attached to a Blacknell saloon sidecar.

(Above) Although it is a two-seater, the Blacknell "Sherwood" by no means dwarfs the machine to which it is attached.

(Right) The sidecar has a good streamline contour, which materially assists high-speed driving. Access to the rear locker is from inside the body.

"RAPIDE"
and
BLACKNELL SHERWOOD" SIDECAR

o.h.v. "Big Twin" and Luxury
on Sidecar Give "Motor
ling" Testers Fresh Ideas on
senger Machine Averages and
Maximums

pushrod, layout enables the engine to run at a much higher r.p.m. than usual with this type and a highly efficient dry-sump lubrication system and the use of light alloy for the cylinders and heads overcome that old bugbear of big twins—overheating on the rear cylinder. Separate Amal carburetters are fitted, with a cable junction box providing compensated control for the throttle

opening and separate levers enabling individual settings to be given for each air slide.

The Lucas magneto has automatic advance and retard mechanism and one of the very few criticisms which can be made of the machine is of the inability of the automatic device to compete with the special requirements of sidecar work—a weakness evidenced by pinking when accelerating sharply on hills.

A separate 50-watt Miller dynamo and voltage control unit, and a 13 amp.-hr. Exide battery attend to the lighting and warning equipment. The Miller head lamp furnishes a broad beam which makes night driving a pleasure and high praise goes to the Lucas " Altette " horn, which has a note which without being frightening, nevertheless gives distinctly audible warning of approach—a most necessary adjunct to a machine which is extremely quiet when running at 50 m.p.h. or less in top.

In semi-unit construction, the four-speed gearbox provides ratios ideally spaced for sidecar work and, addition-ally, there is a choice of rear sprockets which—compared with the more usual tooth-to-tooth change of engine sprocket—gives a far finer selection of gears. After running the road test out-fit for a time with a 56-tooth sprocket —which gave a speedometer maximum of over 90 m.p.h. under favourable conditions—it was decided that a more suitable top-gear performance could be obtained by "cogging down"—in fact,

adding teeth by fitting a 60-tooth sprocket.

With that modification the actual ratios available are 4.56, 5.47, 7.3 and 12.5 to 1. That means a top-gear range of anything from 30 m.p.h. up to 80 m.p.h.—and up to that speed in a mere 31 secs.—without any changing down or lying flat. If the intermediate ratios are used, the jump from 30 m.p.h. to the same figure can be accomplished in as little as 21 secs., whilst the all-out, sitting-up-in-a-great - big - riding - coat maximum is just short of 80 m.p.h. with a passenger weight of one wife and two small children aboard, and the really getting-down-to-it figure with " guinea-pig " Bernal Osborne in the " chair " is no less than 85 m.p.h.

Galloping the outfit with an empty sidecar, an 88 m.p.h. maximum figure has been recorded, allowing for 5 per cent. speedometer error. When obtain-ing the figures recorded on the tester's sheet, it was discovered that the change from second gear to third was none too simple and more than once " miscog-ging " resulted in fabulous—and frightening—surges of r.p.m.

With so much power available, an immediate thought is " do the brakes work? "

They do. There are four of them, two to each wheel of the machine and each of 7 ins. diameter and, provided they are adjusted at fairly regular intervals—for halting 700 lb of motor-cycle and sidecar, plus about 3 cwt. of passengers, is no light duty—they will stop the combination in a d stance which few sidecar outfits could equal. The limiting factors, in fact, are road surface and tyre adhesion—not the brake linings or leverage.

But too great an accent must not be placed on sheer performance, for quite the most endearing attr bute of the Vincent is its ability to gobble up miles effortlessly. Such is the manner in which the " Rapide " surmounts gradi-ents without giving any indication that they even exist, such is its stopping power, and so well does it sweep round bends, that comfortable 35 m.p.h. aver-ages can be maintained with the needle seldom going past the " 60 " mark.

Petrol consumption could be fairly heavy. There have been occasions when no more than 33 m.p.g. has been recorded. Shocking? Hardly, for that figure has been coupled with a " 40 plus " average, on journeys of 150 or 200 miles. At the nominal figure of a maintained 30 m.p.h.—but who in his right senses wants to maintain a steady thirty on the Vincent outfit?—the con-sumption figure rises to 55 m.p.g.

Much the same variation comes in on oil consumption. When the machine is driven really hard—as it has been almost continually since it has been with " Motor Cycling "—a one-pint replen-ishment every second fill-up (every 220 to 250 miles on 3-gallon replenishments) has been normal, yet, when the outfit has been driven sedately for an equiva-lent distance—as when used for daily 16-mile journeys to and from the office —there has been a scarcely noticeable drop in the oil level.

Mention of daily journeys introduces

A phase in the exploratory run to Goodwood undertaken by " Motor Cycling " staff. The photographer forsook the sidecar momentarily to get this picture in the heart of Winchester, with the King Alfred memorial in the background.

BRIEF SPECIFICATION OF THE 998 c.c. VINCENT TOURING "RAPIDE" and BLACKNELL "SHERWOOD" SIDECAR

The Machine

Engine: 50-degree vee-twin: bore 84 mm., stroke 90 mm; 998 c.c.; high-camshaft push-rod o.h.v.; dry-sump lubrication, oil tank capacity 6 pints; Lucas magneto ignition with automatic control; Miller 50-watt dynamo; Amal carburetters.

Transmission: Positive - stop four - speed Vincent gearbox with neutral selector; ratios 4.56, 5.47, 7.3 and 12.5 to 1; rear chain ⅝-in. by ⅜-in.; ⅜-in. triplex primary chain with adjustable spring-blade tensioner.

Frame: Engine comprises frame basis; pressed steel top member, incorporating oil tank bolted to cylinder heads; pivot type, triangulated suspension at rear with adjustable shock-absorbers; front forks patent Vincent "Girdraulic" type with central spring and hydraulic damping

Wheels: Fitted with Avon tyres, 3.50 ins. by 19 ins. front and 4.00 ins. by 18 ins. rear; twin 7-in. diameter brakes.

with compensated control, front and rear.

Tank: Welded steel 3¾-gallon fuel tank.
Dimensions: Wheelbase, 56 ins.; overall length, 85½ ins.; saddle height, 30 ins.; ground clearance, 5½ ins.; weight, 455 lb.
Finish: Black frame and tank, with gold lettering and lining; other parts chrome or cadmium plated or polished aluminium
Price: £265, fully equipped, plus £71 11s. P.T.
Makers: Vincent-H.R.D. Co., Ltd., Stevenage, Herts.

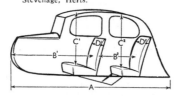

The Sidecar

Chassis: Blacknell "Safety" of single main tube construction; quarter-elliptic rear springs, rubber bush front suspension.
Wheel: Mounted on stub axle with large-diameter taper roller bearings; Avon tyre, 3.50 ins. by 19 ins.
Body: Blacknell "Sherwood" child-adult single-door saloon, coachbuilt with aluminium panelling; folding backrest to front seat; luggage locker behind rear seat
Dimensions: (See diagram) A=81 ins.; B1 =54 ins.; B2=20 ins.; C1=38 ins.; C2=32 ins.; D1=19½ ins.; D2= 18½ ins.
Finish: All-black exterior with high-quality red leathercloth upholstery and fawn lining; separate roll-up hoods for front and rear passengers.
Price: Body £51, plus £13 12s. P.T.; chassis £32 15s. 4d., plus £8 14s. 9d. P.T.
Makers: Blacknell Sidecars, Ltd., New Nuthall, Notts.

the subject of starting. It is making no unfair comment to say that earlier "Rapides" have been fickle in this respect But 1951 modifications to the valve gear and cam contours have virtually "killed" that bother.

Knowing that the model handed over to "Motor Cycling" would come in for more than its normal share of hammering, the Vincent technical staff fitted comparatively "hot" Champion NA8 plugs instead of the standard N8s. Even so, there was little sign of plug-wetting or oiling and, generally, starting was a simple procedure. It was advisable to keep the air levers closed for the first minute or so, and to ease them open steadily, when starting from cold, but once the engine was warm, the mixture controls could be disregarded.

With more damping on the rear springing than would be required for solo use, and with the steering damper just biting, the outfit handled superbly, the weight of the sidecar only making itself evident by a suspicion of handle-bar flap when decelerating below 40 m.p.h. The writer preferred the wide handlebars fitted to the standard short Vincent bars, but would have been even happier had there been a more definite backward curve in the bends. And being very long-legged, he would have liked to have had the footrests lower than the lowest level at which the standard range of adjustment permits them to be set.

From the passenger's point of view, the "Sherwood" gained full marks. Rear accommodation is sufficient to seat a five-footer or two small children in comfort, while the largest adult would not be cramped in the front seat. With the hoods in position, it is easy for the front passenger to get in or out without disarranging her hat. To say that the interior of the sidecar is snug in winter is true but, with only a small hood-flap to provide ventilation, it might become too warm if heavy rain necessitated complete battening-down in midsummer.

The suspension—rubber-bushed at the front end and on quarter-elliptic, multi-leaf springs at the rear—is such that there is absolutely no roll on corners and no unpleasant fore and aft pitching on bumpy roads.

Confirming previous experience on sidecar road tests, it was noted that the weight of a passenger had very little effect on performance figures—as little, in fact, as a mere ⅖ sec. on the "flying quarter." It is the frontal area of the outfit which steals the m.p.h.—particularly over the "60" mark—and, undoubtedly, a contributory factor to the outstanding performance of the Vincent was the excellent aerodynamic contour of the "Sherwood" body.

With the machine costing £265, plus £71 11s. P.T., and the sidecar £106 2s. 1d., including P.T., making a total of £442 13s. 1d, the combination obviously comes into the luxury class. Yet a glance at the tester's report on this page immediately confirms that the Vincent-Blacknell outfit provides a performance, coupled with passenger comfort, which would cost many times that amount if the vehicle had a wheel at each corner instead of two in line and one at the side.

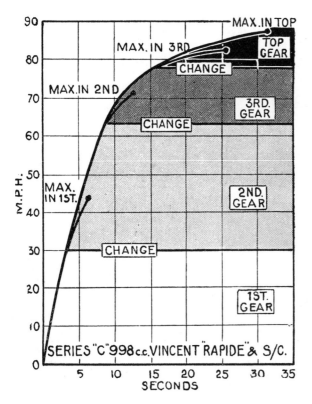

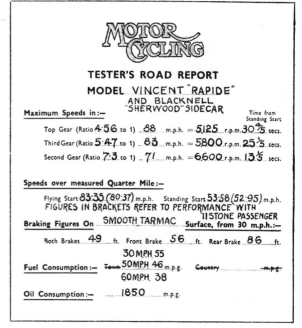

MOTOR CYCLING

TESTER'S ROAD REPORT
MODEL VINCENT "RAPIDE"
AND BLACKNELL "SHERWOOD" SIDECAR

Maximum Speeds in:—

			Time from Standing Start
Top Gear (Ratio 4·56 to 1)	88 m.p.h.	= 5125 r.p.m.	30⅖ secs.
Third Gear (Ratio 5·47 to 1)	83 m.p.h.	= 5800 r.p.m.	25⅘ secs.
Second Gear (Ratio 7·3 to 1)	71 m.p.h.	= 6600 r.p.m.	13⅘ secs.

Speeds over measured Quarter Mile:—

Flying Start 83·35 (80·37) m.p.h. Standing Start 53·58 (52·95) m.p.h.
FIGURES IN BRACKETS REFER TO PERFORMANCE WITH 11 STONE PASSENGER

Braking Figures On SMOOTH TARMAC **Surface, from 30 m.p.h.:—**

Both Brakes	49 ft.	Front Brake	56 ft.	Rear Brake	86 ft.

Fuel Consumption:— 30 M.P.H. 55, Town 50 MPH 46 m.p.g., Country ..... m.p.g.
60 MPH. 38

Oil Consumption:— 1850 m.p.g.

Vincent

Stand 26 : Where Connoisseurs Foregather

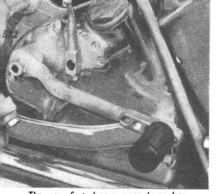

The new foot-change gear lever has direct action and is adjustable to suit footrest position

THE Vincent Stand, as ever, is proving the Mecca of those enthusiastic connoisseurs to whom ultra-high-speed safe travel represents the ultimate form of motor cycling. And judging from the size of the crowds thronging Stand 26, their numbers include many who at present no more than aspire to the ownership of a "Stevenage Special."

All four models of the range are prominently displayed in both sports and touring versions. The former is the type more usually found in this country, with its polished-aluminium mudguards, famous near-straight handlebar and 3.00in- and 3.50in-section front and rear tyres respectively. The deeply valanced black mud-

guards, upswept handlebar and larger-section tyres of the touring versions appeal more specifically to oversea customers and sidecar men.

Four of the twins are shown wedded to various sidecars of Blacknell and Garrard manufacture, and make extremely handsome high-performance outfits.

The twin-cylinder Vincents represent one of the most outstanding British conceptions of the post-war era, and show evidence, not only of design by practical enthusiasts, but also of constant detail advancements. The unique hydraulically damped Girdraulic fork is now universal, as also is hydraulic control of the rear springing.

Recent improvements which Vincent riders are quick to observe concern the gear-change and front-brake control. The former eliminates the previous linkage; a forged, light-alloy pedal now runs direct to the gear box. Lighter and more positive gear selection is thus achieved, while an uncommonly large range of adjustment is

retained by means of splines at the rear end of the lever, plus five optional pedal-mounting holes at the front end.

Most enviable in reputation and handsome in appearance, with the glossy black finish of its power-unit castings, is the Black Shadow—sports edition of the Rapide. Dispensing 55 b.h.p. and capable of cruising at any speed of which a rider is capable, with a maximum in excess of 120 m.p.h., it represents, for many a truly hard rider, the ideal mile-eater.

Also on view are manually operated, sectioned models of both single- and twin-cylinder engines, and of the Girdraulic fork and front brakes, and displayed in showcases is a variety of standard components straight from the assembly line; no special Show finish has been applied.

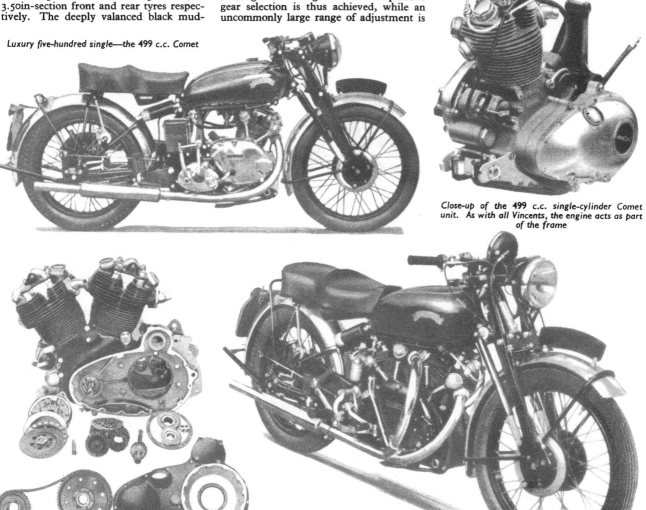

Luxury five-hundred single—the 499 c.c. Comet

Close-up of the 499 c.c. single-cylinder Comet unit. As with all Vincents, the engine acts as part of the frame

Clutch and gearbox internals of the 998 c.c. vee-twin

Three 998 c.c. vee-twin models are produced. This is the Black Shadow, a sports edition of the famous Rapide

Look for this badge at the VINCENT STAND

CONWAY MOTORS
THE
VINCENT
SPECIALISTS

CONWAY MOTORS
THE WORLD'S BIGGEST VINCENT SPECIALISTS

CONWAY MOTORS will be represented on The Vincent Stand at the Motor Cycle Show.

Our representatives will be wearing the badge as illustrated above. They are there to help you, so have a word with them and find out how quickly you can get delivery of your new Vincent, how we can arrange hire-purchase terms to suit your pocket, and ask for details of our fair part-exchange deals.

Find out from them, also, about our works-trained maintenance staff and our comprehensive stock of post-war Vincent spares.

They will tell you about our efficient after-sales service and if you are worried by the price of a new model, they will remind you that you can find a first-class used machine in our London Showrooms.

We always hold a vast stock of used Vincents (and other makes) for immediate delivery and our magnificent show of new Vincents and combinations is always worth a visit.

Now don't miss this opportunity—have a word with one of our men on the Vincent Stand and find out just how easy it is to become the owner of a brand new Vincent.

301-7 GOLDHAWK RD., SHEPHERDS BUSH, W.12.
TEL: RIV. 5725

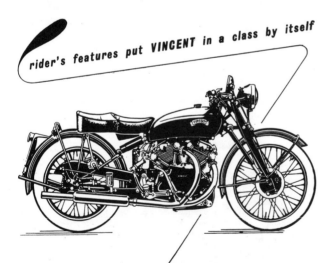

rider's features put **VINCENT** in a class by itself

Before you buy a Vincent you would undoubtedly be satisfied of its high quality of materials and workmanship, you would certainly have heard of the Vincent's outstanding performance and speed. It is most likely that you would have considered the design from the point of view of accessibility. Through the courtesy of a friend you might have experienced the unsurpassed handleability of a Vincent and its perfect comfort at all speeds, but, only as an owner could you possibly hope to appreciate to the full all the many 'rider's features' which to the enthusiast put the Vincent in a class by itself.

See the world's fastest standard motorcycle on
STAND NO. 5

Motorcycles of the future will be judged by the standards set by Vincent today

VINCENT ENGINEERS (STEVENAGE) LTD., STEVENAGE, HERTS, ENGLAND
—*Telephone : STEVENAGE 690-3*—

THE
VINCENT

A STATEMENT ON POST-WAR POLICY FOR
THE LITTLE "BIG TWIN"

★ *"The World's Fastest Motor Cycle"*
the **VINCENT-H.R.D. RAPIDE** must be
Your Choice for the Post War Era!

THE VINCENT H.R.D. COMPANY LTD. Stevenage, Herts

IN 1946 WE PRINTED THIS STATEMENT
OF THE PERFORMANCE CHARACTERISTICS THAT WOULD BE PROVIDED BY OUR POST WAR TWINS. THE MOST MODERN DEVELOPMENTS OF THE BASIC DESIGN WHICH HAVE MORE THAN FULFILLED THE STATEMENT THAT WE THEN MADE ARE TO BE SEEN ON

STAND No. 26
AT
THE EARLS COURT EXHIBITION

THE VINCENT H.R.D. COMPANY, LTD., STEVENAGE, HERTS, ENGLAND.   Tel. : STEVENAGE 670-1

THE MOTOR CYCLE   13 NOVEMBER 1952

CYCLE & MOTOR CYCLE SHOW · EARLS COURT · 15th to 22nd NOVEMBER

Looking forward to meeting all enthusiasts at Stand No. 6

where we shall have on view a most comprehensive selection of current models from the fabulous Black Lightning to the 500 c.c. Comet

VINCENT H.R.D. COMPANY LTD., STEVENAGE, HERTS, ENGLAND. TEL: STEVENAGE 690-3

Vincent

Stand 6 : World's Fastest Standard Production Machines

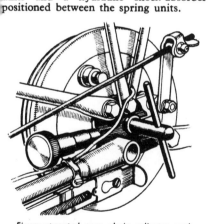

Removal of the magneto cover reveals the large oil-filter chamber and ingenious front stand

MAIN emphasis on the Vincent stand is on the ultra-high performance 998 c.c. Black Shadow, super-sporting member of a family of exclusive thoroughbreds built for hard-riding and discriminating connoisseurs. Maintaining its proud boast to be the fastest standard production machine in the world, this fully equipped mile-eater exemplifies the Vincent post-war policy of frameless construction in its most up-to-date form. The massive though compact 50-degree vee-twin engine-gear unit is bolted to a six-pint, box-section oil tank to form the main frame. Pivoted behind the power plant, the fully triangulated rear fork assembly is controlled by twin telescopic coil spring units and a hydraulic shock-absorber positioned between the spring units.

Front wheel suspension is by means of the now-famous forged light-alloy Girdraulic fork; this features twin telescopic spring units, a centrally disposed hydraulic damper, and ready adjustment of trail and preloading for solo and sidecar work. Exclusive, too, is the use of four 7in-diameter brakes—two to each wheel—and a 150 m.p.h. speedometer with 5in dial.

Observant visitors are entranced with the number of "riders'" features that abound, such as the really quickly detachable wheels, for which no tools are required; the finger adjusters for rear chain tension and front brakes; the knurled battery retainer; gear and brake pedals adjustable for both height and length; and the twin prop stands which combine to form a sturdy front stand. A cutaway model of a complete Black Shadow machine reveals the first-class design and construction.

Though no externally visible modifications are detectable (as compared with the 1952 models), nevertheless the ceaseless search for improvement has continued. Mechanical noise is claimed to be reduced by means of new cam forms employed; gear selection is improved by an alteration to the selector mechanism; and the clutch and brake shoes are fitted with friction linings said to be impervious to oil and water.

With the tractability and exhaust quietness which stem from the large capacity of its twin-carburettor, moderately tuned engine, allied to the stupendous acceleration and maximum speed of over 120 m.p.h.

provided by the available output of 55 b.h.p., the Black Shadow offers the ultimate in usable road performance.

For the slightly less ambitious connoisseur who favours two or three wheels, there is the more docile big twin, the standard Rapide. Externally recognizable by virtue of the unenamelled castings of its power unit and the 3in-diameter speedometer head, the Rapide's salient differences lie in such items of engine specification as compression ratio, carburettor size, and valve-spring poundage. Capable of dispensing 45 b.h.p., it makes an ideal fast-touring solo or sidecar machine. Indeed, for the sidecar enthusiast, Black Shadow and Rapide models with both standard and touring equipment are shown wedded to a variety of imposing sidecars.

Enthusiasts who do not aspire to the ownership of a "thousand" are finding that the majority of the exclusive Vincent features are incorporated in the 499 c.c. single-cylinder Comet.

Maintenance made easy—knurled battery fastener

Small sister of the big-twins— the 500 c.c. Comet

Finger-operated rear chain adjuster and q.-d. wheel arrangement

The famous Rapide in optional touring guise

Drive side of the massive Rapide engine-gear unit

TONY'S FIRST "HUNDRED THOUSAND"

A Private Owner's Self-imposed Endurance Test of a "Black Shadow" Vincent

described by CYRIL QUANTRILL

Cyril Quantrill greets Tony Rose as he brings the six-figure Vincent outfit into the factory for its first decoke. Centre, stands co-driver Jim Reagan.

(Right) It comes to pieces as easily as this! Lifting away the forward section of the Vincent — surely a new "high" in dismantleability.

QUICK wits and sharp eyes are not the only essential qualifications of a real-life Sherlock Holmes. Talking last week to 29-year-old Tony Rose of Liverpool, private investigator (as they call 'em), keen amateur athlete and equally keen motorcyclist, I learnt that an ability to go without sleep, as a camel can go without drink, and an almost infinite capacity for travelling from one place to t'other and back again are equally important attributes.

Tony's working mileage is around the 3,000-mile-a-month figure, and because he likes motorcycling he does it on two or three wheels.

But because he likes motorcycling so much that he openly confesses to being a bit of a fanatic, Tony has almost doubled that figure during the past 16 months. All, oddly enough, as the result of a few moments of Alpine Bar chatter at the 1951 Motorcycle Show.

Tony, at that time, had fairly recently purchased a " Black Shadow " Vincent. It was about the umpteenth machine he had obtained since the war and the first one he really liked. So, as so many private owners do, he bearded " Mr. Manufacturer " at the Show. Phil Vincent in person, as a matter of fact.

Having talked of this and that, Tony happened to ask—" By the way, decoking the thing? After how many miles would you think? "

" Hundred thousand, if you like," said Phil, expansively, and " . . . 'scuse me now, old chap, 'nother fellow waiting to see me. . . . " It's a busy time, the Show, for any manufacturer, and particularly for one who caters for real enthusiasts.

No decoke before 100,000! Kidding, of course! Leastwise, Tony thought so. Until he talked it over with one or two of his friends in the Vincent-H.R.D. Owners' Club. Some of them had done pretty phenomenal mileages between overhauls.

So a few weeks after the Show—the " Shadow " had around 9,000 miles on the clock at the time—there was a phone call, a personal call, to Mr. Phil Vincent.

"At it, lads!" Paul Richardson, Vincent's technician (centre) supervises the stripping of the engine.

Quantrill takes the helm, with Reagan in the Swallow "Jet 80" sidecar.

" This is Rose, Tony Rose of Liverpool, remember me? "

" Yes," said Phil.

" Remember what you said about 100,000 miles? "

" Yes," said Phil.

" Mean it? "

" Yes," said Phil, " on two conditions. You keep below 5,000 r.p.m. and change the oil every thousand."

" Right," said Tony, " I'm doing it."

And if he'd gone a bit further and insisted upon having an A.-C.U. observer about the place—let me see, what *would* it cost, one A.-C.U. observer from the Autumn of 1951 to February, 1953?—Vincents might be in the running now for the next award of the Maudes Trophy.

For last Tuesday week I went to Stevenage to meet Tony coming into the factory at the successful conclusion of his " 100,000."

He had been there a couple of times before, consequent upon seizures due to oil pipe fractures, but on each occasion—at around 35,000 miles and 52,000 miles—no carbon had been removed, I am assured. The first time all that was necessary was the relieving of some high spots on the rear piston. On the second visit, I am again assured, all that occurred was the relieving of some more high spots, the fitting of new rings to the same much-abused piston, and the replacement, for the second time, of the rocker bushes.

The mileage when Tony ran into Stevenage at the end of his self-imposed *course de regularité et endurance* was, so the speedometer said, 100,300-odd. Even allowing for any slight discrepancies which may be produced by a speedometer reading, that is still an awful lot of mileage. During the course of it the Vincent had been run as a solo up to the 18,000 mark, had then been attached to a succession of sidecars—for a long time on the old " Shadow " solo ratios, with a 7.26 bottom " cog "—had reverted to solo status and finally finished with a Swallow " Jet 80 " attached.

It had—because Tony's main concern had been to complete the distance rather than to carry out destruction tests on component

parts—said goodbye to an impressive number of 3.50-in. by 19-in. rear tyres and 3-in. by 21-in. front covers, plus five sidecar " bladders." It had put 25 rear chains and 10 primary chains on the scrap heap. It had seen some 10 sets of sparking plugs fitted and in due course replaced, had had its clutch relined on more than one occasion; had suffered a number of replacements of the clutch push rod and arm; had been fitted with fresh kickstarter mechanism, two replacement exhaust systems, a replacement dynamo (which also failed before the end of the test) and new magneto bearings; had been fitted with many c.v.c. units which had, in succession, ceased to exercise the constant control that they were supposed to maintain, and had had the brakes relined on more than one occasion. Control cables had, of course, been renewed many times, a replacement tank had been fitted—because the original had been rubbed bare by the rider's knees—and nearly 100 broken spokes—mainly, rather unexpectedly, in the front wheel—had been replaced.

But—except for the time when a sidecar wheel collapsed—Tony had never been stranded by the roadside, despite his monthly average of 5,500 miles.

His petrol consumption—42 m.p.g. at the outset—rose to about 35 m.p.g. by half-distance and, rather naturally, never subsequently improved, and oil consumption originally at the rate of one pint every 350 miles, stepped up to one pint every 200 miles, again from the 50,000-mile mark.

Tony is a Filtrate fanatic. He used Filtrate oil the right way through—varying it from SAE 30 in mid-winter to SAE 60 in the hottest months—and always observed the instruction to change it every thousand miles. He used Filtrate oil in the gearbox, and primary chaincase as well, and in every case he had a graphite additive. In his view the oil, plus the graphite, saw him through the trip.

His cruising speed, with a sidecar, he tells me, was a steady 68-70 m.p.h., and at least once a month for the benefit of readers of his progress reports in " M.P.H."—the Owners' Club magazine—he tried the model flat out. Speedo reading dropped steadily

from 105 m.p.h. solo and 93 m.p.h. sidecar, to about 83 m.p.h. with the chair.

But towards the end of the test he was—as is reflected in his notes in " M.P.H."—getting distinctly jittery. I know, only too well, how one can begin to detect " dangerous noises " in a well-used engine, and Tony, by the 75,000 mark, was firmly convinced that one of the big-ends had " gone."

But when I tried the model up the Great North Road, just before the " inquest " took place in the factory, I disagreed with his diagnosis.

The engine still had plenty of compression but it was rough. However, it was my guess that nothing more serious than a badly worn primary chain was the source of most of the harshness, while worn timing gear probably accounted for nearly all the mechanical noise.

Steering was none too good, but that was not altogether surprising. In the first place the steering damper bottom plate was broken and the fork bushes were probably worn, after all that mileage and—certainly the biggest contributory factor—a badly bent chassis, resultant upon a hearty collision with a fallen tree while motoring through storm-swept Ross and Cromarty during the final week-end, had upset the alignment of what Tony describes as the best steering " chair " he has ever had.

With Jimmy Reagan, a 25-year-old toolmaker from Liverpool, who had been putting in several thousand-mile week-ends on the outfit during the last stages of the test, as passenger, Rose covered 2,000 miles in his last week-end, much of it, owing to a desire to visit " Rab " Cook, editor of the club magazine, at his home in Banff, as the 100,000th clicked up, in the teeth of the fearsome gale which swept Eastern Scotland as well as parts of England early this month.

After lunch in Stevenage's excellently appointed Cromwell Hotel, a number of us assembled in a workshop in the old Vincent-H.R.D. factory, for the ceremonial stripping. There were Ken Mainwaring, factory sales manager, Geoff Manning, the resident high-speed enthusiast, and technical " boffin " Paul Richardson; there were Tony Rose himself and Jimmy Reagan; two club members, Derrick Carter and K. J. Dangerfield, who had ridden down from Birmingham for the day to see fair play; me, another Press bod, and T. P. photographer Alf Long.

The experienced mechanics, with a wonderful demonstration of efficiency, had the machine stripped down and the flywheels apart within ¾-hour.

Both cylinder heads and pistons were well coated with carbon—but not excessively —and there was a small amount of scale in the region of the exhaust valves. The barrels looked perfect and all piston rings were free in their grooves. The play in the big-ends— by feel—was very little indeed and neither little-end showed more wear than one would expect to find after, say, one-tenth of the mileage that this " Black Shadow " had covered.

The cams and cam followers showed a certain, but not excessive, amount of wear, particularly where the rear exhaust follower had obviously been chattering through maladjustment of the lifter cable; the primary chain was definitely the worse for wear and

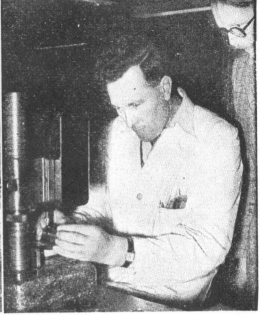

had been hitting one of the holding-stud bosses on the cover—source of much of the mechanical noise—and, another noisy item, the magneto's automatic advance mechanism had broken down.

In the gearbox, the dogs were no more badly rounded than one would expect to see on a component which had served for only one, instead of 100 thousand miles, and there was just a little play in the drive-side main-shaft bearing.

The inlet-valve seats were unpitted, although they would obviously benefit from the application of smooth grinding paste, and the exhaust valves and seats, although pock-marked in places, were only lightly affected and could soon be ground into condition. Rocker spindles, on the other hand, were definitely worn, or so it seemed.

Anyway, there was only one way of telling, so all the engine and gearbox components were scooped into a wooden box and transported to the inspection bay.

And there I received more surprises—agreeable ones, actually, because I happen to be quite a Vincent enthusiast—as the different items were measured. The cylinder barrels, for instance, were only some three " thou." over-size, as tested by the Solex air gauge—not enough to justify a rebore—and the connecting rods showed only two " thou." ovality. The crankpin, checked by the dial micrometer, showed wear of up to .00025 in., the worst occurring, surprisingly to me but not to the several technical bods. in the party, where the separators locating the six rows of needle rollers run on the shaft. The upper valve guides—the Vinc. is unique in having two widely-spaced guides to each valve—showed scarcely measurable wear and the lower ones varied from 1½ " thou." (front inlet) to 2½ " thou." on the rear exhaust. The rocker pads were indented up to 2 " thou." and the rocker spindles and their Duralumin housings were again due for renewal. So were the valve springs—" shrunk " by up to 3/16 in. If

Close scrutiny. Components of the Vincent are examined by (above) members of the technical Press, Jim Reagan and Vincent technician Geoff Manning (in check coat). (Above, right) Crankpin is tested with the dial gauge.

(Right) The two drivers and Paul Richardson take a peek at the "innards" of the engine.

it were my machine I should ask for new cam followers to be fitted, too, and—I think, although I'd check with the price quoted in the spares list first—I should really go to town and have new cams.

In the gearbox there were no components among those tested that were so badly worn that they would not come within the limits set by the inspection department, but I should have called for a new drive-side main-shaft bearing because that, after all, takes so much hard work. And then, if this particular " Shadow " really were mine, I should make sure that there was no re-bushing required on the front forks and that the rear-springing assembly needed no new seal-ing glands. Knowing that they are fitted

with Timken taper bearings, I should be happy about the wheel hubs, although I should take the opportunity of having heavier-gauge spokes fitted, to stand up to sidecar stresses, and an 18-in. rear rim to take a 4-in. tyre. I'd fit a chain oiler, too.

And after that? Why I'd be happy to keep rumbling along, at that nice, steady 70 m.p.h. cruising speed, for the next 100,000 miles, secure in the knowledge that the machine was now well enough run-in to exhibit no teething troubles.

Which. as a matter of fact, is exactly what Tony plans to do. " You know how it is," he explained, " you've done a mile or two on your own outfit. After a while you get sort of confident about its performance."

Handlebar layout of the 123 c.c. N.S.U.-Vincent Fox

Vincent

Stand 5: Famous Twins Joined by Lightweights and Cyclemotor

A T the past few London Shows, the Vincent stand has usually provided a breathing space. The stand has been large, and simplicity the keynote of the decor. The mile-eating 50-degree twins and smaller singles have of late been subject mainly to internal modifications and,

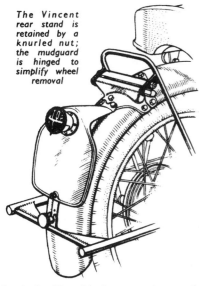

The Vincent rear stand is retained by a knurled nut; the mudguard is hinged to simplify wheel removal

already familiar with the range, the crowds have come (caps in hand!), paused, almost genuflected as they paid their tribute, and filed on.

This year the story is different. Everyone in the exhibition hall wants to see the range of N.S.U.-Vincents. Thousands are apparently interested in the Firefly cyclemotor. The same vast numbers as in past years want to salaam before the big Vincents. Except for those who are prepared to forget that they are gentlemen on hallowed ground (and use their elbows somewhat indiscriminately!), it is almost

Exhibited unaltered for 1954—the Series C Rapide

impossible to see any model at close quarters for very long.

The N.S.U.-Vincents exhibited are the 98 and 123 c.c. Fox models with standard and de luxe specification, the 199 c.c. Lux and the 247 c.c. Max. The Max and 98 c.c. Fox models are four-strokes although, with their finned rocker covers and cleverly concealed valve-operating mechanism, they look rather like two-strokes. Valve operation is by pushrods in the case of the Fox and by an ingenious system of eccentrics and connecting rods in the case of the Max. All models employ robust yet simple spine frames, leading-link front forks and pivoted rear forks. Front and rear suspensions of the Fox are controlled by friction-damped coil springs; hydraulic damping is employed on the Lux and Max models. Not the least discussed feature of the two-hundreds and two-fifties is the oil-bath case enclosing the rear chain.

Two working models of the beautifully engineered Firefly are almost constantly surrounded. Designed for mounting below the bottom bracket, the cyclemotor unit incorporates sliders to allow it to be moved horizontally for engagement or disengagement of the 3⅜in-diameter friction roller. The roller comprises a serrated cast-iron disc rubber-bonded to a steel centre-piece, and it runs at half engine speed. The

Rear chain enclosure is a feature of the 199 c.c. Lux

countershaft gear, which is spur-toothed and of fibrous material, incorporates a compact 9-watt A.C. generator which supplies current for the ignition coil, front and rear lights and electric horn.

Other prominent features of the engine are full disc-type, internal steel flywheels, cast-iron, longitudinally finned cylinder and light-alloy cylinder head. Weight of the unit is 18 lb. Power output is said to be 0.9 b.h.p. at 3,800 r.p.m.

But when all that is said, the glamour of the Vincent stand rests with the big twins. Three, the middle one of which is a

Impressive power unit—engine of the 499 c.c. Series C Comet

998 c.c., 55 b.h.p., 120 m.p.h. Black Shadow, look down on the lightweights from floodlit turntables, gleaming shapes of glistening black, chromium and polished aluminium.

The pure Vincents comprise four models —the Black Shadow, its more docile (45 b.h.p.) sister, the Rapide, the Black Lightning, which is a stripped, super-businesslike racer, and the Comet, a touring single incorporating the majority of the twins' luxury features.

The models have been only slightly modified for 1954, and the widely recognized features, such as the Girdraulic front fork—which provides ready adjustment of trail for solo or sidecar work—twin 7in brakes, and wheel removal and rear chain adjustment that can be effected without the use of tools, are all retained.

EARLY IN NOVEMBER, 1951, Rose, of Liverpool, England sat reading a motorcycle journal. He had finished reading a road test report and idly flipped the pages until he came to the Vincent Company's advertisement, and he studied the slogans: "The World's Fastest Standard Motorcycle" was one, "The World's Safest Motorcycle" another.

He tossed the book aside and lay back in his chair to think of the brand new Black Shadow out in his garage. "I wonder how long it will last without replacements" he pondered, for Tony, who is a Private Tec and covers a huge annual mileage, is a noted motorcycle destroyer and he had already discovered that a big Vincent twin was the machine for his work, in fact, so convinced that he had become Secretary of the Vincent Owners Club!

"I wonder," he continued, "if the Vincent really *is* the world's longest lasting motorcycle," and the more he thought of this, the more intrigued he became with the idea of finding out. So, when the next club committee meeting came along, he startled his fellow officials by asking if the club would sponsor a 100,000-mile road test. Sportsmen all, the boys immediately agreed and it only remained to contact Phil Vincent, president of the club and the brain behind the Vincent machines, to see what he had to say to the idea.

Phil was even more startled by the notion than the committee, for although he knew his machines to be of the best, he had never thought of them as a form of perpetual motion before. But after much deep thought, he decided "Yes, I think it will do it," and so the test was on.

A rather startling feature is that Tony calls his machine "Rumplecrankshaft" but we'll call it "Rumple" for short! A feature which is both interesting and startling is that over three quarters of the mileage was covered with a sidecar attached! Or to be more precise, several sidecars, as it was discovered that while the machine would stand up to cruising at 80-90 and broadsliding around corners, the sidecars were not made of such stern stuff and four were 'used up' during the test. These weren't run to destruction, of course, but sold before their state of disrepair became too evident!

A test of this nature required careful planning with regards to equipment and, after much thought, consultation and experiment, "Super Filtrate" oil was decided upon; the idea being to have an oil with not too much detergent, good clinging properties even when hot and obsolutely no tendancy to form sludge. When asked

Would you believe that a cycle could go 100,000 miles without having the head removed?

WORLD'S LONGEST

what he considers to be the major factor in the success of this test, Tony always mentions the Filtrate and goes on to tell how Rumple's oil tank was always as clean as new when he made an oil change.

Various makes of spark plugs were tried early in the test, but eventually, KLG FE 70 were settled upon as being the best for the job—remember, this test was done on 72 octane English "Pool" gas as it was only in February, 1953, that 80 octane became freely available over there since the war.

Almost every make of motorcycle tire available was tried out, but in the end, Tony came back to the make originally fitted by Vincents, the Avon "New Supreme". Towards the end of the test, though, Avon "Triple Duty" sidecar tires became available and were considered the ultimate for hack work.

The man, himself, had to be kept warm, so a "Barbour" suit was used here with perfect satisfaction. Maybe all this sounds like a commercial write-up on various products, but it was decided that while the test was going, the club might as well find out which of the various accessories were the best.

These tests were in no way sponsored by the manufacturers, with one exception; but this item was found to be so thoroughly bad that it was hurriedly discarded, much to the dismay of the manufacturer concerned!

That particular incident put an end to dabblings with "the trade" but credits are due to Smiths of Cricklewood who supplied and sealed the five-inch speedometer and mileage recorder used throughout. Had this item packed in, things would have become difficult indeed, but it continued to tick off those long weary miles with a monotonous regularity and never did more than break a cable or two.

But now to the cycle itself. After about 4,000 miles, oil got into the clutch and a rather disgruntled Mr. Rose wrote to Vincent's works at Stevenage telling them a few choice things about clutches. They replied that while he had obviously over-filled his primary chaincase, they were introducing new non-slip linings, and would he like to try a set? He would and he did, and the clutch gave no further trouble. These linings are now, of course, standard on all Vincent machines.

At 11,300 miles, the automatic voltage control started to act funny and was replaced with a service unit. Just shortly after this, the first sidecar was fitted "In order" as Tony said, "To be able to hunk around my wife and two screaming brats!" I knew Tony's driving and fully realized why those poor little kids were screaming. When later in the test, he visited my little hideout in the North of Scotland, he even managed to really frighten my iron-nerved wife on a short trip— something which I had never managed.

Friend Rose is certainly some driver and he spent the winter of 51-52 charging that poor outfit through snow drifts that were stopping all other traffic and kept sending me in reports of pass-storming in the Welsh hills, screaming up the length of England flat out all the time and replacing bits of a rapidly deteriorating sidecar. All these reports contained one phrase: "Motor spinning like a top and no trouble to report."

Fitting a sidecar meant that the small garden lean-to Tony used for a garage was no longer of any use as a covering, so the outfit was left outside every night to take its chance with the

lutions and after checking electrics, carb and so on, we diagnosed a weak valve spring. Immediate panic ensued! Was the test all over? Would the motor have to be stripped?

Second thoughts are often best, and when we had cooled down a little and taken time out to think, we realized that due to the unique Vincent method of locating the rocker below the valve springs, it would be possible to alter things without disturbing that carbon— if carbon there should be. As Tony's holiday was almost over, we decided to leave well enough alone. I later heard that an inner spring had been found to have fractured, but that this had been successfully replaced by the method we had worked out. The carbon had not been touched, nor yet the valves ground in or anything else done to the motor.

So the test went on and the mileage grew and grew. Tony began to think that more miles could be piled on if he had a co-driver; so club member, Jim Regan, was roped in. They shortly had a shift system going and the poor old bike practically ran day and night.

I wonder if it is possible to imagine the monotony of covering miles for their own sake; but the boys stuck it, and the monthly reports kept reaching me. New battery fitted as the old one was rather neglected (!), more tires, more chains, more brake linings, new rear sprocket, slightly less speed (but with a start at 125 mph, who was caring?), new exhaust system as the old one rusted through the chrome, broken spokes through taking liberties with pot-holes, replaced fork bushes, another voltage control unit, clutch push-rod and sidecars! At 87,750 miles I got a report which mentioned that the valve clearances had just been adjusted for the first time in 8,000 miles and that only one of them needed more than a quarter turn of the adjusting screw.

And so on it went—as the end grew nearer and nearer, we became more and more excited. If it were to fail now after getting so near.

The motor was becoming noisy through some piston slap when cold, and a very slight rustle was evident from the big ends, but the main bear-

(Continued on page 63)

ROAD TEST

by "Rab" Cook

Speedo actually reads 100,606 miles—end of test.

weather. Not the best way to treat a test machine, and after a month or two of this, rain penetrated the dual-seat cover and froze inside until eventually the cover rotted through. I think this would only have been surprising if it *hadn't* rotted through—what a way to treat such a beautiful cycle, but Tony reckoned that if he was going to test this machine, he was going to do it properly.

Now and then, new control cables would be fitted, new brake linings, tires and chains, but the motor and frame continued as ever with never a murmur of protest. Just around the 50,000-mile mark, Tony came up to stay with me for a holiday and, of course, took along Rumple and the— well, "a" sidecar. I was delighted with this chance to really see for myself and to ride the outfit and I was genuinely amazed with the condition of it. The performance was just as good as that of my own Black Shadow, which had done little over 3,000 miles at that time and was no sluggard.

Just before it was time for Tony to leave us here, we discovered that the back carburetor had an apparently incurable desire to spit back at low revo-

When the speedometer reached 100,000 miles and clicked back to zero, the Vincent Black Shadow was still going strong. However, several sidecars had been worn out.

Engine Restoration Routine for the Forerunner of a World-famous Range of Big Twins

THE 1935-1939 SERIES "A" 499 c.c. VINCENT-H.R.D. COMET

ANNOUNCED in 1934, the series "A" 499 c.c. single-cylinder high-camshaft Vincent-H.R.D. was the forerunner of current machines from Stevenage. Replacing a range of two-stroke and proprietary-engined models, the "A" models were designated "Meteor," "Comet" and "Comet Special," constituting three variations of the same engine in that carburetters, pistons and camshafts were of different patterns. The last-mentioned was fitted with a bronze head.

To aid simplification this article is written mainly with the "Comet" model in mind for the manufacturers do, in fact, advise owners to rebuild their engines to that specification.

With a bore and stroke of 84 mm. by 90 mm., a capacity of 499 c.c. and a c.r. of 7.3 : 1, the high-camshaft unit was equipped originally with an Amal 289/011 carburetter having a main jet size of 180, and a 29/4 slide. Recommended plugs are the Champion L10, K.L.G. F70 or Lodge C14, all 14 mm. short reach types. Approximately 26 b.h.p. is produced at 5,600 r.p.m. and the machine has a maximum of 90-plus m.p.h. pulling a 4.6 : 1 top gear and using a No. 1 fuel, equal to post-war premium-grade petrols.

General

With the aid of four fairly easily-constructed tools a complete overhaul may be attempted. The factory advises the owner to construct a "button stick" to support the piston, a double-diameter drift for extracting valve guides, a simple screw-type pinion remover and a valve-spring compressor.

After removal of the top half of the engine, the oil-bath chaincase, primary drive and clutch assembly, it is possible to split the crankcase. Note that, whilst the engine sprocket is of the self-withdrawing pattern, it may be found necessary to use a blow-lamp to provide heat during the extracting process. The engine sprocket, duplex primary chain and clutch sprocket should be removed in one unit, taking care not to lose the shims behind the clutch rollers; these rollers are uncaged and liable to drop out. Since the engine unit is to be completely stripped, the following will not apply, but it is certainly worth mentioning that for other less extensive work it is possible to split the crankcase without disturbing either the valve or the ignition timing, a unique feature of Vincent design.

After removing the studs which hold the crankcase halves together, the timing-side case can be lifted off—leaving the inner roller-race on the mainshaft—also the distance-piece and shims which lie between the timing-side main bearings, serving to locate correctly the flywheel assembly. The flywheels may now be withdrawn from the drive-side case by using a little pressure with

A Unique Unit of Generous Proportions and Ample Power

two levers, if necessary, but taking extreme care not to damage the faces or spigot of the case. The drive-side main-bearing housing is now easily withdrawn by inserting screws in the blind holes and turning them in a clockwise direction.

Crankcase Assembly

Practical experience has shown that the assembly of the big-end bearing, with the correct clearance is a very tricky job and the wastage of replacement units resulting from incorrect fitting has reached such proportions that big-end components are not now supplied separately.

Crankcase halves and flywheels are no longer available. In cases where these parts are damaged, normal factory practice is to weld broken components or build up worn wheels where necessary. This can be done just as easily by a local repairer. If cam-box studs or cylinder bolts have been pulled from the crankcase, double-diameter studs will have to be fitted.

Connecting-rods are interchangeable with the present pattern and may be obtained polished, as on the "Black Shadow," having a minimum tensile strength of 60 tons. New timing- and drive-side mainshafts are available, so are main bearings.

The drive-side roller bearing, type CFM8, is a press fit in the case and a light press fit on the shaft, and the drive-side ball-bearing,

The 1937 490 c.c. Vincent-H.R.D. "Comet" engine which formed the basis of a series of "singles" and "twins" bearing this name, each of which retains many of the features of the original unit.

type RMS8, is a push fit in the housing and on the shaft.

The timing-side roller-type CRM8 bearing is a press fit in the case and on the shaft and the timing-side ball-bearing, type RMS6A, is a press fit in the case and push fit on the shaft.

Particular care should be exercised when rebuilding the "basement" of the engine, and the following sequence of operations is advised. Lay the timing-side crankcase-half flat on the bench, having first pressed in the ball-bearing. Fit the distance-piece and the roller-bearing. The inner member of this roller-bearing should stand proud of the outer race by 1/64 in.; if not, the inner member should be shimmed-up as necessary. Then fit the flywheel assembly. As shown by the sectional sketch, the sequence of assembly of the drive-side components is as follows: (1) a 1/16-in. washer goes against the flywheel; (2) the .015-in. chip guard; (3) a 1/32-in washer; (4) the roller bearing and spring; (5) the ball-bearing; then (6) another .015-in. chip guard; (7) the bearing cap; (8) a 1/32-in. washer; and, finally (9) the engine sprocket. It is important to check that the inner ends of the rollers do not rub against the lip of the outer bearing. If this does occur, slightly thicker washers will be required—unless it is found that some of the shims have been omitted.

The half-time pinion is removed with the special extractor illustrated and, unfortunately, spares are not available. However, limited supplies of idler-gears and campinions are normally obtainable, but cams will have to be built up and reground. It is recommended that all models be fitted with the 5X cam, which offers an excellent all-round performance. Followers are now not stocked and will have to be built up by the Stellite process. Owners tempted to fit the post-war follower are reminded that, whilst it looks similar, the distance between the centres is quite different from the dimensions of the older component.

Bushes, pins and distance washers are available; so are inner and outer idler shaft bushes. The factory normally stocks the Tufnol magneto gear, sealing washers, the boss collar nut and four retaining screws and can supply the aluminium timing-hole cover.

Lubrication

Oil-pump components can be replaced from stock. The exception is the intermediate steel plate between the body and the cover, which will have to be patterned. There is no stock of the early pattern single banjo feed bolt, but the later separate adjustable unions (1937 onwards) can be supplied.

The engine "breathes" via the timing-chest, exhaust push-rod tube, the rocker box and thence through a union and external oil pipe to a point between the crankcase and primary chaincase.

When reassembling the engine and connecting the various oil pipes with the correct unions, remember that the rear pump-body union takes the oil-tank return pipe; the front body union, the sump scavenge pipe; the adjustable union on the rear of the pump cover takes the cylinder feed and the front union on the cover, the oil tank feed pipe. Remember that the ball and long spring live in the oil-tank feed union, whereas the ball and short spring are located in the rear-cylinder feed union.

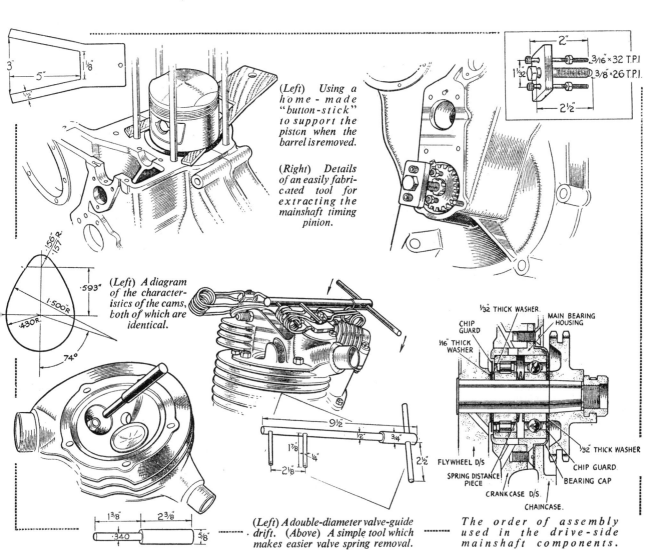

(*Left*) *Using a home-made "button-stick" to support the piston when the barrel is removed.*

(*Right*) *Details of an easily fabricated tool for extracting the mainshaft timing pinion.*

(*Left*) *A diagram of the characteristics of the cams, both of which are identical.*

(*Left*) *A double-diameter valve-guide drift.* (*Above*) *A simple tool which makes easier valve spring removal.*

The order of assembly used in the drive-side mainshaft components.

On earlier models the oil pump had to be dismantled in order to remove the big-end quill, but later types, marked BD, can be removed as a unit. The big-end quills are no longer available but the post-war pattern will fit and are used in works overhauls. It should be borne in mind, however, that these modern quills pass more oil, hence the cylinder and rocker feeds will have to be adjusted accordingly.

Cylinder Head

While cylinder heads are no longer available from the spares department, it is a component which should last the life of the machine. It has been found, however, that cracks may appear between the exhaust-valve seat and the sparking-plug hole. The normal practice is to have the fault welded by specialists such as the Barimar concern. Pocketed valve seats can be built up in like manner. Valves, springs, split collets, the later pattern rockers fitted to 1938-39 models, and the exhaust-valve lifter mechanism are normally available, but the alloy rocker covers, valve collars, tappet guides, valve-stem sleeves, valve-cover and locking plate, rocker pins and bushes, push-rods and adjusters are all out of stock. Push-rod tubes can still be supplied.

Normally the rocker covers will not require replacement but the lip supporting the valve lifter adjustment has been known to fracture and it is recommended that this be welded, drilled out and retapped. A good engineering company with experience of aluminium welding would be capable of this job. Valve collars, covers, push rods and adjusters should be patterned, but the top valve guide can be plugged with cast-iron stick and rebored. Rocker pins should be built up and reground.

Cylinder and Piston

Cylinder barrels are out of stock, but they can be rebored locally and pistons, identical to the present-day pattern, are available .005, .010, .020 and .030 in. oversize. The piston is of the same pattern as that used today and can be fitted in sizes to give compression ratios of from 6.8 to 13 : 1. The E7/7 is the recommended type, giving a ratio of 7.3 : 1. It should be emphasized here that, when the cylinder head is removed, there will be much shake apparent at the piston crown. Indeed, the piston clearances are such that there is a reduction at the top of .020 in. compared with the diameter at the thrust face. This will naturally cause the shake, even when the engine is new, and it must not be assumed that a rebore is necessary without measuring the wear on the barrel, the diameter of which should be 3.307 in.

The end-gap of the two compression rings should be from .016 to .020 in. and the scraper .010 to .020 in. Side clearances of from .001 to .002 in. and .002 to .005 in. respectively are necessary. Overmuch importance is sometimes placed upon ring gaps; the thing to remember is that the gap should not be too small. That causes the ring-ends to abut, because the piston heats up before the barrel. Naturally, broken rings are the result.

Instruction books are available and can be obtained from the works. Whilst they are not illustrated, they do contain valuable information to assist the owner to dismantle and assemble his Series "A" engine.

1935-39 SERIES A 499 c.c. VINCENT-H.R.D. COMET		
Valve Clearance (Cold) Inlet	..	**Nil**
Exhaust	..	**Nil**
Pushrods free to revolve		
Valve Timing (Clearance as above)		
Inlet opens 44° before T.D.C.		
Inlet closes 56° after B.D.C.		
Exhaust opens 68° before B.D.C.		
Exhaust closes 38° after T.D.C.		
Ignition Timing (fully advanced)		
Points break 42° before T.D.C.		
(17/32 inches)		

Startling Vincent Developments

Plastic Enclosure and All-weather Equipment on 499 c.c. and 998 c.c. Roadster Models :
Modifications to Suspension and Ignition Systems : Small N.S.U.-Vincents Continued :
N.S.U. Quickly Autocycle Added to Range

HIGH performance with full weather protection is the keynote of the Vincent roadster programme for 1955. The various factory racing machines seen during the past season have accustomed motor cyclists to enclosure, and many have come to the obvious conclusion about the degree of weather protection afforded to the rider.

Windscreens and legshields have become common additions to road-going machines, since many riders find little pleasure in extensive dressing up to guard against the elements. Valuable as are such accessories, they rarely look other than extras because the manufacturers have to design them to fit a large number of different makes and models. Vincents have made the logical decision to build such protection into their standard machines.

Since Vincent mounts are already endowed with above-average performance, the aim is not streamlining and consequently higher speed, but to provide

accessibility which is not generally inferior to that of the earlier models, and in certain respects is markedly better. Finally, Vincents claim that the handling, particularly in gusty winds, is improved by the enclosure. During a run on a prototype machine, a member of *The Motor Cycle* staff, clad in a lounge suit on a day of blustering half-gale, found a complete absence of unpleasant effect attributable to the fairings, even at very high speed.

The enclosure is applied to the three Vincent roadsters, and the machines have been given new names which are more in

With the new enclosure, the 998 c.c. Black Prince has flowing lines and thorough weather protection

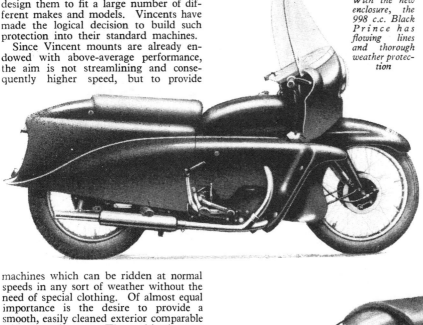

keeping with their much-altered appearance. Black Prince, Black Knight and Victor replace Black Shadow twin, Rapide twin and Comet single respectively; all three bear the designation Series D.

For those unacquainted with Vincent machines, it should be mentioned that the 998 c.c. vee twins and the 499 c.c. singles have light-alloy, high-camshaft, o.h.v. engines with a bore and stroke of 84mm and 90mm respectively, and several unconventional features. The single is, in effect, half of the twin engine but differs further in having a separate Burman gear box driven by a 1in-pitch single chain, in place of the unit-construction Vincent gear box and $\frac{3}{8}$in triplex chain of the twins.

In each case the engine forms an integral part of the machine structure and eliminates a normal tubular frame. Front suspension is by Girdraulic fork, which is of the parallel-ruler type but

machines which can be ridden at normal speeds in any sort of weather without the need of special clothing. Of almost equal importance is the desire to provide a smooth, easily cleaned exterior comparable with that of a car. These objectives are achieved by the use of a voluminous front mudguard, a frontal fairing with integral windscreen, side panels which conceal the power unit and embody legshields, and a completely enclosed rear end on scooter lines.

Such comprehensive "coachwork" at once raises questions of its effect on noise, weight, accessibility and handling. The first two points are met by the use of glass-fibre-reinforced plastic material for the major components. As is well known, the material is extremely strong for its weight; hence the enclosure adds but little to the all-up weight of the machine; some of the surplus is offset by weight reductions achieved in other directions. A further advantage of the material is its non-resonant qualities, so that, instead of amplifying sound (as sheet metal would tend to do), it has a subduing effect.

Careful design has achieved a degree of

Another view of the Black Prince, which clearly shows the measure of protection from the elements

has forged light-alloy blades, side-mounted springs of unusual length and a central hydraulic damper. The rear suspension differs only in detail from that fitted to all Vincent machines since the late '20s; it comprises a triangulated fork pivoted on taper-roller bearings, with the suspension unit located under the seat and connected to the apex of the fork.

Deeply valanced, the front mudguard is unsprung and of sufficient width to embrace the fork members. The rear of the mudguard is contoured to match the rear of the tail fairing and thus provide continuity of styling. The deep, curved section gives the guard considerable inherent stiffness; it is attached to the fork at the bridge and is further braced by the tubular front stand.

Unsprung weight of the front-wheel assembly has been appreciably reduced by transferring the headlamp to a sprung position. The 7in-diameter lamp, of Lucas manufacture, is mounted in a one-piece plastic cowling which embraces the steering head and turns with the handlebar; the sides of the cowling are extended downward to overlap the front

mudguard, and a tubular-steel stiffener is bonded to the interior.

Hand protection is given by detachable cupped extensions mounted on the cowling. Although the cups could have been embodied in the main moulding, it was felt desirable to keep them separate for ease of replacement in the event of damage. At the top, the cowling forms a semi-circular dash panel inclined at an angle to give easy visibility of the speedometer and ammeter mounted thereon. Also on the panel are the lighting and ignition switches.

Full access to the underside of the instruments and switches is readily obtainable by removing the steering-damper knob, undoing the clamping nut beneath it and slackening the two bolts which attach the stiffening tube to the fork assembly. The complete cowling can then be pivoted forward through a right angle.

Imposing frontal aspect of the 499 c.c. single-cylinder Victor. The headlamp is recessed, except for its rim, and the handshields are detachable

Each side panel is a single plastic moulding flared outward at the front to provide leg protection and also to direct air on to the engine. At the top-front the panels have a forward projection which reproduces, on a smaller scale, the nose of the front mudguard. The panels extend from the underside of the tank to halfway down the crankcase and chaincase castings.

Three-point attachment of the panels is by means of knurled screws. Removal of the panels is a matter of seconds only and gives complete accessibility to the engine.

A smoothly contoured, one-piece plastic moulding forms the tail shell and is bonded to a light, tubular-steel sub-frame which carries the attachment and pivot brackets as well as the pillion footrests. The extreme rear of the shell incorporates a flat portion on which is painted the registration number. Above the number is fitted the rear lamp and below it the regulation reflector; both fittings blend neatly into the general lines.

The dual-seat, embodying springs and foam rubber, sits directly on top of the shell and is therefore fully sprung. Below the seat is a moulded-in tool compartment of ample size, exposed when the nose-hinged seat is raised.

Attention to the rear wheel, chain or

battery is unobstructed. The sub-frame pivots from the rear cylinder-head bracket and is held up when required by a stay which can be unclipped from the interior and swung down to engage with a lug on the rear fork. The structure is rigidly secured in the down position: at each lower-front corner of the sub-frame is a substantial C-bracket which engages with a clamping bolt behind the gear box. There is no rear mudguard as such, but a short, aluminium shield is mounted ahead of the wheel to protect the power unit and rear springing from mud and water.

Unlike previous post-war Vincents, the oil tank no longer forms a box-section bridge between the steering head and the rear cylinder head. Of unchanged capacity, the tank is housed in the rear shell with its filler orifice under the seat. Since the orifice is at the rear of the tank, there is no risk of spillage when the shell is hinged up, and the flexible oil pipes are so positioned that the operation does not subject them to any load.

The tubular top member of the frame is brazed into modified steering-head and rear cylinder-head lugs. The rear lug incorporates brackets to support the fuel tank and the seat nose, and forms a side-car-connection point. Fuel-tank capacity has been increased to four gallons as a result of the transfer of the oil tank.

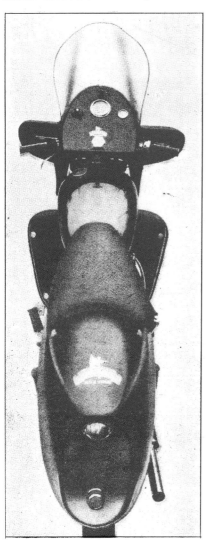

Seen from the rear, the 998 c.c. Black Knight has a clean and businesslike appearance

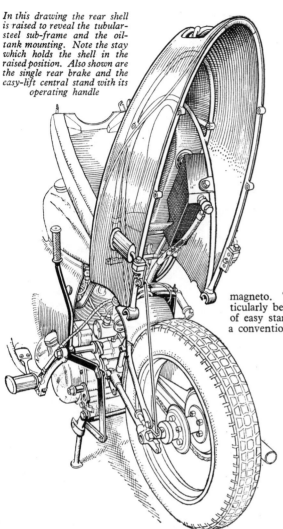

In this drawing the rear shell is raised to reveal the tubular-steel sub-frame and the oil-tank mounting. Note the stay which holds the shell in the raised position. Also shown are the single rear brake and the easy-lift central stand with its operating handle

Previously 3.00in front and 3.50in rear tyres were standard equipment, with 3.50in and 4.00in sections as optional alternatives. For 1955 the position is reversed and the larger tyres are standardized, although the smaller tyres can be specified if preferred.

To reduce unsprung weight, only one rear brake (of the ribbed, Black Shadow pattern) is fitted and the leverage has been increased so that there is no reduction in braking efficiency. The stop-light switch is operated by the balance beam of the front brakes and not from the rear-brake mechanism. On the Black Prince, ribbed drums are employed for the front brakes as well as for the rear brake.

Action of the front-wheel springing has been softened and a small Armstrong damper replaces the previous Vincent-made component. At the rear, a full six inches of wheel travel has been achieved with the aid of a single, large Armstrong spring-and-damper unit which has a spring rating of 300 lb per in. Unsprung and all-up weights have been reduced by this modification.

Rear and prop stands are superseded by a very ingenious and effective central stand. Operation is by a lever which, with the stand up, lies horizontally along-side the primary chain-case. A very moderate upward and backward pull on the rubber grip of the lever suffices to lift the machine on to the stand with the rear wheel well clear of the ground. The actual pull required to raise either of the twins is stated to be only 30 lb, or no more than the weight of a heavy suit-case. A gentle forward push on the lever brings the machine down on to its rear wheel again.

Extensive modifications are not confined to the cycle parts; the power units, too, have come in for their share of attention. The most important change to the engines is the adoption of coil ignition in place of a magneto. This change has proved particularly beneficial to the twins in terms of easy starting and slow running; with a conventional magneto it is impossible to obtain maximum intensity for both sparks.

The Lucas distributor is mounted in the same position, on the front of the crankcase, as was the magneto; the coil is fitted on top of the primary chaincase. Both units are accessible on removal of the left-hand side panel. A Lucas 60-watt instrument, the dynamo is driven from the primary chain or timing gear in the case of the twins and singles respectively. To give better audibility, the horn is mounted over the front cylinder head.

Amal Monobloc carburettors are fitted and have necessitated modified induction elbows for flange fixing. A small increase in power output has been effected on the twins by the fitting of the same pattern of head to both cylinders. Both heads are of the former front type, so that both carburettors are on the left and both plugs on the right.

The idler-gear shaft assembly of the latest engines is in one piece instead of two as previously. One or two cases of

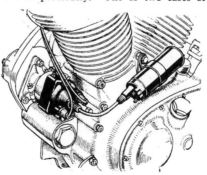

Distributor and ignition coil are readily accessible on removal of a side panel

excessive oil leakage on earlier engines were traced to the timed crankcase breather. To obviate the trouble the new breather is a simple pipe leading rearward from the inlet rocker-box plug of the front cylinder. On the twins, the engine-shaft shock-absorber has been rendered more robust by the incorporation of four additional pairs of springs.

For the touring enthusiast, special pannier equipment will be available for the three new models. Made from the same plastic material as the enclosure panels, the panniers attach rigidly to the rear fairing and blend with its form.

Exterior finish is in black, with gold lining. The timing cover and outer half of the chaincase are black so that their exposed surfaces maintain the colour scheme.

No alterations (other than the modified breather and shock-absorber) are made to the Series C Black Lightning racing model, which retains the "backbone" oil tank and magneto ignition. The engine is, of course, specially tuned, but the detailed specification can be varied.

The lively 48 c.c. Firefly cyclemotor also is continued with no change. It is a two-stroke, horizontal-cylinder unit which attaches to the bicycle bottom bracket and provides geared-roller drive to the rear tyre. An A.C. generator provides current for coil ignition and lighting.

N.S.U. Models

Finally, there are the two N.S.U.-Vincent Fox models and the N.S.U. Quickly autocycle. The Quickly is imported complete from Germany, but in the case of the Fox machines numerous items, including electrical equipment, wheels and tyres, are of British manufacture.

The two Fox models are identical save for the engines. One has a 98 c.c. o.h.v. unit (of the same basic type as that used by Gustav Baum in the record-breaking "flying cigar"), while the other is powered by a 123 c.c. two-stroke engine. Each has a four-speed gear box and a Miller flywheel magneto. A pressed-steel spine frame is employed, and front and rear suspensions are respectively of the leading-link and pivoted-fork pattern.

Of 49 c.c. (40 × 39 mm) engine capacity, the Quickly is one of the most advanced machines of its type. It has a spine frame comprising two steel pressings welded together along the edges. Gear primary drive and a two-speed transmission are included in the specification. Direct lighting is provided by the Noris flywheel magneto. A leading-link front fork and 2in-section tyres ensure satisfactory riding comfort.

The manufacturers and concessionaires are Vincent Engineers (Stevenage), Ltd., Great North Road, Stevenage, Herts. Prices of the Black Prince, Black Knight, Victor and Black Lightning will be available later. Prices of the other models (in which total price includes purchase tax) are as follows:—

	Basic Price			Total Price		
	£	s	d	£	s	d
Firefly, 48 c.c.	25	0	0	No p.t.		
N.S.U.-Vincent Fox, 98 c.c. o.h.v.	104	0	0	124	16	0
N.S.U. - Vincent Fox, 123 c.c. two-stroke ..	99	15	0	119	14	0
N.S.U. Quickly, 49 c.c. autocycle	49	18	4	59	18	0

48 c.c. Vincent Firefly

An Admirable Cyclemotor with Good Traffic Manners and Excellent Performance

ORIGINALLY designed by H. Miller and Co., Ltd., the electrical concern, nearly two years ago, the Vincent Firefly is one of the latest cyclemotors to appear on the British market. The all-round excellence of the unit's performance places it immediately among the very best of its contemporaries. It is intended for fitting below the bottom bracket of a cycle frame.

The controls of the Firefly are orthodox for a cyclemotor; a combined throttle and compression-release lever fits on the right-hand side of the handlebar while a drive-engagement lever clamps on the left-hand side. Pulling the latter lever towards the handlebar engages the friction roller with the rear tyre; an automatic, spring-loaded catch locks the lever in the engaged position.

Starting the engine was a simple matter, particularly when it was warm. The method most commonly used was to pedal the machine away from rest with the drive disengaged and the throttle partly open; after no more than one-and-a-half turns of the pedals, the drive was engaged. There was invariably an immediate response from the engine, which would then pick up lustily without pedal assistance. An alternative starting method was to pedal away with the drive already engaged and the throttle lever moved outward to operate the compression-release valve; as soon as a speed of approximately 4 m.p.h. was attained, opening the throttle produced an immediate start.

When the engine was started from cold, it was necessary to close the carburettor strangler; it could be opened almost as soon as the engine fired. No difficulty was experienced in opening the strangler with the left foot while the cycle was in motion. Only after the Firefly had been left outdoors overnight in damp weather was it necessary to pedal for more than a very few yards in order to obtain a start; under such conditions pedalling for 30 yards might be required.

The Firefly was used extensively in London traffic, yet pedal assistance was never necessary except when moving off from a standstill, this in spite of frequent baulks on steep, main-road gradients. Used to the maximum, the engine's acceleration and speed capabilities were sufficient to enable the rider easily to maintain station in a moving stream of London traffic. According to the whim of the rider, the machine could be ridden in-

The Vincent Firefly unit fits neatly below the bottom bracket of a cycle frame

definitely at low, moderate, or maximum speeds. No vibration was perceptible, the exhaust note was pleasantly subdued at all times and mechanical noise was notably absent.

Frequent traffic halts presented no difficulty. The hub brakes on the cycle used for the test were below the expected standard; consequently frequent use was made of the engine's retarding effect by closing the throttle and opening the decompressor valve (one movement of the lever) when a halt was required. Once the cycle was at a standstill, the drive was disengaged and a restart duly made by the method first described, namely, engagement of the drive, with the throttle open, after one-and-a-half turns of the pedals.

With more powerful brakes, it would be possible to come to rest with the drive disengaged and the engine running. This scheme offers no advantage, however, since it is necessary in any case to pedal for a few yards when restarting. Additionally, the

---

INFORMATION PANEL

ENGINE: 48 c.c. (38 x 42 mm) two-stroke with cast-iron cylinder barrel and detachable, light-alloy cylinder head. Roller bearing big-end; ball bearings supporting crankshaft. Compression ratio, 5 to 1. Petroil lubrication.

CARBURETTOR: Amal lightweight, type 308; handlebar-lever throttle control. Combined air filter and strangler.

TRANSMISSION: Rubber-bonded friction roller mounted on countershaft and gear-driven at half engine speed.

IGNITION AND LIGHTING: 9-watt A.C. generator incorporated in countershaft gear; current supplied to ignition coil in base of fuel tank and to front and rear lights.

FUEL CAPACITY: 5 pints.

FUEL CONSUMPTION: 160 m.p.g. ridden moderately; 130 m.p.g. ridden hard.

WEIGHT OF UNIT: 23½ lb complete.

ROAD TAX: 17s 6d a year; 4s 10d a quarter.

PRICE: £25.

MAKERS: Vincent Engineers (Stevenage) Ltd., Stevenage, Herts.

DESCRIPTION: *The Motor Cycle,* 31 January, 1952, and 4 June, 1953.

---

engine's tickover was not reliable unless set fairly fast. The drive-engagement lever was rather stiff to operate; a nipple pulled off the cable during the test.

In view of the ease with which the Firefly surmounted main-road gradients, a series of tests was undertaken on a quarter-mile-long hill with a maximum gradient, for the last 50 yards, of 1 in 7. From a full-throttle approach, the Firefly crested the hill at 10-12 m.p.h. With a half-throttle approach followed by full throttle opening when the speed fell appreciably, the hill was surmounted easily at 6-8 m.p.h. A restart was readily accomplished halfway up the hill; the engine would continue to pull unaided down to 4-5 m.p.h. on the steepest part of the gradient. Only if the speed fell below this figure was pedal assistance—light pedal assistance—required to keep the engine pulling.

In wet weather, no roller slip was experienced so long as the rear tyre was kept inflated really hard—50 lb sq in or more. The rear tyre was of the tandem type and the inner tube was fitted with a Schrader valve. After dark, adequate intensity of front and rear lights was ensured by the A.C. generator.

(Continued from page 57)

ings kept running along and vibration was unknown. The oil pump kept delivering oil, the valves kept holding in the explosions and the steering was typically Vincent—perfect.

Tony and Jim soon became like the woman who knitted fast lest the wool would run out and they stepped up the mileage to fantastic figures. I was shortly told that they were blasting the outfit north through the winter to visit

me and that they hoped to reach that 100,000th mile more or less outside my front door. They did just that, on February 3rd, and it was all over, bar the shouting and the engine stripping. I had a run on the outfit before they left and apart from a bit of a clank from somewhere down in the engine-room when pulling slowly, it was wonderfully good. I later heard that

when the parts were measured up against new ones, even Phil Vincent was astonished at their good condition.

I guess Tony now just sits at home twiddling his thumbs and trying to think up some new scheme to astonish the world with. Good luck to him, but it will have to be a beauty to even equal the World's Longest Road Test. The things some people do. . . . . !

VINCENT

STAND 174: Enclosed Models Cause Show Furore

WITH their built-in weather protection for the rider and almost complete enclosure of the machinery, the spectacular Series D vee-twin and single-cylinder Vincent models are creating enormous interest. It is fortunate indeed that the Stevenage firm has a large stand to accommodate the crowds swarming in the shadow of the monster V emblems.

The new models represent a big step forward in motor-cycle development, both

A model everyone is queuing to see—the 998 c.c. Vincent Black Prince

turntable. Two additional Black Princes, two 998 c.c. Black Knights and two 499 c.c. Victors (developed from the former Rapide and Comet respectively), and one immensely potent-looking Black Lightning racer, complete the display of solo Vincent models.

Many sidecar fans are coveting the fully sprung three-wheeled exhibits—a Black Prince with Blacknell Bullett sidecar and a Victor with a Canterbury Victor family model.

Modifications to the Series D mounts are not confined to the exterior. The knowledgeable are commenting on the coil ignition, the single rear brake (instead of the long-established twin rear brakes) and improved rear-suspension layout.

The 123 c.c. two-stroke and 98 c.c. overhead-valve N.S.U.-Vincent Foxes are attractive, spine-framed lightweights which have a luxury specification in keeping with that of the larger models on display. They embody many British components although the major items are of German manufacture.

as regards the basic conception and in the use of light but strong glass-reinforced plastic material for the bodywork. Accessibility of all major components remains remarkably good in spite of the high degree of weather protection achieved.

Pride of place goes to the magnificent, sectioned 998 c.c. Black Prince, developed from the former Black Shadow and mounted on a raised and illuminated

Left: At the lower end of the capacity scale—the 123 c.c. Vincent N.S.U. Fox

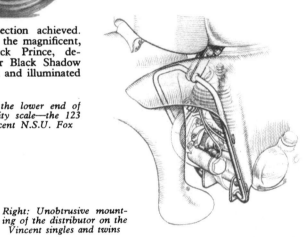

Right: Unobtrusive mounting of the distributor on the Vincent singles and twins

Office bound, wearing a mackintosh and walking-out gloves, the author sets out on the Black Knight. Coil ignition makes for easy starting

At most roadside halts, as at this petrol station the distinctive appearance of the Black Knight evoked interested comment

Between Breakfast and Teatime

VIC WILLOUGHBY Covers 500 Enjoyable Miles Behind the Windscreen of a 998 c.c. Plastic-enclosed Vincent Black Knight

YOU might think that a rider who covers 500 miles during a winter's day in Britain when he has nowhere special to go, is a candidate for a mental home. Probably you would be right. But, though I did just that on the Sunday of Show week, I hope I shall escape the charge of insanity, for there was indeed a purpose in my journey.

The previous evening I had borrowed a 998 c.c. Series D Vincent Black Knight, and I was anxious to put it through its paces as soon as possible, for time is at a premium during Show week. Hence the day's mileage. Actually, the machine I rode was a prototype—a well-hacked test model. That I was able to complete the scheduled distance without a hitch on a machine to which I was quite unaccustomed says much for the Vincent.

Purpose of my test was to find the answers to several pertinent questions which arose from the bold and comprehensive plastic enclosure of the Series D Vincents. How would the enclosure affect the exemplary handling of the big machine? What degree of weather protection would be afforded to the rider? Would the level of noise reaching the rider's ears be more or less than with earlier series models? What, if any, would be the effect on fuel consumption and performance? Additionally, there were other modifications the effects of which I was anxious to assess—coil ignition, Amal Monobloc carburettors, proprietary shock-absorbers and 3.50 × 19in front and 4.00 × 18in rear tyres.

As a basis for comparison, I relied on previous experience of my own Series A and B Rapides and a friend's Series C Black Shadow all of which I had used extensively for long-distance, high-speed travel.

It was not difficult to approach my task with an open mind, for earlier experiences had long since banished pre-conceived prejudices in respect of weather shielding, enclosure and streamlining. Tests carried out by *The Motor Cycle* in September, 1953, revealed that the fitting of a windscreen to an orthodox machine actually brought about a small improvement in petrol consumption and maximum speed. On the other hand, I had abandoned the use of a most effective screen on my machine after a short trial, since I could not tolerate the reflected mechanical noise. When riding the Dolphin-type, streamlined, two-fifty N.S.U. racer near Belfast last August, I had been impressed by the weather protection afforded by the fairing: I wore an ordinary lounge suit which remained unruffled at two miles a minute, while my shoes retained their shine in spite of slight drizzle. A ride in the fantastic N.S.U. "flying hammock" had convinced me that scientifically designed streamlining can be perfectly safe at speeds within the compass of contemporary production machines.

I have an inherent dislike of riding without a particular destination. Consequently, when planning my trip, I sought an objective. I decided that, since the house of Vincent has always been on the Great North Road (A1), it was appropriate to use that famous highway for my journey. A return trip from London to Scotch Corner seemed to fill the bill.

Even at 6.20 a.m. on the Sunday, when I crept out of the front door, the Vincent was receiving rapt attention—from the newspaper delivery boy. It was dark and the London roads were covered with rime which gave way to water as the early miles slipped by. Behind the beam of the Lucas headlamp I cruised happily at 70-75 m.p.h. except in restricted areas. To my surprise, traffic was not quite so sparse as I had anticipated; there was quite a number of tradesmen's vans and heavy vehicles already on the roads.

When 25 miles were recorded on the Vincent speedo-

The Black Knight made light of high-speed cruising. A two-piece riding suit and warm under-garments were sufficient for the 500-mile winter run

meter, an eerie yellow glow to my right heralded the dawn. After another 20 miles I was able to switch off the lights and push up my cruising speed, where conditions permitted, to 80-85 m.p.h. My route lay along A10 and A14, to join A1 near Alconbury.

As the Vincent swept through the counties of Middlesex, Hertfordshire, Cambridgeshire and Huntingdonshire in the cold early morning, I was surprised to note the degree of bodily warmth retained as a result of the weather shielding. I wore a Bell two-piece plastic riding suit and short over-boots over a tweed jacket and corduroy slacks. The only special precautions taken to keep warm were to wear an old pair of pyjama trousers beneath my slacks and to replace my usual sleeveless pullover with one of the long-sleeved, roll-neck variety. Yet I felt warm except for my gloved hands. The reason for their coldness was that the Vincent was not, at that time, fitted with handshields. Subsequent journeys with handshields in position revealed that my hands kept warm when wearing only walking-out gloves.

Smoke issuing from domestic chimneys indicated that the wind was blowing from the north-west, was moderately strong and was certainly gusty. The roads continued to be streaming wet. Periodically I inspected my legs and feet and found that, though the left leg remained substantially clean the right leg gradually became splashed with water which eventually dried into a very thin film of mud. This fouling, however, was much less than would have occurred had I been riding an orthodox machine under the same conditions, and it was obvious that the Black Knight could be ridden in cyclist's waterproof leggings where riding a conventional machine would necessitate the use of waders.

In Northamptonshire and Lincolnshire, the Vincent's speedometer regis-

tered a steady 90 m.p.h. on the long, straight stretches between Stamford and Grantham. A series of checks provided the answers to the other questions in my mind. The exhaust note was virtually inaudible from the saddle. I offer that as a plain statement of fact and not as high praise for, in any case, the exhaust note of a Vincent twin is one of the most pleasant and inoffensive I know. As to mechanical noise, there seemed to be an improvement. The glass-fibre panels are positively non-resonant and, in addition, tend to insulate the rider from the noise of the engine.

The height of the screen was such that its top edge was well below my line of vision, and I found my ears buffeted by a blustery backwash of eddies and my goggles slowly dirtied. Lowering my head an inch or two had a remarkable effect, for I then found myself in a calm, quiet pocket of air. Gone was the buffeting of the wind and, with the exhaust inaudible and only a faint whirr of machinery detectable from the "engine room," I had the impression of being in a high-powered sports car. It was quite feasible to dispense with goggles altogether in the lower position, and my line of vision was still above the top edge of the screen. Had the screen been adjustable for height, I should have raised it one or two inches and enjoyed this pleasant sensation all the time.

To appreciate the extent of the screen's influence, even when I was not crouching, I stood up on the footrests and was immediately assailed by the full blast of the machine-made gale. A subsequent journey in drizzling rain confirmed these impressions.

Possible impaired stability of the machine as a result of the enclosure proved to be a complete myth. At no time during the run did I feel the slightest anxiety. The only occasions when I detected any wind effect were when pulling across the turbulent bow wave in the wake of a large, fast-moving vehicle. Even then, the effect was no more pronounced than with a conventional machine.

The impression of speed has always been deceptively reduced on a Vincent twin, owing to its high gearing (the solo top-gear ratio is 3.5 to 1) and its steadiness on the road. The Black Knight is even more deceptive, particularly when one is down behind the screen. Steering was typically Vincent—inclined to be heavy at very low speeds but otherwise rock-steady, extremely positive and guaranteed to inspire confidence.

Heading south. The Vincent circles the Royston roundabout to join the A10 road

The new suspension is as good as any I know and furnishes superb road-holding. It is lighter than previous Vincent patterns around the static-load position and is so well damped that neither bottoming nor pitching was experienced. When I wanted to slow or stop, the brakes pinned down the heavy machine as smoothly, safely and relentlessly as only Vincent brakes can. This was mostly due to the excellence of the twin front brakes, for the rear brake on the particular machine used was heavy in operation and lacking in power. As to the engine's power delivery, it was at all times smooth and effortless. Normal upward gear-changing speeds were 35, 60 and 80 m.p.h.

I carried on non-stop through Rutland, England's smallest county, and Nottinghamshire before entering England's largest county, Yorkshire. On the north side of Doncaster I made a 10-minute refuelling stop and was flabbergasted when the attendant expressed neither surprise nor interest in the unusual appearance of my mount. Probably he would refuel a flying saucer without batting an eyelid. Wetherby, Boroughbridge, Leeming Bar and Catterick were all left behind and, eventually, the brick-red hotel at Scotch Corner loomed into view. The time was 10.25—much too early to expect lunch. So I circled the roundabout, stopped to clean my goggles and make a few notes, then started on the southward run.

Favourable Wind

At first I found the sun's reflection from the wet roads troublesome, but it was not long before I realized that the wind direction was more favourable on the return trip: on suitable stretches of road the speedometer registered 90-95 m.p.h. without conscious increase in throttle opening on my part. I noted, too, that it was the turn of my left leg to become lightly fouled with water from the road surface.

On a straight, deserted dual carriageway near Boroughbridge the Vincent reached 100 m.p.h. with the same rock-steadiness, the same effortlessness and, whenever I lowered my head, the same uncanny quietness.

In due course I approached Doncaster again—this time from the opposite direction, of course—and conceived the notion to shatter the phlegmatic garage attendant by calling for my second three gallons of fuel within a period of 2½ hours. But he was as unimpressionable as before; so I asked him to recommend a good eating house. With 311 miles on the trip recorder, I felt I had earned an early lunch.

Steaming tea, several rashers of bacon and fried eggs restored my vigour. I chatted with some Sheffield riders, brought my notes up to date and listened to the entertaining remarks of some bystanders before taking to the road again. For the remainder of my journey, the roads were wet and dry in patches. On the dry sections I was able to renew my experience of the comparative ease with which a big Vincent twin can be heeled at speed through bends and corners.

As London was approached we encountered dense traffic. When I neared home at 3.30 p.m. I found my mileage was 26 short of the scheduled 500, so I made a detour round the North Circular Road to make up the deficiency. It was an unfortunate decision, for the road was chock-a-block with Sunday afternoon trippers. The remaining mileage occupied three-quarters of an hour, during which time the Vincent's top gear was virtually ornamental.

I pulled the Black Knight on to its hand-operated centre stand and noted its appearance. After 501 high-speed miles, approximately 400 of which had been over wet roads, a thin film of mud had formed on the rear surfaces of the legshields and on the sides of the tank. The film was much lighter than would have appeared on a conventional machine, and five minutes' work with a piece of mutton cloth restored the exterior to the condition in which it had been when I collected it.

A check of fuel consumption revealed an overall figure of approximately 53 m.p.g.—some seven miles a gallon better than I used to achieve on my Series B Rapide in similar use. The improvement is probably due to the combined effects of the weather shielding, coil ignition and the Amal Monobloc carburettors. Incidentally, coil ignition has resulted in easier starting. A less hearty swing of the kick-starter than hitherto brings the engine to life.

At the conclusion of the run I was conscious of two sources of physical discomfort. First, I was saddle-sore, for the seat had proved rather hard. I understand the point has already been raised with the suppliers and that production seats are considerably more softly sprung. Secondly, my hands ached. This was largely due to the long reach from the handlebar grips to the clutch and front-brake levers; the possibility of obtaining differently shaped levers is being considered. Also the plane in which the levers were set was too high, and adjustment was strictly limited by the narrowness of the slots in the head cowling. Possibly, too, the semi-crouching riding position, which has made post-war Vincents so tireless to ride at high speeds for long periods, throws slightly too much weight on the rider's wrists now that his body is no longer subjected to wind pressure.

These small criticisms will doubtless not apply to production models. The Series D Vincent merits high marks as a bold step in the direction of what I foresee as an inevitable trend in motor-cycle design. Whether other designers will follow the Vincent pattern or obtain similar effects by a gradual process of styling development remains to be seen, but built-in weather protection will, I am certain, eventually become recognized as an essential feature of all machines.

Parking the Vincent was merely a matter of exerting a moderate pull on the centre-stand lever

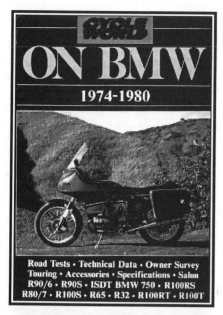
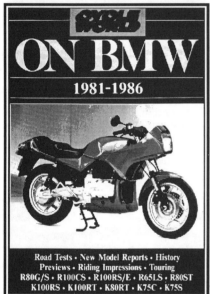
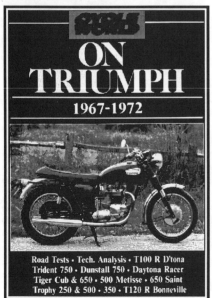

Side view showing the effective enclosure of the 998 cc. Black Prince twin.

New Fiberglass Bodies
For Vincent

VINCENT motorcycles have always been noted for unconventional design and high class workmanship and the Vincent engineers have now broken entirely new ground with their 1955 "Knights of the Road", a spectacular range of fully enclosed high performance motorcycles.

The Vincent is the first British touring motorcycle to use total enclosure with fiber glass reinforced plastic. The new design, a well kept secret, was one of the sensations of the British Motorcycle Show.

The prime reason for adopting the covering is weather protection for the rider and not an increased top speed on account of better streamlining. The photos clearly show the extent of the fairing: a wide front fender, a frontal cowling with the nicely blended in windshield and handle bar "cups", the side panels which cover the engine and gearbox and the rear end fairing reminiscent of scooter practice.

The use of fiber glass reinforced plastic has many advantages: it is light and strong for its weight and its tensile strength is comparable to good quality light alloy sheeting. It has a high resistance to fatigue and is non-corrosive. This plastic material is particularly suited for the suppression of noise as it has none of the resonance tendencies of sheet metal. This is particularly important in view of the fact that it is used to shield a motorcycle engine, where vibration can be of a high order. The Vincent company claims that the handling has been improved by the enclosure and even sudden gusts of wind are easily dealt with. Overseas road test reports bear this out completely and the silent speed and the sheltered effect by windshield and enclosure are reported to be truly remarkable. On the proto-

type the steering lock was rather limited but this has been improved on the actual production models.

The three enclosed models which have the designation series D, have now been named Black Prince, Black Knight, and Victor. The latter is a single cylinder machine. Engine outputs are respectively 55 hp at 5700 rpm and 45 hp at 5200 rpm for the 1000 cc V twins, and 28 bhp at 5800 rpm for the single.

Names of the previous models were

The tail section can be lifted up. The oil tank to be seen inside the shell is raised with the assembly and is fitted with flexible lines. Note the lever operated central stand.

68

All models in the Vincent for "55" line are equipped with bodies which fully enclose the entire machine.

Black Shadow twin, Rapide twin and Comet single.

The Vincent engine is of a high efficiency, slightly unconventional design. The twin and the single are similar in design, both being light alloy high camshaft engines with a bore and stroke of 84 x 90 mm respectively. The unconventional overhead valve actuation is a unique Vincent feature.

The twin engine is built in unit with the gearbox but the single has a separate Burman gearbox driven by a 1 in. pitch single chain, whereas the larger engine employs a ⅜ in. triplex chain.

Front and rear suspension follow the design that Vincent machines have had for many years. The triangle rear fork pivots in taper roller bearings and the suspension unit is located under the seat. An Armstrong hydraulic damper is now used which effectively controls the rear wheel suspension travel of 6 inches.

The front wheel is suspended by the well known "Girdraulic" parallelogram fork which employs special heat treated light alloy blades of taper oval section, and long side springs. Suspension movements are checked by a completely new design centrally mounted hydraulic damper. The light weight fork members and the fact that the head lamp has been transferred to a sprung position has reduced the unsprung weight considerably.

The front fender however is unsprung. It is wide and deeply valanced and should give very good rider protection.

The new Lucas F 700 headlamp represents the latest in motorcycle lighting equipment and it is mounted in a one piece plastic cowling which covers the steering head. The cupped extensions which protect the riders hands are made separate so they can be replaced in the event of damage.

The "Perspex" windshield has been specially designed by Vincent and is a standard fitting. Its base surrounds the semicircular instrument panel which is slightly inclined to give the driver full view of the speedometer and ammeter. The panel also contains the ignition and lighting switches.

The legshields are part of the engine cowling and they serve a dual purpose in that they also form the air intake for the engine cooling air. The panels have a three point attachment by means of knurled screws and removal of the panels is only a matter of seconds.

The tail shell is a one piece plastic moulding and the shell has been made very rigid by bonding it to a light tubular subframe which also carries the pivot and fastening brackets and the pillion foot rests. The subframe is hinged from the rear cylinderhead bracket and it can be held up by a prop stay specially provided for the purpose.

The dual seat which contains springs and foam rubber sits on top of the shell and is fully sprung. A large tool tray is exposed when the seat is hinged upward.

The rear shell is rigidly secured in the down position by a clamping bolt behind the gearbox.

There is no rear fender but a short aluminum shield ahead of the wheel protects power, transmission and suspension units from mud and dirt. The oil tank is placed in the rear shell, moves up with it and is therefore fitted with flexible pipes. The filler orifice is at the rear of the tank to avoid spillage when the assembly is raised. Previous Vincents had the oil tank in the shape of a box section member between steering head and rear cylinderhead. Because of the oil tank transfer, the fuel tank capacity has been increased to 4.8 gallons.

Only one rear brake is now fitted to reduce unsprung weight, but brake leverage has been increased to keep the same braking efficiency. On the Black Prince ribbed drums are fitted front and rear.

Very convenient is the new center stand which is lever operated. With the stand up the lever lies horizontally alongside the primary chain case. Only a moderate pull (30 lbs) is required to lift the machine on to the stand. An important modification in the power unit is the adoption of coil ignition in place of a magneto which has made the machine easier to start and has improved idling. Amal Monobloc carburetors supply the mixture. The electrical equipment includes a Lucas 60 watt generator. Cylinderheads are now interchangeable and both carburetors are now on the left and the spark plugs on the right.

A new crankcase breather pipe has cured excessive oil leakage that was sometimes experienced in the earlier models.

On the twins the crankshaft shockabsorber now has four additional pairs of springs.

The machines are finished in black with gold lining, and the timing cover and outer part of the chain case are black to match the exterior finish.

The new models are fitted with larger section tires, 3.50 in. front and 4.00 in. rear, but the smaller section tires previously used (3.00 front, 3.50 rear) can be had if specified.

The Vincent line is distributed in the U.S. by the Indian Company of Springfield, Mass.

The Vincent Victor 499 cc. single cylinder displays the same handsome design typical of the Vincent line.

Built for Speed No. 30

JOHN GRIFFITH describes a

1959 Vincent "Black Lightning"

A RACING "THOUSAND" BUILT FROM NEW PARTS BY PARKSTONE ENTHUSIAST REG PESKETT

Light alloy is employed for the plates carrying the footrest and the gear change pedal. A Series D-type breather is fitted to the exhaust rocker cover on the rear cylinder.

THE last Vincent "Black Lightning" to be made at the factory was built in 1955—or so it is generally believed. But Dorset enthusiast Reg Peskett has recently made a little bit of history by assembling such a machine from new spares which he had acquired over a 10-year period as a Vincent owner and rider. Reg is head salesman for Huxhams (Motor Cycles), Ltd., 149-155 Ashley Road, Parkstone, Poole, and his beautifully built model is currently on display in their showrooms.

As Vincents made it, the "Black Lightning" was finished appropriately, but Reg has polished most of the parts that were originally enamelled, so it seems only reasonable that he should have improved his tank transfer with the single word "Lightning."

The engine unit has been modified slightly in the light of knowledge gleaned by Reg during his riding and workshop experience of this marque. The crankcase castings and the chaincase, timing, and gearbox covers have all been polished inside and out to give a really

IN BRIEF

Engine: 50° Vee-twin o.h.v. in unit with gear-box ; 84 mm. bore x 90 mm. stroke = 998 c.c.; c.r. 9 : 1; estimated output, 70 b.h.p. at 5,600 r.p.m.

Ignition: B.T.H./T.T. manually controlled magneto.

Fuel: 3½-gal. steel tank.

Oil: 6-pt. tank integral with frame member.

Wheels: Light alloy rims carrying Avon racing tyre, 3.00-in. × 20-in. at front and Dunlop racing tyre 3.50-in. × 19-in. at rear.

Spit and polish! Some idea of the excellent polish is given in this view. Note the modified transfer.

wonderful mirror finish. I shudder to think of the hours upon hours that Reg must have given to this work alone.

The flywheel-con.-rod assembly has been polished to the same standard as have all the smaller moving parts. A caged ¼ x ¼-in. roller big-end bearing is employed. The standard main-bearing arrangement—two sizes of roller bearings on the timing side and one large roller and one ball bearing on the drive side—is retained.

Since the machine is initially to be run on petrol (as Reg puts it, until he can use all *that* power), Specialloid pistons giving a 9 : 1 c.r. are at present fitted, but a pair of high-compression pistons for use with alcohol fuel are already in stock against later requirements. The valves and their ancillaries are all standard " Black Lightning " parts; so are the twin front-pattern cylinder heads, but one exhaust rocker cover is fitted with a Series D-type breather.

Sparks are provided by a manually controlled B.T.H./T.T. magneto. This, I am told, is one of the two parts which are not new. The Smiths rev.-counter assembly is the other. Both components have been overhauled to original standards.

Champion NA12 plugs fire the mixture provided by 32-mm. bore Amal 10TT

carburetters. The latter have bolted-on float chambers at present, although it may be necessary at some later stage to turn to remote positioning. The carburetter air controls have been disconnected.

Gearbox internals are to " Black Lightning " specification, although " Rapide " ratios are employed in order to secure a lowish bottom gear. With a 22-tooth gearbox sprocket and 50-tooth rear wheel sprocket, the overall top gear ratio works out at 3.6 : 1. A 45 t. cog is fitted on the other rear brake drum, so that wheel reversal can give a 3.32 : 1 gear.

With a Vincent there is little in the way of structure beside the mangle-unit itself. The frame spine holds the oil and steering column bearings, and also joins the cylinder heads; at its rear it

provides anchor points for the two spring units and one damper which control the pivoting fork. Front-end guidance is provided by the well-known " Girdraulic " forks; an outrigger plate has been attached to the brake balance beam to eliminate some of the inherent sponginess in operation. Hubs and rims have been Peskettized, but the brake drums and backplate have been left black to help dissipate heat.

Many cycle parts and small pipes have been satin-chromed—a very pleasing finish—and a few parts have been stove enamelled. These include the two long stays which fully spring the seat, leaving the old joints free to be used as separate, and additional, friction dampers.

Here's to the summer, to see how it goes.

Front and rear. An extra steady-plate is fitted to the front brake balance beam The seat is fully sprung so that the original fittings are used purely as dampers.

A 998 c.c. VINCENT SPECIAL

110 m.p.h. roadster

extensively modified

to owner's requirements

Specification

ENGINE

Type	50° V-twin four-stroke
Bore	84 mm.
Stroke	90 mm.
Cubic capacity	998 c.c.
Valves	Overhead (push-rod)
Compression ratio	7.3 : 1
Carburetters ..	Amal 1⅛-in. bore " 289 "
Ignition	Lucas magneto with automatic control
Generator ..	Lucas E3L 6-v. 60-w. dynamo with A.V.C. and boosted output
Makers' claimed output	55 b.h.p./5,500 r.p.m.
Lubrication ..	Dry sump with double-output rotating-plunger pumps
Starting	Kickstarter

TRANSMISSION

In-unit gearbox with footchange	
Ratios (48t. rear sprocket)	3.7, 4.4, 5.9, 9.4
Speed at 1,000 r.p.m. in top gear ..	21 m.p.h.
Speed equivalent to revs. at maximum power rating:	
Second gear	73 m.p.h.
Third gear	100 m.p.h.
Top gear	118 m.p.h.
Primary drive	Triple-row chain in oil bath
Final drive ..	Single-row exposed chain (both chains by Renold)

Clutch	Norton multi-plate in " dry " compartment
Shock-absorber ..	Spring-and-cam type on engine shaft

CYCLE PARTS

Frame ..	Box-type backbone with power-unit as structural member; bolted on sub-frame
Front suspension ..	Girdraulic forks modified enclosed coil springs; two-way Armstrong hydraulic damper with limit stops
Rear suspension	Swinging-fork with hydraulically-damped Armstrong units; 85-lb. springs. Wheelbase 53 in.
Tyres ..	Dunlop ribbed 3.25×19-in. front, studded 3.50×19-in. rear, both held by security bolts and balanced
Brakes	Duo front, single rear, all 7-in. dia. racing parts. Total lining area, 30 sq. in.
Fuel tank ..	3½ gal.; two taps
Oil tank	Hollow upper frame member, 6 pints
Lamps ..	Marchal: 45/36-w. adjustable head, 48-w. spot, 48-w. fog. Lucas: twin 6-w. side, 18/6-w. stop/tail, one 3-w. speedometer
Horns	Twin Lucas Windtone

Battery	Lucas 12 a.h.
Speedometer	Smiths modified 130 m.p.h. with trip
Seating	A.M.C. q.d. two-level twinseat
Stands	Centre, prop, front jack
Toolkit..	Too large to list; includes full tyre and chain repair equipment
Toolbox ..	Open compartment beneath seat
Finish ..	Black cycle parts, power unit in natural alloy, glass-fibre enclosure in silver with black trimmings; usual parts chromium or cadmium plated

OTHER EQUIPMENT

Modified Avon Streamliner; q.d. panniers and rear carrier; Triumph tank-top luggage grid; tyre pump; special engine breather; pillion footrests; oil-temperature gauge; mirror

PRICES

Machine	Listed in 1951 at £336 11s. (inc. £71 11s. P.T.)
Tax ..	£3 15s. p.a. (£1 7s. for four months)
Makers	Known in February, 1951, as Vincent-H.R.D. Co., Ltd., of Stevenage, Herts., now Harpers Engines, Ltd., of same address

'Motor Cycling' Test Data

Conditions. *Weather: Dry, cold (Barometer 29.85 Hg. Thermometer 36°F.). Wind: N., 8–10 m.p.h. Surface (braking and acceleration): Dry asphalt. Rider: 11½ stone, 5 ft. 10½ in., wearing two-piece suit, safety helmet, normally seated behind screen throughout. Fuel: "Super" grade (101 Research Method Octane Rating).*

Venue: *Motor Industry Research Association Station, Lindley.*

Speed at end of standing 1,000 yd.:
East	102 m.p.h.
West	94 m.p.h.
Best certified M.I.R.A. maximum (rider upright behind screen)	109 m.p.h.

Braking from 30 m.p.h. (all brakes): 9½ yd.

Fuel consumption:
At constant .. 50 m.p.h.	60 m.p.g.
70 m.p.h.	46 m.p.g.
500-mile overall figure ..	53 m.p.g.

Speedometer
30 m.p.h. indicated =	30.5 m.p.h. true
40 m.p.h. indicated =	40.3 m.p.h. true
50 m.p.h. indicated =	50.1 m.p.h. true
60 m.p.h. indicated =	60.4 m.p.h. true
70 m.p.h. indicated =	70.5 m.p.h. true
80 m.p.h. indicated =	80.4 m.p.h. true
90 m.p.h. indicated =	91.9 m.p.h. true
100 m.p.h. indicated =	101.8 m.p.h. true
110 m.p.h. indicated =	110.8 m.p.h. true

Mileage Recorder .. Over-reading ½%

Electrical Equipment
Top gear speed at which generator output balances:
Minimum obligatory lights..	28 m.p.h.
Headlamp main beam ..	36 m.p.h.
Headlamp and either spot	Not capable

Weights and Capacities
Certified kerbside weight (with oil and 1 gal. fuel)	540 lb.
Weight distribution rider normally seated:	
Front wheel..	43%
Rear wheel..	57%
Tank capacity (metered):	
Total	3½ gal.
Reserve	1¾ or 6½ pints

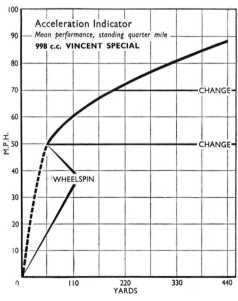

Acceleration Indicator
Mean performance, standing quarter mile
998 c.c. VINCENT SPECIAL

CHANGE

CHANGE

'WHEELSPIN'

M.P.H.

YARDS

We close the year with a Road Test that is different. It deals with a privately owned machine of a make which (regrettably, many feel) is no longer in production. The subject is the 10-year-old "Shadowized" Vincent "Rapide" owned by staffman Bruce Main-Smith and modified by him to his personal requirements. Its history includes a spell of solo and sidecar racing.—Ed.

NOW at a mileage of 132,000, Bruce Main-Smith's 1951 1,000 c.c. o.h.v. V-twin Vincent "Rapide" has been converted by the owner to meet his own priorities. These demanded the ability to cruise indefinitely on motorways at 90 to 100 m.p.h.; outstandingly good acceleration and braking to deal with week-end traffic on the A29 and A3/A283 London-South Coast routes; first-class roadholding; protection from the weather; luggage-carrying facilities; and especially good lights. Further, the machine had to be as suitable for the owner's wife on the pillion as it was for the driver.

Accordingly, the following non-standard equipment has been fitted, some of it of the

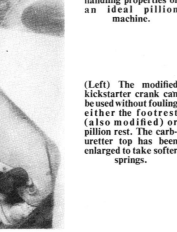

Tailored for two, the Main-Smith Vincent has the power and the handling properties of an ideal pillion machine.

(Left) The modified kickstarter crank can be used without fouling either the footrest (also modified) or pillion rest. The carburetter top has been enlarged to take softer springs.

owner's design and construction: "Shadowized" engine with "Picador" two-start oil-pump worm, doubling the rate of circulation; "Lightning" brakes; "conventional" swinging-fork rear suspension; an "Avon Streamliner" full-frontal fairing; q.d. panniers and luggage carrier; and an A.M.C. twinseat.

The immediate impression on seeing "Pig"—as the Main-Smiths call it—is of cumbersomeness. This was not dissipated when one wheeled the machine around. Steering lock was restricted, even below the limited Vincent standard, and the frontal overhang was a nuisance.

Against this, the enclosure was completely successful in keeping the rider clean and dry—even his hands and feet—and in relieving him of fatiguing wind pressure. (The Vincent "leaning on the wind" position has been eliminated by moving the foot rests forward and fitting Ariel handlebars.) At speed, goggles were necessary. The passenger received some air buffeting, though

less than on a "naked" model. Really fast cruising in rain was practicable. Water could not pass the front-fork gaiter.

Internal leg panels tidy up the enclosure, allow the stiffening boxes to be used to carry full puncture and chain repair outfits, and direct air more onto the cylinders. Either shield could be taken off in 30 sec.

Diminished cooling by radiation made the engine run hotter than standard at low air speeds—without, apparently, any ill effects. A pleasant warmth was imparted in the wintry test period; in summer, the owner's riding kit consists of sports jacket and flannels, with light outerwear for rain.

Once under power, the steering was faultless. There was no heaviness at low speeds. Although the standard steering damper had been removed, the Vincent was 100% wobble-free even when thrust hard over bumpy roads. It never nodded its head or wagged its tail.

There was undiminished ground clearance. The enclosure could not be touched down.

In the wet, sheer weight aided adhesion, the mount being both quick and extremely safe.

Roadholding was equal to that of any mount in current production. Indeed, it was "Grand Touring" in the car sense of the term. The ride was exceptionally comfortable for this level of handling, the Girdraulic front forks making a major contribution.

Behaviour was free from pitching or any associated faults. There was no change of trim, no matter how hard the excellent brakes were applied. Application of the nominal 55 "brake horses" produced only a trace of lifting at the front; jack-knifing at the rear pivot, not unknown on standard Vincents, was completely absent.

The front forks clicked on being moved from lock to lock, indicating wear at the eccentrics. The metal-bush-pivoted rear fork was rigid laterally. The use of closed lug ends in this component, however, made rear wheel removal complicated and messy.

Steering generally was a revelation for a mount weighing 540 lb., conceived in 1945 and home modified. A pillion passenger was no handicap—if anything, an asset. The front forks have Series "D" trail limits, an Armstrong hydraulic unit and one Norton clutch spring supplementing each inner main spring.

The tailored riding position proved perfect for a man of much the same size and build as the owner. The tank could be both narrower, to reduce splay at the knees, and larger, to hold more than 3 gal. The fixed footrests were just right; both their associated pedals, modified to suit, were well placed. The pillion rests have been lengthened and cranked for the comfort of a 5-ft. 1-in. passenger.

With the flexibility and output of a "Shadow"-type engine, the machine had an abundance of smooth power. The crankshaft, Hartley balanced, mounts Irving-designed caged big-ends.

A continuous motorway cruise in the upper nineties revealed no vibration. But there was a protracted period, in the forties in second and fifties in third, which produced tremor rather than vibration—an effect probably accentuated by the general smoothness. Top gear could be held down to 35 m.p.h., below which speed the extra backlash suggested a change down.

What optimum use of the gears could achieve is shown, strikingly enough, by the graph and tabulated figures; but under road conditions change-points were by no means critical. Although third could be held to 90 or even 100 m.p.h., this was quite unnecessary. The machine has been fettled to give shattering acceleration in top gear at 45 m.p.h. Good results were forthcoming at 40; at about 43 one felt everything get into phase—then one had to hold on very tight. And pick-up persisted at 100 if the half-open throttles were suddenly fully lifted.

The gearbox has the low " Rapide " bottom. Top and third have been given extra backlash. Also non-standard is the multi-plate dry clutch, made from Norton parts.

This combination gave faultless gear-changing. A Vincent can be stiff to put into top around 90 m.p.h., but this did not occur. Neutral was easily found from bottom or second. The gear pedal, however, had too long a travel.

The clutch was excellent, light and jerk-

Fixed main footrest and modified brake pedal are details seen in this nearside view. Both crankcase breather pipes enter the pannier rail so that discharge occurs at the machine's rearmost point.

(Left) The home-brewed swinging-fork rear end, with Armstrong damper. The axle lug is cut from solid high-tensile steel. The pannier frame is q.d.; the wheel is not.

free. There was no overheating, slipping, or need for adjustment during the test.

Carburation was unhesitant throughout. The modified mixing chambers permitted light wrist action. General fuel consumption was 53 m.p.g. over an extended period of really hard driving. " Super "-grade petrol was essential to avoid pinking.

Main jet size is 190 instead of 180, to promote reliability at prolonged high speeds. PJO 846 has not been recently decoked—in accordance with the widespread belief that this process is simply unnecessary with a " 1,000 " Vincent.

The handbook advice of " straight " oils —SAE 50 summer, 30 winter—is normally followed. In deference to the high-speed work at MIRA, we kept to heavy oil this month and paid the penalty with an engine stiff to crank when cold. No chokes are fitted, nor were they needed; a good flood was enough. The rear float-chamber is sensibly mounted on the left so that the petrol may be left on when the prop-stand

is used; its tickler is extended for easy access. The standard Vincent drill of raising the footrest before kickstarting was not necessary; the pedal-piece to the rebent crank is fixed permanently out; it did not foul the leg.

Vincent braking has always been superb, and indeed set the road-test record for a long time. The " Lightning " racing anchors on this mount were first-class. Pedal pressure on the single-drum back stopper was less than standard for the marque. Neither it nor the Ferodo-lined dual front brake was affected by heat or rain.

The Marchal lights were admirable, especially the asymmetrical cut-off to the dipped beam of the headlamp, the set of which is adjustable from the saddle to compensate for load. The " flamethrower " spot is aimed 30 yd. ahead, aligned on the verge of the centre strip of M1. The fog lamp gave a spread pattern at short range.

The note of the twin Lucas Windtone horns, set to fire up the left airscoop, was

lethal at 150 yd. during 90 m.p.h. motorway cruising. Boosted dynamo output kept the battery up, though charging as heavy as 8 amp. was seen at times.

The power unit was oiltight with the exception of the kickstarter cover, a " dry " compartment anyway! Oil consumption, however, was high at 200 miles per pint. There was considerable engine-to-chaincase transference, which called for levelling, and probaby accounted for most of the oil loss. K.L.G. FE75 plugs were used. They never fouled, even in prolonged central-London work (inlet valve and rocker drainage has been improved).

Exhaust silencing was up to the usual Vincent standard, which is good. Mechanically, the engine was clatttery, but wear may account for some of this; for example, the cams are the originals. There was slap from the cylinder group, which has done some 90,000 miles and is due for renewal.

Many detail points are worthy of comment. The special prop-stand is excellent— easily found with the foot, always supporting the machine firmly, and tucking up well. The centre-stand is really repair-maintenance equipment, so its heavy lift may be overlooked. Neither grounds on corners. Regrettably, there is no front stand, but a small jack is carried.

The handlebar mirror is free from vibration-blur and was a boon. The speedometer, which had been regeared to remove optimism, was accurate. There are 16 attachment points for elastics on the luggage equipment.

To sum up. Here is a 1945-designed, 1951-built machine that has been modified for a particular purpose. The success of those modifications in dealing with certain known Vincent shortcomings provokes, inevitably, thoughts of the mount which Stevenage might have been producing today —and points sadly to the gap left in the British production pattern by the death of the big twin.

TERRY'S BIG 'ED

A London dealer valued this machine at over £600

Not every Special is built specifically to take part in competitions. There are a number of very interesting road models circulating the country. One of the most interesting of these is Terry Hart's fabulous Vincent, " Big 'Ed."

Originally a 1951 Series "C" Rapide, the glittering Vincent of ex-regular Army Sergeant Terry Hart, must be one of the most eye-catching machines in the country, if not the whole world. It is now so much of a Special, that it is almost impossible to discern where the original finishes and the beautiful modifications of this skilled engineer/owner begin.

Save for the petrol tank, it is virtually a chromium-plated motorcycle. Terry's wife says jokingly that he'd have the tyres and petrol chromed if it were possible! Emphasis has been on rider comfort and economy rather than performance during the years of tailoring. He has fitted a pair of high compression pistons, but that has been his only bid for more speed.

Rear-end Alteration

One of the biggest structural alterations has been to the rear end. By adding a special "D" bracket the dualseat has been converted to a fully floating variety. That is to say that the suspension travel all takes place beneath the rear end of the saddle and that part of the machine no longer jumps up and down. Apparently this has made quite a difference to comfort, particularly on a long run.

Probably the most non-standard part of this unique machine are the electrics. All the circuits, save the horns, go through one fuse so that the balance of current can be checked at any time from the ammeter. The master fuse, from a Post Office telephone, is strategically placed so that should any electrical trouble arise, it can be nipped in the bud immediately.

All cables are fed inside the frame tubing, handlebars etc., and when Terry told me that it took him eight hours to feed the rear-light cable alone, it emphasised the vast amount of hours he must have spent on his favourite hobby. Two of the most interesting electrical modifications are the fitting of a front brake stop-light and an anti-thief magneto cut-out. The front-brake stop-light is combined with a battery charger and wander-light plug, and the whole lot is in one neat cluster just inboard of the front brake lever which works the switch.

At the front end the plain glass headlight (Terry feels that the beam is thrown further that way) is, like the saddle, fully floating and independent of the front fork movement. A twin cable front brake has also been made up.

Latest Addition

One of the latest additions has been the fitting of a cluster of breathers. These include the standard mechanical breather, three more from the rockers, two from the primary chain case, and another one which constitutes a gearbox selector cover drain.

Although everything looks very expensive, Terry, with the ingenuity of a true craftsman, is not averse to using " available " material ! There are grease catchers in the front and rear hubs which have been made up from Nescafé tins, and the induction reservoir for the Trico horn is a brazed-up Woolworth's oil can—chromed of course.

Although Terry likes nothing better than to shut himself in his well-equipped workshop, the Vincent is far from being just a showpiece. He is in the saddle whenever possible and enjoying 1,000 cc motor cycling for the price of a 350 cc. By changing the rear wheel sprocket, by fitting a 4.00 rear tyre instead of the standard 350, and by being gentle with his throttle hand he has got as much as 85 m.p.g. on a long run. ●

Riders' view of the Vincent front— surprisingly the extra weight does not affect handling at any speeds

Not a racing frontal area but one that certainly causes some eyebrow raising and the occasional gasp

Just in front of the rear wheel can be seen this array of breather pipes fitted on to an aluminium plate

The chrome reservoir for the horn was at one time an old oil can—now it gleams alongside the rear pot

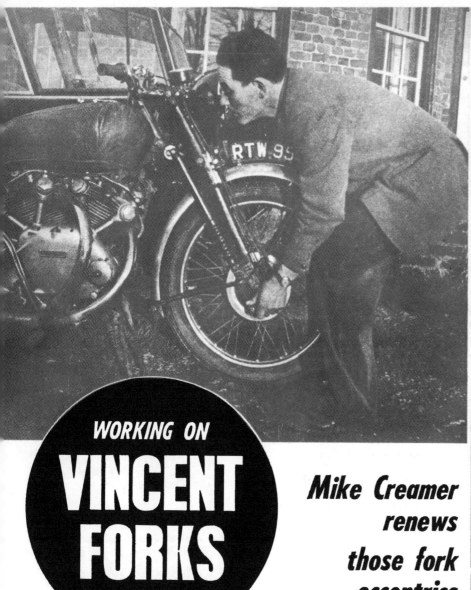

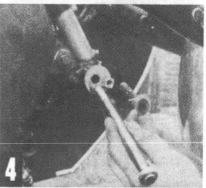

WORKING ON VINCENT FORKS

Mike Creamer renews those fork eccentrics

THERE is nothing quite like the Vincent front forks. A cross between the old girders and modern teles, some people say that they combine the best of each. Other people say they combine the worst of both.

But whatever your feelings, if you have a Vincent you will have to put up with these forks. And make no mistake about it, they are superb for road-holding and stability—provided they are in good condition.

A frequent cause of poor steering are worn eccentrics. Check them by placing the machine on the front stands, and rocking the lower part of the forks back and forth (as in the heading picture). If there is any wear in the eccentrics you will notice it at once.

Start by removing the front fork spring boxes and the front damper. Remove the locknuts on the bottom spindle, slacken off the pinch bolts and drive the spindle out with a suitable drift (picture 1). It is important not to forget the pinch

bolts, else the spindle will be damaged. The forks can now be lifted forward clear of the wishbone and placed on a box (picture 2).

Undo the nut on the front fork eccentric spindle and drift out.

When new eccentrics are fitted it is essential to fit new bushes as well. Sometimes the eccentric flange will lock solid on the bush. In this case fit a suitable shim. These are available from .002 to .010. Note the shim on picture 3.

When replacing the bottom link great care must be taken to line up the eccentrics, shims, thrust washer and trail stop. When replacing the spindle you should use a bullet, otherwise the shims will be damaged. The bullet is made from a piece of 9/16 round bar tapered at one end and tapped out to 7/16 BSF the other end (picture 4).

To replace the spring boxes first replace the lower bolt, then loop one end of a piece of rope round the spring box as shown (picture 5). Take two turns of the other end round the brake cam boss. Pull the spring box into the vertical position, when you should be able to replace the top bolt quite easily. ●

HOW TO RENEW SHOCK ABSORBER SPRINGS

DON McLEAN describes this work on a 1,000 c.c. Vincent

It takes two clutches to tame this 55 b.h.p. monster! And all 1,000 Vincents also have a unique shock absorber unit mounted on the end of the crankshaft.

A triplex chain is used for the primary drive, giving some idea of the loads on the transmission. All parts must be extremely strong with a high resistance to fatigue.

This shock absorber unit is fitted in order to reduce the risk of damage, due to transmission snatch. It also provides the driver with a more comfortable ride.

Servicing this unit and the primary drive chain is easy. Firstly remove the clutch cover. Put the machine in gear to prevent the clutch pressure plate turning when you undo the screws. Then take out the clutch plates and the secondary clutch and centre. Take off the clutch drum and the primary chain case can be removed.

Check the condition of the chain tensioner blade. It should have four grooves in it when properly " run in," so don't scrap it because of this. However, it must be replaced if a new chain is to be fitted. The chain cannot be removed without damage unless the engine and clutch sprockets are withdrawn at the same time.

Release the shock absorber nut and take off the ring plate, springs, cam, cam sleeve, and engine sprocket sleeve. The complete primary drive can now be removed for cleaning.

Reassembly is in the reverse order, but there are two tips which can help you. When replacing the ring plate on Series C machines, put the smooth side facing the springs. This will prolong the life of the springs. When fitting this plate it is easier if the sleeve is pulled out about a ¼ inch. The splines can then be lined up more easily. Then put the primary chain case back and refill with oil. Replace the clutches and cover and that's it.

The shock absorber springs will last 10,000 miles of hard driving and at only 10s. the lot, it is just as well to replace them to maintain their efficiency.

1 Remove clutch cover. Then undo nine screws and take off pressure plate. Remove clutch plates, taking care not to lose the spring behind them

2 Unscrew main clutch centre nut and withdraw the secondary clutch and centre. Undo the six screws holding in the clutch drum and remove it

3 Drain oil and remove primary chain case. Check condition of the chain tensioner blade. It is essential to replace it if new chain is fitted

4 Release the shock absorber nut— first gear will have to be engaged to do this. Remove the ring plate and the 36 shock absorber springs

5 The shock absorber cam may now be taken off the cam sleeve. Always make sure that sliding parts are clean and greased on reassembly

6 Now the shock absorber cam sleeve can be withdrawn from its splines on the end of the crankshaft. Again these must be clean on reassembly

7 The engine sprocket sleeve should be right inside the sprocket. Make sure that it goes back there. Face of cam must be smooth and greased

8 Check for wear by trying to pull the chain away from the sprocket. Engine sprocket, clutch sprocket and chain must all be removed together

An immaculately maintained example of the 1955 Vincent Black Lightning factory built racing model, owned by Bill Cottom of San Pedro, California. The 50 degree, V-twin, displaced 1000cc (61 cubic inches), employed huge dual Amal carburetors, wide angle large valve heads, and was rated at 75 horsepower! Polished parts were standard; these machines were hand assembled and sold for over $1,500. A similar model achieved 160 mph at Bonneville, proving the claim to the World's fastest motorcycle. (Photos by Leon Callaway).

The Fabulous VINCENT

The beginning, reign and decline of one of the most fantastic eras of motor-cycling from which came some most remarkable machines, and an incredible heritage.

BY VAUGHN GREENE

The popular series "D" Vincent Rapide.

IN APRIL 1917 a young British flying officer was shot down and captured by the Germans. To while away the monotonous hours of his captivity, the young flier dreamed of building the perfect motorcycle. This was Howard Davies and after the war he started building the motorcycle he'd dreamed about, the HRD. It was a hairy, temperamental machine with a powerful fascination but, ironically, the HRD name never became widely known until it was added to another great name, the Vincent.

Davies' background for building an outstanding motorcycle was good. As a boy he had been apprenticed to the AJS factory and at 17 became a tester for the Sunbeam factory. A year later he entered the Isle of Man TT and his Sunbeam tied for 2nd with an Indian ridden by O. C. Godfrey. Then came the Kaiser war and after a stint as a motorcycle dispatch rider he joined the Royal Flying Corps. After the armistice Davies worked for a carburetor firm, then in 1920 became competition manager for AJS. In 1921 he won the Senior (500cc) Isle of Man TT on a 350cc AJS, a feat that has not been duplicated since. He would also have won the Junior (250cc) TT had not a flat tire put him back to 2nd place.

In 1924 Davies and an ex-motorcycle manufacturer, Massey, teamed up to build the HRD. After being shown at the Olympia display late that year, the new marque set the motorcycle fraternity on its ear by winning the Senior TT in 1925 with a 4½ mph gain over the course record. Never has a new machine gained fame so quickly. Much of the credit must go to Davies' advanced ideas on frame design but credit must also be given to his taste in components—JAP engines, Webb forks, Burman gearboxes, and so on.

The tiny company gained a secure reputation and came into the limelight again by winning the 350cc Isle of Mann TT in 1927 ridden by the famous engineer Freddy Dixon.

The next year, 1928, young Philip C. Vincent became attracted to the HRD company. After a bit of haggling, Vincent bought out the old firm and it was re-named "Vincent HRD Co., Ltd." Howard Davies left motorcycle manufacturing at this time to start another company which he still controls today.

Phil Vincent, with an engineer's degree from Cambridge, designed a fully sprung rear frame for the HRD and thus arose the Vincent company's unique claim that they were the only motorcycle company never to produce a rigid-frame motorcycle. There had been previous attempts at sprung frame machines (Matchless, ABC, Raleigh, to name but three) but it was left to Vincent HRD to produce a few prototypes, display their ability at races and scrambles, and demonstrate the superiority of their rear springing system.

In 1930 Vincent HRD displayed their machines at the annual London Motorcycle Show for the first time. They attracted great interest because they abounded in features almost unknown in those days; 4-speed foot-change gearboxes, prop stands and all-welded triangular sprung frames. All the machines displayed used 500cc JAP engines with the exception of a grass tracker with a 350cc JAP.

After further improvements, including replacement of the triangle type frame with the diamond style, the Vincent HRD continued to attract favorable attention. It was at the 1934 London Motorcycle Show that the company really blossomed out. Seven different models were displayed including 500 and 600cc JAP models, the famous "W" model with 250cc water-cooled Villiers engine, plus four 500cc models equipped with engines built by Vincent HRD.

The model W was 20 years ahead of its time with its inaudible water-cooled engine, battery-operated parking light, 4-speed Albion foot-change gearbox, aluminum

The 1952 single 500cc cylinder Vincent Grey Flash was in effect one half of a Black Lightning. The model shown here, owned by Sydney Dickson of Eastom, Maryland, has been altered somewhat from the original. For one thing, the seat is off of a Honda, and several other lesser items. 135 miles per hour was claimed for this 35 hp machine which was designed for racing. (Photos by Neil Winstone).

The 1000 cubic centimeter, V-twin, overhead valve Vincent engine, cut away for display purposes.

head, stainless steel radiator, fully enclosed engine and inconspicuous legshields. The result was weather protection for the rider and a motorcycle that could be ridden in any weather with only the tips of his shoes getting soiled.

Though several unusual machines were introduced, including a sidecar version with a radio transmitter, it was the brand new Vincent engine that attracted the most attention. This engine, so sound was the engineering involved, retained many of the same features until the last Vincent was produced in 1955. In fact, many of the parts in the first and last Vincent engines (valves, pistons, rods, chains, etc.) are interchangeable.

The chief designer, whose accomplishments were later to become legendary, was none other than P. E. Irving, author of *Motorcycle Engineering* and *Tuning for Speed,* two standard reference works in the motorcycle world.

This Series "A" Vincent engine is worth examining in detail. With a bore and stroke of 84 x 90mm (3.207 x 3.543 in.) the only difference in the original series and later engines was that the "A" had a 5-stud head while the later series used four through-bolts secured deeply in the massive alloy crankcase. Unusual features of the "A" included the quickly-detachable driveside main bearing, engine sprocket, magneto and oil pump. Twin valve guides were used to obtain cooler springs and the Series "A" used hairpin springs exposed directly to the air. A high camshaft wide-angle pushrod valve train was used, quite advanced for its day, and the rockers were forked to catch the valves. The rocker arm bearings were quickly detachable and the entire assembly could be pulled out by removing one bolt. This feature was retained on all later series, as was the 4-bearing lower end. A Burman gearbox was used and was interchangeable with postwar models.

Innovation did not stop with the engine. There were twin drum brakes (one on each side of the hub), the wheels were quickly detachable and, since the rear wheel had two drums, two sprockets could be carried. Thus, by reversing the wheel, the gearing could be altered in a minute. There was also lavish use of stainless steel in the new Vincent HRD; axles, brake rods, thumb nuts, motion blocks, gas tank, etc. A dream machine indeed.

The next year engines by other manufacturers were dropped with the exception of 20 special-order Model "W's" with the 250cc water-cooled Villiers. Through 1939 the Vincents remained essentially the same except for minor detail improvements. These models were the "Meteor" (25 hp, 75-80 mph, black and gold), "Comet" (26 hp, 85-90 mph, maroon and stainless steel tank), "Comet Special" (detuned racing engine in standard frame, 28 hp, 100 mph), and "Comet TT Replica" (bronze head, 34 hp, 110 mph).

In the 1935 Isle of Man Senior TT, Vincent HRDs took 7th, 9th, 11th, 12th and 13th places. Not bad for a standard touring machine that cost $800. In 1936, Jock West came in 8th, in spite of breaking a primary at the last minute. Zoller type superchargers were experimented with that year but there was too little time to work

the bugs out.

The fabulous Vincent "Rapide" was first shown in October 1936. As a 61-cu. in. V-twin with 45 hp, a conservative 115 mph and weighing 400 lbs., it had nothing in the way of competition. The cylinder angle was 47 degrees and many of the parts were identical with the Vincent single. Weakness later corrected included the 4-speed Burman gearbox that wasn't up to holding the power fed into it and pushrods that wore very rapidly. The Rapide sold for $420 and another of the interesting features was the Smith's 8-day clock to match the 120 mph speedometer.

In 1937 Phil Irving returned to the Velocette factory, not to return to Vincent until the war when he became chief engineer to develop a special engine for airborne lifeboats.

In 1939, just before the war, Vincent announced a new series, the "B" range. Though only one "B" Comet TT Replica was built, it was a most interesting machine since the frame seemed to have disappeared. The front and rear forks bolted to the oil tank which was hidden by the encompassing gas tank. The engine was suspended from the oil tank member and appeared to be hanging in mid-air.

Like other manufacturers, Vincent HRD was engaged in war work during WW II. Because the plant was small it attracted little attention from enemy bombers and consequently, in April 1945, was the first English motorcycle manufacturer to announce a postwar machine. There was a tremendous response (some who ordered in 1945 had to wait two years for delivery) and the factory therefore decided to concentrate its production on Rapides.

The average motorcycle offered for sale in 1946-47 could only be described as miserable in both design and construction. Thus the Rapides became even more highly prized. Nor did the Vincent name go unnoticed in the U.S. Eugene Aucott, Philadelphia, became the first American Vincent dealer. Soon, Vincent H. Martin, Burbank, Calif., was also importing Vincents and the rush was on.

America had always been V-twin country and the odd-looking, ugly Vincent with its skinny tires and girder forks was immediately compared with the Harley-Davidson — thus creating a controversy that still goes on to this day.

The Vincent Series "B" Rapide which so startled the post-war world had a high-cam 50-degree V-twin all-alloy OHV engine with 4-speed unitized synchromesh gearbox. Aluminum alloys were used extensively; crankcase, cylinders, barrels, heads, hubs, shock absorbers, brake adjusters and so on. Unlike American practice, the Vincent used two male connecting rods which not only afforded interchangeability but also gave better cooling through the necessary 1¼-in. offset of the cylinders. The liners were deeply spigoted into the crankcase, held in place by long bolts through the heads and attached to the head brackets. These in turn fastened directly to the box section oil tank and the effect was such a strong, vibrationless structure that no other support was needed for the engine.

The lower end assembly was massive. Three roller and one ball bearing support-

1955 Vincent fully enclosed Black Prin...

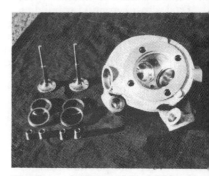

The Burns & Wright "big port" head, a... American innovation.

A beautiful series "A" HRD Rapid...

Many Vincents have been seen in com... petition, this at the Isle Of Man durin... a 1000cc Clubman race.

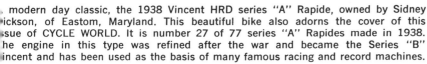

modern day classic, the 1938 Vincent HRD series "A" Rapide, owned by Sidney Dickson, of Eastom, Maryland. This beautiful bike also adorns the cover of this issue of CYCLE WORLD. It is number 27 of 77 series "A" Rapides made in 1938. The engine in this type was refined after the war and became the Series "B" Vincent and has been used as the basis of many famous racing and record machines.

the mainshaft and the nickel chrome steel rods ran on a casehardened crankpin and each was supported by three rows of uncaged roller bearings. The result was phenomenal bearing life. One Vincent, the famous "Rumplecrankshaft" of Tony Rose, was given a 100,000-mile road test without any apparent wear on the bearings and that same machine is still running with over a quarter-million miles on the clock.

The timing-side mainshaft drove the rotary plunger oil pump. The drive-side mainshaft was splined to accept an engine shock absorber. The materials throughout were the best available; the timing gear was aluminum, the pushrods silver steel, the pushrod tubes stainless steel, alloy rocker bearings, valve seats of aluminum bronze and austinitic cast iron, valves of DTD 49B steel and Silchrome steel, and so on.

In the gearbox there was a beefy set of internals designed to transmit up to 200 bhp and all shafts were supported by ball bearings. A weakness, if it can be called that under such conditions of abuse, showed up in America where lead-footed types stomped a too-weak cam plate bevel to death and this was replaced by a foolproof design in 1953. This bevel had more to do with losing sales for Vincent than any other factor since its replacement demanded that the entire engine be dismantled, which entailed removing the front and rear forks, exhaust pipes, magneto and generator, gas and oil tanks, and so on. Not that the riders lost interest. It was the dealers who rebelled, some stating that they were willing to sell Vincents but not to work on them or honor their guarantee.

Through this gearbox "weakness," another undeserved Vincent legend began. The actual fact is that the Vincent is a wonderfully easy machine to work on and, given anywhere near normal care, malfunctions are very rare. The clutch is an ideal case in point. Phil Vincent wanted that ideal, a dry plate clutch in a wetsump chain case. To achieve this, synthetic rubber seals were used. These seals wore in time, resulting in a slipping clutch as oil leaked in, but three-quarters of the trouble came from owners needlessly messing around with the clutch and gearbox housings. But who could blame them when that clutch-gearbox complex is so easy to dismantle?

The clutch, incidentally, consists of two clutches; a 2-shoe servo clutch and a single-plate clutch disc, and this results in an unusually light clutch lever action for such a powerful machine.

The Rapide framework also had many interesting features. All four brakes could be adjusted by hand from the saddle, both wheels could be removed without tools in less than a minute, the rear chain could be adjusted in a minute, the left and right prop stands could be swung down to make a front stand, and the oil tank contained a check valve so the oil would not run out if the lines were disconnected, very handy for overhauls. An experienced mechanic could completely dismantle a Vincent in an hour, including the lower end.

Other nice touches included hand-operated fittings to disconnect the wiring, raise the rear fender flap, and lower the rear stand. The battery could also be quickly removed by loosening a handwheel. It was also the first British machine to have dual "buddy" seats and there was a sliding tool tray under the saddle.

The rear brakes used a combination cable and rod system but the front, cable-operated brakes seem, at first glance, incapable of working. A single cable runs to a balance beam mounted on the front fork so when the handlebar lever is pulled exactly the same pressure is applied to each brake, thus equalizing any torque and greatly lessening the chance of a skid.

Other features include screen filters in the oil and gas lines and the famous short Vincent handlebars of 25-inches width. All handlebar levers, the handlebar itself, the saddle, footrests and foot levers are individually adjustable.

A year after the introduction of the Rapide, the famous "Black Shadow" was first shown. Costing $200 more, it had a claimed cruising speed of 100 mph and a top of 125 mph. It had polished rods and rockers and lightened gearchange components, finned cast iron brakes instead of the pressed steel variety and a very gory-looking 150 mph 5-inch Smith's speedometer. The only concessions to speed were carburetors 1/16th of an inch larger and a slightly higher compression ratio. The entire engine was painted in black enamel to assist in heat dissipation.

Upon the heels of the Black Shadow came the "Lightning," the fastest racing motorcycle sold to the public. This sold for $1,500, had 70 hp and was rated at 150 mph. The Lightning was a stripped-down Shadow with aluminum wheel rims, magnesium brake plates, twin straight pipes, twin racing carbs, the compression ratio was to order and all stressed parts were polished and streamlined. Lightnings were

Vincent Rapide, circa 1950.

put together by hand in a small shop and each was gently ridden for 100 miles on a test track and individually timed.

One of the first "B" Lightnings was owned by John Edgar, Los Angeles, and in 1948 veteran rider Rollie Free set a record of 160 mph with it at Bonneville. This was to start a round of record breaking at the Utah Salt Flats that still continues.

At the 1949 Earl's Court Show in London, the "C" range was introduced. These were essentially the same as the "B" except for a new front fork called the "Girdraulic." This was a combination of girder and telescopic fork with aluminum alloy blades made by Bristol Aircraft Co. It featured a hydraulic damper and self-lubricating bronze bushes and is the strongest motorcycle fork ever made.

Also in 1949, the single-cylinder models were reintroduced; the Meteor, the Comet and the Grey Flash. The Meteor was a cheaper version of the $900 Comet and the Grey Flash was a racing model with 135 mph on 35 hp. A small number of speedway engines were also made. These were similar to the Grey Flash but with total loss oil systems and magnesium crankcases.

Speaking of speedway racing, Vincents dominated the tracks in Australia, where that sport is very popular. Vincents competed against Harleys, Indians, Excelsiors, double-engined Triumphs, JAPs and came off with the honors. In 1949, at Victoria, Tony McAlpine won every race he entered with his Shadow sidecar special.

Phil Vincent had assured John Edgar, owner of the "B" Lightning that had gone 160 mph, that the record should stand for 10 years. Only two years later, however, the same Rollie Free who had ridden for Edgar bought a "C" Black Lightning (as the "C" racers were known) and went 156 mph. In 1953, Joe Simpson, Stockton, Calif., upset the applecart with his "C" racer, one of the first sold in this country, and went 160 mph at Bonneville. Phil Irving was sufficiently impressed to ask Joe how he did it. As Joe put it, back in those days the British thought they were doing you a big favor by offering anything larger than a one-inch carburetor so, calling on his hot rod experience, he used bigger carbs, installed larger valves and so on. It was from Simpson's experience that the factory developed the famous "Big Port" heads with carbs up to 1 9/16th-inch diameter.

Long before this, in 1948, the Vincent Owners Club* was started in England by Allan Jackson. It was, and still is, one of the most highly regarded clubs in England. The VOC has produced several reporters

and an editor for the English motorcycle magazines and one woman member, Margaret Ward, is now secretary of BEMSEE. Rab Cook, a staff member of *Motorcycling* and former editor of *MPH,* the monthly VOC magazine, was one of the first to advise wearing crash helmets. The VOC started the custom of wearing helmets which soon spread throughout the world.

After the "C" series Vincent was introduced in 1950, they remained almost unchanged until the "D" appeared in 1954. The company's policy was to include improvements as soon as they were developed rather than indulge in the razzle-dazzle "brand new model" stuff every year, so the new "D" promised to be something special. And it was. It was the first standard motorcycle to offer complete streamlining in the form of a fiberglass shell. The motive was not increased speed or better fuel consumption, though these were improved, but to give complete weather protection to the rider. The fiberglass panels were quickly detachable by Dzus fasteners and the rear shell pivoted upwards to give access to the rear wheel. This rear shell also held the oil tank and there was a spacious tool box beneath the hinged saddle.

In these new models, the "Black Prince," "Black Knight" and "Victor" corresponded to the Black Shadow, Rapide and Comet models. The Series "D" Black Shadow and Rapide were naked models, without the streamlining, and were basically the same as the "C" version except for detail improvements. Coil ignition replaced the magneto, a center stand was introduced which was operated by a hand lever, larger tires and a fully-sprung saddle made for a much more comfortable ride.

Phil Irving was chief designer for these remarkable machines and the Vincent company was also building several types of small marine, agricultural and dairy machines. There was a cute little water scooter, a fuel-injected engine based on the Lightning for target drone aircraft, an unusual 3-wheel fiberglass car with standard Rapide engine and the firm also produced a very reliable little moped known as the "Firefly" which could run three miles on a penny's worth of gas. The name of the company was now "Vincent Engineers, Ltd.," the "Vincent HRD Co., Ltd.," having been changed in 1952.

It was against this background that New Zealanders Burns and Wright, using the "Big Port" heads, made their historic runs in February 1955 when Wright set a new world's record at 174 mph and Burns established a new world's sidecar mark at

162 mph. The next year Wright wen 185.15 mph (not a record, but a 1-wa run of 198 mph was achieved) and Burn upped the sidecar mark to 176.42.

It was indeed a shock then when Phili Vincent announced in the summer of 195 that he would no longer manufactur motorcycles. For several years it ha proven unprofitable; the big hairy machin was a thing of the past, felled by th 250cc motorbike. Knowledgeable rider flocked to put in last minute orders fo the Vincents remaining. When the last c the 100 "D" Rapides was sold a total c 13,000 machines had left the factory.

The postwar history of the Vincer might be compared to a skyrocket. A first it was unknown, then it started t gain fame and rose in a rush. There wa a time when it ruled over all, but the in evitable slump came, the descent, an then, the end. There were many reason for this. Although the pre-war compan supported works race teams, the late company concentrated on touring ma chines. The Vincents were also the mos expensive motorcycles in the world at th time. Racing sells motorcycles and, natu rally, the riders chose to buy cheaper ma chinery. Therefore, though the single were as powerful as any OHV machine ever built, they were never too popula The twins, though capable of tremendou power, suffered from heavy weight as con pared to, say, a Manx Norton.

Although no longer manufacturing mo torcycles, Phil Vincent promised that a long as a Vincent was still on the roa spare parts would be made. This is sti true and it is easier to get parts for Vir cents than many 1962 motorcycles. Th Vincent company's troubles continue however, finally going into receiversh and was eventually bought by the Harpe group of companies. After various trouble Harper Engines, Ltd., is enthusiastical doing repairs and making spares.

Will Vincents ever be made agair Most doubtful. Phil Vincent once said h would build 50 new engines only at $80 each. There was also a shop in Englan that was making "new" Vincents fro spares and another fitted Vincent engin into Manx frames.

No, the gallant old V-twin is forgotte Or is it? Clem Johnson recently turne 149 mph in the standing quarter on a Vi cent. Dave Matson was building a engine Vincent to run at Bonneville befo he was drafted. Joe Simpson owns th world's most powerful motorcycle, a 1 hp fuel-injected supercharged Black Ligh ning. George Brown recently set a ne world's record for the standing kilomet on his famous "Nero." Simpson, and handful of others, intend to capture th world's speed record soon.

The Vincent is fading away, having bee out of production for more than sev years, but not nearly so fast as its con petitors would like. Most often, the "fa ing away" is that of a black-engined m torcycle showing its license plate to lesser machine. ●

*For information about joining the Vi cent Owners Club, write Vaughn N Greene, P.O. Box 7724, Rincon Anne San Francisco, Calif.

WHAT do you do, when you live in a terrace-type house, haven't a proper workshop, yet want to build yourself a snorter of a road-racing outfit? If you're like Bob Taylor, a Birmingham welder, you clear the furniture out of the front room and build it there.

But it takes time, when you are on overtime working. So Bob's 998 c.c. Vincent kneeler represents some 15 months of weekend toil, and of nights when the activity in the parlour went on into the small hours of the next morning. And when it was done, there was the problem of getting it out into the street.

That meant removing the front door from its hinges, dismantling parts of the outfit and sliding it through the opening tipped up on end. Ted Young built the frame, integral sidecar chassis and front fork, based on the design of his own E.T.Y.-Vincent. But the real interest lies in the engine, which began life as a 1951 Rapide unit. All that remains of the original are the crankcase castings (and Bob Taylor spent six weeks on buffing each half inside and out), one cylinder head, and the outer shells of the two barrels.

For the rest, there is now an oversize, high-tensile steel mainshaft carrying Alpha, caged-roller big-end bearings for each of the connecting rods, and hand-finished and matched Hoffman main bearings. The rods themselves are Black Lightning, polished, and balanced so that they are identical in weight. The cylinder barrels were shortened to give a compression ratio of 10½ to 1, and thick-wall liners were shrunk into the original shells.

Cams, too, are of Black Lightning origin, and the cam followers are tipped with Stellite pads for long life and ground so that the theoretical valve timing is smack on for each cylinder. ("And as Vincent owners will know," comments Bob, "to achieve that is something like winning the football pools!")

Carburettors are $1\frac{9}{32}$in-bore

Parlour-built Racer

GP Amals, fed by home-built, weir-type chambers; the S.U. pump is mounted in the sidecar nose and the fuel supply is drawn from a tank on the platform rear. Exhaust pipes are genuine works jobs, of no less than 2in diameter.

The Vincent's wheels are 16 in. diameter (the front is spoked to a B.S.A. Gold Star hub, with 190mm-diameter brake and fully-floating shoe plate) while a 12in-diameter wheel is used on the sidecar. Total cost? Bob purses his lips and hazards a guess of £530 minimum.

It hasn't yet appeared on a race circuit. Nor will it with Bob Taylor at the helm, for within a fortnight he will be emigrating to Canada.

The household goods are already packed, but the outfit must be left behind. That's a heart-breaking decision for anyone to make, but family needs, of course, come first.

But at least Bob has had a chance to hear the song of the Vincent. It was a Sunday morning, with the usual suburban street scene of householders busily grooming their cars, when Bob wheeled the Vincent out of the shed which is now its home, gave a hefty push then dropped the clutch.

The bellow which resulted, he chuckles, brought immediate chaos to that street scene—with upset water buckets and flying chamois leathers everywhere. But all the neighbours enjoyed it!

Bob Taylor tries his home-brewed 998 c.c. Vincent kneeler outfit for size. Above: Originally a 1951 Rapide unit, the engine has been extensively rebuilt

by DAVID DIXON

continental EXPRESS

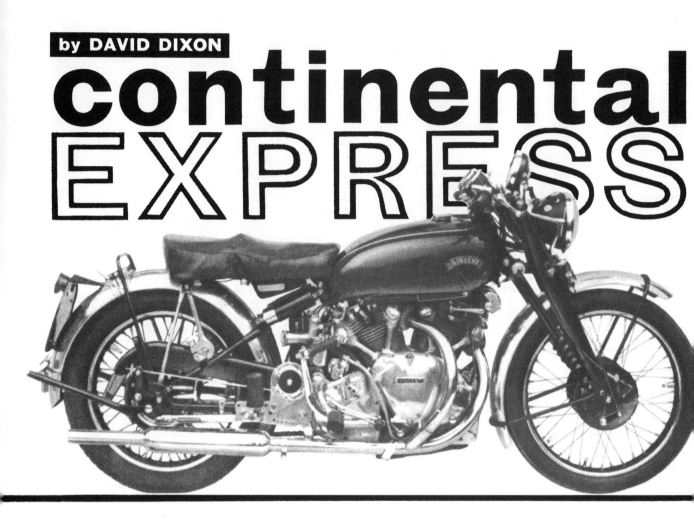

WHY, of all machines, embellish a Vincent? "Simple, really. You begin with a basically fine machine intended for the true enthusiast. That's a pretty good start. I have merely done what Phil Vincent would have liked to do, had he not been handicapped by commercial considerations." That's how 39-year-old school teacher, Edward Stevens, explains his masterpiece, a superbly prepared 1950 Vincent Series C White Shadow.

One can hardly call this Vincent customized because, as he says, it remains almost standard in appearance "as a true Vincent should be." Sounds like a one-make fanatic? A perfectionist, certainly, because the motivation for this painstaking, 200-plus hours' labour of love was inspired by practical, rather than aesthetic, thoughts.

You see, Edward Stevens is of Anglo-French stock. Reared in France, he fled to this country in 1940 and joined the RAF. And although he married and settled down here after the war, many of his friends and relatives are scattered throughout France. So he spends a couple of months in the summer, during school holidays, touring there and in other continental countries.

Now what machine is better for the long, straight French roads than the supremely effortless gait of a 998 cc Vincent vee-twin? But Stevens wanted to make the model even more suitable.

Priority was given to preserving the finish, as with Vincents out of production, there would be no chance of getting a new one at a later date. He went all stainless-steelminded. Costly, true, but the chromium-plated parts which required regular attention to avoid deterioration, were to be replaced by stainless items.

Although stainless nuts and bolts were easy to get. in the absence of a mechanical buff, they all had to be polished, by hand, on the kitchen table.

Fair enough, but what about those many bright items which make Vincents a delight to the enthusiast's eye? To have had these copied in stainless would have meant the sort of ransom money no one has.

So teacher Stevens set about learning how to use a lathe. Pretty effectively, too, because over the past seven years or so he has made more than 200 parts!

LATHE WORK

You doubt that there are 200 bits he could copy? Well, five and a half meticulously detailed pages of a copy book account for 107 standard items, from brake-anchor pins to carburettor ticklers and steering damper plates.

Of course, some pieces—such as exhaust pipes and silencer—are obtainable in stainless steel

Left: Functional and practical, the Vincent *looks* standard; closer examination reveals scores of alterations, result of 200 hours' labour. Right: Edward Stevens goes for a canter

Visible alterations here include the windtone-horn compressor beneath the steering head, longer carburettor venturi, air scoop for the clutch, light-alloy rear brake pedal, domed engine nuts and quick-release battery

model for continental travel. In 1954, Stevens started to alter the specification to his own taste. Compression ratio was raised to 8 to 1—a shade high, he now admits, for some continental petrol grades.

Beautifully oil tight, the engine now uses Royal Enfield Bullet decompressors instead of the standard exhaust-valve lifters which could never be kept oil tight.

BOSCH COIL

The magneto was discarded because of spares scarcity on the Continent and Bosch coil ignition substituted; the battery was taken care of by a 60-watt Lucas dynamo.

That brings us to lights. For his needs, Stevens found the original Miller lamp inadequate. First he replaced it with a French Marchal unit. Now he is using a Cibié with a 45/40-watt main bulb.

A vital piece of equipment for high speeds on French roads, where huge lorries abound, is a penetrating horn. Stevens goes one better—he has two. One is for the passenger's benefit, a genteel English tooter

to Vincent owners through their club. But they are pricey—a silencer costs about £9.

A further two pages of the log demonstrate originality in the form of stainless brackets, clips and distance pieces. And not just fiddly bits, for the complete safety-bar assembly is also home made.

Enthusiasm at the lathe stretched to turning replacement spacers, certain nuts and push-rod tubes in light alloy.

Hours were spent on such things as cutting out and finishing light-alloy engine plates and the rear-brake torque arm. Risk of corrosion? Well, when I saw the model all the alloy parts were burnished fit to dazzle. They looked as if they had just been made, although they had been in use for years.

Remember the underlying objective—to make a better

which few can take exception to.

A "rabble rouser" is what Stevens calls his Italian Boss wind-tone twin horns. Driven by a Marchal compressor, they made me leap a yard in the air when demonstrated!

WHITE

Puzzled by the *White Shadow*? **So was I, until Stevens explained that the model started life as a Rapide but was now virtually to Black Shadow-cum-Lightning specification. But as, externally, the engine remained unpainted—the production Shadow and Lightning units were black—he opted for White Shadow.**

Obvious Lightning parts include the dual front brakes, revmeter, sprung pillion-rest assembly. Not visible are the Lightning clutch drum, friction disc and plate carrier, and some minor engine items. Made for Vincent Club members is a cast clutch cover with air scoops.

Slightly improved fuel consumption is claimed for the spun-aluminium carburettor venturis; petrol consumption abroad is approximately 45 mpg.

What staggered me was the incredible attention to detail. Here are just a few examples. The engine breather is led rearward to meet the breather from the rear inlet valve cover. Both flexible pipes join stainless steel pipes which take excess oil well clear of the wheel.

Then there are the stainless-steel (of course!) tabs from the battery terminals. The end of

each tab forms a connection with an accessible screwed knob. These, in conjunction with a special light-alloy carrier with quick-release strap, make battery maintenance only a minor chore.

Bracing the balance beam of the front brakes is an alloy outrigger plate which eliminates any suggestion of flexing when the anchors are clapped on really hard.

View from the saddle takes in quite an eyeful. The vast speedometer is calibrated in kph; alongside is the revmeter and on the other side is an eight-day clock.

Also on view is a thermometer (centigrade) for atmosphere temperatures. It was

David Dixon getting the gen. Edward Stevens frequently takes his bike to school to give his pupils a treat!

Rear-end details include stainless-steel breather outlets and chain-guard extension, and light-alloy brake torque arm

Impressive handlebar group, showing clock, speedometer (kph) thermometer, and revmeter. Three buttons on left are for horns and flasher

showing one degree above freezing when I saw it!

Extremely useful is a headlamp flasher operated by a button on the left. Headlamp dipping is by a Britax twistgrip on the left and, on the headlamp itself, is a tumbler switch for speedometer and ammeter illumination.

Amal light-alloy clutch and brake racing levers are used—without adjusters as finger adjusters are standard Vincent practice. In case anyone should try to pinch the model, a Britax locking twistgrip is used.

A *concours* Vincent? Yes, surely, but a well-used one. Total mileage is now 110,000—on one replacement big-end since 1954!—and 90,000 has been logged since the high-kick pistons were fitted. Oil is changed every 1,300 miles; SAE 40 or 50 is used in summer, 30 in winter.

Cruising around the 80 mph mark wears down rear tyres in about 6,000 miles and rear chains in 4,000. Then they reappear on Edward's hack 1951 Comet.

If you ask Edward Stevens how much his super Vincent cost him, he just smiles—or was that a shudder? Certainly, the stainless steel *alone* **worked out at about £70! Still, you cannot evaluate such a dream bike in vulgar £sd.**

BY VAUGHN GREENE

THE BLACK PRINCE

PHOTOS BY B. R. NICHOLLS

wo views showing a 1955 Series D Black
Prince with engine painted stove black
s on Black Shadow series Vincents.
orns are not standard equipment.

A GOOD WAY to start an argument where-
ever motorcyclists gather, is merely
to mention the name "Vincent." Instantly
there will be fierce cries of praise or deri-
sion. Some will tell you the Vincent was
the greatest motorcycle ever built. Others,
snorting, will ask what races were ever won
on a Vincent. Then, other riders will point
to many international speed records Vincents still hold, while others tell gory tales
of unreliability . . . and so it goes.

Just how good is a Vincent? This may
come as a considerable shock and surprise to many self-anointed experts, but
it is my belief that there are not over a
dozen people in America qualified to pass
judgment. I base this assertion on the
fact that the last type of Vincent made,
the "D" series, is quite rare in America.
To my knowledge there are but eleven of
these machines in the United States and
Canada. Interestingly enough, three of
them are in Iowa. Probably 5,000 Vincents
were sold in the U.S.A. so there are many
riders who know the machine well. However, the only fair way to appraise the
Vincent potential would be to examine one
of the last type built — a "D."

Before doing so, let us find out just what
is meant by this "Series" business. The

Vincent-H.R.D. Co. began in 1928 when a young Cambridge graduate, Philip Vincent, bought Howard R. Davies's small motorcycle factory. Until 1934 the fledgling firm used various engines, such as Rudge and J.A.P. in its machines. At the 1934 motorcycle show the company introduced their own engine. To celebrate the new design, the machines were called the series "A." These consisted of the Meteor, Comet, and T.T. Comet — all high performance singles. In 1936 the legendary series A Rapide was introduced. This was a 1,000cc V-twin virtually created by mating two Meteor barrels to a common crankcase. With a 110 mph top speed, it sported such luxury touches as a stainless steel gas tank and eight-day clock.

Nonetheless, the Rapide did have various weak points, major of which was the clutch. To cure this, a series "B" was laid down on the drawing board, but war delayed its introduction until 1946. The B Rapide outwardly looked similar to the A. The primary difference was a new crankcase with unitized engine and gearbox. There were many critics of this scheme, as it made work on the engine internals laborious. Nevertheless, it did save considerable weight. The other major change in the B series was an ingenious combination oil tank and upper frame member which did away with the conventional frame. The B consisted of the 110 mph Rapide, the 125 mph Black Shadow, and the 150 mph Black Lightning. The singles were not pro-

THE BLACK PRINCE

duced, due to heavy demand for twins.

At the 1948 Earls Court motorcycle show the Vincent H.R.D. Co. introduced their own answer to the telescopic fork. In honor of this new patented design, the range was called series "C." The "Girdraulic," as the new front fork was named, answered the huge post-war demand for telescopic forks and rear springing. Vincents have always had rear springing. In fact, one of their famous claims was that they were the only motorcycle factory in the world which had never built a rigid frame. The Girdraulic was to have combined the best features of the girder and telescopic forks. Or perhaps, as some disgruntled riders claimed — the worst features. Be that as it may, the Girdraulic was certainly the strongest and most expensive fork ever built. And, in good condition, it handled quite well indeed. Other than the new fork and the inclusion of hydraulic dampers, the machines remained unchanged. However, increased production enabled the Meteor and Comet singles to be re-introduced.

Perhaps it would be best to point out here that Vincent Engineers, Ltd. (the name was changed in 1951) did not indulge in yearly model changes. Detail improvements were added to the range when-

ever they were devised. Inevitably, a "D" series would have to be created, and inevitably, it would have to be something special. It was!

When the new Series D models were unveiled at the 1954 Earls Court Show they created a sensation. Crowds mobbed the stands to see the machines which had remained until then a closely guarded secret.

The Ds bristled with innovations, not the least of which being that they were the world's first totally enclosed motorcycles. The new models were called the Black Prince and Black Knight — corresponding to the "naked" Black Shadow and Rapide, which were also re-introduced a few months later. Around this time two Lightnings in New Zealand captured the

Removal of side panel does little to mar handsome lines. Rubber tipped lever on left side operates floor stand on bike.

Rider is well protected from the elements. Turn indicators are non-standard.

The author, Vaughn Greene, astride his own recently-restored Black Prince.

world's speed records for solo and sidecar. Therefore, it was a double shock when Vincent Engineers, Ltd. shut down production in 1955, with fewer than 500 Series Ds having been built at the Stevenage works. (Only two D singles were produced — a "naked" Comet, and its clothed counterpart, the Victor.)

So much for history. Was the D series really any better than the A, the B, and the C? Indeed, many claimed the D was a mistake, a retrograde step which drove the company out of business. Let us compare a D to a C and find out how good the last Vincents really were.

At the time the Ds were being developed, racing fairings were in their infancy. Nevertheless, far-seeing types claimed fairings would some day be commonplace on all motorcycles since they increase speed, cut down gas consumption and, above all, protect the rider from the elements. The fairings used on the Prince and Knight were developed primarily to shield the rider from wind and rain. Indeed, the sensation while riding one of these machines is like being in a sports car, and goggles can be thrown away. Leg shields, hand muffs, and an aerodynamically designed windshield enable a rider to take long trips in ordinary clothing without discomfort.

Although rider protection was the aim of the fairings, a number of other advantages were incidental dividends. For example, the leg shields act as air ducts, and the engine actually runs cooler. Another advantage: in the event of a crash, the frontal fairings act as crash pads, protecting the ride like the padded dash of a car. Cleaning up time is reduced to about one minute's use of a damp rag. This was an idea appreciated by the really hard, fast Vincent rider who didn't care to spend his Sunday afternoons polishing a two-wheeled mountain of chrome. Speaking of chrome — it was virtually eliminated (except for muffler and handlebar), as were all decorations. True, many riders apparently like to spend their time polishing innumerable little bits and pipes. But Phil Vincent felt it was about time the old adage that "a motorcycle is the only vehicle with its guts hanging out" was changed. A further benefit of hiding the

engine and frame was that the unit price could be lowered. Expensive polishing and plating could be eliminated from parts that usually require these operations for the sake of appearance.

In regards to accessibility, the fairings present no problems. The two engine shields are held by three quick-disconnect Dzus fasteners each. The rear shell pivots up to be retained by a prop, just as with a car hood. The dual seat also pivots up, to reveal a large tool compartment molded into the rear shell. Incidentally, future plans had intended that large fiberglass saddlebags would be available, that would screw into fittings on the shell.

Theories may be all right, but how did the fairings stand up in actual practice? Most riders reported that where they used to do 70 mph, they now found the same impression of speed at 90 mph. Handling in strong winds improved, due to the aerodynamically designed shell. No longer were clumsy gauntlets and heavy leathers required. Further, the machine was quieter, and far more comfortable. The reason for the latter was not only because of the fairings, but for a number of other reasons.

In the interests of a more comfortable ride, softer springs were used together with softer shocks. The dual seat, for the first time, was fully sprung. Larger section tires also helped, as did Mark III cams which were quieter than the former pattern. Again, this sort of radical change alienated some of the old guard die-hards — but you can't have things both ways.

In addition to full fairings, larger tires, softer ride, and coil ignition, still more radical changes were made. The complicated Vincent front stands were scrapped and replaced by an ingenious lever-operated center stand. When riding, the lever lies parallel with the rider's left foot. However, on giving the lever a gentle tug, the bike virtually rolls itself onto the stand. The stoplight was now operated by the front brake, since most riders use it at high speeds anyway. Other changes included: a better voltage regulator and headlight, a more powerful generator, and a leakproof battery. Also utilized were leakproof dampers by Armstrong, better grade clutch and brake linings, a larger gas tank, louder horn, Monobloc carbur-

etors, and redesigned steering damper, engine shock absorber, primary chain tensioner, gear change mechanism, clutch chamber sealing, and engine breather. I might add that many of these later parts are definite improvements, and should be added by owners of Series B and C Vincents.

Thus it was that the hairy, temperamental Vincent of old was tamed down to a smooth road burner that could have had fascinating possibilities on our long distance freeways. But, too late! Too late! The gods of finance had struck down this futuristic machine which even today has no equal. Perhaps it was just and fitting, when the movie "1984" was being filmed, that 12 Vincent Black Prince motorcycles were included in the props. ●

Footnote:

Many readers by now have, no doubt, a desire to actually ride one of these mythical beasts. The writer recently satisfied ten years of a similar desire by importing a D Vincent from England. There are perhaps fifty D Vincents left lying around in various shops in England. After vainly scouting, by mail, a number of these establishments, I finally chose one of the largest dealers in London. They had a selection of D Rapides, Shadows, Princes, and two Knights. I chose one of the Knights at $500. The "naked" models run less, and the Prince about $150 more. The Knight was described as being in "average condition for the year." A further $150 was sent to the shop, which then paid to have the bike crated for ocean shipment and shipped by the Royal Mail Lines.

Frankly, I was somewhat disappointed. The machine certainly looked neglected. The tank and engine had been gone over with house paint, and both engine shields needed some cracks mended. It was obvious the former owner had been a bit of a kook, and worse, had apparently been lugging about a great dirty sidecar at one time. Rust and dirt were abundant.

Was it worth it? To me, yes — perhaps to another, no. There are still expensive items to get, not the least of which is the license. There is a great deal of restoration to do. But if the end result is truly a Knight of the road, it will be worth it. Ⓖ

TED PEEVER OF CONWAY MOTORS SHOWS HOW TO REBUILD A

SHADOW BOX

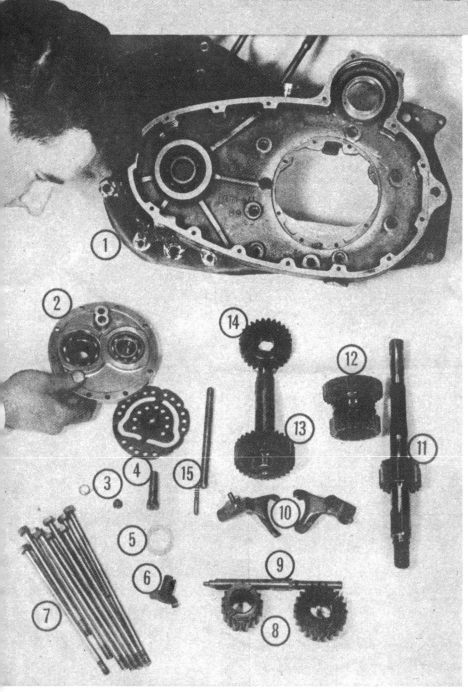

JUDGING by the continuous demand for the big twin Vincent among motorcycling enthusiasts, it would appear that the Vinny is as popular now as it was during its heyday. These immensely powerful machines made the ton look easy even before the war when they were called the HRD. Naturally, with so much poke at the rider's disposal the gearbox has to be very robust. Well, it is—and notably simple too.

In this feature, Ted Peever, works foreman for Conway Motors, Goldhawk Road, Shepherd's Bush—the world's biggest Vincent specialists—shows how the famous Black Shadow gearbox is assembled. All components are part-numbered to make things easier. Unlike the 500 c.c. Comet, the big twins have gearboxes incorporated in the engine unit. In order to completely dismantle it is necessary to split the crankcases. This entails complete removal of all primary drive components to carry out the work.

The engine and gearbox unit has to be removed, and with a Vinny it isn't so much a case of lifting the engine from the frame so much as removing frame parts from the engine.

You will notice that this feature deals only with the correct sequence of assembly for the gearbox, and when fitting the crankcase halves together a lot of work will have to be done on the engine. Remember when rebuilding to renew all gaskets and oil seals to keep the motor oil-tight.

KEY TO PARTS

1, Crankcase/Gearbox Half. 2, Gearbox End-Plate. 3, Bevel Gear Retaining Spring and Screw. 4, Camplate Spindle. 5, Mainshaft Bearing Spacer. 6, Camplate Bevel Gear. 7, Gearbox Retaining Bolts. 8, Gear Pinions. 9, Selector Rod. 10, Selector Forks. 11, Mainshaft. 12, Gear Pinions. 13, Gear Pinion and Layshaft. 14, Gear Pinion. 15, Camplate Plunger and Selector Fork Rod.

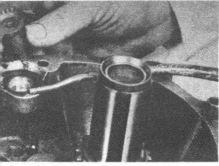

1 First position modified bevel-gear (original now obsolete) seeing that the boss is lubricated first. A hair-spring and screw holds gear

2 Assemble layshaft cluster next. First gear pinion is positioned and is followed by sliding-gear. Note selector fork locating groove

3 Next locate the second sliding dog and slide on second gear pinion. This completes layshaft cluster which should be clean and oiled

4 Now mate large double gear with the layshaft cluster and position the first selector fork. Note that the solid fork mates with double gear

5 Position the second fork (this is the grooved one) on the first and second sliding gears on layshaft. Push-fit both with selector spindle

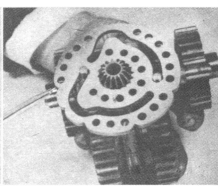

6 Gear selector camplate can now be located on to selector fork pegs. Place in first-gear position; turn anti-clockwise to line up spindle

7 Mate crankcase halves. Use jointing compound and bolt up tightly, then locate gear clusters. Note that the bolt heads are drawn into crankcase

8 Locate bevel gear shaft on timing side of crankcase. Note that it must be fully located so that the shoulder is flush with the bearing

9 Feed gear cluster into crankcase. Support layshaft with screwdriver. Juggle slightly to locate splines on double gear over hollow shaft

10 Hold bevel gear shaft in first gear with spanner; locate camplate spindle through hole in crankcase top. Tighten after bearing plate

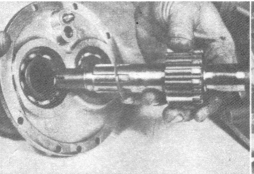

11 Fit mainshaft to gearbox end-plate after ensuring that the 31 thou. shim is positioned between mainshaft constant gear and end-plate

12 Locate gearbox end-plate and mainshaft into gearbox shell. Ensure camplate plunger and spring are correct. Lock plunger with wire

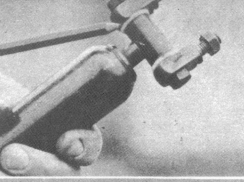

1 Removal of the hydraulic damper is the first step. There is one pinch-bolt at the top and two more ½ in. nuts located under the lower link

2 Test damper at this stage. If worn replace under the exchange service scheme. Note that felt washers must be in good condition to stop rattles

3 Remove bridge plate held by two ½ nuts and flat washers and two ½ bolts. Make sure that brake bal— beam is free with pivot lubric—

7 Now loosen off the fork spindle lock nuts (⅜ in.) and then the fork spindle pinch bolts (¹⁄₁₆ in.) as shown. Washers are fitted under both

8 Punch out top fork spindle with a suitable drift. If the spindle is at all shouldered where it locates against the bushes you must replace

9 With top fork crown and link assembly removed, examine the bush as shown for excessive wear. If w— replace; do not reamer the origi—

TED PEEVER (
CONWAY MOTORS SHOW
HOW TO STRIP THE.
FAMOUS GIRDRAULIC FOR—

FORK
FACTS

Now remove spring damper units by shifting lower holding bolt then tensioning spring with a screwdriver. The bolt can be withdrawn

5 Remove damper shrouds and lubricate main springs with a medium grease. Sidecar springs are available but in any case renew if tension is lost

6 Remove the head stem and then, carefully using a hide mallet, tap up the top fork lug over the fork stem. Do NOT use a metal hammer!

The head crown spindle is removed in same way as fork crown spindle. All spindles should be checked for trueness on a proper surface plate

11 Drift out lower fork spindle; this allows two fork blades to be withdrawn. Check trueness of these blades. Exchange service is available

12 Finally withdraw lower eccentric spindle, eccentrics and snail-cam plates. Note that these are shimmed. The clearance must be just 3 thou.

THE big-twin range of Vincents are among the most powerful road bikes ever built. With so much power readily available all components must be beefy to cope. Because of this the standard Rapide or Shadow is a heavy bike and this has led to a frequently heard myth that the Vinny doesn't handle well. Well, as any enthusiast will tell you this just isn't true. Once certain steering peculiarities are mastered the Vincent handles as well as most bikes and mainly responsible for this are the unique Girdraulic front forks. What must be stressed about the Vinnys, however, is that maintenance must be of a very high level to keep ALL parts functioning properly and this applies particularly to the front forks. In this article Ted Peever of Vincent specialists Conway Motors, Goldhawk Road, Shepherds Bush, shows how to strip the Girdraulics and what to watch out for when you do it.

The correct drill, given in full detail in the picture strip, is to first remove headlamp, speedometer, handlebars, front wheel and mudguard. Undo the pinch bolt on the top head lug and remove damper complete. Withdraw spring boxes from the lower end, tap up top head lug and lift forks free. There are 40 ball bearings in the steering races, so don't lose any! In pictures 10, 11 and 12, dealing with head crown, lower fork and lower eccentric spindles, remember that absolute trueness is essential. So if in doubt get an expert to check them. When refitting make sure that clearance between eccentrics (Picture 12) and the bushes is exactly three thou.

At this stage we must stress again the absolute necessity for replacing any worn components. Vincent parts do tend to be somewhat expensive but the finished job is well worth it.

VINCENT

TEN YEARS have passed since Philip Vincent announced that the Vincent HRD Company, Ltd. would no longer manufacture motorcycles, but in those ten years the Vincent legend has grown, rather than diminished, and it would be substantially correct to say that there are more people interested in the bike today than when it was being produced. The reason for this is not much of a mystery: the Vincent may be gone, but everyone remembers the big, vastly powerful V-twins that set so many speed records. Rollie Free rode an unstreamlined Vincent to a 160 mph record back in 1953, and these machines hold so many other records that it would be futile to attempt a list. But, just as important as the records, there was the indisputable fact that you could walk into a Vincent dealer's showroom and purchase a touring machine that would run away from anything you are likely to encounter on the public roads by a comfortable margin. Even more impressive, if the Vincent were being made today, it would *still* be the fastest thing on the road.

All of the above is the substance of the Vincent legend, but because of the bike's tremendous speed, and exceedingly unorthodox mechanical layout, a myth is beginning to rise up around it that threatens to obscure any mere fact. The danger is all the more real because very few Vincents are still in circulation in this country, and those few are owned by people who are dyed-in-the-wool Vincent enthusiasts, who tend to be something less than objective in their evaluations. Thus, in the interest of historical accuracy, we decided to obtain an example of Vincent's art for test purposes, and we were extremely fortunate to find an ideal specimen to use. Mr. Bill Cottom, a most ardent Vincent fancier, loaned us his 1955 Black Lightning — one of the last Vincents built, the quickest model, and one that had been run only 2800 miles when delivered into our irreverent hands.

To say that we were excited at the prospect of doing a road test of the *Vincent Black Lightning* does not begin to describe the level of emotion around these offices. A

THE VINCENT BLACK LIGHTNING

ouple of our number had ridden Vincents, very briefly, many years ago, but none of us had ever been given the opportunity to really wring one out.

The machine that faced us incorporated some rather far-out engineering — even by modern standards. The engine is an all-alloy V-twin, with a "unit" crankcase that also houses the 4-speed transmission. The bike quite literally has no frame: the oil tank bolts into place over the cylinder heads, and the steering head is an integral part of this tank. The rear wheel is held in a swing-arm that pivots on plates fixed directly to the rear of the main engine cases, and is supported by springs that butt against the previously mentioned oil tank. There are certain disadvantages to this type of construction — for instance, the motorcycle must be dismantled for anything beyond minor engine adjustments — but it makes the machine lighter than would otherwise be possible. Our Black Lightning weighed only 403 pounds with oil and a half-tank of fuel.

The Vincent's front suspension is of the girder-fork variety, which was retained by this British company long after everyone else had changed to either telescopic or some form of leading link forks. There was, of course, some justification for Vincent's adhering to the girder forks. Up and down motion with a girder fork is accommodated by pairs of more-or-less horizontal links up at the steering head, and the relative angle and length of these links can be arranged so that front wheel travel is substantially vertical through most of its range of movement. This principle of "constant wheelbase" is no longer considered necessary, or even desirable, but it was when the Vincent was being manufactured. Incidentally, the Vincent's springs, front and rear, were carried separate from its dampers. At the front, coil springs are housed in long tubes leading down almost to the axle, while a hydraulic damper was centrally located up at the top of the forks. The rear springs are up under the seat, on each side of a short, large-diameter damper. The braces supporting the seat lead into friction dampers where they connect with the rear suspension, and

these dampers can be adjusted by tightening down on a pair of large knobs. Quite frankly, the bike's hydraulic dampers need all the extra help they can get, as they are so weak as to be almost useless.

Another of the more interesting features on the Vincent's "chassis" is its brakes. There is a total of four separate drums, two to each wheel, each with one leading and one trailing shoe. Balance bars are provided to distribute brake-control pressure evenly, and these brakes are marvelously smooth. Our test bike, being the "racing model," had special finned brake drums, which were supposed to make them dissipate heat faster. However, the truth is that these brakes are so weak that it would be hard to tell if they were fading; they feel badly faded on even the first application. The brakes will stop the bike, eventually, but they are not anything like being equal to its formidable speed. Very smooth, yes; powerful, no.

Inside the Vincent's engine you will find one thing the like of which has been used in few others. This is

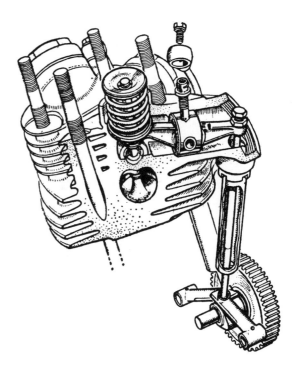

the valve gear, which is arranged so that the rockers reach in *under* the valve springs. Below the valve spring, there is a chamber cast into the cylinder head, and the rocker is located in this chamber. The valve stem diameter is reduced at this point, and a sort of button is slipped on; the rocker has a forked end, and this works against the button to push the valve open. Advantages of this arrangement are that the valve springs are not quite so near the hot combustion chamber area, and that the pushrods are considerably shortened. Further shortening of the pushrods has been accomplished by placing the cams high on the side of the engine.

A lot of imagination was also employed in the design of the Vincent's clutch — which is constructed very much like a drum brake. There is a single clutch disc, intended to give a smooth engagement, but the bulk of the torque is transmitted through a pair of brake shoes. In effect, the engine drives a drum, and the shoes transmit the drive to a "backing plate" on the transmission input shaft. The shoes are linked to this backing plate in such a way that when the single clutch disc is engaged, torque forces the

shoes out against the drum. With this arrangement, the gripping action of the shoes always increases as torque increases. In theory, the Vincent clutch should be absolutely free of slip; in practice, it is infamous for its lack of grip.

Knowing in advance that the Vincent's clutch was likely to slip and that the transmission could be difficult, and that riders who know about these things consider its handling to be "different," we nonetheless looked forward to a scheduled trip to the Riverside road-racing circuit. We knew, no matter what, the whole thing would be an experience — and so it was. Our test machine being the racing model, we half expected it to be fussy about starting, but it fired immediately. This was due in part at least to the fact that Marty Dickerson, one of the leading Vincent exponents and holder of several Bonneville records on a Vincent, prepared and tuned our test machine. Marty is Service Manager at Conejo Honda in Thousand Oaks, Calif., and is still immersed in Vincents. It was apparent from the beginning that we would not suffer from any lack of sheer power with the Vincent; while warming the oil we noticed that just blipping the engine would cause the bike to lift at the front, as a reaction to what was obviously absolutely thunderous torque. Then, with a set of fresh plugs installed and the engine nicely warmed, we set off

around the track.

At the end of one lap we knew that we had a tiger by the tail. Sheer speed the Vincent has, but it is virtually without brakes and the handling was enough to make brave men blanch. Someone had once told us that the Vincent felt as though it had a hinge in its middle, but in riding the beast we quickly discovered that the hinge to which they referred was a ball joint. No motorcycle we have ever tested has flexed in so many different directions at once. Get the bike into a fast turn, trying hard, and it sets up a really heart-stopping shudder and waggle. The Vincent would, fortunately, track quite nicely when running straight, but on a road course — or even an ordinary road, sooner or later you have to turn, and that's when the trouble starts. Also, it is necessary to decide well in advance what you intend to do about a corner, because the brakes aren't good enough to permit any last-minute changes in plans.

We suppose that the Vincent has its charms. It is fast, and reasonably smooth, and we think it would be reliable. However, the example we rode had to be shifted very deliberately, and even then it would sometimes pop out of gear. Its clutch slipped furiously, too, and what with this

and the sometimes bulky transmission it was impossible to get much of a standing-start quarter-mile time. Our best effort was 14 seconds flat, which is not really bad, but at least 1.5 seconds could have been trimmed from that time had the drive system been functioning properly. We do not know what the top speed would be: the Vincent would gather speed by leaps and bounds, but the Riverside straightaway is not overly long and the bike's poor brakes made it necessary to shut down much sooner than is our usual practice.

The Vincent Owners Club will not love us for some of the things we have said—and they will love us even less for what we are about to say: The Vincent motorcycle may be fast, but it is an evil-handling beast, with simply awful brakes. Potentially (and by this we mean unless ridden with great restraint) it is the most dangerous motorcycle ever to come our way: and we are not sorry in the least that it is no longer being made. We are a bit sorry that we found this most revered of Vincents, the series C Black Lightning, to test. Most of us began to believe the legend, and the legend is so much better than the motorcycle that we cannot but feel that in abandoning the legend for the truth we have made a bad exchange. ☻

VINCENT BLACK LIGHTNING

SPECIFICATIONS

List Price	$1500
Frame Type	none
Suspension, front	girder fork
Suspension, rear	swing arm
Tire size, front	3.00-21
Tire size, rear	3.50-20
Engine type	V-twin, 50°
Bore & Stroke	3.31 x 3.54
Displacement, cu. in.	60.9
Displacement, cu. cent.	998
Compression ratio	(optional)
Bhp @ rpm	70 @ 6,400 rpm
Carburetion	2 32mm (1.26") Amal TT
Ignition	magneto
Fuel capacity, gal.	4.35
Oil capacity, pts.	7.8
Oil System	dry sump
Starting system	push

POWER TRANSMISSION

Clutch Type	self-energizing shoe
Primary drive	duplex chain
Final drive	single-row chain
Gear ratio, overall:1	
4th	4.10
3rd	4.88
2nd	6.30
1st	8.45

DIMENSIONS, IN.

Wheelbase	56.5
Saddle height	31.0
Saddle width	8.0
Foot-peg height	13.0
Ground clearance	6.5
Curb weight, lbs.	403

PERFORMANCE

Top speed,
Test strip too short for time
Max. speed in gears @ 700 rpm

4th	137
3rd	115
2nd	89
1st	66

Mph per 1000 rpm, top gear

SPEEDOMETER ERROR

30 mph, actual	24.7
50	41.2
70	57.5

ACCELERATION

0-30 mph, sec.	2.7
0-40	3.3
0-50	4.3
0-60	5.4
0-70	7.3
0-80	8.9
0-90	11.2
0-100	13.5
Standing 1/4 mile	14.0
speed reached	102

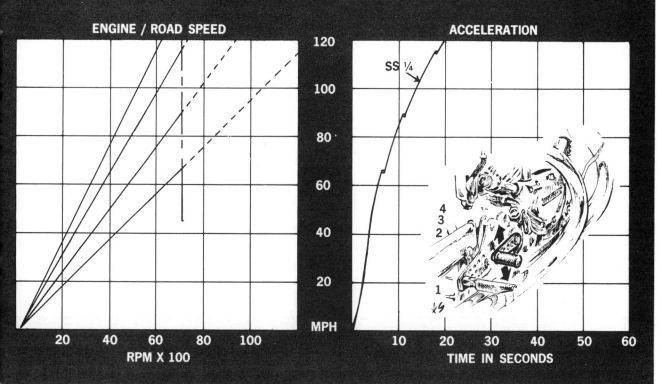

ENGINE / ROAD SPEED

RPM X 100

MPH

ACCELERATION

SS 1/4

TIME IN SECONDS

ROAD TEST

TWO-MILES-A-MINUTE!
MM TESTS THIS FABULOUS
REBUILD OF THE 65 b.h.p.

BLACK

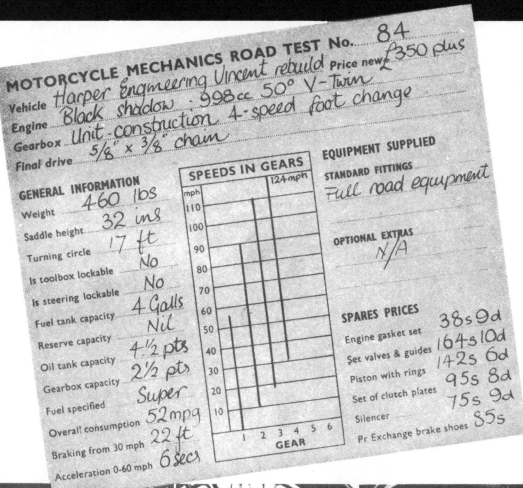

MOTORCYCLE MECHANICS ROAD TEST No. 84

Vehicle Harper Engineering Vincent rebuild **Price new** £350 plus

Engine Black shadow - 998cc 50° V-Twin

Gearbox Unit-construction 4-speed foot change

Final drive 5/8" × 3/8" chain

EQUIPMENT SUPPLIED

STANDARD FITTINGS Full road equipment

GENERAL INFORMATION

Weight	460 lbs
Saddle height	32 ins
Turning circle	17 ft
Is toolbox lockable	No
Is steering lockable	No
Fuel tank capacity	4 Galls
Reserve capacity	Nil
Oil tank capacity	4½ pts
Gearbox capacity	2½ pts
Fuel specified	Super
Overall consumption	52 mpg
Braking from 30 mph	22 ft
Acceleration 0-60 mph	6 secs

OPTIONAL EXTRAS N/A

SPEEDS IN GEARS

124mph

SPARES PRICES

Engine gasket set	38s 9d
Set valves & guides	164s 10d
Piston with rings	142s 6d
Set of clutch plates	95s 8d
Silencer	75s 9d
Pr Exchange brake shoes	85s

NEVER mind about your 50
and 650's. Forget about th
for a minute while I tell y
about a MAN'S bike.
460 lb. monster that chu
out the revs. with all the econo
of a Tory M.P. handing out
Daily Worker in Westminster.
65 b.h.p. V-twin that will see
off in second, 110 in third and
thunderous 124 in top. Capaci
998 c.c. Make? Obviously—
fabulous Vincent.

And what are we doing road t
ing a Vinnie? Well, this is
nearest thing you can get to a n
one since 1955; a Harper Engine
ing rebuild of an excellence t
would bring tears trickling do
the leathery cheeks of the Vinc
Owners' Club. Properly ma
tained, it's a bike that will still
blowing anything else off wh
some contemporaries are just r
stains in a breaker's yard.

It's been many years since I r
a standard Shadow. So the fi
thing I did when I took it over v
to kick it over. I couldn't. Th
I rediscovered the valve-lift—
this case a hefty lever in the on
usual place underneath the left b
Half-way through my power stro
I released it and off the Vinn
went with that delightful exha
note that has left so many vehic

Powerplant. The 50-degree V-twin motor has high-compression pistons, Lightning cams and develops around 65 b.h.p. at 6000 r.p.m.

Safe anchorage. The twin brake drums outstop anything else on the road. Front brake alone stopped in 32 ft. from 30 m.p.h.

Strength and simplicity is the keynote of the Vinnie's rear-end. The saddle is well clear of wheel giving a comfortable ride

Twin Monobloc mounting is sh
here. Also note single cen
suspension unit and easy-to-w
propstand. Foot controls are

SHADOW

its wake. Clutch in, first gear,
few revs., clutch out—whoops!
that was another thing I'd forgotten. Still, I didn't stall it and the
steaming monster idled its way up
the road like a rocket.

When you ride a Shadow you
enter a new world of motorcycling.
The first thing that goes by the
board is your impression of speed
formed mainly, I think, by the way
the motor's working. At 55 you
would swear you were only doing
thirty. This false impression chases
the speedo needle right round to
the ton mark. After that you know
you are on a Vinnie and you know
you're shifting!

Equally deceptive is the braking.
At low speeds the brake shoes hit
the 3 drums with such a wallop
that you finish up on the headlamp.

At higher speeds the fantastic
brakes cancel things out and I'll
never forget an emergency stop I
had to make at 115. If I'd been
doing anything else I wouldn't be
writing this now.

Finally, the Shadow makes its
own unique demands on gear-
changing. It will wuffle through
town in top gear at 30. But if
you want to steam away the drill
is to change down twice. It's easy
to forget just what gear you are in
but you have to make an effort

because bottom gear ratio is so low
that if you select bottom at anything over 20 the back wheel locks
with a shriek of rubber and you
had better be in a straight line on
a dry road or else!

This apart, the much-maligned
Vincent gearbox proved practically
faultless. There was no tendency
to select neutrals nor did it drift
out of gear on over-run. Selection
was positive at all times although
a trifle clunky occasionally. Care
had to be taken selecting bottom
from standstill and revs. had to be
at a minimum. The clutch—a
Lightning unit in this case—stood
up to everything that was handed
out and was far less dramatic than
many Vincents I have ridden.

The high-camshaft 50-degree
twin unit has been lovingly reassembled using all new parts.
Special bottom end, high-compression pistons, 1⅛" Monoblocs, triple
valve springs and polished internals
account for the Rapide-plus performance and the mill is fired by
coil ignition. Really incredible
acceleration sees the ton off from a
standing start in a mere 22 seconds.

Despite this tremendous performance, to my mind the most
endearing thing about the Vincent
is its durability and built-in rugged-

continued on page 145

brake on rear is large area
very effective. Again note
depth of design and ease and
flexibility of adjustment

It could only be a Vinnie! There's
a complete lack of drama about
the controls although the bike's
the most powerful of 'em all

THERE'S nothing else for it—I'll just ha to buy a Vincent again, take a cou on V-twin internals and join the V cent Owners' Club. Then I might able to test one without offending ar one. Still, when Conway Motors, of Go hawk Road, Shepherds Bush, offered m 1951 Rapide for a second-hand road t feature, I accepted. There's a new gene tion of motorcyclists who know nothi of Vincent motoring and for about £ down and the rest on the drip there's excuse for it.

Whether it was just the luck of the dra or that Conway's won't let a Vinnie unless it's a good one I couldn't say, t this particular Rap was the nicest o I've ridden and all sorts of new mach ery languished in the garage while t Rapide ran up many more miles on time-honoured clock.

Apart from slightly stretched cab there was nothing to fault. The tickov was as regular as an athlete's heart b and at the other end of the scale t Vinnie did the length of the M.1 in nineties with plenty of steam in han Only once did I forget that the bike star its career way back in 1951, and that w when I had to put a gormless great Jagu back in its place. The Rap scorched ba past him with 110 on the clock and me straight in the saddle as a V.O.C. vetera

I don't know the history of the bike the previous owner was obviously an thusiast. Everything had been w looked after and the only trace of rust w on the twin damper units under the sadd

Other good points that the next ow will inherit are a positively violent a horn driven from the rear tyre, a power spotlamp on the offside crash bar and electric clock which kept perfect time a was mounted rev counter fashion oppos the 120 m.p.h. speedometer!

The twin front brake was fabulous a right up to the most stringent Vinc

HERE'S A '51 VETERAN THAT OFFERS TON-PLU PERFORMANCE FOR £130! IT'S THE VINCEN

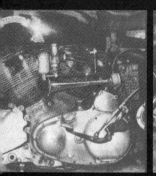

heart of the matter—the
nsely powerful slow-revving
.c. V-twin power unit

Twin-drum front brake is a fantastic stopper.. Note the unique and effective Girdraulic forks

Impressive? Some say you don't know what motorcycling is until you've ridden a 1,000 c.c. Vincent

Drive side view of rear wheel. Gadget on tyre at top of picture powers impressive shrieker horn

dards. Light and progressive in normal it could be as dramatic as an emer-y and the knowledge that the Rapide ld stop as well as it went took the on out of high speed cruising. The gs were down a little on the rear brake h needed slight adjustment to bring o standard.

echanically, the bike had worn well. big power unit was easy on the oil as as the eye and engine noise was very There was no chatter from the timing and the entire unit was oil tight. ins and sprockets were relatively new no adjustments were necessary dur-he course of the test.

rankly, it was people's reaction to our d at Earls Court that decided me to a second-hand Vinnie. There was so h reaction to the hot bikes on the d, and so many rather despairing com-ts from the boys who wanted high ormance but at a price they could rd, that a test on a Vincent in the £120 e range seemed the answer. A good ide or Shadow will outpace most bikes cost a good deal less. The spares tion is still healthy (on a par with e new bikes I could name!) and even rices are relatively high a good Vin-is unbeatable value.

nd although this was a perfectly stand-Rapide, not even the most ardent burner could find fault with the bike's ormance. We took things fairly ily in deference to its age, but even acceleration in second and third gears e than held a new twin-carb six-fifty cal twin, while top gear performance rely Vincent-90-plus cruising with an ost ridiculous lack of fuss and an omy of revs that would make the y Wheel perform like a works fifty! he gear change seemed to have mel-d with use and the slightest pressure sted the cogs quickly and cleanly al-gh the travel was a little lengthy. The

MOTORCYCLE MECHANICS ROAD TEST No. 6

SH.

Vehicle Vincent Rapide L
Engine 998 c.c. 50° V-Twin
Gearbox Positive stop 4 Speed
Final drive Chain to rear sprocket

Price new £130 SH £

THE VINCENT

GENERAL INFORMATION

Weight	455 lbs
Saddle height	30 ins
Turning circle	16 ft.
Is toolbox lockable	No
Is steering lockable	No
Fuel tank capacity	3¾ gals
Reserve capacity	Nil
Oil tank capacity	4½ pts
Gearbox capacity	2½ pts
Fuel specified	Premium
Overall consumption	46 mpg
Braking from 30 mph	24 ft
Acceleration 0-60 mph	7 secs

SPEEDS IN GEARS (mph) — GEAR 1 2 3 4 5 6

EQUIPMENT SUPPLIED

STANDARD FITTINGS

EXTRAS Spot lamp, shrieker horn, clock

SPARES PRICES

Engine gasket set	38s 9d
Set valves & guides	144s 0d
Piston with rings	71s 3d
Set of clutch plates	18s 10d
Silencer	75s 3d
Pr Exchange brake shoes	2l5 6d

clutch was vintage Vinnie—abrupt at first but fine once one got used to it. I staged one traffic spectacular soon after leaving Conway's when I skipped down Hammersmith Broadway in a series of neck-breaking jerks. It's happened to better men than me, too.

The oft-maligned suspension was in first-class order which produced a firm and undeviating line on bends with a powerful self-centralising effect when one began to straighten out. It's a funny thing about Vincents, they don't seem to corner as well as a Norton, say, but you find you are going round them just as quickly just the same! The normal riding position with straight bars and the standard dual seat puts the pilot very close to the controls, but it's a position that pays big dividends in comfort on long runs.

The only trouble the big Vinny gave during the test was when the carbs and electrics were swamped by a very heavy downpour while I was three miles out at sea doing a little fishing. A friend towed me six miles but after drying everything out the thing still wouldn't fire. Luckily, sprint ace Basil Keyes came to the rescue from his Worthing motorcycle business and the trouble was traced to the magneto and quickly rectified.

So there you are. For around £130 a good second-hand Rapide offers matchless touring performance and acceleration and top speed at least equal to a 1965 650. A Shadow, of course, is considerably quicker.

But a word of warning. If you are going to buy a Vinnie, do it through the Vincent Owners' Club or a specialist dealer like Conway's. A good one is a wonderful bike; a clapped one can be a disaster.

RAPIDE!

101

Spacers are fitted above and below the original Vincent headstock to supplement its height up to Norton specifications. Oil tank mounts in centre of petrol tank

The upper fork yoke on the Norton tele has to have $\frac{1}{8}$ in. milled from it to allow space to fit the top steering race into the Vincent cast-steering headstock

The exterior of the large timing ch is alloy—and the normal enthusi polishes it. Ian had a matt sh blast finish for better cool

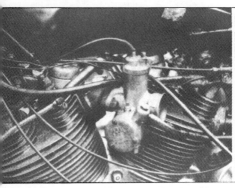

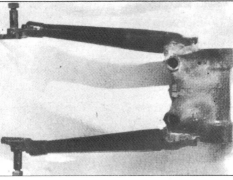

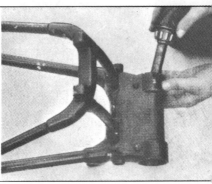

Picador cylinder heads are fitted, with special stubs carrying $1\frac{3}{16}$ in. Amal Monobloc carburettors. Apparent untidy cables are free routed for easy action

The rear swing arm is made up with Velo forks brazed into the original pivot housing which is very strong. The casting has to be cut back to fit wheel in

Top view of the housing which is mounted in the original frame with rollers. Heavy triangulated o Vincent suspension tubes are cu

SOMETHING SPECIAL

SUPEI

Sorting the handling on this 1,00

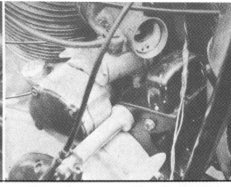

petrol tank is basically modelled on d Star lines, with underside altered form deep pockets to let it sit over centre-mounted Vincent oil tank

An extension plate is riveted to the original battery carrier allowing old battery position to be moved to the right to clear new carb mountings

Picture shows new position of carb, which is normally on other side. New arrangement gives straighter flow across head. Old battery position now carries AVC unit

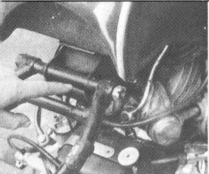

original Vincent seat bolt mountings take the Girling sub-frame which was stituted at the rear. These lugs are ned by end of the unaltered oil tank

The full loop rear member, shown from above. Support tubes at each side run down to rear of engine, while cross-strut carries two $\frac{5}{16}$ in. holes for seat

The original offside front brake plate together with the speedometer drive is shifted to the back wheel, with a drive sprocket fitted on to the machined drum

SHADOW

given engineer Ian Forrester a 130 mph dream

The rear wheel remains unchanged, along with the quick release spindle. Spacers fill space formerly occupied by second brake drum, removed on Series D models

● Take a standard Vincent motorcycle —and add one owner with sporting ambition and proved engineering ability; sprinkle in a liberal helping of initiative. Allow the mixture to simmer in a garage until the owner experiences a tank-slapping speed-wobble at around the ton while production racing.

The result? In this case, a 130 mph Black Shadow Special with unique suspension and a shattering performance.

Owner Ian Forrester, of Luton, is an accomplished engineer with a taste for the race game, and when he experienced the unnerving speed wobble he decided something would have to be done to cut down the large amount of unsprung weight carried in the normal Vincent front and rear

rather heavily built suspension.

The heavy triangular rear end was scrapped and Velo rear fork units—a popular item with Vincent special builders because of their strength—brazed on in their place. Norton forks and front hub replaced the original hydraulic girder front layout.

Down in the engine room, the breathing of the rear cylinder was improved by fitting a front cylinder head—which gives a one direction crossflow of gas through the carb being on the nearside instead of on the right.

Other engine mods have been carried out and have given Ian an incredibly powerful production racer, still in full road trim which "handles like a dream".

Standard clutch has been replaced with a multiplate version, but retained in the cast iron drum, which is deeply slotted and reinforced with radial steel strips

CONFESSIONS OF A VINCENT LOVER

Highlights of a 15-Year Romance With England's Famous Big Twin — the Vincent

Report and Photos by George Hays

ALTHOUGH the wheels have brake drums on each side, the brakes are not as efficient as they look. Rapide drums are smooth; Black Shadow drums are finned.

I FIRED up the Vincent Black Shadow and headed for an open stretch of road where I could put it thru its paces. The motor chugged along slowly with such lack of fuss that I found it hard to believe I was going as fast as the speedometer indicated. Closing behind a car at 65 mph, and preparing to pass, I grabbed a handful of throttle. The bike leaped forward, accelerating so suddenly that it seemed as if the throttle were geared directly to the speedometer, and by the time I passed the car the speedometer pointed an accusing finger at 100 mph. "Good Lord, what have I got hold of?" I thought, as I snapped the throttle shut.

With wind-blown tears streaking my face, I returned the bike to my friend who had allowed me to take a trial spin. Thus ended my first ride on a Vincent. I decided then and there that I had to have one of the magnificent beasts. With the impatience of youth, I had mercilessly flogged three other bikes, advertised as road burners, to death. Brand X died of a broken crankshaft, Brand Y died of oil pump failure, and Brand Z chronically seized its pistons when pushed hard on the road. The 1000cc Vincent Black Shadow, guaranteed capable of 125 mph off the showroom floor, promised to be the only bike that would keep up with my desire to ride far and fast.

In 1952, when I began shopping for a Vincent, they were selling new for around $1350. Quite a price in those days, when new 650cc Triumphs were going for $950, so I began looking for a used Vincent in good condition. I found my bargain in, of all places, a Harley-Davidson store. The bike was less than a year old, had only 7000 miles on it, looked new, and was priced at only $650, less than half new price. At the time, many Harley-Davidson fans hated Vincents with a passion, because they were the only machines on that road that could romp away from their big 74's, and the dealer seemed to be anxious to get the Vincent out of his store before it claimed one of his regular customers. The only draw-back: the model was a Rapide, similar to the Black Shadow, but with milder cams, lower compression ratio and a top speed rated at only 110 mph.

Naturally, as soon as I got my hands on the monster, I set about putting it thru its paces to see if it lived up to its reputation. On a straight stretch of remote desert road, I opened the throttle wide and left it there. The speedometer needle climbed until it passed 100, and kept climbing steadily, even though I was sitting upright. It's alarming how fast the scenery flies by at that speed; the telephone poles flashed by like pickets in a fence, and a town that should have been far off in the distance suddenly popped up on the horizon. The speedometer was edging by 110, and the bike felt as if it had more speed left, when I lost my nerve and eased off the throttle. That kind of performance was good enough for me, and that was my only all-out speed attempt, although at times I cruised the open highways at 105 mph with a hard-riding group known as the Vincent Owners Club.

My Vincent, with its saddlebags, windshield, air cleaners, stock muffler, and low compression pistons is set up for touring rather than for top speed, but it can still turn in a creditable performance. On rare occasions I open the old girl up to see if she still has what it takes. Riding thru the desert while returning from the Death Valley Tour a few years ago, I overtook another rider on a huge V-twin of domestic manufacture. Having an uppity English bike pass him on the road seemed to irritate him, and he opened his throttle and left me behind. This process was repeated several times and I finally decided to see how irritated I could make him. The next time I overtook him, I opened my throttle wide and left it open until I approached the next

ABOVE: *Rear wheel has brakes and sprockets on both sides and is designed to be quickly reversed for a change in gear ratio. Rear brake arms were lengthened by owner for better braking action.*

TOP LEFT: *'Rapide engines were left unfinished, while Black Shadow and Black Lightning engines were painted solid black. Owner painted the Rapide cylinders black for better cooling. Air cleaners were added to carburetors for maximum engine life.*

LEFT: *Magneto and oil filter are hidden under an aluminum cover at front of engine. Finely machined gearbox dipstick and cap reflect the quality design and workmanship found thruout the machine.*

town. With windshield, saddlebags, and heading into the wind, top speed was 95 mph, and I expected the big Milwaukee charger to rumble by at any moment. Reaching town, I stopped and looked back down the road. No one in sight. Finally, a few minutes later, the other rider rolled into town, so mad he wouldn't even look in my direction.

On another occasion on the open highway, I overtook a BMW R-69 equipped with windshield, saddlebags, and carrying a passenger, as I was. The other rider opened his throttle wide and I did likewise, not really expecting to keep up with such a fine, modern machine. But the old Vincent slowly crept ahead of the other bike and gradually widened the distance, leaving it behind.

Even those who hate the Vincent have to admit it has quite an engine; it has set speed records that still stand. Nevertheless, as with any mass-produced vehicle, some go, some don't. A friend owned two Black Shadows, and his hobby was making speed runs every Sunday morning at dawn when the freeway was deserted. One of his Black Shadows was a real performer; it could make the back wheel smoke at 100 mph, and would exceed its rated top speed of 125 mph, while no matter how he tinkered, tuned and adjusted his other Black Shadow, it would barely do 100.

Although its high speed performance is outstanding, the stock Vincent isn't much of a dragster. Shifting is slow and deliberate, and a well-tuned 650cc vertical twin can take one thru the gears. But once above 65 mph, there are few bikes

that can outrun it even today.

But enough about top speed. I'm a touring rider, not a racer, and the Vincent serves the purpose well. Gas mileage averages out to about 59 mpg. The Rapide engine runs nicely on regular. The gear ratio in high is 3.5-to-1, and the low revving, vibration-free engine has real hauling power. The speeometer needle can be hung on 80 and left there between gas stops, regardless of windshield, saddlebags, head winds and hills.

Starting the 1000cc engine is easy, provided it's in good tune. The long starter pedal swings in a large arc down the side of the machine, but can't be budged until the compression release lever on the left handlebar is pulled. The rider stomps on the starter pedal with all his weight, letting go of the compression release lever in mid-stroke. You can work up quite a sweat if the huge engine doesn't fire in the first few kicks.

The bike is so geared that starting out in low is like starting out in second or third gear with other brands; you have to slip the clutch much more than usual while getting under way. Another characteristic of the Vincent, the saddle and suspension are a little too firm for maximum comfort, but the rider can cover 500 miles in a day without becoming unduly tired.

The Vincent's main claim to fame was its speed, but it had many other good features, some far ahead of their time. It was one of the first with unitized crankcase and transmission, and frameless construction, with the wheels seemingly bolted to each end of the engine.

The extensive use of aluminum limited the weight to 455 pounds, light for a bike its size.

The road-holding ability of the Vincent has to be experienced at length to be fully appreciated. To the uninitiated, the bike feels top-heavy and awkward, and takes some getting used to. True, it's a bit unwieldy at slow speeds, not a good traffic bike, but the faster you go, the better it handles. At speeds above 65 mph, it is rock-steady. I graduated from a 650cc English bike to the Vincent, and at first I had the feeling of sitting on a fence, the saddle height is so high. But after a few thousand miles of riding, this went unnoticed. Not long after acquiring my Vincent, I gained a deep respect for its stability. Cruising at 80 mph, I was suddenly confronted with a hole in the pavement about 12 feet across and 10 inches deep. From my experience with other motorcycles, I expected to be unloaded, but the Vincent took it so smoothly I wasn't even lifted off the saddle.

The forks are one of the best engineered front ends ever put on a motorcycle. The have been ridiculed as a rehash of the old Indian front end, but only by those not having extensive experience with both. The "Girdraulic" forks have a long, soft travel, similar to that of telescopic forks, but the lateral rigidity of the Vincent front end provides a feeling of stability at speed that is far superior to that of telescopic forks. To illustrate the point, try this experiment. Position the side of the front wheel of almost any machine equipped with telescopic forks against a telephone pole or some similar object. Then, with the handlebars, try to turn the wheel in the direction of the telephone pole. The forks will spring sideways, allowing the handlebars to move several inches without moving the front wheel. Try the same experiment with a Vincent, and you will find that there is no give in the front end at all. The heat-treated aluminum alloy forks are so sturdy that they are not bent by accidents that collapse front wheels.

The rear wheel is designed so that sprockets can be mounted on both sides, and fitted to the bike so that the wheel can be removed, turned around, and replaced for a quick change of gear ratios en route to suit road conditions. According to the Rider's Handbook, this operation can be done in less than 10 minutes with a minimum of tools, although in practice I've found that it takes closer to half-an-hour. An intriguing arrangement, but in 75,000 miles of touring, I found it to be an advantage only once, when a friend and I decided to follow a dirt trail up a mountainside. Incidentally, Ye Olde Vincent handles quite well on a dirt road, swinging into easily controlled broadsides like a barn door.

The Vincent is ideal for sidecar work, and a sidecar can easily be mounted on either side of the machine. Mounting

BOTH right and left sides of the machine have kick stands. Front and rear footrests are the folding type.

VINCENT

points are built in, and a simple adjustment on the front forks changes the trail and effective spring strength for better handling with a hack.

Although the Vincent has four brakes — two brake drums on each wheel — the brakes leave something to be desired. They were purposely designed so that they can't lock the wheels, making it safe to apply them full force at high speeds without inviting a skid. But this makes them inadequate at lower speeds, particularly when carrying the added weight of a passenger. I would rather have brakes that can lock the wheels tight, and use my own judgment on how hard to apply them. Braking action can be improved somewhat by lengthening the cam arms, re-enforcing the backing plates, and by installing high quality brake lining of a soft grade.

No bike is perfect, and the Vincent has its share of shortcomings, although many of its faults can be lessened or eliminated by modification. The shock absorbers drooled and had to be refilled with oil every 3000 miles. This problem is eliminated by replacing the original seals with an improved type.

It has been said that there never was a Vincent clutch that didn't slip. This may be true in some cases, but on my machine, the clutch works almost too well; it takes hold so firmly that it's difficult to start out in low gear without stalling the engine or screeching the rear wheel. True, Vincent clutches are known to become oiled, but this can be avoided by installing oil-resistant clutch lining, and by replacing the clutch chamber seals when necessary.

It takes a strong man to lift the Vincent up on the rear stand, and it's almost impossible when the bike is loaded with luggage. The Vincent is blessed with side stands, both right and left, but they are a little short. The rider has to be careful how he parks, lest the machine topple over. This trouble can be cured by brazing steel pads onto the bottom of the side stands, thus lengthening them slightly and preventing them from sinking into soft surfaces.

Saddlebag set-ups aren't available, so equipping the bike for touring is a small engineering project.

Not long after acquiring my Vincent, I was accelerating around a curve on a bumpy road, when the bike suddenly went into a violent speed wobble. The front wheel seemed to clear the ground and leap from side to side, leaving black marks on the pavement about 40 feet apart. I crouched low over the tank, eased off the throttle, and after several violent gyrations, the bike straightened up. After riding slowly to the nearest dealer, I was advised to keep the steering damper snugged down lightly. Tightening it too tightly invites heavy steering at low speeds, and a tail wagging effect at high speeds. Following this advice, I experienced no further trouble.

Some problems exist that I haven't been able to solve. The engine breather slobbers oil, leaving an embarrassing puddle wherever the bike is parked. The brakes quit working when the linings get wet, which almost always happens when the bike is washed or ridden in the rain. The original voltage regulator was erratic and impossible to adjust properly, and was replaced with a Harley-Davidson regulator. The generator has a charging rate of only 8 amps, barely enough to run the lights. Also the generator doesn't charge at full capacity at speeds under 50 mph, so it's difficult to keep the battery charged during stop-and-go traffic driving at night.

Parts are hard to find, and priced outrageously high when you locate them. But fortunately, the Vincent seems to be exceptionally reliable and durable, and I haven't had to buy many parts. Aside from routine maintenance, the engine hasn't been touched, but I have had to overhaul the magneto, generator, clutch and brakes.

My '51 Vincent is one of the "C" Series. In 1954, shortly before the factory suspended the manufacture of motorcycles in favor of more profitable government contracts, the Series "D" was produced. It featured many improvements over the Series "C" models, such as optional fiberglass panels that completely enclosed and streamlined the bike, improved suspension and electrical system, and a large lever on the side of the machine for lifting it effortlessly onto the rear stand.

I'm prejudiced, I admit, but in spite of the Vincent's age and shortcomings, there isn't a motorcycle on the market that would better serve my touring needs. You can't help but love a bike that brings you home time after time without trouble, from the far reaches of the continent. While leafing thru the rider's manual in Acapulco, I came across a phrase advising the owner to "ride slowly to the nearest dealer" in case of mechanical trouble. I suddenly realized that the nearest dealer was more than 3000 miles away, and in case of a breakdown I would be helpless. While riding across a vast expanse of prairie one night, I was caught in a snow storm. If you can keep rolling in extreme heat or cold, your morale remains high and you can endure extremes in temperature, but if you break down, you've had it. I began wondering what would happen if the bike should quit running, and concluded there would be nothing to do but sit on the roadside, cry, wring my hands and wait for death. But as always, the old Vincent brought me home.

On another occasion, I blundered into the California desert in the 120° heat of August. As I rode along with spots swimming before my eyes and sweat trickling down my legs and filling my boots, I noticed a peculiar knock in the engine. Realizing I would be in serious trouble in case of mechanical failure, I headed for home. After the trip I found that the engine was knocking because half the teeth on the magneto drive gear were worn completely off! How the mag kept turning, I can't understand.

How can you part with a bike like that? After so many years of faithful service, it would be like selling an old friend.

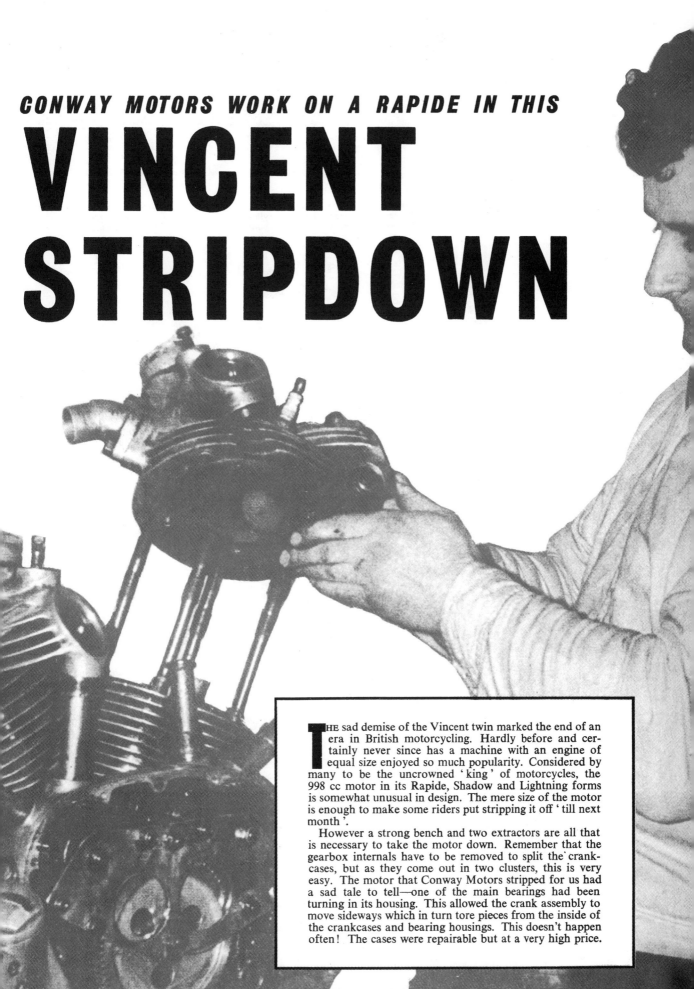

CONWAY MOTORS WORK ON A RAPIDE IN THIS
VINCENT STRIPDOWN

THE sad demise of the Vincent twin marked the end of an era in British motorcycling. Hardly before and certainly never since has a machine with an engine of equal size enjoyed so much popularity. Considered by many to be the uncrowned 'king' of motorcycles, the 998 cc motor in its Rapide, Shadow and Lightning forms is somewhat unusual in design. The mere size of the motor is enough to make some riders put stripping it off ' till next month '.

However a strong bench and two extractors are all that is necessary to take the motor down. Remember that the gearbox internals have to be removed to split the crankcases, but as they come out in two clusters, this is very easy. The motor that Conway Motors stripped for us had a sad tale to tell—one of the main bearings had been turning in its housing. This allowed the crank assembly to move sideways which in turn tore pieces from the inside of the crankcases and bearing housings. This doesn't happen often! The cases were repairable but at a very high price.

VINCENT RAPIDE STRIP

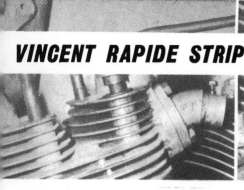

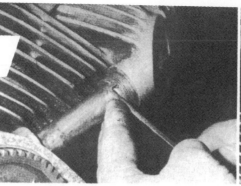

The cylinder heads come off complete with all the rocker gear. To remove them, take off these nuts and the carburettors

The push-rod tubes are secured by threaded flanges which screw into the cylinder head. Release them with this 'U' spanner

The complete cylinder head can be lif clear of the barrel. Do this carefu and then examine the joint condit.

With the cover out of the way, the gear change and kickstart mechanisms are exposed. Remove the cover from timing chest

Actuating arm of the gearchange complete with its ratchet and pawl should be removed from their shafts. Check condition

Use a pair of pliers to pull the kic start return spring from its pegs on t pawl. Replace spring if it is very

Still with the engine locked, undo the nut on the half-time pinion. This nut has been off several times and is damaged

An extractor is necessary to pull the half-time pinion from its place against the large idler. Don't try to lever pinion

The two camshafts and the central st idler will now pull out from their po tions without the use of any extracte

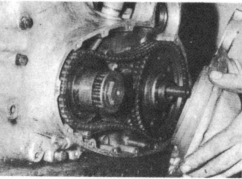

Six cheese-headed screws hold the clutch drum in position. Take these out and then pull the drum out. Check condition of drum

Turn now to the primary drive. Drain all the oil from primary chaincase and release all securing screws to remove case

Again lock the engine with a bar throu the small end of con-rod and undo the on mainshaft and remove shock-absorb

he push-rod tubes are a push-fit in ming chest and they should be pulled out. lean insides of tubes on re-assembling

Take the circlips out and then warm the pistons with a rag dipped in boiling water. The gudgeon pins will drift out easily

Take the kickstart lever, gear indicator and gearchange lever off the kickstart cover. Then undo screws and remove cover

circlip holds starting pinion and ratchet. Remove it and slide the ratchet, inion and spring from their place on shaft

The advance-retard unit is self extracting. Undo the centre bolt until it gets tight, tap it and continue to remove unit

Here the magneto is being removed. The motor should be locked with a bolt through con-rod to extract the advance-retard

ndoing two clamping screws will release e dynamo from its housing, having already ulled the dynamo sprocket from shaft

Take off the outer clutch cover, undo the screws in the spring ring and remove it along with springs and all clutch plates

The inner clutch plate and clutch shoe assembly can be withdrawn when the retaining nut is undone. Lock the motor for this

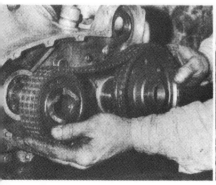

he complete primary drive consisting of gine sprocket, triplex chain and clutch rocket can now be pulled from position

Behind the clutch sprocket there is the gearbox cover plate. Drain all oil from gearbox and remove plate with mainshaft

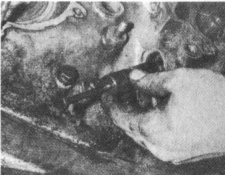

Gears come out in one cluster. Remove cover to oil pump, insert bolt to act as extractor and pull the oil pump from housing

EGLI-VINCENT

THERE ARE, among men's creations, certain machines that induce animated conversation, that illuminate the eyes of enthusiasts. Among automobiles there are the Mercedes SSK, the Cord, and the Blower Bentley. Among aircraft there are the Sopwith Camel, the DeHavilland DH4, and the Lockheed Vega.

Among motorcycles there is the Vincent.

Those men who rode Vincents when they were new, glistening black and silver, tend to engage in overspeak, describing the feel, the thrill. Youngsters who don't know what they're seeing still stand in awe of the restored Shadows and Lightnings that appear in motorcycle exhibits from time to time.

The Vincent H.R.D. Co., Ltd., of Stevenage, England, manufacturer of handcrafted magnificence, was felled in 1955 by the avalanche of assembly line manufactured vertical Twins from other British factories. To the financial detriment of Vincent H.R.D., these less costly Twins found rider acceptance worldwide. The firm announced it soon would close its doors.

Then, and only then, did the dying company's sales department encounter a rush of orders for the huge, powerful, rapid monarchs of two-wheeled transport. The expression of faith was too late in coming. The great 998-cc ohv V-Twins no longer underwent one-at-a-time assembly, hand polishing of ports, individual fitting of carefully selected matched components. The Vincent H.R.D. plant was closed. Remaining engines and miscellaneous parts were left to gather cobwebs and dust.

Then, in 1967, an enterprising Swiss, Fritz Egli of Bremgarten, acquired the remaining Vincent powerplants and spares, and license to use the Vincent name and trade marks. He established a manufacturing and assembly plant, and started production of the Egli-Vincent. The manufacturing part is for the Egli frame; the assembly part is where the frame, supplied components and Vincent engines are joined to create Shadows and Lightnings reborn.

From this plant are delivered, f.o.b. Bremgarten, a pure racing Egli-Vincent Lightning, tailored to the purchaser's requirements, a sports model Egli-Vincent Lightning with an engine tuned for racing, rated at 73 bhp at 6500 rpm, but equipped with full touring gear; and an Egli-Vincent Shadow, a fast touring model, also fully road ready.

It was the latter machine that was made available to CYCLE WORLD for evaluation. Air freight and customs difficulties past, the motorcycle was unveiled for general inspection. If one word were to describe staff members' first impressions, that word would be: "Awesome!"

There are the black-finned, elegant massiveness of the engine, a great humped fuel tank, a plethora of levers and cables, wires for instruments, wide pedals, a cage of tubes and an extended racing saddle, all seemingly outsized, as if for a rider somewhat larger than life.

When the initial shock had worn away, a check of engine casing serial numbers revealed the Egli-Vincent Shadow's powerplant to be a series B Standard Rapide unit of approximately 1949 vintage. As with all 998-cc Vincent engines, bore and stroke are 84 and 90 mm, respectively. This particular engine first saw the light of day with a 6.8:1 compression ratio. However, Egli has raised the engine's compression to 8:1 to better deal with more modern fuels.

The Vincent valve train, for those who may recall, and for those who've never become acquainted with the king of V-Twins, is unique in motorcycle practice—radial aircraft engines, yes, but not in motorcycle engineering. Gear driven cams actuate followers which raise and lower short pushrods, which move rocker arms. The forked end of the rocker engages the valve stem at a button *below* the valve spring. This configuration results in short pushrods, which don't flex, hence are less subject to wear, and valve springs which are well away from high cylinder head temperatures, thus are less likely

to fail as the result of metal fatigue. The topside valve spring location makes changing springs an easy chore. A threaded cap above the spring is removed, a keeper released, and, presto, the valve spring can be withdrawn. No complex removal of rocker arms is required.

Cam profiles provided by Egli with the neo-Shadow show the engine is not equipped with the mild configuration of the original. The series B Rapide engine was fitted with 40-60-degree intake, and 72-28-degree exhaust cams. The new cams show 52-82, 80-50 configuration, with 9.5 mm lift.

Another Vincent variation from run-of-the-mill motorcycles is the clutch. When the clutch lever is released, a small dry, drive plate type clutch engages a face plate to which are attached two shoes, each with two pads of friction lining material affixed thereto; this sets the face plate/paired shoes arrangement spinning and, actuated by centrifugal force, the shoes make contact with the inner surface of a very brake-like drum; the clutch drum is bolted to the primary duplex drive chain shaft and sprocket.

Ignition requirements on the Egli-Vincent Shadow are met by a Lucas KVF magneto. Lighting needs are accommodated by a 6-V, 50-W Lucas/Miller generator.

Carburetion—and a great deal of feeding is required for what amounts to a pair of 500-cc engines—is accomplished by a pair of 32-mm Amal concentrics. On the test machine, these were equipped only with velocity stacks, with no provision for air filtration. The Vincent powerplant demands better treatment in a land where abrasive grit is the rule, rather than the exception.

The Vincent siamesed exhaust headers join a Dunstall style conical baffle muffler Though this so-called silencer proved unsatisfactory to police during highway and city test riding, the muffler could only be a joy to the true enthusiast who appreciates the distinctive bass crackle of the Vincent V.

The Egli frame is built around a large diameter tube backbone, which extends rearward from the steering head, and serves as the engine's oil reservoir. Triangulated struts of smaller diameter extend downward and rearward to provide a measure of rigidity, and to locate the swinging arm pivot point. Additional tubing provides support for the upper rear shock absorber mountings and saddle. The frame is a rather non-complex structure. Test crewmen at first thought the frame would not prove stiff enough, would not provide the resistance to torsional stresses that is a requirement of a high performance touring machine. These fears were groundless. The frame is not marked by any new departures in construction techniques, or any great attention to finish. The test bike's frame showed gas welds that were the equivalent of mass produced machinery, and not what enthusiasts have come to expect in custom frames in this era of aerospace metal working techniques. The frame's welds were sufficiently strong, but not neat or tidy.

The swinging arm is of built-up welded construction, heavily gusseted, filleted, ground and filed—with many file marks remaining in the metal. A pair of flattened oval tubes carry thick axle mounting tabs at the rear. The left tube is slotted for brake caliper mounting adjustment. The tubes are welded at their forward ends to a large diameter pivot tube.

The front suspension for the Egli-Vincent is a Ceriani fork. The test machine's fork was equipped with spring rates insufficient to meet the demands of 600 lb. of machine and rider. The adjustable Ceriani coil spring/hydraulic shock absorber units at the rear were able to cope with the majority of roadway irregularities.

The Egli-Vincent is fitted with Campagnolo mechanical disc brakes, double discs in the front, a single disc on the left at the

rear. Test crewmen agreed unanimously that brake pedal and hand lever effort was excessive, and that braking efficiency left something to be desired. In an effort to increase efficiency of the braking mechanism, the manufacturer has bolted 2-in. extensions on the existing Campagnolo front brake actuating levers—while not repositioning brake cable ferrule retainers above the levers. This places the brake cable stress point rearward from the ferrule bearing point. When hand lever tension is applied, the result is biting drag at the ferrules, and excessive cable wear. The best of brakes, with the ultimate in easy stopping capability, should be standard—no, mandatory—on a machine that is capable of 130 mph.

Alloy rims, 19 in. in diameter front and rear, carry Avon road racing style tires.

The Egli-Vincent Shadow's instrumentation is comprised of suspiciously Volkswagen-like VDO trip odometer/speedometer, tachometer (which confusingly reads counterclockwise), and an oil temperature gauge mounted in a crudely finished alloy bracket atop the handlebars. An ammeter is located almost out of sight of the rider in the top of the headlamp.

The Egli-Vincent was taken to Riverside Raceway, the 2.7-mile Southern California circuit, for final testing. Loafing around the course, at speeds of 80 mph or less, the machine proved surprising. It handled well, much better than anticipated. Though somewhat top heavy, the big machine clung to the road in bends something closely akin to road racing fashion. Once leaned over in a bend, the rider was required to pick up the machine bodily to make a straight line exit.

Speeds well in excess of 100 mph were achieved without difficulty. A flat-out run was not attempted, however, because of the braking capabilities of the machine in relationship to the running room available.

Over the quarter-mile, the Egli-Vincent, even though it was apparently running overly rich, and even though it was ridden with care in deference to its owner, proved itself capable of consistent 94-mph trap speeds, with e.t.s in the low 14s. The legendary Vincent V-Twin is as strong as ever.

Though ride, handling and performance of the Egli-Vincent Shadow were deemed adequate, close inspection showed a number of things wrong, definitely out of order with this particular machine.

Oil leakage became a messy problem, the result, apparently of faulty seal insertion. Smoke and exhaust gasses escaped past the exhaust header clamps, perhaps because a copper ring gasket was missing or too tightly compressed. Apparently no seal had been fitted on the generator gearshaft at the top of the primary case. These difficulties looked to CYCLE WORLD staffers to be results of lack of pains taken in assembly, rather than faulty original design. Exercise of more care could but result in a much more acceptable motorcycle.

A 250 lb. behemoth cannot kick the Vincent engine's starting crank downward against compression. The trick is to tickle the carburetors to overflow (Vincents like a lot of gas); release compression with the left-hand lever, feel (with an educated foot) when the No. 1 (rear) piston is just ready to reach the firing stroke; start the downward kick; flick in the compression release; repeat anywhere from three to 11 times for a start. Once the technique is learned, the Egli-Vincent starts hard—but it starts.

What place has the Egli-Vincent in the present world of motorcycling? The neo-Shadow has a niche, and that is ownership by a man who is first a connoisseur of Vincents, second a lover of motorcycling, and third a mechanic/machinist of greater than average skill. An Egli-Vincent must be appreciated, well loved and well maintained. ∎

EGLI-VINCENT

SPECIFICATIONS

List price	(f.o.b. Switzerland) $2000
Suspension, front	telescopic fork
Suspension, rear	swinging arm
Tire, front	3.00-19
Tire, rear	4.00-19
Engine type	50-degree ohv V-Twin
Displacement, cu. in., cc	60.9, 998
Claimed bhp @ rpm	62 @ 6000
Carburetion	(2) 32-mm Amal concentric
Ignition	magneto
Fuel capacity, gal.	3.75
Oil capacity, pt.	11.5
Oil system	dry sump
Starting system	kick, folding crank

POWER TRANSMISSION

Clutch	self-energizing expanding shoe
Primary drive	duplex chain
Final drive	single-row chain
Gear ratios, overall:1	
5th	none
4th	3.66
3rd	4.38
2nd	5.84
1st	9.49

DIMENSIONS

Wheelbase, in.	56.6
Saddle height, in.	30.6
Saddle width, in.	10.25
Footpeg height, in.	11.2
Ground clearance, in.	8.5
Curb weight (w/half-tank fuel), lb.	432

PERFORMANCE

Zero to 60 mph, sec.	4.9
Standing 1/8th mile, sec.	8.92
terminal speed, mph	78.80
Standing 1/4th mile, sec.	14.26
terminal speed, mph	94.04

Realisation is better than anticipation –in the case of

THE EGLI-VINCENT

A FAST RIDE through the spring countryside to Silverstone. Sun, new friends and the unforgettable experiences found racing one of the most magnificent motorcycles ever. Could a more pleasant way of spending a day possibly exist? On occasions, I almost envy myself, and this was one of them.

We on MCI have been extraordinarily lucky over the past few months regarding our test machinery; most of it has been big stuff—Interceptors, "Three's," BMWs; fine motorcycles all, any one of which I would be proud to own.

Now a journalist should, I suppose, ideally be a calculating, flesh-and-blood computer, just gathering facts without acknowledging his own personal preferences, yet relying on his personal experiences, icily separating the good from the bad. He should be detective and judge, but not jury, and should certainly remain unmoved by passioned councils. Possibly some men could write in such a manner, and others find their spelled graphs entertaining, but my Achilles Heel is in my enthusiasm. I will forgive a good many motorcycles anything up to a point, for a good number of reasons set by entirely my own standards (not necessarily the right ones). It could be because the machine has been conceived by a manufacturer to be the way to producing a first-class, low-cost product, i.e. the Ariel Arrow, or is an attempt by a small man to point the way to an entirely new avenue of thought like Paul Wright and his Scorpion. (That an unconventional machine, especially one without the backing of a multi-million-pound organisation fails, is not necessarily an indication of unsound design, but generally unsound market research, a very different kettle of fish.) As a rule the machines finding least favour with me are those conceived twenty or thirty years ago, still in production, and whose success is directly proportional to the gullibility of the motorcycling public. Racing successes bear no relationship to roadster suitability. Vast sums of money are spent modifying a machine for a task for which it is completely unsuitable, and against which, its racing counterpart bears not the slightest resemblance.

A lot has been written in the past few months about the bad sportsmanship of "that" Spanish factory. Using a racing expansion chamber, indeed—tut, tut. They were not disqualified for using an expansion chamber. Disqualification came about for one reason only—the modification could be seen easily. Why one of our most successful factory's motorcycles was not pulled in for inspection is beyond me. It was an open secret that the camshafts were special, but the obvious modification was to the cylinder heads. The inlet tracts had been repositioned, and so brazenly that welding scars were plainly visible. It was carried out on the advice of one of our famous racing car drivers and designers following gas-flow experiments. The price of the machines involved shot up from say £400 or so to probably £1500; that's what I mean about "relationship".

But man is a creature of emotional, not rational, thought, and to that I plead guilty. If there is one thing I enjoy more than a little one bettering a big one, it's the thrill of discovering an old machine, maybe because of its legendary past, still capable of trouncing the motorcycles of today.

It must be plain by now, although we try as hard as possible to hide it (cross my heart we do), what admirers of Vincents the Editor and I are. Even their most ardent lovers must now though, especially under pressure of some of the large capacity designs of the past year or two, admit their equalling. Up to six or seven years ago nothing surpassed them. A Vincent was faster than everything, outbraked anything, and properly set up, held the road better than all (with the exception of one make). Then imperceptably at first, but with gathering momentum, the argument changed from not so much what it does, as to the way it does it, for the 650 twins were speeding up. With the advent of 750 twins and threes and even bigger ones promised, "The way it does it" fades unless used to denigrate. Vincents, despite the practically suggested leads taken by so many of their owners, are still a rider's machine, not glittering museum pieces, so how can an owner update his big twin to bring it once more to its rightful place ahead of the crowd?

Countless owners and dealers have attempted the task but instead of improving, most have simply altered. The most popular method was to shoehorn a Manx or Featherbed frame around the power unit, but that upset everything, even adding to the overall weight in many cases, and certainly raising the centre of gravity to uncomfortable heights. Probably the most successful modification I have ever seen utilised a pair of Norton forks at the front, and Velocette swinging arm on the other end, but retaining the Vincent oil tank spine. For all that, it was still a one-off "Bitza", however handsome.

The answer can be found in Fritz Egli's beautifully engineered new creation. For £170 any Vincent owner could transform his dated twin into a machine no less modern than a Honda "four". Performance? That's up to you. Midlander Roger Slater, the sole Egli concessionaire, sells only cycle parts under the Egli-Vincent scroll. He will as he always has, repair, improve and/or tune engines, but that is entirely your concern, requiring separate pricing, and within certain limits outside the interests of this report.

A dream materialised. Because of the Egli's use of conventional suspension, it should appeal to a broader section of motorcyclists than its forerunner.

Photo/report: DAVE MINTON

You may if you interest yourself with motorcycling activities of our American cousins, have read a test report of the USA Egli-Vincent and noticed the magazine's surprisingly critical appraisal. Personally, I think it counts for nothing; not after putting two and two together anyway. Our libel laws, being what they are, make things difficult, but work it out for yourself. Even our palsy-walsy motorcycle world suffers from commercial politics; at least, I think so.

Fritz Egli decided to start production of Vincents again. He signed a contract with one of the big USA motorcycle importers to supply 1500 new machines. On the strength of this he visited Harpers, the Vincent holding company, with £250,000, enough money to purchase the manufacturing rights from them. A German engineering company had agreed to produce the engines, crankcases and all; these were not to be the old twins we know now but vastly improved engines. However, before production was under way the magazine in question wanted a machine to test so urgently it had to be airmailed over with an old engine. Now, the proprietor is also an importer and manufacturer himself, with some ideas of his own regarding the resurrection of the old Indian motorcycles—"V" twins and with new Featherbed-type frames, but these have only side-valve engines, scarcely a marketable proposition in the face of ohv competition with a name like Vincent. After the test was published the order for 1500 was cancelled. Fritz Egli lost a fortune. Luckily the German company agreed to free him from his contract with them. The Harper/Vincent purchase fell through and that was that, the end of a brave attempt to start production of a great motorcycle. Luckily, from the ruins, Fritz salvaged his frame and decided to continue production of that alone. Back to Silverstone and the sun.

This machine is owned by Reay Mackay. He is the man you see riding a thundering great black, girder-forked twin amongst the rainbow enamel and chrome of the others in production and even "open" races. If you are really lucky and it's raining, then you will probably see him in front. The engine was originally from his Black Shadow and departs only a little from its old specifications. Manx pistons are fitted, raising the compression ratio to 9.5:1 and the carburetters are 1⅜in GPs, and of course it has been assembled with loving care and attention. Roger Slater fitted an AMC/Norton clutch plus one extra plate, and the gearbox is standard early Shadow using a close-ratio cluster. Bottom gear is 7.5:1 and top 3.56:1. Lots of Reay's and Roger's own mods are included in the engine of course, but I tried to keep my interest around the cycle parts where it should have been.

Initially I thought how similar in concept the Egli was to a standard Vincent. Spine-type oil tank; swinging fork from the engine plates; all solid Vincent in fact, but it was not. Unlike a Vincent, the Egli did not require the engine as a frame member, although it appears to hang in the same manner. The top tube, or spine, is 4½in diameter and holds the oil. The rear part of the frame is ⅞in diameter tubing. Both are in 16 gauge weight material. Prodding around the bike, I suddenly noticed a bolt missing, one normally used in cap-

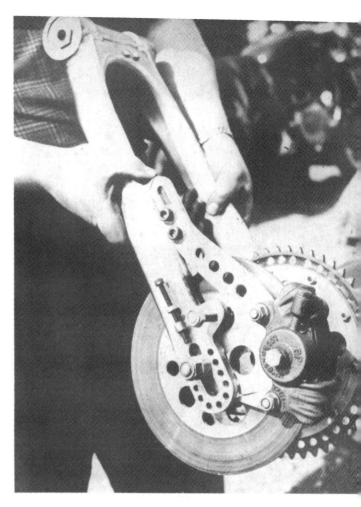

Another Egli fabrication, a disc brake to replace the standard one. This fork is of necessity different from the normal Egli; note the standard Vincent pivot bearings.

turing the rear cylinder head to the frame. Roger smiled, and explained how unnecessary it was. The only engine attachment points are at the front cylinder head and the rear gearbox mounting plates; one is provided for the rear cylinder but it was not found essential. The swinging fork is attached in the usual Vincent manner to the standard engine plates. Here at last is a fork that I think possibly even Phil Vincent would appreciate, even though it is not triangulated. Its bearings are the normal taper roller style, and the rest is fabricated from sheet steel and welded. Each one is hand-made by Fritz Egli, flame-welded and then cleaned with a file before chroming.

In place of the usual uniform round-section tubing, each leg is approximately two inches deep, and three-quarters wide. Two Girling units supply springing and damping movement. In this country the front forks are Metal Profiles, but on the Continent and USA are Ceriani. Reay's bike has a single Vincent rear brake and a Robinson double twin-leading-shoe front brake. Weight is 352 lb and approximately 70 bhp is turned out at 7000 rpm, although the motor will rev to 7200 rpm in safety. Incidentally the 500 cc Comet single can also be so modified and this weighs only 257 lbs!

Roger Slater has half a dozen basic price guides, starting at £78 for the bare frame and swinging fork. The complete conversion kit for the original Vincent is £175. This price includes fitting. Unless it is found impossible for one reason or another for Roger to build the machine, kits will not be sold like a great box of Meccano, although any separate items can be purchased as spares. Next on the list, including the kit, plus extra touring components and lightweight alloy equipment is the £275 specification. For £475 a complete machine with an as-new, thoroughly overhauled engine is listed. Top of the list is a racer equipped with a fully-tuned engine. GP carbs, 9 in double twin-leading-shoe front brake and so on, but the price is still only £530.

It's a lean-looking beast seen from this end, and this is the view that the majority of other riders will . . .enjoy . . .?

Remembering some past experience with a Vincent at speed, to say I rode from the paddock eagerly would not be entirely true; full of anticipation maybe, for I was anticipating just about everything, so for the first lap I toured around.

Next lap, a bit faster. Third time around and I was driving it round the bends and opening the throttle hard against the stop on the short straights. On the fourth and fifth laps I began to find out a bit about Silverstone and then during the next two I had time to think about the machine; and in the seventh I felt that tiger rising, and discovered what a dream of a machine it really was. Then, on the eighth, overstepped myself and blessed the Robinson brake, and on the ninth the chairs went out for practice and I came in.

Just nine laps . . . ah! But nine laps of sheer bliss. Fritz Egli and Roger Slater, you are producing the most perfect examples of well-engineered motorcycles that I have ever laid eyes upon. After my ride I am sure Roger must have thought me a bit simple, for I said, I think, very little. In all honesty, I did not know what to say; it was such a fantastically good motorcycle. On most test occasions, something stands out on a machine that makes it worthy of a few superlatives, rarely is everything good. If only one or two things are, conversation is so easy, there is so much to discuss, but when everything is so perfect, I at any rate, feel such a chump, grinning like a happy idiot, drooling nothing but, "It's lovely. It's lovely". Reay Mackay encouraged me to go around Maggotts—a poorly-surfaced shallow left-hander, flat out—"As fast as you like", so after five or six laps I was, and every time I came out feeling like a king and pretty sure I could do it at 200 mph at least.

On the track with me were, amongst racing Bantams and wee Hondas, a few Manx Nortons and PR Bonnevilles; fast motorcycles indeed, but we swept past the lot. No credit to me, mind, I am no regular racing man and do not doubt the ability of the Manx and PR riders to better me on similar machines. But on the Egli, not a chance of it; I was unbeatable and not only because of the enormous power output either, but around the bends as well—Maggotts I took faster and faster at each successive lap. Becketts, a tight, shockingly-surfaced right hander, found me over so far that my right foot, flat on the rest, kissed the tarmac (and you don't

catch me leaning over that far on a broken surface if I am conscious of it). Around there in second and after banging open the throttle hard at the next two changes up along the half-mile straight to Woodcote, I waited for the rev-counter needle to reach 6000 rpm in top—that's why my foot touched at Becketts. The faster I went around, the faster I left, and the sooner I was in top gear. Lap after lap I tried, forgetting all about my careful analysis of the Egli side of things. At first it was only 5600 rpm, then by lap five or so 5800 but not until the last lap but one did 6000 rpm show. Just a fleeting glance of the needle, just a shy hesitant kiss, but it did. On that gear 6000 rpm works out to 130 mph, and that was not all; lots more revs lay awaiting a more daring fist than mine. Peter Davies, the PR racer, was riding through to another 200 revs, approximately 135 mph, and there was still more to come! Moreover, for safety reasons revs through the gears were limited to 6000, so without a doubt speeds would have been higher had the maximum power range at 6,500 rpm been used.

Alas, the point of the riding was with the frame, so the frame it shall be. I can only say that for me it was faultless; perfect. Despite some attempts at provocation (and some other attempts to get round at all) everything went smoothly. No warping or swaying, and the tyres felt glued to the tarmac. Everything contributed to it. The soft, beautifully damped, long-action forks, the light rigid frame, and the immensely strong rear fork. What more can I say? It was much too good for me to find its limits.

After my stint, Peter Davies took over and he really showed what a potential race and sales winner the Egli machines are; remember, the engine, though tuned, is not a scarcely-tamed devil, happy only when running wild. Reay hides no tuning secrets in his twin's immense black chest; even the valve timing is standard. Most Vincent owners could bring their twins to the same pitch. Peter held the revs to the 6000 limit, but that was still 500 below maximum so the Egli's ultimate power remained just out of reach. Roger also changed the GP rear tyre for a triangular racing one. I must admit to discovering the ease with which the rear wheel would move sideways if too much sudden throttle was applied before recovering completely from a bend. The entry at Woodcote, a right-hand curve connecting the short circuit up to the main one in front of the grandstand and paddock, was a bit rubbery; this, combined with the light weight and high power of the bike, invited disaster if too heavy a hand

Continued on page 150

Roger Slater just duster servicing the Egli. The rear engine plates support the rear sub frame and fork pivot in much the same manner as the "D" series.

Roger Slater overhauls

The mighty Vincent V-twin

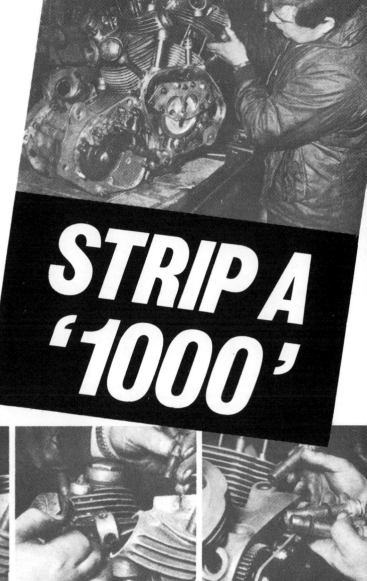

When Vincents were available new from the factory, their high price and to some extent their tremendous power kept them for an exclusive type of enthusiast.

He was usually knowledgeable enough to keep the bike in first-class condition or he had enough money to have it done for him.

Unhappily the scene has altered somewhat over the years and although many fine Vincents are to be seen, some are no longer maintained to the standards this fine machine deserves.

MM went along to Roger Slater and watched him strip and build a 1000 cc motor at his workshop in Bromsgrove, nr. Woodcote, Worcestershire.

We barely scratch the surface here, owing to limited time and space.

The Vincent is no motor for the amateur or ill-equipped mechanic. If you feel you have the necessary know-how to tackle the job and the necessary tools, it is essential that you get the workshop manual.

Much of the Vincent is simple to work on, but there are special operations, common only to this machine, which could cause vast trouble and expense to the man who is not familiar with the make.

The gear adjusting mechanism, for instance, is relatively simple—once you know how, but it can seem very confusing if you don't.

Incidentally, Paul Richardson's Book of the Vincent covers that particular aspect of the bike comprehensively.

Lastly, if you do get hold of a Vincent, it is well worth joining the Vincent Owners' Club. There you will meet true enthusiasts who live and breathe Vincents. What's more they are always ready to help other members with advice.

Remove cylinder head brackets. Note which way they are offset. Undo head holding nuts and push-rod cover nuts. Use the KI spanner

Get the cylinder on compression before removing the clearance adjusters. Use thin-nosed pliers to lift push-rods through rocker holes

Take out rocker feed bolt which locates in the valve rocker bearing. The rocker can then be pulled out. Check bearings for undue slackness

Knock push-rod tubes down before trying to lift heads. No gasket is fitted; heads are ground on to barrels with valve-grinding compound

With timing cover off you will see steady plate over timing wheels. Take careful note of position of gears, washers and timing marks

When reassembling, do not forget the two thrust washers which fit on the camshaft spindles. Both go behind steady plate in order shown

Always fit a steel idler wheel-gear for it to last. Slacken idler shaft nuts and lift up idler to get correct pinion tooth mesh

Any tightness or slack is corrected by replacing the half-time pinion ET49 by any of the over or under-sizes available from −20 to +20

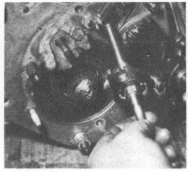

The front exhaust cam spindle is the only screw-in one and has a washer on either side. Loose camshaft spindles should be copper . . .

. . . plated to restore their fit. Use extractor or screwdriver to take off engine shaft pinion. These are usually loose and extract easily

Take off gearbox cover to reach gear ratchet shaft and kickstart quadrant. No oil should be in the cover unless a seal or bush fails

On the left is the modified carrier centraliser. The ears this version restrict sel arm movement and help cha

With these bolts out and the camplate spindle removed, a blow with a hide hammer on the mainshaft will allow gear cluster removal

Here we see the final drive shaft and third gear pinion being withdrawn. The gears are very robust but renew the two G16 Oilite bushes

When assembling gearbox, fit selector forks and cam plate in position and turn cam plate anti-clockwise into the first gear position

When parting crankcases, make the studs stay in their co positions as they are all d ent lengths. Don't lose three do

On the timing side mainshaft is the oil pump worm which drives the oil pump. Roger Slater supplies a complete pump with larger output

To withdraw oil pump (arrow) in order to drive out the timing side main bearing, it is necessary to heat the case and use . . .

. . . one of the $\frac{5}{16}$ in. BSF bolts and a long tube to act as an extractor. With enough heat on the case, pump body should easily extract

Again, with cases suitably he and using a large soft drift can drive out the inner bearing in the normal ma

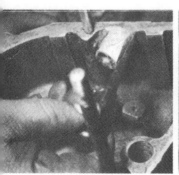

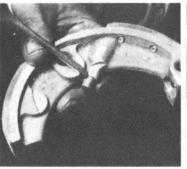

Watch this boss for cracks. The series D had a strengthening web which cured the problem, but on B and C models cracks are common

Vincent valves are different to conventional. The rocker arm acts on the collar midway up the stem instead of on top of the valve

There must be no play in this plunger on the clutch shoe assembly. Service exchange shoes are available if linings are worn

Renew oil seal PD 26/1. Smear pound on the face of the which contacts the chainwheel, up screws (shake-proof). Smea

ove circlip, starting pinion
et spring and bush. Make sure
there is no play on bush as
can cause kickstart failure

The long nuts (arrowed) must be
replaced in their correct positions.
Failure to note their places
can lead to great confusion

Loosen crankcase bolts to relieve
pressure before trying to lift
barrels. If levering is necessary
use only the short tough fins

Dismantle the clutch, primary drive
and undo the set-bolts on the gearbox drive-side plate. Another bolt
is wired to index plunger cap

n reassembling, the outer bearing
in after cases are joined.
von't go in before (with oil
p in position) it fouls the worm

Make sure that the alloy distance
piece is firm between inner bearing
track and circlip and that the
oil thrower ET77 is a snug fit

Here we see the drive-side inner
bearing track coming out with the
large alloy distance piece behind
it. Circlip is still in position

This crankpin nut was damaged by
the bearing coming loose. Watch for
polished outer bearing cases—a
sure sign of looseness in housing

outer bearing will have to be
rried" out with a tool similar
he one shown. An old screw-
er, heated and bent, works well

When you come to replace the oil,
pump drive, reverse the method
used for extraction and be sure to
get the locating holes lined up

Here is the older type pump with
straight teeth (single start worm).
The later type has angled teeth
and has a double start worm

Fit the ratchet bevel and spring
before joining crankcases—it's
easily forgotten. Small bearing
rarely wears, but check anyway

e compound on the splines of
clutch shoe carrier before
g. Now fit clutch carrier,
, retaining nut and washer

The clutch driver pin sleeves
can be fitted after the inner
clutch plate. Never fail to renew
the oil seal in carrier centre

Tighten carrier nut, making sure
it goes right home and that the
locking spring ear locates in the
slot in line with hole in shaft

With the floating plate assembly
and outer plate in position, all
that remains is to insert springs
and cups before final adjustments

MOTORCYCLE MASTERPIECES

MCM looks at the greatest of all the V-Twins
Story: Roger Cox

VINCENT

In the motorcycling fraternity there is one marque which can be relied upon to generate more controversy than any other; it is that of the Vincent. It is now 17 years since the last machine was assembled, but despite this they still maintain a high level of interest, a fact which is emphasised by their now escalating second-hand price. Like the 4½-litre vintage Bentley, they now command a higher price second-hand than they did when they were new.

Mention of the Vincent usually draws a particular picture in the enthusiasts mind, namely that of the Series C model, the model of which most were produced and the one that achieved the greatest fame in racing, sprinting, speed trials and world-record breaking. Yet an analysis of the lineage since the C's introduction goes back to the 1930s. It is perhaps remarkable that a machine whose basic design concept was so old could, 20 years later, establish so many records; it is even more remarkable that 15 years after that, they could still be so pre-eminent in so many racing fields.

The history of the Vincent, from its inception to its final design philosophy and ultimate demise in the 1955 Series Ds, Black Princes and Black Knights, covers a period of over 30 years during which time the factory turned out nearly 11,000 assorted machines. Its history is also irretrievably intertwined with that of its makers, the Vincent Engineering Company, and that of its prime progenitors, Philip Vincent and Philip Irving. It tends to be a very personal history, liberally sprinkled with many colourful characters, ideas and inspirations, for whatever else may be said of the Vincent motorcycle, it was a machine built by enthusiasts for the enthusiast to enjoy.

The inception of the Series C really goes back to around 1935, although the HRD-Vincent company had been in existence for a number of years prior to this. The machines prior to 1935 were not spectacular. They were very quick for the period, quicker than most of the competitors. They used proprietary engines—the Rudge Python being among the favourites —and they used many proprietary cycle parts. Later models did see some innovations in the frame design, innovations that were to remain with Vincents until the day that they ceased production.

HRD was a company formed by Howard R. Davies, a man who had enjoyed considerable success riding his own machines in the Isle of Man TT. He is still the only man ever to have won the Senior mounted on a Junior machine. Because of his successes, his company—and hence the machines that he made— were held in high esteem throughout the motorcycle world. Philip Vincent decided that his fledgling company, Vincent Engineering, might be able to profit from the esteem that HRD's had acquired. And so the association of the two companies began and the HRD-Vincent company was formed.

The main item Vincent was not content with on contemporary motorcycles in the years preceding 1935 was that concerning the frame design. Practically all motorcycles of the era demanded that the riders had cast-iron spines, for the provision of any sort of suspension was considered to be well in the realms of the luxurious. It was towards rectifying this deficit that Vincent turned his attention. The result was a machine that, while embodying the normal Webb-type front suspension, had a rear suspension which was entirely to P.V.C.'s own design and for which a subsequent British patent was granted. The suspension took the form of a triangulated rear fork, the rear apex of which carried the wheel, the bottom apex was pivoted to swing up and down, and the top apex carried the spring

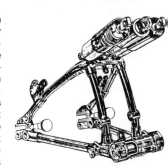

Top: The renowned Shadow, 1953 model modified for world record attempts. Above: Layout of Vincent's triangulated rear suspension

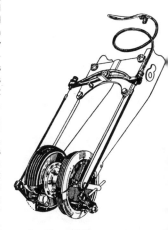

An innovation at the time—twin drum front brakes with balancing caliper mechanism

The prototype Series A "Plumber's Nightmare"

Photographs reproduced by permission of "Motor Cycle"

boxes. The whole fork pivoted up and down in a concertina sort of fashion and hopefully absorbed all the shocks. This sounded all very dubious and was only matched by its very unconventional appearance. However, a consideration of the theory of suspension reveals that the basic idea was very sound.

While Vincent worked away at his machines, over in the Velocette works a young Australian engineer was working out a few of the design details of their machines. The most notable was the introduction of helical-cut timing gears into the various ranges of Velocette, the idea being to cut down noise and improve transmission. As it worked so successfully for such a long time it is amazing that this was never carried out on the Vincent when it was finally designed; it would have been a major improvement.

It was destined that the two engineers, Vincent and Irving, should meet, and that the net outcome of this meeting should be some thoughts on an entirely new home-brewed engine to power the HRD range. Vincent outlined the ideas that he had for the new engine and Irving translated these on to paper. It was 1935 when the first of the new range saw the light of day: the Series A had arrived. As was to become typical of Vincent's thinking in later years, the engine embodied a number of unusual features which at once become apparent when compared with those of contemporary engines. Not least of these features was the high camshaft/short pushrod configuration,

and the novel arrangement of the valves and valve gear. It was this approach that enabled the Vincent to cover huge mileages in between decokes, also enabling the valves to run at an exceptionally cool temperature. The 500 cc Series A came in four ranges: the Meteor, the Comet, the Comet Special and finally the TT Replica—the last two really being hotted-up versions of the first two. Performance was very good on all the models, remembering the era. The Meteor developed 25 bhp at 5300 rpm and had a top speed of 80 mph; the Comet achieved 26 bhp at 5600 rpm and had a speed of 85–90 mph. The Comet Special and the TT Replica achieved 28 and 34 bhp respectively, and the TT version could achieve speeds of 110 mph, although often at the expense of reliability.

All the machines were received quite well by the motorcycling public but it still seemed to the designers that much more could be accomplished. Ideally, what was needed was a machine which had the speed of the TT engine but could do it with much less fuss and bother. After some deliberation it appeared that an answer might be found if one merely "doubled up" on the 500 cc Comet engine.

And so was born the fore-runner of the Series C range, and the type of motor which more than any other was to be characteristically Vincent. It was the Series A 998 cc Rapide. This approach took the motor-cycling press by storm when it first appeared. Its power output was 45 bhp at 5500 rpm and it

could haul the machine and rider to 110 mph at a very quick rate of knots. In 1937 there were other machines around that did have nearly the same performance—machines like the Brough Superior SS 100—but not quite. In motorcycling events all over the country the Rapide quickly established itself as being in a league by itself. The factory Rapide, in the hands of people like George Brown riding the legendary "Gunga Din", established hill-climb records, speed-trial records and innumerable others all over the country.

pipework

Of course, the machine did have its faults and its detractors. One unkind wag, eyeing the mass of pipework surrounding the power unit, christened the Series A as the "Plumber's Nightmare", a name which has forever stuck. Also, because of the tremendous power that the motor churned out, and because transmission techniques had not quite caught up to these sort of power ratings, the clutch was always a constant source of bother. Too much enthusiasm with the throttle produced only the smell of burning clutch plates. In later years, this clutch problem, and the attempt to solve it, was to have side effects that would forever plague Vincent owners.

The Series A could have gone on to greater things if it had not been for the inconvenience of Hitler starting the Second World War. Inevitably, due to the factory being geared into the war effort and to shortage of supplies for use in motorcycle manufac-

ture, progress in further development became curtailed.

Despite the war, both Irving and Vincent had realised the shortcomings of their machines and consideration was given as to how they could be improved. Irving, in 1945, presented a paper to the Institute of Mechanical Engineers, where he outlined his proposals for what he thought "the ultimate machine" should be. In his paper this "theoretical machine" was described in some detail, particularly the performance aspect. Although the paper was fully reported in *Motorcycling*, generally it aroused little interest. Within a year the Vincent-HRD Company had produced a 998 cc machine which, curiously enough, bore a striking resemblance to that machine which Irving had described in his paper. This was the birth of the Series B Rapide, a machine that some pressmen said "opened up new vistas in high-speed motorcycle cruising". The Vincent company had completely redesigned their machine, obviously having taken to heart the statement of "the plumber's nightmare". Gone were all the external oil pipes which had so littered the earlier Series A. In its place was an all-alloy motor whose external lines were as simple as the A's were complex. The massive crankcase casting was cast integral with the gearbox, making it over a decade ahead of its rivals. Irving had also given much attention to the transmission side. The gearbox internals were extremely robust, bearing more resemblance to a tank gearbox than a motorcycle. Irving was still suspicious of multi-plate clutches. They had their place, but not on machines that had so much bottom-end torque and such prodigious power output. The device which took its place has often been called a self-servo clutch, despite the fact that it was no such thing. It was, in fact, a single-plate clutch of the normal pattern which could be operated with the pressure of two fingers. The primary clutch operated through on to another clutch which in appearance looked like a brake-drum with two brake-shoes. The primary clutch, through a system of pins, collars and linkages, caused these "brake-shoes" to expand on to the "brake-drum", this secondary clutch taking up all the primary power. In principle the system was very good, the primary clutch alone was capable of taking the main power up to speeds of 60 mph. In practice, however, the clutch operation could be a little violent and did often give impressive standing-start getaways. But at the time there was simply not another type of clutch that was up to the sort of treatment that the Vincent could dole out.

massive

The frame, too, had not escaped attention. As Vincent was to write 20 years later, he could not see the point of having such a massive engine without using it as part of the frame construction. The engine was so massive that it certainly would not be given to the flexing and twisting that even the most sturdy of duplex frames was prone to. And so the characteristic Vincent frame was born, the engine being the main frame member. The frame still employed the patented Vincent rear fork which was now hinged straight on to the rear of the gearbox casting. The front of the rear spring boxes came up underneath the saddle and were attached to the rear of the oil tank. This oil tank was a sheet-steel girder-box type that looked as if it owed its construction to a battleship designer. The oil tank, too, formed part of the frame, and the oil-tank filler neck poked its way through the petrol tank which sat, saddle fashion, over it. The front of the oil tank carried the head races to which were attached the Brampton girder forks. In all, the total frame design proved to be immensely strong and free from any of the flexural defects which bothered its contemporaries. Also, something quite novel for the time,

the roadholding was well above average.

Other aspects, too, had received attention. To cope with the machine's high speeds Vincent fitted two brakes to each wheel. In case of a puncture there was no need to resort to the toolkit: both wheels were capable, through a tommy-bar arrangement, of being removed with fingers only.

With the introduction of the Series B Rapide Vincent could have left it at that, but there had to be a "sports" version. This marked the entrance of the Vincent-HRD Company's prima donna in 1948. It was the appearance of their most famous machine, the 998 cc Vincent Black Shadow, a machine whose capabilities and performance were not matched anywhere in the motorcycling world for over 20 years. Its power output was 55 bhp and its performance was in excess of 120 mph. With its introduction the praise lavished on it by the motorcycling press was extensive. *Motorcycling*, in their famous road test of 1948, had much to say about it, examples of which were phrases like ". . . how it feels to hit the atmosphere at two miles a minute . . .", ". . . acceleration that was constant and colossal. . ."

As the Rapide had given rise to the Shadow, so the Shadow gave rise to the Black Lightning, an even more potent version of the Shadow. This 998 cc variant was the out-and-out competition model supplied strictly for racing and record-breaking. Power output was in the order of 75 bhp, depending on the state of tune, and top speeds of around 150 mph were possible. A short while after its introduction it set many national and world speed records. 1950 saw the evolution of the Series B into the Series C range. Essentially they were the same in outward appearance as the B, with the exception of the front forks. The former Brampton pattern gave way to Vincent's own design, the highly unusual Vincent "Girdraulic". These were supposed to combine the lateral rigidity of the Bramptons with the greater shock-absorbing characteristics of the telescopic. The whole principle looked unusual, was unusual and was expensive to put into practice. The Bristol Aeroplane Company manufactured the greater part of them from L64 aircraft alloy and of course this added to the cost. Other detailed modifications

took place. Perhaps the most symbolic was the removal, along with some exposed oilways, of HRD from the timing-case cover, to be replaced with the word "Vincent". Also, the rear suspension now had the added luxury of hydraulic damping to try and smooth further the unusual suspension activities of the rear frame.

unusual

The series C stayed in production until the 1954 trading season when it was time again for the factory to produce a highly unusual machine. The Series C evolved into the Series D and more significantly saw the introduction of the Black Knight and Black Prince models, an announcement that once again caused a considerable stir.

The Series D range in general—of which both the Black Knight and Black Prince were part—saw the biggest modifications carried out to the rear suspension and spine-frame design that had evolved on the B. The rear frame now had a single Armstrong shock absorber unit instead of the earlier two separate springs and separate damper. The hand-adjustable friction dampers connecting the seat to the rear frame were also dispensed with and the rear seat, by utilising a subframe that was attached to the rear engine pivot mounting, became fully sprung. The former central oil tank was removed from being a main frame member, to occupy a position under the seat. A hand-operated centre stand was fitted, eliminating the need for all Vincent men to have Herculean strength. The Amal Standard carbs—always prone to leaking—gave way to the Amal Monobloc. The whole electrical system was revamped, and finally, the cylinder-head design became standard on both front and rear heads, in short, the front head was fitted to both.

The Prince and Knight wer[e] structurally both the same a[s] the D. The difference was in th[e] fact that these two mode[ls] became totally enclosed in glass fibre shrouds, making the Rapid[e] and Shadow look like grown-u[p] Ariel Leaders. When announce[d] in 1954 it was a radical depar[ture] from motorcycle practice[.] Vincent had paid great atten[tion] to design and much wor[k] had been involved in using win[d] tunnel testing to finalise th[e] eventual shape. One press roa[d] tester tested a Knight for 50[0] miles in pouring rain and only go[t] the back of his trousers wet, whic[h] bears testimony to the outcome.

Unfortunately, while Vincen[t] was always hard at it producin[g] new machines, rumblings wer[e] coming from the firm's financ[e] department. The firm had been i[n] the hands of the Officia[l] Receiver since 1950 and th[e] cessation of production had, fo[r] a long time, been just aroun[d] the corner. The Vincen[t] had always been an expen[sive] machine. After the war an[d] into the early 'fifties there wa[s] not the money available from th[e] public coffers. And so, at a tim[e] when Vincents were producin[g] their most unusual machine[s] they decided to call it a day[.] The legacy they left behind ha[s] always been a source of contro[versy] versy in motorcycling circle[s] were their machines ever an[y] good? As good as Vincent owner[s] always said they were? Tha[t] question is for the individual t[o] answer. What can be said i[s] that they produced a desig[n] which managed to span the 'thirties and 'forties into the 'fifties and survive longer tha[n] most: that in the early 'fifti[es] they established and broke mos[t] major records that were worth having—including several worl[d] records: and that for nearl[y] 20 years they remained in *Th[e] Guinness Book of World Record[s]* as "the world's fastes[t] standard-production machine".

The 1946 Series B Rapide

VINCENT BLACK SHADOW

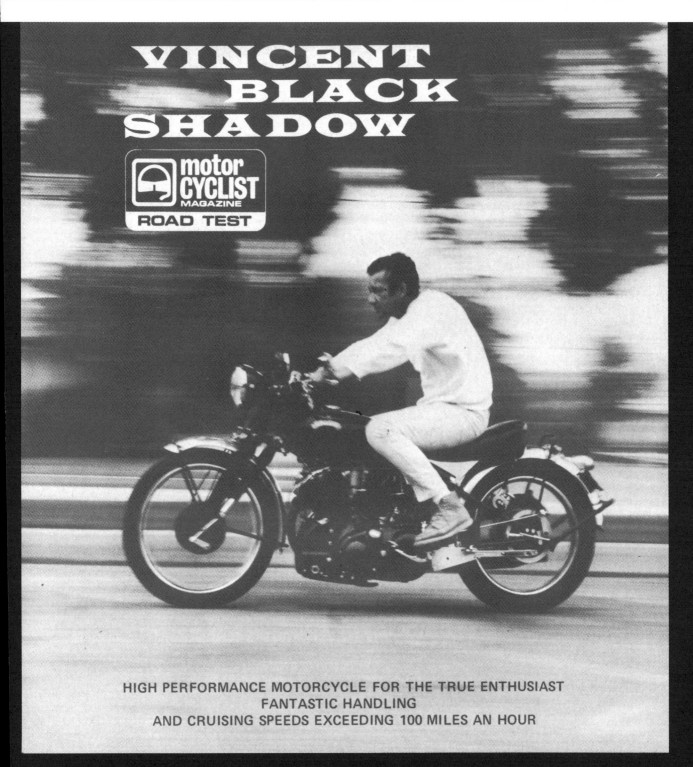

motor CYCLIST MAGAZINE
ROAD TEST

HIGH PERFORMANCE MOTORCYCLE FOR THE TRUE ENTHUSIAST
FANTASTIC HANDLING
AND CRUISING SPEEDS EXCEEDING 100 MILES AN HOUR

THE MOTORCYCLE that you see in these photos is a Vincent Black Shadow. Its Vee twin overhead valve engine displaces 998 cubic centimeters, and produces 68 horsepower at 5,400 rpm. It has a top speed of almost 125 miles an hour, will travel from 0-60 miles an hour in six seconds, and at 60 miles an hour, engine turn-over is only 2,700 rpm. How does this compare with the motorcycle that you are riding today?

Everything about the Vincent Black Shadow is unusual, and this includes the big Vee twin engine. The upper faces of the paired cases are machined to accept two cylinders at 58 degrees in Vee formation. The rear cylinder being offset 1½ inches toward the timing gear for improved cooling and con rod alignment with the crankshaft bearing. The timing case is shaped and machined to accept the camshaft for both cylinders and

their appropriate operating gear. As the twins have a unit construction gearbox, the gearbox housing and the inner half of the oil dab for the primary chain are cast integrally with the crankcase. A separate camshaft is provided with each cylinder mounted very high on the timing case with pushrods only six inches long. These pushrods operate inside stainless steel pushrod tubes. The Lucas magneto is gear-driven from the timing gear thru a Lucas automatic advance and retard unit. The aluminum alloy pistons have two pressure rings and one scraper ring.

Lubrication is by the dry sump system. A large double acting rotary plunger pump is worm-driven from the timing side of the mainshaft. The pump draws oil from a 6-pint oil tank, thru a gauze filter and a large bore pipe pumps it thru a 5 square-inch full flow fabric filter and then directly to the big

123

end assembly, camshaft bearings, and the rear of the cylinder walls. Return oil is scraped from the flywheels and pumped back into the oil tank. Four large diameter bearings are provided to support the crankshafts. Three of these are roller bearings and the fourth is a ball bearing for endwise locations of the crankshaft.

You'll also find bore and stroke interesting in relation to the motorcycle you are now riding. The bore is 84mm and the piston stroke 90mm. What this means, is that the engine is barely turning over in order to get its horsepower and the amount of torque available is virtually unlimited. The cylinders are cast iron which have been shrunk into aluminum alloy barrels. The cylinder heads are aluminum alloy.

Carburetion is by two vertical Amal touring carburetors with 20mm (1-1/8 inch) choke size. Air filters can be supplied as an option, but were not fitted to our test bike.

The engine sprocket with its 35 teeth, drives a 56-tooth clutch sprocket. The engine shaft shock absorber is of the 3-lobe cam type with 36 light coil springs which enable it to operate extremely smooth. A single plate clutch provides the expanding pressure to work a pair of shoes in a nickel chrome alloyed cast iron rib drum. We found the operation of the clutch to be extremely light, but yet the clutch itself refused to slip no matter how hard we pushed the bike. The positive stop foot-controlled gear box has the following ratios: fourth 3.5-1, third 4.2-1, second 5.5-1, first 7.25-1. If you look carefully at our test bike, you'll see that there is an extra sprocket fitted at the other side of the rear wheel. You'll find that one sprocket is for around-town use, and the other is for touring. If you want to utilize the secondary sprocket, all you have to do is undo the finger adjustment, lift the fender, pull the wheel, and turn the wheel around. No tools are needed for this job, and the whole thing can be completed in a minute or less, depending on how fast you are.

The engine itself, is the major portion of the Vincent frame. A large headlug bolts to a forged steel bracket on the front cylinder head. From there, a strong triangulated oil tank which also forms part of the frame makes against a similar lug on the rear cylinder head. The rest of the frame consists of the rigid triangulated rear forks and the plate which secures this fork to the rear engine unit. Rear suspension provides a fairly soft action of about six inches travel, controlled by a hydraulic damper, the same as used up front on the Girdraulic fork.

A combination of muscle, know-how, and finesse are needed to start the Vincent Black Shadow engine. Those 61 cubic inches aren't that hard to kick over, but you've got to know the correct starting drill to go thru before you start kicking. We found that the easiest way to start our test bike was to get both carburetors good and juicy when the engine was cold, and it would usually start on the second or third catch. With the engine warm, you had to be very careful not to flood it, but usually with luck you could get the engine running again on the second or third kick. If you flooded the two cylinders, you could kick all day without having the engine do anything more than pop and try to kick you over the handlebars.

Once the engine was started, it would settle down to one of the most beautiful rumbling idles that we had ever heard, even when cold. If you dig Ferraris and Maseratis, you'll certainly enjoy a Vincent, as the engine is very noisy mechanically. Even so, it's nice to know that all those clattering parts are doing what they're supposed to be doing in there. The noise has actually become part of the Vincent legend.

We could almost do a complete test on the wheels and brakes fitted to our test bike. We already told you that the rear wheel could be yanked off in under a minute without using any tools, turned around and put back so the other sprocket could be used. This is just one feature of many.

Did you know that for many years, Vincents have all been fitted with **four** seven-inch diameter (178mm) internal expanding brakes! Our test machine was fitted with heavy-duty, nickel chrome alloy cast iron drums. The idea of having a brake on each side of each wheel is that braking stresses are spread over all the brakes, and the resulting perfect balance of forces provides the Vincent with controllability and safety which may very well be beyond the standards that are found on competitive motorcycles. For a motorcycle weighing in at 462 pounds with gas and oil, stopping was impressive. At 30 miles an hour, for the first two stops, all the action could be brought to a halt in 33 feet. After two stops, things were no longer impressive. Braking gradually worsened until we wondered how it would feel to take a bike this size down a winding mountain road where the brakes had to be applied over and over. Brake fade is something that we just don't like. Brakes fitted to this Vincent were adequate, but really nothing more.

A ride on a Vincent, is in no way similar to any other motorcycle that you've ridden before. The ride is "heavy." This is the only word we can use to describe what we mean. Even with the steering damper loose, at 100 miles an hour, the bike feels secure and safe. The suspension works, and works well, but yet it also has that "heavy feeling," as everything seems to operate slowly.

The engine is also the same, as with its long stroke, unlimited torque and unbelievable lugging power, it's very much different from anything on the market today. The engine feels like it's just loafing along at 100 miles an hour, and if you worked out our specifications, you'll see that it is. For an approximate base to work out your rpm at speed, figure that the engine is turning over 1,392 rpm at 30 miles an hour at top gear.

Other than the rear brake lever, which took a muscle man to operate, everything else on the bike operated smoothly and easily. As far as clutches go, the one on our test bike was a dream, and it could be pulled in with your pinky. The front brake lever could be operated also with one finger. The shift lever feels tight, but yet will operate just as fast as you could get your foot to wiggle. Shifting is fast and accurate. Our test bike would jump out of second, third, and fourth gear if accelerated hard, but there again, under average riding conditions we had no problems at all.

Acceleration is fierce, but for some strange reason, doesn't seem that way. As we said earlier, the Shadow will go from 0-60 in six seconds, and that's moving right along. In first gear, you can run at almost 70 miles an hour before you have to shift into second. In second cog, you can hit 87 miles an hour, and in third, 110. Fourth gear will get you 123 miles an hour. The factory claims 125, but we couldn't get this Vincent to give up those extra two miles. Just like everything else on the bike, acceleration is "heavy." If you're not watching that gigantic Smiths speedometer, and you're not noticing the wind, you don't really have the feeling that you're moving at such a terrific speed. Even at the top speed that this model would go, there was no wobbling, hopping around, or feeling of general uneasiness. Of all the bikes we've ever tested, the Vincent Black Shadow has come the closest to being the most roadworthy. The gear pedal and brake pedal moves with the foot pegs, so if you're not happy with your seating position, all you have to do is move the pegs forward or rearward, depending on your size, and length of your legs.

Lighting is by today's modern standards, adequate, but not excellent. The electricity is provided by a Miller 6-volt, 50-watt oltage regulator controlled generator. This is driven from the rimary chain, and if you so desire for racing, the sprocket is asily detachable. The battery fitted to our test machine was a tock 13 amp hour Exide battery that was fully shock-absorbed. ighting up front was crisp and clear, but the tiny taillight in he rear is definitely not acceptable. Because of this, the owner ad changed to a taillight that he felt was more visible from the de. The Lucas horn was loud and more than piercing enough o attract the attention of anyone in a car with the windows olled up.

When it comes to looks, the Vincent Black Shadow is a ard one to beat. All the enameled parts are bonderized and finished in Pinchin Johnson's Best Cycle Stoving Enamel. The brake parts are mostly polished stainless steel or aluminum, and others are chromium or cadmium plated. On the Black Shadow, the power unit is Pyluminised and most distinctively enameled glossy black. There is just about no chrome on this bike, but yet the machine is so impressive that no matter where you park it, it immediately collects a crowd of people who just admire beautiful machinery.

If you know motorcycles, you know what a Vincent Black Shadow is. We're not going to devote a bunch of space in telling you any more than we already have. Just a check of the specifications will show you what you could have bought for $1,250. You look and you decide, and we think that you'll agree with us, that the Vincent Black Shadow is one of the world's most fantastic motorcycles.

SPECIFICATIONS: VINCENT BLACK SHADOW

Make	Vincent
Model	Black Shadow
Engine	Vee Twin, OHV
Compression Ratio	7.3 to 1
Horsepower @ rpm	68 @ 5400
Carburetion	Two Vertical Amal Touring 29mm
Ignition	Lucas Magneto
Starting System	Kick
Lighting	Miller 50 Watt Generator Exide 13ah 6 V Battery
Transmission	4 Speed
Gear Ratios	1st: 7.25 to 1
	2nd: 5.5
	3rd: 4.2
	4th: 3.5 to 1
Tires	Front: Avon Speedster 3.00 x 20
	Rear: Avon Supreme 3.50 x 19
Brakes	Front: Internal Expanding 7 inch Double
	Rear: Internal Expanding Double 7 inch
Suspension	Girdraulic front fork with twin helical compression springs and hydraulic damping. Link action. Pivot action rear springing hydraulically damped.
Fuel Capacity	3¾ Gallons
Weight	462 pounds
Wheelbase	56 inches
Ground Clearance	5 inches
0-60 mph	6½ seconds
Top Speed	123 mph
Price As Tested	
Los Angeles Area	$1,250.00

ENGINE	Excellent	Good	Fair	Poor	Unsatisfactory
Starting	•				
Throttle Response	•				
Vibration		•			
Noise			•		
TRANSMISSION					
Gear Spacing	•				
Clutch Smoothness	•				
Shifting speed	•				
CONTROLS					
Handlebar position	•				
Ease of operation	•				
Location	•				
BRAKES					
Lever pressure	•				
Pedal pressure				•	
Fade resistance				•	
Directional stability	•				
Stopping distance	•				
SUSPENSION					
Front	•				
Rear	•				
Ride control	•				
Dampening	•				
APPEARANCE					
Paint	•				
Construction and welds	•				
Chrome and trim	•				
ELECTRICAL					
Wiring	•				
Headlight	•				
Taillight				•	
Horn		•			
GENERAL					
Spark plug accessibility	•				
Instrumentation	•				
Side stand	•				
Center stand	•				
Seat comfort		•			
Muffling	•				
Tool storage space					

COMMENTS: Unbelievable torque. Excellent braking system, but bad fade characteristics. Cruising speed up to 100 miles an hour. Fully adjustable foot levers and pegs. A motorcycle with a real future here in the United States.

THE VINCENT

The elements of a legend:

THE ENGINE: A 998-cc pushrod V-Twin that developed 45 bhp in its early days. Later refinements pushed output to 70 bhp. Weighing less than some of today's Superbikes, the hotter versions could churn out 100-mph-plus standing start quarter-miles and top out at 125 mph. Beginning with the post-war B series Rapides, the engine was of all-alloy construction, with 50-degree cylinder angle. Following the Rapides came the faster Black Shadow and finally the ultra-fast 150-mph Lightning.

A FAR-OUT CHASSIS: It utilized the engine itself as the primary structural member to save weight. Unusual was the rear frame section, actually a triangulated swinging arm pivoted off the engine plates and sprung from a short top tube. The front forks were of the girder variety, accommodating up-and-down movement through horizontal links near the steering head. Wheelbase was thus kept nearly constant through the entire range of fork movement.

THE CONTROVERSY: It was the fastest bike of its time, giving forth to the mistaken impression that it should be a road-racer, not merely a good roadster. So it was praised for its speed and smoothness. And damned for its handling, which wasn't bad—for its intended use. Its brakes were only passable, if you're of the mind that a manufacturer should stop you as fast as he accelerates you. What finally killed it? A trend towards smaller machines, and the high cost of unautomated production.

THE VINCENT V-TWIN:
BORN 1934–DIED 1955

THE Vincent, Phil Irving's design masterpiece, ended a 19-year run in 1955 with the Series "D" models, most of which were equipped with total streamlining. Although this provided the rider with protection from the elements, engine and drive train, public opinion was not with the factory, which had recently been through a series of financial reversals. Eventually, the factory went into receivership, and production was stopped during the early fall of 1955.

In addition to the financial problems the factory was encountering, British motorcyclists were beginning to turn toward the smaller, lighter machines being produced. Price was also a consideration: the Vincents were the most expensive machines manufactured in the world at that time.

But the Vincent name will be a long time in dying. Enthusiasts all over the world are maintaining Vincents in perfect condition, and the Vincent Owners Club chapters are some of the most enthusiastic to be found.

Although complete engines are no longer available, certain of the more important spares, including remanufactured engines and frame kits, are still available from Roger Slater Engineering in Worcestershire, England. The Vincent factory in Stevenage, England, now called Harper Engines Ltd., is also making spare parts, but Conway Motors in London probably does the most business in parts. They are expensive, but are all of high quality.

Aching for a closer glimpse of the fabled Vincent, we went over to Dave Furst's shop at 1127 N. La Brea Ave., Inglewood, Calif. to see one of his. Dave is considered one of the men to see on the West Coast for Vincent spares and information. He has recently return-

(Continued on page 140)

WHATEVER HAPPENED TO THE VINCENT?

A Purist Who Is Keeping The Vincent Legend Alive

ONE OF THE MORE pleasant short motorcycle jaunts on the East Coast is the run along Rt. 125 through the Andover Hills to Haverhill, Mass. After the concrete drabness of Interstate 93 out of Cambridge, you turn off at the Andover Exit onto 125, and boom along through rolling countryside dotted with ancient weathered farmhouses, crumbling stone walls, and tiny herds of cattle.

Now and then, the winding blacktop road plunges into a silent pine forest; there is no traffic, and the speedometer of your machine climbs close to the ton as you sweep around the gentle bends in the cool shadows of the pines. Then you crest a hill and explode once again into farm country and dazzling sunshine. Soon you find yourself coasting down into Haverhill on the Merrimac River.

This old manufacturing town, once famous for its leather goods and woolens, is now full of decaying 19th century mills and sleepy clapboard tenements. It looks like it should long ago have been consigned to the dungheap of industrial development, when similar milling towns went bust all over New England during the Great Depression. But through some unknowable combination of native orneriness and unwillingness to recognize or compromise with economic "reality," Haverhill held out.

Haverhill isn't exactly a boom town

THEN CAME BENSON

Benson pulls away from the curb on his magnificently restored Black Prince.

PHOTOS AND TEXT BY CHARLES TAYLOR

THEN CAME BENSON

by contemporary standards, but it still manages to chuff along at a moderate pace. Its economic life is based on the variety and small successes of dozens of tiny enterprises. There are welding shops in profusion, places which undertake nickel and cadmium plating, stove enamelers, and half a dozen antique shops specializing in Victoriana. And there is Coburn Benson's Merrimac Motorcycle Sales, which deals in Triumphs, BSAs, and caters to the Northeast's die-hard Vincent freaks.

BENSON'S VINCENT WONDERLAND

From the outside, Benson's shop at 125 River Street is just another unprepossessing piece of false-fronted Victorian clapboarded real estate. Step inside, and you're in a kind of "you-don't-see-many-more-of-these-anymore" motorcycling never-never land: Vincents, Vincents, Vincents, a cabinet full of Manx parts, a Norton International, a 1938 Brough Superior SS 100 in for a top-end overhaul, a 1911 Indian Racer . . . and even a contemporary Triumph or two.

Standard Tricor signs and displays take up a small amount of space in the showroom window; pride of place goes to an immaculate remanufactured Series

"D" Vincent Black Prince over which hangs an immense six-feet-long Vincent banner in black and gold. A Merrimac M/C Sales News Bulletin, detailing the latest racing exploits of Benson's 1950 Grey Flash, is prominently displayed on the wall next to the side entrance to the shop.

On a given day, Benson is likely to have several used Vincents for sale, as well as a Harper's Engines remanufactured machine or two for the customer with an ample pocketbook. Harper's Engines Ltd., a large English manufacturing concern, took over the production of Vincent spares several years ago, and, up until June 1969, were offering works-overhauled machines for sale on a limited basis. The spares supply continues, manufactured in the old Vincent plant in Stevenage, Hertfordshire. Some of Philip Vincent's original employees still work there. Spokesmen for Harper's Engines say that as long as the demand for spares holds up they will do their best to meet it; but alas, the works overhauled machines are no longer available.

The remanufactured machines are beautifully finished. Welds are almost invisible, and the deep-gloss black enam-

Benson's shop crew puts the Vincents out in front before beginning the day's work.

THEN CAME BENSON *Continued*

eled tank and cycle parts are set off with perfectly applied gold-leaf striping. The wheel rims have black enamel centers and chromed sides separated by delicate red pinstriping. As on the original Vincents, there is liberal use of stainless steel and polished alloy components.

They are fitted with higher compression pistons to take advantage of modern fuels, and the old side-float pattern carburetors have been replaced by Amal concentrics; otherwise, the machines are completely original. They are virtually brand-new from the crankcase up, and come with the traditional 6000-mile, four-month warranty, and a detailed list of the parts replaced during the overhaul.

Asking price is $2000, which, while a bit steep, is not all that bad in this day of $1800-$1900 "superbikes," and not bad at all when you think of the prices asked for many used Vincents in the classified sections of CYCLE WORLD. Best of all, the customer knows that a remanufactured Vincent will be set up *right*. Many Vincent owners have almost as much money tied up in their worn machines, and they still can't get them to perform the way they should.

THE REBUILDING PROJECT

At one time, Benson was thinking seriously of rebuilding and guaranteeing Vincents himself. He acquired some working space at Jay's Motorcycles in Cambridge, Mass., and bought 10 running but shaggy Shadows and as many wrecks for spare parts, and shut himself up for the winter.

His plan was to assemble 10 machines from new and sound used parts, and sell them for $1000 apiece in the spring. Unfortunately, he was only able to assemble seven and sell five. He barely managed to break even, and decided that the whole scheme was not worth the effort, in view of the long hours involved and the difficulty of obtaining really large quantities of warrantied new parts.

But he did end up with one of the largest collections of used Vincent spares and machines on the East Coast. He still has a barn in Concord, Mass., on the old family farm, well stocked with wrecks and good used parts, and a shed behind the shop in Haverhill which, at last examination, contained two Shadows, a Rapide and a ratty-looking Comet Single.

His Vincent work now consists most-

(Continued on page 138)

John Clark on Benson' racing Twin on his way to 3rd place in the 1000-cc Junior event a St. Eustache, Deu Montagnes, Quebec.

Jody Nicholas, On An Impeccable Rapide

THE AURA OF THE first Vincent I ever rode, some 15 years ago, has never been obscured by any of the many motorcycles I've ridden since. I can distinctly remember having to have the owner start it for me, balance the machine while I climbed aboard, give me a shove to get me underway (because I couldn't touch the ground then) and catch me after I finished the ride.

I shudder to think what would have happened had I found it necessary to stop, or had I stalled the engine, but my brief 10-minute introduction to the world of the Vincent was one which I'll never forget.

During the ensuing years, I've only ridden a few scattered examples of the machine which has developed a following that few other machines will equal. Vincent owners, for the most part, are loath to allow "outsiders" to ride their machines, and it is quite difficult to find a truly "standard" Vincent. The owners are fairly consistent in that they prefer to use genuine parts, but they don't seem to mind swapping them around with other Vincent models. You're quite likely to find a Rapide with Black Shadow pistons, or Lightning cams, but the exterior looks quite like it did when it left Stevenage.

Vincent Owners Club member Don Halliday, of Hollywood, Calif., has a machine that I wanted to ride: a 1952 Series C Rapide in nearly original condition, which he has owned for many years and kept in immaculate shape.

When I arrived at Don's house that brisk Sunday morning, he was busy installing the exhaust pipe which had just been replated and was making a few minute adjustments here and there. I waited impatiently for him to finish, watched carefully as he went through the starting drill, and forgot my gloves in my haste to get aboard when he returned from a warm-up run around the block.

Don explained that he had installed the stiffer sidecar springs front and rear because he and his wife usually ride together and carry quite a lot of luggage. He also admonished me to remember to tighten the steering damper ever so slightly before taking to the freeway, and listed a half-dozen other hints which I immediately forgot. I needn't have worried, however, as the big Vincent was deceptively easy to manipulate.

Despite what you may have heard about starting a Vincent Twin, there is no reason why one shouldn't start on the first kick. Don's bike proved to follow suit, as it never failed to start immediately and begin idling like a BMW. The machine's excellent throttle response is due, no doubt, to its fine mechanical condition and the substitution of 32-mm Amal Concentrics for the

(Continued on page 140)

RIDING THE VINCENT

Sidney H. Dickson Photo

Dan Hunt, On A Well-Ridden Rapide/Shadow

THE THING ABOUT riding a funky old bike like the Vinnie is that you have to have perspective. It's old. And it will never be new again. So you have to project yourself back into what must have been its newness.

I rode a 1955 mixture of mostly original parts—a Rapide with Series D chassis, Series C Rapide engine with Series D heads (both heads are front heads) and 7.5:1 Black Shadow pistons. The bike belongs to Dean Wixom, the fairing manufacturer, who acquired it a year ago through a friend who was returning from England. It has many thousands of miles behind it, and is ripe for an upper end job. Nonetheless, the machine was healthy.

The 1000-cc Vincent is a new machine to me, so I was able to have substantially the same reaction to it as the bystander who comes upon the more ubiquitous two-wheel marvels of today. I noticed, for example, that it is much easier to get involved visually with its mechanical "being," than with current biggies like the Honda Four or the Mach III. There are more places for the eye to rest and linger—a valve cap here, a machining mark there, a patterned lever there. Individuality everywhere. Sculpturing. All evidence of a machine that was mostly hand-made.

The starting drill is easy. Flood the float bowls. Pull the compression release and drive the engine through once. Kick again, releasing the compression release lever about halfway. The engine is heavy to turn over, but not too heavy, even for this 155-lb. weakling. Two kicks or so will do the job, and the magneto ignition sparks the powerful V-Twin into life.

As you pull the foot lever up into first and get under way, you'll find that the clutch action is smooth, but a trifle sudden. First gear is taller than you would expect. As it sounds like two Singles loping along, side by side, the Vincent feels like it is going slower than it really is. Therefore, a temperate blast in first gear to 35 mph is followed by another shot in second gear to 50 or 55 mph, and before you realize it you are breaking the in-town speed limit. Then you discover that the machine takes kindly to very slow running—30 to 35 mph in fourth—and you can practically count the firing pulses. At 70 or 80, the tempo is just as relaxed, and vibration is minimal.

On the handling side, the Vincent scores well, too. It is somewhat ponderous below 40 mph, and tends to heave on acceleration or deceleration, much in the manner of the H-D Sportster or the Moto Guzzi V7. Above 50 mph, the bike becomes more settled, more nimble. If you can disregard the antique aspect of the suspension components underneath you, and the disorienting effect of a gigantic speedometer that

RIDING THE VINCENT

moves up and down with the suspension like Big Ben on a yo-yo string, you have to admit that this old warhorse handles extremely well. Not well enough to race, but well enough to please about 90 percent of the riders on street machines today. It tracks well, goes where it is pointed, absorbs bumps stiffly, but with little wobble.

The Vincent's two weakest points, as they were when the bike was new, are the gearbox and the brakes. The gearbox requires deliberateness to avoid overshifting—passing the desired gear and arriving in the next false neutral. While the front brake was not what a Vincent enthusiast would deem well-maintained, it is obvious that the unit does not have enough swept area per pound of machine weight to deliver modern-day stopping power. The back brake, which has the least work to do, is passable.

Like Dean Wixom says, and he says it not as a purist, but as a casual collector who likes to get his rigs running with as little fuss as possible and then ride hell out of them, "What else was there in 1955?" There wasn't much, and I can

only wonder what an evolved Rapide or Shadow, production-line 1971, would be like. My guess would be an engine of basically similar configuration running in a double-loop frame, with telescopic forks and conventional swinging arm. It would be like a NorVin. The separate gearbox would remain traditionally separate, only it would shift faultlessly and rapidly like Norton's Commando gearbox. The front brake would be an 8- or 9-in. drum, with double leading shoe. Borrowing from H-D's success, it would have optional electric starting. With hardly any increase in horsepower from 1955, the 1971 Vincent would still run with the fastest of today's Superbikes and be smoother (in the sense of calm) and more docile than most of them. And it would run on regular gasoline.

All these projected changes are minor, intended only to broaden the bike's market appeal, and make it easier to ride. The 1955 machine had most of the required elements to please a 1971 enthusiast; it just hadn't gotten itself "together."

I rode a '55 Vincent and survived. And I survived in style, thank you. ◙

Had The Vincent Gone On To Meet The Superbikes Of The Seventies, It Would Have Looked Much Like This.

IF THE 1000-cc VINCENT had been perfect, as some of its hardiest devotees claim, then why is the NorVin one of the most popular engine/frame conversions among British and American Vincent enthusiasts today?

A NorVin, quite simply, is the mating of the big. V-Twin engine to the superb Norton Featherbed chassis. The benefit is obvious. A better handling motorcycle. Better braking. Lower profile. Better styling. All for the rider who wants the ultimate cafe racer, not just an excellent touring bike, which the Vincent was.

Had Vincent continued production into the Seventies, it would have had to meet the Superbike market head on. Honda Fours, Mach IIIs, Commandos, Sportsters, etc.

For that purpose, the classic NorVin swap is ideal. The Vincent engine and the Featherbed frame seem made for one another. Together, they represent what the Vincent of the Seventies might have been. The Ultimate Weapon for the pavement, giving quarter to no one.

Typical is Dave Furst's NorVin, assembled with painstaking love and care from the finest components available today. A Norton wideline Featherbed frame was chosen for its fine handling qualities, its availability, and because the large Vincent engine fits in, barely.

Shoehorning the Vincent into the Featherbed is exacting work. Once in, the frame seems designed for the Vinnie. Dave fitted Ceriani road racing forks and a four leading-shoe front brake. The rear wheel from a Honda Superhawk is used. Good brakes are essential to a machine with the potential of this one, and the combination works very well indeed.

The handsomely finished fiberglass seat and tank (which also contains the

THE NORVIN

oil supply) are made in England by Duguid Motors especially for the Featherbed frame.

Close to 70 bhp are obtained from the engine, which features Vincent Black Lightning cams, 10:1 pistons and 1¼-in. Amal Concentric carburetors. Dave opted to do away with the complicated and often troublesome standard Vincent compression release mechanism and instead fitted modern-day two-stroke decompressors into the cylinder heads.

Other modifications include a dual-point contact breaker assembly and a twin-coil ignition, which offers a hotter spark at cranking speeds and eases the starting chore.

Replicas of this machine are available from Furst Motors, 1127 No. La Brea Ave., Inglewood, CA 90302. Price? About $3500 a copy!

THEN CAME BENSON

Continued from page 132

ly of repairs on customers' machines, special racing modifications and speed tuning. He has more than enough to keep him busy. The last time I made the trip to Haverhill to pick up some parts and rap for a while, Benson was making the following modifications to a customer's Shadow engine: Alpha big-end assembly, theoretically disaster-proof up to about 7500 rpm, which is really flapping for a 1000-cc V-Twin; cams of his own (classified) design; 10:1 pistons; porting and polishing the heads to take 1 1/4-in. TT carbs (easier to tune than the GPs, says Benson); and judicious lightening and polishing of the valve gear.

These modifications, in conjunction with a straight-through exhaust, should give the customer something like 75 bhp to play around with on the street. The standard Black Lightning, with similar internals, used to deliver upwards of 70 bhp with slightly smaller carburetors and a 9:1 compression ratio, so Benson's estimate of power output is probably on the conservative side.

One of the nice things about the Vincent engine, says Benson, is the extent to which it can be modified before it becomes truly "strung out" and unreliable. The engine's robust internals, including the four main-bearing crankshaft, the 2-in. crankpin, and the massive I-section, high-tensile steel rods riding in an impressively strong and rigid crankcase, make it virtually indestructible.

The old Black Lightning engine, while delivering an honest 70 bhp from 998cc, was in a relatively mild state of tune compared to, say, a Triumph Bonneville engine producing 52 bhp from 650cc. The prospective engine tuner can confidently expect to get into the 80-90 bhp range on gas before encountering serious reliability problems. So when Benson twirls his drooping moustache and gestures in the direction of the aforementioned customer's machine, saying ". . . and it'll be fully streetable and idle down like a Buick Eight," he isn't putting anybody on. Well, not much, anyway.

A GREY FLASH GUINEA PIG

Benson—his two assistants and close friends call him Ben—does most of the research and development work that eventually finds its way into customers' machines on his ancient Grey Flash road racer. This is a 500-cc production racer made in limited quantities by Vincent in the early Fifties.

The machine, as delivered from the works, used to produce about 35 bhp on an 8:1 piston at 6200 rpm. Benson's modifications, including an Alpha big-

end, 11:1 piston, 1 1/4 Amal GP carburetor, home-brew cams, and extensive lightening and polishing of the valve-gear and other highly stressed internal components, have resulted in an engine which puts out close to 50 bhp—almost as much as a Norton Manx.

The engine's reliability and the machine's relatively light (300 lb.) weight make it competitive with most of the classic British single-cylinder production racers still being campaigned all over the world. Since a Vincent Twin is, in effect, two Singles on a common crankcase, information gained from modifications to the Flash can be applied directly to the Twins. The advantages of the Flash as a vehicle for experimentation are obvious: it is simple, and if anything breaks, the damage will be less extensive and expensive than on a Twin.

ON HANDLING AND STOPPING

What about handling and stopping, the alleged twin failings of all Vincents? "Ever since that CYCLE WORLD road test on a Lightning a couple of years back," says Benson, "I've been running into people who put down Vincent handling and braking, and the clutch too. And you know," he continues, "half of them haven't even seen a Vincent, much less ridden one." Benson gets worked up over the phenomenon of "Honda generation" critics of the Vincent legend, and magazine criticism from "people who should know better."

"Let's take the matter of the clutch first: is it reasonable to assume that all Vincent clutches slip, just because the one in the CYCLE WORLD road test did? I mean do you think that Phil Irving *designed* it that way? If the Vincent clutch is assembled carefully with new oil seals and religious attention is given to cleanliness, and if you keep an eye on the oil level in the primary case, there's no reason why you shouldn't get trouble-free service from the unit.

"I know people who've driven around with the original Vincent clutch for years without any problems at all. In fact, they claim they get better mileage and dependability from it than from an ordinary multiplate clutch." (The Vincent unit is a serve-clutch operated centrifugally by engine revolutions.)

(One of these "people" who can attest to the reliability of the Vincent clutch is this writer, who, in the course of the last five years, has owned three Black Shadows and a Rapide, none of which has needed anything other than routine maintenance in the clutch department—but, naturally, I'm biased.

"Handling?" says Ben, ". . . well, let's be for real. Vincent handling was

great compared with whatever else was around back in the Forties and early Fifties. Remember all those plunger BSAs, sprung-hub Triumphs, and rigid-frame hogs? Compared to them, the Vincent handled like a road-racer; in fact, about the only thing you could get that handled better were the early Manxes and Velocette production racers.

"Vincent went out of production in 1955, at just the time when the rest of the industry was beginning to make real advances in suspension technology. If Vincent had stayed in production, they would have had to come up with a new frame and suspension to maintain their reputation for fine handling.

"By today's standards, their handling would be judged only fair. They *do* get kind of snaky when banked over hard for a fast corner on a poorly surfaced road, but if you don't push them, they're okay. Most of the people who put down Vincent handling are incapable of driving the machine to its limits anyway.

"When it comes to straight-line highway cruising in the 90- to 100-mph range, though, I'll take a good Vincent over just about anything on the market today. Seems like the faster you go, the steadier those Girdraulic forks become. There's absolutely no wandering and hunting like you get with even the best telescopic forks at those speeds, and the suspension dampening is more than adequate for most surfaces." (The Vincent "Girdraulic" fork, introduced in 1949, combines the twist-resistant characteristics of the old-fashioned girder fork, and the hydraulically dampened springing of the telescopic fork.)

"Now remember, I said a *good* Vincent," continues Benson. "They've been out of production for 15 years now, and not all owners have the know-how to do first-class maintenance work on their own machines, and, excepting certain parts of the country (like Haverhill), you can't just go down to your friendly local Vincent dealer to get the work done.

"Most bike dealers don't want to take the responsibility of working on such an old and rare machine, or say they can't get parts and so forth. In fact, if you don't know about people like Harry Belleville in Marysville, Ohio, Gene Aucott in Philadelphia, the Vincent Owners Club, or *me*, you really *can't* get parts. And things like shock absorbers, hydraulic dampers, spring-boxes, fork spindles and so on tend to wear out fairly quickly, while they're often the last things that a motorcycle owner is going to replace, especially if he thinks parts are hard to get.

"So the result of all this is that there are a powerful lot of truly shaggy rat-Vincents with shot suspension systems running around in the woods. The

THEN CAME BENSON

well maintained, properly equipped Vincent is somewhat of a rarity. Needless to say, all those privately maintained rats don't help the Vincent reputation.

"Christ, the other day some New Hampshire farmer came in with a '51 Shadow which had an old tabacco tin for a clutch cover, bone-dry dampers, no brakes at all, and 'Vincent Black Shadow' scrawled on his tank in white house paint. The letters were 4 in. high and looked like they'd been put on with a broomstick. He said all he needed was a tune-up. Fastest farmer in Plaistow, N.H., eyup."

... AND BRAKING?

On the subject of Vincent braking, Benson has this to say: "The stories about Vincents not being able to stop are ridiculous. Again, it's a question of lots of Vincents on the road having worn linings and out-of-round drums. If you look back at some of the early road tests of brand new machines, you'll find that the Twins (and we're talking about a 460-lb. motorcycle), could stop in something like 22 ft. from 30 mph. The Singles stopped even quicker than that. That's damned good stopping even by today's standards.

"The old Vincent duo-brake system, which some of today's road racers are just beginning to use, really worked; it was reasonably fade-resistant—let's face it, lining materials *have* improved in the last 15 years—and it stayed dry, thanks to Vincent's system of light-alloy water excluders on all four brakes.

"If anything, the Vincent had too much stopping power. The factory recognized this, when, in the last year of production, they left off one of the rear brakes altogether, relying solely on the front duo-brakes for serious stopping and leaving on the single rear brake as an auxiliary, more than anything else.

"Old Man Vincent was so confident of the stopping power and controllability of his machines that he often drove his prototypes up to 100, and then seized up the front wheel to demonstrate these qualities to sceptics. That's one of the reasons he's got a steel plate in his head and has lost most of his coordination." (Author's note: Phillip Vincent was involved in a serious crash in 1947 while road testing a prototype Black Shadow. He suffered internal head injuries and a partial loss of coordination, and as a result was never able to ride a motorcycle again.)

"Of course there *are* things you can do to improve the handling and stopping of the standard Vincent," Benson continues. "You can get rid of the snakiness during hard cornering by replacing the standard rearsprings with heavy-duty sidecar units. The dampers can be filled with 50-weight oil instead of the normal 20, if the damper seals are

still good or, better yet, Koni makes a special damper to fit the Vincent. They cost about twenty-two bucks apiece, but if you want fine handling, that's not too much of a price to pay.

"If you want good, consistently fade-resistant braking, replace the original linings with Ferodo 'green stuff'... and be sure to synchronize the brakes on each wheel, especially the front. That's a point a lot of Vincent owners overlook."

Vincent front brakes are synchronized by adjusting the position of a torque arm which picks up the motion from the two brake cables and transfers it to a single cable connected to the brake lever. There are four points of adjustment, and synchronizing the brake can be difficult if it is allowed to get out of whack, and different wear patterns on linings and drums develop.

"That's all very fine," I told Benson, "but isn't the necessity for all these modifications proof that the Vincent is basically an unperfected machine?" Benson smiled, and poured himself another cup of coffee from the old tin pot which was bubbling merrily on the electric plate that doubles as a cylinder liner removing aid.

"Yes and no," he resumed. "In 1950, the heyday of Vincent's prestige, a Vincent Twin was the most 'perfected' motorcycle you could buy. It represented the quintessence of pre-war handcrafting, and post-war materials and technology. Today, it's 'unperfected' in the same way a Bugatti or a Bentley racing car is 'unperfected.' It's unfair to judge an older machine out of the context of the technology of its own time.

"But the interesting thing about the Vincent is that it *can* be updated so easily, and that so many people are willing to spend a lot of time and money to do just that. I always tell the doubters that the Vincent is the best 'kit' do-it-yourself motorcycle around today; you get the best metals, the best workmanship ever, and you can assemble it anyway you want.

"Starting with the basic machine, you can make yourself a real 'Superbike,' and in this day of Honda-generation, disposable beer-can-metal motorcycles, that's saying something. When you've finished 'perfecting' your Vincent, you've got something that sets you off from the rest of the crowd, that says 'This guy really knows his machine.' Why I imagine that most of the people you see riding around on Honda Fours have exhausted the limits of their technical knowledge when they remember to turn on the gas before punching the electric starter button."

PROSPECTS FOR AN EGLI FUTURE

What does Benson think of the Egli-Vincent, that latest in a long line of attempts to bring back the Vincent? "Well, Egli's basic concept is sound: put the old engine-transmission unit in a new, lightweight frame, use Cerianis up front and disc-brakes. All the road tests I've read on the Egli-Vincent seem to indicate that the new combination handles quite well for a big machine.

"But the performance figures of the Eglis don't jive with the claimed bhp; in fact, if you look at the old road tests from 20 years back, you'll see that the 'New' Vincents are slower than the old. The Egli-Vincents turn in mid-14-sec. quarter-mile times. That's about as quick as a 1948 Black Shadow on 7.3:1 pistons and post-war 'pool' gasoline, using a whopping high 7.2 bottom gear to boot! A good Series C Shadow (1949-53), with 9:1 pistons and the stump-puller bottom gear which became standard on all C Twins, should run in the middle 13s with a trap speed of slightly over 100 mph, and this on 55-60 bhp, as opposed to the 65-70 bhp claimed for the Egli.

"I think what is happening is that some of the old hand-assembled qualities of the early Shadows have been lost. Each Shadow that came off the assembly line was, in effect, blueprinted. All parts were carefully selected within the limits of manufacturing tolerances. For instance, Shadow pistons and barrels were graded into four sizes for perfect fit. All the pieces that didn't come up to Shadow standards were put back on the shelf, or were assembled into Rapides, the basic work-a-day Vincent Twin. This is a mighty expensive and painstaking way to make a motorcycle, but it worked. And when Vincent claimed 55 bhp and a top end of around 130 mph for his machines, he wasn't lying.

"Egli appears to be taking reworked old Rapide engines, stuffing high compression pistons, Lightning cams and fat concentric carbs into them, and then making outrageous bhp claims for them which just aren't borne out by test results. Still, I wouldn't mind putting one of my Shadow engines in an Egli frame. I understand Gene Aucott (Philadelphia) has several frames for sale, as well as complete Egli-Vincents."

Benson would appear to be not far from the truth on the matter of old-time Vincent performance. Recently *Super-Cycle*, an East Coast publication dedicated to "The Big Bike Enthusiast," road tested a 1952 Black Shadow loaned them by Ghost Motorcycles of Port Washington, Long Island. The machine was fitted with Black Lightning cams and high compression pistons; otherwise, it was completely stock. Its quarter-mile time was 13:0⊦ at 106 mph. Top speed was 144 mph, with full road equipment, lights, muffler and *no* fairing, certified by NHRA clocks. There is no road machine being manufactured today which can turn in a better all-around performance. A stock Black Lightning, needless to say, should be even faster.

Benson is not overly optimistic about the future of the Egli-Vincent: "If, in 1970, they can't put together a motorcycle that'll outhandle, outstop *and* outperform the original Vincent, if they can't build a machine which sells for slightly over $2000, finished with as much attention to detail as the original, then they're doomed to failure.

"Cost is not the object in America, and it never was with the Vincent: the old Shadows used to cost upwards of $1400 in the Fifties—the price of a good car. But when someone lays out that much money for a motorcycle, he wants to know that he is getting the best. Twenty years ago, the Vincent *was* the best. Today, the Egli-Vincent doesn't seem to be as good, all told, as the original. You might as well go buy a

Honda Four."

Benson is 35 now, makes a good living as a Triumph and BSA dealer, and still manages to find time to work on customers' Vincents and tend to his own private stable of exotic machines. He's got a representative of every postwar Vincent made, and he's looking around for an early series A pre-war Rapide onto which he can graft the upper works of two pre-war TT Replica 500s. "Imagine cruising down the turnpike at 115 in third on *that* oozing plumber's nightmare, and then shifting into fourth as you pass some poor mind-shattered bloke on his showroom-new Triumph Triple."

He's continually toying with new schemes to enhance the Vincent legend. Right now, he's talking about building a Vincent to go after the 24-hour production record, and you never know, he just might do it. "If I could just get away from my Triumph and BSA customers long enough to put some serious work into the Vincent project, shut off the phone, bolt the door, hang out a sign saying "Gone to Stevenage on Business, be back next year," and retire to the farm in Concord—but that's like talking about installing gaslights at the Pentagon." ◎

RIDING
Continued from page 133

standard carburetors.

Clutch action is amazingly light; onl two fingers were necessary to depres the handlebar lever. Feeding the clutcl back out resulted in a smooth star contrary to what one usually finds witl the Vincent. A properly adjusted Vin cent clutch is capable of delivering a ultra-smooth start. There was no slip page at any time during the ride.

Shifting is very smooth, but it pay to take one's time as it's easy t overshift and go through the next gear With an overall top gear ratio of 3.5:1 the big Twin idles along quite happily a 45 mph in high, and the Rapide's lacl of "camminess" and brute torque make it possible to accelerate smoothly an smartly from a lower speed withou down shifting. Even though a sligh vibration is noticeable, it is more com forting than objectionable. The Vin cent's forte is high speed touring, an with an engine that is apparently jus loafing along at legal freeway speeds and the low, English-style handlebar that allow the rider to lean into th wind, long trips are much easier t enjoy.

Vincent brakes have been objects o criticism from nearly every motorcycl publication at one time or another, bu I found that a Vincent with properl set-up brakes stops nearly as well as an road machine available today. The brak backing plates must be perfectly fre from distortion and the drums must b perfectly true, but when everything is i order, braking is consistently straigh and rapid, with little sign of fade.

Stiff suspension certainly does littl for the comfort of a rider of my weight but a series of fast, sweeping bend (with the steering damper screwed dow a little) brought back a thrill which ca usually be found only on a full-blow road racer. The large diameter wheel and small cross-section tires contribute immensely to the Rapide's rock-soli tracking and precise steering, and th stiff suspension felt reassuring excep when the road got really rough.

Due to the limited suspension trave I wasn't able to be completely objectiv about the ride's comfort factor. Bu Don assured me that the machine is ver comfortable with two aboard.

Most Vincent owners are purists wh don't mind the extra effort involved i keeping their machines spotless an mechanically sound, and the Vincen Owners Club members are a tight-kni group who know and love the big Twin (and Singles) from Stevenage. It's reall a shame that they are no longer bein manufactured, but if they were, the would undoubtedly lose some of th mystique that surrounds them. ◎

WHATEVER
Continued from page 129

ed from a trip to the factory in England, where he picked up a load of spare parts and a great deal of information.

Dave graciously went through a partial strip of his own "Lightningized" Black Shadow engine to give us a closer look at what makes it tick. He's grafting it into a Norton Featherbed frame (the sixth NorVin he's constructed) and should have it completed in a couple of months. With 11:1 compression pistons, Lightning cams, 1¼-in. Amal carburetors and a Dolphin Motors dual point set-up, which allows precise ignition timing, the completed machine promises to be a real bomb. Modifications to the Norton Featherbed frame include Ceriani forks, a Ceriani four leading-shoe front brake, and a Honda rear wheel. Dave has promised us the privilege of testing it as soon as it's completed.

We had heard several stories about the demise of the Vincent, one of which Dave was able to confirm. He maintains that, aside from the factory's financial problems, the biggest single cause of the halt in production was Britain's reaction to the streamlined models. "Big Lambrettas, they called them. The Englishmen just weren't ready for them, nor, evidently, was the rest of the world.

"I talked for quite a while with George Brown, owner of Nero, the

world record holder for drag racing motorcycles for a number of years. George was also Vincent's development engineer during the last years of the company's existence. I asked him if it would be possible to begin manufacturing Vincents, or at least new Vincent engines again, and he said that he estimated it would take 1 million pounds sterling (almost $2.5 million!) to get production into full swing again, and that he was sure it would never happen."

We asked Dave what happened to the dies for the crankcase, cylinder and cylinder head castings. "Well, it seems that all the dies were out in a shed beside the works. The shed was on the property of a school next door and the school was planning to expand and tear down the shed.

The people at Vincent were told to get their stuff out of the shed, but somehow the dies were left and the wrecking crew carted them off to places unknown. So, it's just not possible to get those parts now. The cases you see in the corner of the shop were the best used set I could find in England, and at $150 I wouldn't have considered them a couple of years ago."

And so, the fabulous Vincent is slipping further and further from the picture, but people like Dave Furst and Coburn Benson are helping to keep the legend alive. ◎

bike HALL OF FAME

Compiled by Peter Watson

MUNDANE and exotic, ride-to-work and ride-for-the-hell-of-it, there are some bikes which have stamped their imprint upon the British biking consciousness. This month we begin a series devoted to these machines, taking a close look at individual evolution and development as well as casting a sidelong glance at the men who built and rode them.
But no way is this going to be an exercise in rose-tinted nostalgia: we'll be taking a hard look at overblown reputations and perhaps puncturing a few myths, as well as helping to highlight the strange and underrated. Some of our choices will surprise you and all the bikes will be post-war, so stay with us. For starters we've taken that black beast of untold expense and mystique, the highly individual all-time British hot-shot Vincent vee-twin, pictured above.

HALL OF FAME

IT WAS just starting to look a little overcast as we pulled into Charnock Richard services on the M6 and began queueing once more to fuel the RE-5. In front of us, about ten yards away, a Vincent HRD twin was being filled up. The rider's small, black leather clad wife turned her silver pudding basin helmet in our direction and after a brief covert glance her husband obviously confided all there was to know about Japanese rotaries in one short but doubtless polite expletive. His lip-read comment made my lip curl in response. Smug middle of the road, middle-class, dyed-in-the-wool bastard. I'll show you what 500 cc of modern motorcycle can do to a piece of 25-year-old superannuated scrap.

We set off down the road about ten minutes after the Vincent and its twee leathered crew and I wound the Suzuki up to the red in every gear going down the slip road and back on to the motorway. Five minutes passed. Ten minutes, twenty; and still no sign of those stupid silver helmets bobbing up and down with the strange spring frame. Must've turned off, done an endo across the Armco, vaporised. Then they appeared, cruising at an unconcerned 70 mph down the inside lane, back end waving up and down like an epileptic's hand, but pudding basins motionless. We droned by, turned, and smiled a genuine smile. A hi there guys 'n' gals smile; a nice to know there are still some old fogies like you around smile. We might as well not have existed. The Vincent continued to fall behind and then turned off, its passengers enveloped in a coccoon of self-sufficiency, secure in the knowledge that only right-minded people ride the Beast.

It must be envy that causes such despicable thoughts to flit across my mind whenever I meet a rabid Vincent owner on the road. Perhaps it's a secret longing to join a club where members converse in genteely lowered tones of P.V.C., M.P.H., Series D, and look at each other with faintly pained expressions should you commit a blunder while talking of The Thing and It's Life Here On Earth. The Vincent twin may not have been canonised yet, but I have it on the best authority that a Papal decision on its beatification cannot be long delayed.

What makes a motorcycle achieve such legendary proportions? Speed? A 1948 Black Shadow would cruise at a genuine 100 mph. Racing success? The Norton boys threatened to stay at home and sulk if George Brown turned up to race his 998 cc bolide. Exclusivity? At £315 (excluding purchase tax) for a Series C Black Shadow in 1949, when the average industrial wage was about

£10 a week, Vincent twins were reserved for the monied classes. Longevity? A Shadow owning private detective called Tony Rose clocked up 100,000 miles at an average speed of around 70 mph in 15 months with less failures and breakages than you'd expect of the latest 750 Four. Oh, and for 80,000 of those miles the Beast was lugging some sort of sidecar. Originality? Every Vincent bristled with unconventional features, new metals, avant garde design work. But those factors in themselves can't explain the aura of mystique and machismo that continues to surround a name which ceased production in 1955. Plenty of bikes as worthy are forgotten, many that don't belong in the same league have achieved similar glorification and price inflation. I suppose it just happens.

Philip C. Vincent, a young Harrovian and Cambridge undergraduate studying mechanical science, was blessed with rich parents. You didn't get to a public school like Harrow or Cambridge university without them in the 1920s. And since he was fascinated by motorcycles and motorcycle engineering he was bought, at the age of 19, Howard Davies' far from going HRD 'concern' for £400. In 1927 it was up for grabs from OK Supreme Motors and Vincent with a MD appointed by his father — at once

began producing Vincent HRD machines that bore little resemblance to Davies' motorcycles which had achieved such incredible racing and abysmal commercial success. HRD remained on the tank until it was deleted in 1949 following P.C.V's discovery that dumb Americans were confusing it with *Harley D*. Ho, hum . . .

Early days were not encouraging. The Stevenage firm — like so many others — used proprietary engines like JAP and the Rudge Python, but with a triangulated pivoted sprung fork at the rear which was decidedly adventurous for the twenties, or thirties, or forties . . . Today we'd call it cantilever, but in those early days the readers of the motorcycle press called it other, less polite, names. That didn't bother Vincent, who, to judge by his writing, is a man who lets little trouble him. Like Butch Cassidy in *Butch Cassidy and The Sundance Kid*, P.C.V. reckons he has vision while the rest of the world wears bi-focals.

The twin was sparked from an equally remarkable individual, Phil Irving, who joined the firm after returning with a strange Yorkshireman called Gill on the pillion of a Vincent HRD 600 cc (JAP) sidevalve Model E and sidecar from his native Australia. Gill's passenger for the outward overland jaunt in 1929 had wisely decamped in the Antipodes. After

aving Liverpool the intrepid explorer anaged to plot a course for London that ok in Henley, Oxfordshire. Well, he was m Bradford. ·

What Irving did — merely a year after ncent had gone into production with his vn high-cam pushrod 500 cc single gine — was to come up with the idea a 47 deg vee twin by lining up the ankshaft gear and idler wheel on a cing and drawing of the timing side of e new engine. It was 1936. Hitler had en in power for 3 years. Stanley ldwin was Prime Minister and Jimmy thrie took the Senior TT for Norton ain at nearly 86 mph. The average dustrial wage was 3½d a hour . . .

The Series A Rapide engine, with its vo Meteor top ends and maze of ternal oil pipes was a rather strange oking device. A 47 deg, 998 cc twin ith short splayed pushrods lying parallel its valves with the rear pot offset to aid oling and avoid a Harley-type forked nrod. But with the exposed hairpin lve springs of the period as well as an f-the-shelf four speed gearbox and utch from Messrs. Burman, both of hich were simply unable to cope with e massive torque shovelled out by the gine. But as long as the transmission ld you could lap Brooklands at over 00 mph. George Brough might *claim* at you could get one of his SS100

Brough Superiors of the period to lap at the ton, Philip Vincent's vee twins actually made it happen on the track.

You leave your signature upon any piece of work you've laboured over for a long period. Writers leave trails of half-remembered phrases, motorcycle mechanics leave broken fins, and looking at a Vincent twin you conclude that the engineers who built it must be almost as interesting as the monster they produced. The Vincent twin is individual and unconventional enough to have been dubbed "several engineering solutions in search of problems" and "one of the greatest designs of all time". The men who built it looked the world in the face and spat right in its eye.

Take the spring frame. Right from his undergraduate designs Vincent believed in a spring frame, at a time when this was rank heresy. He even had to *hide* the springs which controlled the pivoted fork's movement under the saddle to pretend it was rigid, although perhaps they'd have found their way there anyway. You must remember that it took motorcyclists literally years to accept overhead valves. Who cared if sidevalves were less efficient? Bury your head in the sand and progress will pass on by.

But, of course, Vincent was racing the future. His spring frame needed damping and all he had to start with was the sort

of friction damping you can find on the head stem of any bike with sporty pretensions today. Vincent couldn't wait for gas-oil shox and multi-rate springs, by 1955 it was all over and the last — Series D — twins were about to leave the factory.

The 1949 Series C with its Irving-designed Girdraulic forks at the front was prey to the same lack of really adequate damping. To design front forks based on the pre-war girder when all around were apeing BMW and Matchless with telescopics takes the sort of mind which believes it can produce the goods in its own way.

In his book *The Vincent H.R.D. Story* Roy Harper — no, not *that* Roy Harper, rock freaks — quotes Vincent as saying that he has "always regarded with absolute horror the long springs of telescopic forks which project the best part of two feet below their lower mounting to the head lug, the whole two feet being completely unsupported and subject to whip". Therefore, the attempt to get the best out of girder forks with forged aluminium legs fitted with large diameter spindles to brace them and one-piece forged links to resist twisting. Hydraulic damping came from a single central Armstrong unit which controlled the movement of very long springs — enclosed in tubular boxes — joining the lower end of the fork crown direct to the fork ends. These were the soft, high pre-load coil springs which give good teles their supple action. As a keen sidecar pilot, Irving also incorporated a cunning eccentric adjustment on the new forks which both altered the pre-load on the springs and adjusted the trail for solo or sidecar use in minnies.

The natural break provided in production by WW2 gave Vincent and Irving their chance to re-design the big twin completely. Only the 84 x 90 mm bore and stroke (998 cc) remained from the A Series Rapide engine as well as such features as the duplex brakes back and front with the spokes laced into a separate hub to provide exceptional strength and resistance to distortion. Yep, a four-drum motorcycle.

The engine was now a 50 deg twin in unit with its gearbox which was much stronger than the Burman, and a typically ingenious self-servo clutch which has been known to give real trouble if not fully understood, like the Velo. (Writes our man in the DR mac.) The frame was the famous spine-type with a head lug of drop-forged steel bolted to the front pot — both cylinders being attached to the crankcases by four high tensile steel through bolts — by a bolt itself firmly attached to the 16 gauge 6 pint oil tank

unit. The engine, therefore, formed an integral part of the frame, and the back end — wheel, brake, pivoted fork, seat and so on — could be removed *en bloc* by displacing three bolts and splitting the chain.

It would take about two complete issues of *Bike* to provide an accurate run-down on all the Rapide, Black Shadow, Black Knight, Black Prince and Black Lightning intricacies as the twin developed from 1946 to 1955. All the famous features like the five-inch Smiths' speedo and all black engine — introduced on the Black Shadow, a 'sports' version of the Rapide, in 1948 — the mass of stainless and alloy parts Vincent used because he loathed chrome, the wheel spindles with integral tommy bars make an endless list of the weird and wonderful.

Motor Cycling tested the new Black Shadow in '48 and turned in a 122 mph top whack. Fuel consumption was 51 mpg, with the engine turning over at a mere 5,485 rpm at 122 mph in top. Tester Charlie Markham also managed to produce a braking figure of 22½ ft from 30 mph, although he completed this sitting on the oil filler cap. Painful.

Of course, road tests of this vintage — you might almost say any road tests — give you no more of an objective view of the big twin than a ride on one would today. Most have been rebuilt with inferior, pattern spares. It would be interesting to know how *Motor Cycling* carried out their timing — probably by stop watch — and anyone who goes brake testing knows how easy it can be to come home with freak figures you couldn't possibly imitate on the road. I wouldn't want to damage my testimonials on the oil filler of a Shadow,

for one. Mr Markham also noted that it took him two days to get the hang of starting the Shadow and that although it would pull away from 22 mph in top, the front plug soon oiled up if you tried this too often. The gearbox apparently 'drifted' out of gear on the over-run and was difficult to persuade into third at anything over 65 mph.

Nevertheless, for £381 (plus £2 7s. 6d. for the double sprocket rear hub) you could buy 457 lbs of 998 cc motorcycle capable of "constant and colossal" acceleration from 0-100 mph at a time when the average family saloon was pushed to see 65. And the Shadow was undoubtedly slightly over-geared as standard. Fit a sidecar and you could still take the wife and kids out for a 16.5 sec standing quarter and see over 80 mph. A measure of the myth has got to be the performances turned in by Vincent motorcycles and Vincent engines in the hands of factory-sponsored record breakers as well as sprinters, drag racers, club scratchers and the ever-keen road riders long after production ceased.

Star of the Vincent riders is George Brown — no, not *that* George Brown, stupid — who left the factory in 1951. At a time when younger men were easing their arthritic joints into armchairs, he was piloting his blown big twin Super Nero along the runway at Elvington. Doing 190 miles an hour when you're 61 must be quite a blast.

Brown's two most famous machines, Nero and Super Nero, were really incredible projectiles for the period (fifties, sixties and early seventies). For

sprinting on the unsupercharged Nero the Vincent frame gained AMC teles and a Velocette swinging arm because George found the Girdraulics and cantilever rear end just a touch lively in a straight line.

Brown had been experimental tester at Stevenage, conveniently situated for the Great North Road (A1) which apparently formed part of his test strip. But other public highways were employed, like a stretch of the Newmarket Road where one day Brown had to cross a minor road at 110 mph on a Vincent/Indian concoction. He narrowly avoided making a large hole in a police car which wanted to cross the major road at the time. His boss was keeping a lookout and flagged down the fuzz, who he conned with a story that they were carrying out important work on behalf of the Chancellor of the Exchequer, whom Vincent insinuated needed the dollars from US Vincent sales so badly that any lawbreaking would be officially condoned. Some people will believe anything . . .

Stateside, Rollie Free made that amazing 150.313 mph pass at Bonneville on a stripped Black Lightning in 1948. Amazing, because, having torn his leathers, he lay flat on the bike in his bathing trunks for the final run. Free was in his late forties.

Nearer home, drag fans may recall the Vincent-engined Pegasus campaigned by Ian Messenger, Mick Butler and Derek Chinn. Its best time ever was a 9.8 sec run and in 998 cc form the bike still holds the litre class record for Santa Pod at 164 mph. It consisted of 1948 Black Shadow crankcase, Series C heads and special barrels with Venolia pistons. The conrods were standard but they naturally

HALL OF FAME

used the larger crankpin and MK II cams. A Shorrock supercharger fed the motor and the clutch was a Norton unit grafted on.

They gave up the Vin after it had been hogged out and cut about to obtain 1,500 cc. It never ran in this guise and spares were becoming extremely difficult to come by in 1972. Plus the fact that the Vincent engine required endless machining time for this sort of application. The same reason — shortage of spares — ended Laverda importer Roger Slater's brief flirtation in the late sixties with the Fritz Egli framed Egli Vincent road racers.

Writing one of this *P.C.V.* pieces in *Motorcycle Sport* of December 1969, Philip Vincent observed that he didn't share Vincent Owners' Club members' indignation at the idea of his engine in a Swiss frame. "Why should I take offence, when Fritz appears to have paid me the greatest compliment accorded to any manufacturer of motorcycles or cars in the 85 years' life of the industry to date? It is as though Monteverdi, Bristol or Jensen were to fit Rolls-Royce, Cadillac, Packard or Hispano Suiza engines bought off scrap dealers and reconditioned as new in their determination to offer their customers the best available engines . . . but they don't."

The road-going, racing Vincent twin still survives today, when many owners are just beginning to think about their first big end replacement. Ray Elger, a toolmaker from Cassington, near Oxford, recently rode his 25-year-old Egli-framed Shadow to an NSA sprint, near his home, two-up, ripped off 17 standing quarters with a best of 12.19 and dropped by Didcot on the way back for a total fuel bill of £1. Because Ray can't afford to run

the bike just for sprints he has to keep it in genuine street trim, with stock Shadow gearing. That includes a 46T rear sprocket producing the classic Vincent 100 mph at 4,600 rpm. Non-standard items are 36 mm Concentrics, a multiplate Norton/Vincent clutch and 9.9:1 (as opposed to 7.3) compression ratio. The bike's best quarter time is 11.91 sec, with a top terminal of 116 mph, both recorded last year. Anyone care to try and match that sort of performance with a genuine street bike tomorrow?

No-nonsense instrumentation — just a single, five-inch 150 mph speedo.

On the road, the legend continues. Of 11,000 Vincent motorcycles made, less than half that number probably survive worldwide. Morini Riders' Club organiser Simon Pancheri owns a 1955 Rapide — naked version of the all-enclosed Series D models — which he bought for £350 in 1972. It isn't as quick as his 3½ Strada and it vibrates a lot more, but he doesn't have to whizz up and down the box so much. The Rapide handles strangely on pre-cling rubber Avons, but then it is *100 per cent* original. The lights are weedy six volt glimmers, but the ignition was by coil in 1955 so it starts well. Once you buy a

Vincent it's vee twins all the way . . .

Today the Vincent name is owned by Matt Holder who also has Scott and Velocette on his list of motorcycle firms. Vincent always ran close to the financial precipice. Attempts to sell the Air Ministry a vee twin powered target aircraft to save the firm's motorcycle production failed in 1953. Even the news from New Zealand that Russell Wright and Bob Burns had succeeded in breaking the world record for both solo and sidecar with a basically standard unblown Lightning failed to boost sales in 1955. Perhaps, as Vincent himself observed in Roy Harper's excellent marque history, "This . . . proved beyond doubt that the usual motor-cycle enthusiasts' talk about speed and performance was not genuine." P.C.V. wasn't the first manufacturer to discover that show often sells more bikes than go . . .

The Vincent Owners' Club continues to flourish, with over 1,500 members worldwide, and one of the best club magazines — M.P.H. — that has ever been produced. The VOC Spares Company Ltd., a public company with 50,000 shares, was recently formed to keep Vincents on the move and seems to operate amicably with Matt Holder, who is tooling up to produce parts for the remaining examples of the handbuilt British performance motorcycle at its best.

Despite its not inconsiderable faults the Vincent twin remains a monument to engineers who produced the world's fastest production motorcycle without the benefit of cost accountants, computers or a vast income from moulding plastic garden gnomes. Of course they went bust; naturally people stopped buying a machine for which *Motor Cycle* could find "Nowhere . . . to obtain fastest speeds". This is Britain, after all. ●

Continued from page 99

ness. At 100 m.p.h. in top gear the engine still has 1,000 r.p.m. in hand. This, of course, accounts for the machine's very long engine life and, properly ridden, the big unit should outlast any two high-revving competitors.

Handling improves as speed increases. At low speeds in London's traffic the Harper Vincent is a handful. A certain amount of physical effort is necessary to thread its purposeful bulk through the traffic and it's not advisable to nip in and out like one would on a lightweight. But once on the open road the picture changes and the limits to which you can crank her over are dictated by the clutch cover. The Shadow holds its line on long sweeping curves like a train and the handling didn't give me a moment's anxiety in a thousand fast miles.

Road shocks are absorbed by the usual Vincent system of Girdraulic front forks with cenarl compression damper. The rear units are triangulated pivot-type with adjustable shock absorbers. I would say

that this was the first time I have ever ridden a Vinnie on which all these units were in first-class order and the result surprised me considerably. The steering was beautifully positive and there was no pitch whatsoever. I had an elderly Rapide once which developed my arms to Mr. Universe standards fighting tank-slappers. Not so with this one!

Mind you, with about 65 b.p.h. on tap, wet-weather handling demanded extreme care. You just can't take any liberties at all and braking, accelerating and changing up and down has to be done very cautiously. But this, of course, is in no way a criticism. The same thing applies to any bike, particularly big, powerful lots.

A stop light is fitted to the front brake, there's an ignition warning light mounted in the ammeter and the motor is fitted with two front heads. A tool box is fitted on the near-side of the comfortable dual seat and the oil tank is opposite. Access to the filler is gained by pivoting the seat upwards from the front, but the design

of the tank is such that it's difficult to see the actual oil level. A 150 m.p.h. speedometer is fitted into the big headlamp which throws out a beam of light almost powerful enough to allow the Shadow's vast performance to be used at night to the full.

Throughout the road test I tried to analyse the charm of a big-twin Vinnie and, frankly, to justify the machine at a time when smaller, neater jobs give almost the same performance. The answer, I think, lies in the rider himself : you either like Vincents or you don't, just as you may or may not like spinach, cricket, 40 headlamps on a scooter or filling in idiotic readership surveys for " Motorcycle Mechanics." Every man to his own.

I like the Vincent and I always have. It has a unique vintage feel, a complete lack of fussiness coupled with r nsational performance and ruggedness. Long may Harpers and other enthusiasts continue to resurrect the beast. There'll always be a number of reactionaries to ride 'em— me for one!

How's this for a long road-test?

A blow-by-blow account of 85,000 miles on a vee-twin Vincent

WHAT is a road-test? Perhaps 1,000 miles in a couple of weeks, hopefully with an experienced person if anything useful is to be concluded. A reader's report can sometimes be illuminating, although restricted to a letter. There have been more ambitious ideas, *Motor Cycle* used to compile a Readers' Report based on a large number of questionnaires, and once, back in the mists of time, Tony Rose took it on himself to do a 100,000-mile road-test on a Vincent (it had to be a Vincent, didn't it!).

Well, if you like road-tests the following was compiled after 85,000 miles (I wanted to do a Tony Rose but, after all, my bike was approaching 20 years old at the start!). However it is more than that, it is a story of travelling, meeting new friends and horizons. The bike is a Vincent and I have learned most of the myths and truths of the legend. I will give you my subjective impressions, and also the cold facts, warts and all, which I have been keeping in a log for the last few years.

I'm not certain exactly when my interest in Vincents started. It was my father who bought the 1,000 c.c. Rapide PUB335 in 1962. At about the same time I came across a pre-war Comet owned by another apprentice. It was in bits, and to save it from the scrap heap I took it over and put it together. Meanwhile PUB was run with a chair as my father's transport until vandalized, whereupon he took it apart for an overhaul. Did it need one! For instance, there were 12 teeth missing from the clutch sprocket (mostly on one row of teeth), and I am quite serious in stating that when the contents of the oil tank were drained they stayed in a pile, taking over a week to run into a level pool.

Eventually it became clear that the rebuild would never be finished, so once again I took on the job. I keep vowing every time never to take on bikes in boxes, or building up bikes from spares, but I keep on doing it. Bear in mind that in the mid-60s apprentices were not the richest of people, so anything that was serviceable was reused. Replacements were, therefore, as follows:

Big ends and main bearings.

Rebore and new pistons.

New timing chest spindles, good second-hand cams and followers.

New sprockets and chains.

New seals and gaskets of course.

New steering head cups and cones, fork spindles, bushes and eccentrics.

New carburetter slides, needles, and jets.

A repaint by hand with Belco.

Just as significant is the list of items not replaced, which goes:

The cylinder heads were untouched, no valves, guides, not even springs replaced.

Nothing inside the gearbox proper, not even bearing, was renewed, although springs in the selector positive stop mechanism were.

All wheel swinging arm bearings (taper roller) were untouched.

The clutch was reassembled with only new seals and bushes. This was a mistake as, unknown to me, the linings were oil soaked, and I failed to notice a corroded area under one oil seal.

The brake linings, and a sidecar rear sprocket were reused. It was obvious they would quickly have to be replaced but the money would not run to it when all else was ready (remember a Vincent has four brakes). One loose rocker was reused with Loctite, but not successfully.

After about five years it was complete again, having cost me about £150 (pause for everyone to sigh "those were the days"), although I gave my father very little for the tea chest of bits which had originally cost him about £100. It puzzles me to note I spent about £10 on missing bits, but it had been a complete bike? Long suffering wives

A tired, neglected but ever reliable "PUB" at 67,000 miles —having just journeyed to every corner of England, Scotland and Wales

and mothers might like to note that the rebuild was done in the front room. At first the engine would be hauled out then put away again. Becoming too big for that, it was hidden in a corner, and finally built up into a bike one Christmas when I was home, and wheeled out. Since it was cold outside. I excelled myself in inventing reasons why it couldn't be moved while I fitted bits in the warm!

This, then, is the machine whose performance is to be gone over. Not a new bike, nor even an expensive rebuilt model.

At the time I had gained entry to a University postgraduate course. but after

handing in my notice my grant application was turned down. My professor managed to get me £7 per week (and there is no summer vac. on postgrad. work) so the mileage in 1969 when we took to the road was limited. Nevertheless from May '69 until October '75 it has been my everyday transport. although I ride sundry vintage machines and rubbish occasionally.

A period of "debugging" took place. I have all the receipts but my log did not start for a couple of years so my records here are from memory. Fairly quickly the brakes were relined, and the 56t sprocket changed for 48t on numerous recommendations, then changed, as will be seen later, for the standard 46t which I prefer. The clutch slipped, as Vincent clutches are reputed to do. However the linings were replaced, also the faulty carrier which was corroded and was replaced secondhand. The Miller dynamo worked. as Miller dynamos are reputed to do, poorly and with frequent breakdowns. It cost me little as I did the repairs myself—usually new brushes. a clean, resoldered wire, and adjust. However after 5,000 miles it would fail again. I persevered for a long time but eventually changed it for a Lucas and cured the trouble. There must have been an explanation but I never found it.

After this initial period the bike was very reliable, with mileage rising to 20,000 a year. Listing the work done on it makes it sound a lot because of the mileage—after all, tyres every 10,000, chains the same, oil changes every 2,000, etc.. meant a steady flow of regular maintenance which must be borne in mind.

Two other things became apparent. First, driving carefully (by someone rather more used to a Fanny-B at the time) I found that consumption was 60 plus—eat your hearts out, strokers! Secondly, a little quirk, a

valve stuck then freed. Running was not affected, only compression. Very occasionally, maybe 10,000 miles later, it would happen again, in France or Scotland, just to frighten the daylights out of me, then go away again. Something else I never tracked down properly, which was aptly described by a chap I met in the TT queue as "character".

No log for 1969.

I still was not keeping any sort of log in 1970. That did not start until it became obvious I was on to a good thing. I kept records once with an ancient Royal Enfield 125 and nearly gave up motorcycling when

LONG ROAD-TEST
You can be sure of hard facts... I began a detailed log of all repairs, replacements, even petrol and oil used

I found it was costing me about 3s 9d per mile. Not a recommended practice! Anyway I started getting about and meeting people—Dragon rally, TT, various Vincent rallies, etc. Being very slow to make friends, and considerably slower to manage the courtesy of remembering any of their names, this was only the start of a long but rewarding process.

One or two odd notes survive. As already mentioned, I did not like the 48t sprocket and fitted a standard 46. I just love "tall" gearing. The original platinum points, hammered away. They were almost unobtainable, and frantically expensive, so tungsten Comet ones were used. Neither this nor the manual magneto conversion is recommended for a Vee-twin mag. but with exactly the right technique first-kick starts were the rule, and I was only 10½ stone, down to nine at times. Dynamo trouble persisted. The clutch-retaining nut, retained by a tag, came loose. At long intervals this recurred—no great problem but annoying, until I had a brainstorm, fitted two tags, and it never happened again. There was a spot of bother when screws in the positive stop came loose, the cure for which was of course to tighten them. However here I learned the lesson "if it's working well leave it alone!" There is a later modified bit which is intended to stop over-selection of gears. Until the loose screws I had no such problem but fitted it anyway. Remember that the gearbox had been untouched. The backlash inside at the selectors and wear of the positive stop outside were no problem. However take out one, and leave the other, and the result is under selection! The cover had to come back off, the old bit was put back, and all was well thereafter. I suppose we all learn the hard way at times!

Still no log in 1970.

Mileage at the end of 1970 was still modest as I lived in the Midlands near most friends and family. However in '71 I really got it together with the bike. Late in the year I moved to Somerset and hopped on after work most Fridays to travel up to Warwickshire. As I recollect, even in the 50s the weeklies ran articles on "preparing your bike for the Dragon rally" whereas now any bike is expected to be capable. The Japanese bikes take some of the credit, but a lot of it is surely just that nowadays the average rider has a serviced near-new bike,

not a wire and string old banger.

The year took in most of the usual events (e.g., the TT), and I note a road-safety rally. I remember that. The first test was a mini-trials section—and me on a 470 lb Vincent plus panniers! A later section could not have been done by an articulated moped, but at least it was impossible for everyone. Mainly by carefully reading the regs and choosing low penalty failures, I managed second place in the motorcycle section.

From occasional notes I see the speedo gave a bit of trouble, also the (Miller) dynamo flung off a retaining wire. Lucas don't suffer that trouble because they do not fit one. It does seem a pity that Miller go to the trouble of fitting such a nicety, then suffer increased instead of reduced problems! Failures to charge I did not bother to note. The only real failure worth mention seems to have been a worn rocker bearing, which squeaked when its oil feed blocked. While replacing this, I also replaced the rocker which was loose on its pin (mentioned in the rebuild comments) since this defied Loctite, swear words, prayers, etc., and insisted on pivoting on the wrong bit. Someone had given me an old one, undamaged in its bore, but which he had replaced as worn out at its tip. Since it looked just like the rest of mine, I fitted that and cured the looseness! On a Vincent the rocker/bearing comes out through the inspection cap so it was no sweat. By now I stopped worrying that I had not put it together properly so it must be about to go wrong, and started worrying that it had done enough miles to make big-end failure likely. A born pessimist am I. Actually I did note a rattle when shutting off after a motorway run, which I swear *was* the big end.

Nineteen-seventy-one—mileage at the end of the year 26,000, start of log.

By this time it was obvious even to someone with my outlook of gloom and despondency that I was on to rather a good thing. I began a detailed log of all repairs, replacements, even oil and petrol used (subsequent years I settled for regular consumption checks). Thus from now on you can be sure of hard facts.

As I run Vintage machinery and retain my previous bikes in use, I did not use the Vincent for all events, e.g., the TT, but nevertheless attended many. Nor does this make much difference to mileage as a lot of it is general transport (no car at all). Most of the major rallies do not need describing as they are familiar to all. One, however, stands out, on its own account, and because it was my first trip abroad. Taking the latter point first, I joined a party of Vincent owners going to the first continental club rally in France, organized I seem to recollect by Jean Paoli. This actually involved me in the maximum possible distance as I was on one side of the country and the party were travelling from the other, but being a worrier, I preferred to make use of someone else's experience first time. On the way there the sticking valve already mentioned reappeared to scare me (which it did). As usual it went away on starting, the only snag being that short of one of its compressions it did not want to start. In spite of a crowd of eager French lads dying to push-start a

Vincent, and the rest of the party being impatient, I stubbornly refused to bump it (never having failed to kickstart it before, and in fact the only subsequent occasion it needed bumping was when the kickstart shaft sheared). The bike equally stubbornly refused to start. Eventually I won, but my scientific knowledge that it is just a machine and that there is an explanation for everything cannot submerge the feeling that it was just playing up because we were a long way from home and in an embarrassing position. Having had its game, it reverted to normal, first-kick starting.

A couple of us got split up on the way there. The return trip was worse. The start was delayed for one, then another wanted to stop, someone else for petrol, and so on. Eventually we broke up and all went hell for leather independently. If you like travelling alone, do so, if not keep to the smallest groups. However the event itself was great. On arrival at 2 a.m. hot punch was poured down me and floor space found indoors. I never did unpack my panniers! Add to that people such as Paul Richardson, ex-service manager for Vincents and author of a good book on the Vincent marque, and what more could one ask?

Another interesting aside—this time testing my honesty somewhat. The speedo occasionally read funny, so it was sent to a specialist. When it failed to return I wrote to them. They said they couldn't trace it. Now everyone knows what you mean by a Vincent clock—one of those 5in dinner plates. So they did the obvious thing and returned me one, with quite a sizeable bill. Even so since mine was an ordinary 3in it was cheap, but of course I told them their mistake. Mind you, it took me a fortnight!

To return to the bike's performance, not much seems to have gone wrong although there was plenty of routine maintenance. The plugs and points were checked rather often, suggesting slight unhappiness with starting, and two tubes mean two punctures—I seem to get one or two every year. A kickstart spring broke, the clutch nut loosened as I had not yet thought of two lock tags. The clutch possibly needed a degrease, according to whether I caught the nut early or not. Two mirrors and a pair of handlebars indicate mishaps. Taking the heaviest model the factory turned out greenlaning does for mirrors quite quickly. Messrs. Miller also get some of the blame. Down a strange lane one night I peered at the ammeter (not illuminated, subsequently "modded" in this respect) to try and see why the battery was flat. I should have looked at the road because when I looked up there it was—gone. As the road disappeared to the left I braked and ran into the ditch. With around 5 cwt only desperation and a complete lack of anyone else for miles got me out. Later in the year I chucked the Miller for a Lucas set-up made from an assortment of bits in my loft.

Oil consumption has always been good for a Vin—900 miles per pint usually. The first proper costing becomes available, including fuels, repairs, tax, insurance, in fact everything except the rider's clothing. For 1972 it worked out at 1½p per mile.

1972:

Mileage: 14,000 (40,000 total).

Routine work: seven oil changes. Checked tappets three times, points five times. Plugs, cleaned twice, replaced twice. Two new tyres. One new chain. Two new tubes. Relined rear brakes (now regard this as routine, checked whenever a tyre is changed).

Repairs: Two new mirrors. New handlebars. New kickstart spring. Clutch nut tightened, lock spring replaced (twice), Miller dynamo/regulator changed for Lucas (E3L, MCR1) secondhand.

Data: Petrol: 55 m.p.g.
Oil: 900 m.p.p.
Repairs: £3 per month.
Total cost: 1⅛p per mile.

The Lucas regulator caused a bit of teething trouble. The spring seemed to be soft and needed frequent adjusting (old age or perhaps because the MCR1 was not intended for an E3L dynamo). Temporarily the Miller was replaced, but caused trouble again. Meantime the spring was unriveted and replaced. This resulted in a very interesting fault when the Lucas set was refitted. The cover was left off while I arrived at the right adjustment, then put on. Straight away the charge began to creep up. As darkness came on the lights were switched on, but the charge continued to climb. All the lights on and an 8 amp. charge is unheard of on a Vincent—nor is it good for the dynamo! The cover was taken off again and the rest of the journey done at low revs. The explanation is easy. Together with the spring Lucas incorporated a bimetallic strip for temperature compensation and I had refitted it backwards, getting away with it so long as the unit was open to the air. Cure was simply to turn it round (a riveting job) after which my electrics troubles were virtually cured.

Vincent front fork eccentrics (which adjust spring and trail for sidecar work) are prone to wear, and at 50,000 miles they and their bushes were replaced, not exactly something to complain about! The other spindles and bushes were fine. A new silencer and (secondhand) pipes were needed. Complaints about modern chrome are not just wishful thinking. That silencer was very old, worn through the chrome to nickel and steel in one place and tatty from knocks through the years, but only needed renewing because the baffles loosened and blew out in time. Cheap replacement pipes and silencers rot away in a couple of years or so, like car items.

An incipient fault began to show. A rear-wheel bearing was found to be loose, Loctite etc. applied and a couple of spokes broke. The real cause did not reveal itself for quite a while longer. The clutch and valve lifter cables needed repair but the only other repairs were caused by a very unfortunate incident in the island.

Just before TT week I saw an advert, from a chap with no transport for the week, and since I travel alone I had a pillion seat to offer. Ivor, however, got a bad bargain! The week passed quite well until Friday. Along the tiny Druidale road the front wheel picked up a nail and deflated at once, throwing us off. Injuries were not really bad but warranted a trip to Nobles. My leg did not stiffen up immediately because I was busy fitting a new tyre but Ivor could hardly make the trip to Douglas and went home by train. As the hours on the boat and bike passed, my leg stiffened. Because of tiredness I had to break my trip home—reluctantly. It is useless to play with the kickstarter, only a full-blooded kick will do. Imagine yourself with a stiff, painful leg, and 1,000 c.c. of silent motor. You know how much it is going to hurt, you know you have to put your back into it, and you have too much time to think about it. Anyway home was reached and a few days off work put things right, no real damage to me (or Ivor as far as I know), and just a bit of mudguard damage to the bike, plus a written-off home-made pannier.

1973:

Mileage: 13,300 (53,000 total).

Routine work: Six oil changes. Checked tappets once. Points three times. Plugs, gapped four times replaced once. Two new tyres, one tube. Two chains. Relined front brake shoes.

Repairs: One mirror. New silencer, secondhand pipes. New fork eccentrics and bushes. Three rear spokes, Loctite loose outer race in hub. Mudguard fibreglassed, pannier repaired. Clutch and valve lifter cables repaired. Clutch degreased. Dynamo/regulator changed over twice.

Data: 55 m.p.g.
Oil: 1,000 m.p.p.
Repairs: £4 per month.
Total cost: 1⅓p per mile.

In the first few weeks of 1974 I hit some roadworks temporarily patched for Christmas but unsignposted, coming off as a result. After numerous letters I did get payment for damage from the company responsible, nevertheless I have included the repairs and costs below. Whether this incident affected the rear wheel I cannot be sure, but the reason for previous loose bearings came to light—the hub was cracked. Even on a 23-year-old bike it is not nice to think one's hubs might break up, but inspection showed this one to have just cause. Vincent drums and spoke flanges are bolted on using special bolts with off-centre heads fitting closely to the bearing housing. It is not possible to put the bolts in wrongly, at least it should not be. However armed with a 2 lb lump hammer and a strong arm it can be done. The heads bend over 10 degrees and carve a $\frac{1}{32}$in deep groove in the alloy but they do go in. This was exactly how the previous owner (whom I shall not mention here) did the job and the wonder is that it took so long to show up.

The one and only occasion the bike needed bump starting then occurred. After work at a remote site the kickstart crank broke. Actually it was bumped twice, I stalled it first time! The second attempt proved that I am man enough to bump a Vin once and once only. I got the works policeman to give me a push.

I must briefly mention my personal circumstances because they considerably influence the story. Nineteen-seventy-three had started very well, with my meeting a girl

Round-Britain Rally shot of the Vincent. Th tower is at Lake Vyrnwy in Wales . . . enjoyab riding country for high-geared bikes!

I thought the world of. When it went wron I was left as low as I have ever been. Thos who know PUB 335 may find it hard t believe but it used to be cleaned and eve polished fairly often. Cleaning and every thing except essential maintenance stoppe and for a while even riding dwindled. Unt 1974 most riding was for transport to famil or one-make gatherings, most of my friend (whom I was very glad of) being VOC mem bers. In some way 1974 mirrored the pre vious year rather cruelly, but not as regard motorcycling. I was persuaded to enter Tin Stevens' "Round Britain Rally" which too me to every corner of this island. The Nort and Scotland were done on a fortnigh holiday, being my first real touring holiday Sightseeing was a bit limited by the nee to cover so many places, but I shall be re returning. As far as the bike was concerne it did 3,500 miles in two weeks, with only one nipple pulling off. If it sounds like a boast, perhaps I should record that on thi particular trip I travelled along with Heathe MacGregor, who went everywhere on he Triumph outfit carrying two children. Tha should put a lot of riders in their places and surely shows that we should expect a bike to do this sort of thing nowadays!

On another weekend devoted to the same rally was suffered the only serious breakdown ever. The fibre magneto pinion stripped. It's funny but I knew it was serious although all that happened was that the engine stalled on tickover. Something about the way it did it, I suppose? Fortunately the spares I carry, other than soldering nipples etc., are front and rear tubes, clutch cable, fibre pinion (secondhand at the time) so it was repaired at the roadside. It is not trivial for a very annoying reason—the inspection cover is a bit smaller than the gear (pre-war the gear comes out), so the timing cover must come off, for which on a twin the exhaust must come off. The designer's ears should have been singed that weekend because I had 1,000 miles of varied going to fit in, and with no flash on my camera could not make good use of night.

Mileage began to pile up as I spent a lot of weekends at rallies, not one-make but

LONG ROAD-TEST
Replacements were mainly routine ...except for the clutch

Ted Davis shows off one of his "yesteryear's masterpieces"—a 1955 Series D Vincent Black Shadow with monoshock triangulated cantilever rear suspension. . . .

where I would meet some new faces, although as many keen motorcyclists know, one keeps meeting the other keen types everywhere, even abroad! Since the clock was around 60,000, cleaning nil, maintenance minimal for the continuing reason mentioned previously, I think it a tribute to the machine that I could travel so much, and cheaply—which I am grateful for.

Replacements were mainly routine, and other work was trivial—like overcharging cured by cleaning a corroded earth. The clutch, however, needed degreasing a couple of times and when it slipped again it was decided to replace all the oil seals. Vincent clutches feature three or four and will not tolerate oil! The job involves removing the primary chaincase, so a new tensioner blade was fitted, and broken shock absorber springs replaced (which to be honest was most of them). Otherwise punctures were the only problem, about 1½ per year. A reward to the man with a foolproof cure, but I am very sceptical, goo for treating tubes has been advertised since the 1920s.

974:
Mileage: 17,000 (71,000 total).
Routine work: Nine oil changes. Checked tappets once, points twice. Plugs cleaned once, replaced once. Two new tyres. Two new chains. Two new tubes. Relined rear brakes.
Repairs: New mirror, licence holder, prefocus unit, handlebars, grips, secondhand rear wheel (£10), kickstart crank, spring, ratchet bush. New battery. Two clutch cables (first faulty), new inner for valve lifter cable. Cleaned regulator. Clutch degreased twice, fitted new oil seals, primary chain tensioner, shock absorber springs, secondhand magneto pinion (64,000 miles).
Data: Petrol: 55 m.p.g.
Oil: 800 m.p.p., 600 m.p.p. at various times.
Repairs: £5 per month.
By 1975 I was really hoping to emulate Tony Rose's 100,000-mile feat (performed as the longest road-test in the world for the VOC in the early 50s). However the year had other ideas. As a friend keeps saying—'smile and be happy, things could be worse", so I smiled and was happy—sure enough things got worse! Actually that really applies a little later as far as the bike is concerned. Indeed early on it continued to perform faultlessly as indicated by a trouble-free trip to the Elephant rally, where it started in freezing conditions first kick as usual (albeit with great care over priming) to the chagrin of all the Bee Emms which were being bumped all over the place.

Hardly a weekend was spent in my flat—so much rallying, etc.—that there was no time for bulling the bike even if I had the inclination. The Round Britain Event had a rather less interesting format, so I aimed for only a bronze, intending to use a pre-war model but in fact falling back on PUB quite often. Mention of the number again reminds me that I owe quite a lot to it. I am really very shy, and have an awful memory as an additional handicap to getting to know people. Fortunately they remember the number which helps a lot, leaving me only with the problem of placing someone I know quickly enough, and trying to cope with rarely being able to remember their names!

If I had wanted to see it, however, the end was coming into sight. First sign was the chain jumping the gearbox sprocket. This together with the less worn rear sprocket was changed, restoring chain life which had been shortening. Petrol consumption got the wrong side of 50 m.p.g., though recovering after a twiddle with carb, and so on. Then came TT week. As the week progressed starting deteriorated, and oil consumption rose a bit. By the end of the week it was obvious that the rear exhaust valve was burnt although it still went satisfactorily and got me home. This was very disappointing as it meant opening the engine up for the first time in nearly 80,000 miles. A new valve was fitted, without doing anything else at all, and I continued, hoping perhaps to coax another 20,000 if I was gentle. A few thousand later the clutch began to grab really badly. The clutch shoes needed replacing, not because of lining wear which I have never known, but because the pivot holes had worn. Although the parts were needed at perhaps the worst ever time for Vincent spares (just before the VOC Spares Co. was formed) they were obtained by return of post. Eat your heart out —— owners (fill in as required. What is also interesting is that I have yet to see rebushed shoes. The exchange items were of course relined, but

hole wear was more than the better of my old ones. If they are all 20 years old now this may explain some of the clutch's reputation. Nevertheless the replacements did the trick.

A few more rallies clocked up 80,000 and the oil filter was changed, tappets adjusted as usual. Only the very last bit of front exhaust adjustment was hardly enough—so what do I do next time? Worry about that if and when it comes. Occasionally the speed rose to keep up with a group, but mostly it stayed around 60 per, because a knocking noise was becoming impossible to ignore (remember the motorway noise mentioned at 26,000—the same noise). As long as I rode the bike I worried, for the first 10,000 in case I had put it together wrong, and from then on expecting it to wear out, but it was no longer pessimism, just recognition of the facts. Even so a trip to the Bol d'Or race meeting had been arranged, so off to France we went. Quite impressive, these 24-hour races. Typically, the bikes which circulated using only one headlight (or even less!) through the night were the British ones. After the race I could not resist the temptation for a blast round the circuit, in spite of the engine noise having got to a stage where my friends asked me to stop the engine while looking at maps because they couldn't stand it. A tour had been intended, but I went a bit sick, then the weather went a bit sick, and the bike was already sick even if still game. With a couple of other Vincent owners a rather indirect return trip was made to get a bit of touring in. The only trouble it should be pointed out was a minor one, a broken kickstart spring. This I reckon to be another manifestation of machine character. It was old, tired since its last overhaul and obviously in need of another, dirty and neglected. An aerolastic holding up the kickstart completed the picture to a tee, or could be taken as a plaintiff cry that no machine could endure much more without letting me down!

On reaching home I rang a friend, who could let me use his garage which has heat and light, and took it out for the last time over to Bristol where it was dismantled.

1975 (9 months only):

Mileage: 12,000 83,560 total).

Routine work: Six oil changes. Tappets checked twice. Points checked twice. Plugs replaced once, reset twice. One new tyre and tube. Two sets of brake shoes.

Repairs: New clutch lever. Two new bulbs. Replacement exhaust pipe and silencer. New speedometer inner cable. New rear chain and sprockets (71,500). New rear exhaust valve (78,000). Exchange clutch shoes (81,000).

Data: Petrol: Sometimes dropped below 50 m.p.g., recovered to 55 m.p.g. Oil: 1,000 m.p.p. (January) dropping to 500 m.p.p. (June). Repairs: £8 per month (9 months only, and inflation). Total cost: 2¼ pence per mile.

How did the bike strip? A lot better than I expected. A lot of work and money were needed to clean it up, repaint, blast and polish to restore some of its glory, and fix up the mechanics. But the latter was surprisingly little as listed below.

Front forks: Bushes worn, some wear on spindles, eccentrics unworn (but replaced once already).

Frame: Swinging arm, steering head, and wheel bearings all sound, front wheel rim dented.

Gearbox: Bushes worn, kickstart spring broken, all gears, shafts, and ball races sound.

Primary drive: Chain badly worn (rust set in due to neglect at one time), sprockets and clutch sound.

Bottom end: Big-end terrible, 10 thou play and all tracks pitted, mains satisfactory, but one shaft loose from turning inside race, one mainbearing moved out of its housing.

Timing chest: Cams sound, one cam spindle worn, one worn a shocking amount as was the respective bush (explains lack of tappet left), two followers worn a bit, two sound.

Top ends: Pistons very clean bore wear under 2 thou, valves and guides clapped (except the replacement exhaust valve, the rest being over 100,000 miles old), rocker pins and bearings varying from little to a lot of wear (but oddly the worst being definitely the one which had been replaced by new—something to do with quality!)

The Vincent legend is of a fast, long-lived quality machine. And this is certainly lived up to. Suspension draws all sorts of comments. I have found it lacking little in handling, though a rough ride by modern day standards. The unenviable clutch reputation is only partly justified. It needs understanding and care, but will do its job and suffer a lot of abuse in some ways. The lights are awful and always were. It is

a machine with character and my ? judgment is surely proved by the fact ? I could sell my wreck and with the proce? plus the overhaul price buy almost any b of my choice (and I try them wheneve get the chance), but instead I buckle de to managing without for a while, and do the overhaul because I have yet to fine bike I personally like riding more, nor which can promise better service than have just had. I have not said much ab performance because I am not a fast m cruising usually between 60 and 70 m.; acording to weather, although figures in high 80s have been sustained at times considerable distances. Either at the TT some other time during the year I usu get 100 m.p.h. on the speedo just to it still does it. Since the model is the To ing Rapide, only reckoned to be good 110 m.p.h.. I can only suggest that spe would have pretty well lived up to re tests, with a little fall off during the ye as the miles piled up.

I am not arguing that I have a better b than your favourite machine, Jap or oth wise, but make no mistake that it can h its head up in any company. Certainly has its weak points and idiosyncrasies, so have I. One of mine seems to be runn against the tide and enjoying just th features which are tending to be least evid in current machines. And I like living w a legend.

Long live the Vincent.

PETER BICKERSTA

Continued from page 116

controlled the throttle. Maybe the "triangular" helped, maybe not; but whatever, Peter, although keeping to 6000 rpm, after only a few laps was lapping regularly at 1 min 9 sec. On this track, only Phil Read on the works Yamaha is noticeably faster. During a racer-test, David Dixon raced Lance Weil's Harley around at a fraction under 1 min 8 sec and Lance Weil did 1 min 10 sec. Now these were the best times obtained. Peter is certain that should it be necessary (and it will be), he could comfortably knock a second from his lap speeds, especially when he uses the extra, and important, 600 rpm. Incidentally, in the second round of the European hill-climb championship held in Austria, Fritz Egli beat a fully race-kitted Triumph "Three" engined special. Racing carbs, megaphone exhausts, and Rickman frame, and although it left black rubber strips on the bend exits, Fritz on one of his own machines, beat it. The course was eight miles long.

Peter will probably be riding for Roger Slater and Reay Mackay during the coming season on an Egli (isn't it just too easy to imagine what "Egli" will be rudely called by rival entrants and riders). From what I saw at Silverstone, the racing scene is in for a few surprises.

Despite its obvious racing talents, Roger is not aiming the Egli primarily at the competition rider, but the tourist. For half the price of a new factory machine a man can have himself a unique motorcycle equipped to his, and his only specification, either to suit his pocket or his requirements or both. Obviously the best way to improve performance is to reduce weight (on the motorcycle as well), but seriously, consider the position of a Rapide owner. His machine is 15, even 20, years old, tired and in need of an extensive overhaul and stove-enamelling job; but assuming he overhauls the engine himself, then providing absolutely everything is not completely worn out, £50 should cover the cost of spares. Depending on his choice of Egli components another £200 should see him with not merely a new motorcycle but one he is familiar with and probably has a garage stacked with spares to fit; it will moreover be one tailored exactly for him. The shedding of over 1 cwt (112 lb) from the overall weight from his Vincent offers countless improvements—handleability and roadholding, braking, acceleration, petrol consumption, top speed, wear and tear. Doubtless, the stick-in-the-mud purists will hate the breakaway Egli-Vincent owners, cursing them for destroying the "last" of the great motorcycles; contributing to the death of living legend, and soon all the familiar old war cries. It's just so much bunkum,

of course—they, the purists, are the preservationists.

As Titch Allen cried out in a moment of high emotion during the VOC annual dinner after the announcement of the factory's closure: "The Vincent is dead. Long live the Vincent." It was a brave toast to a bleak future, but now it rings strong and true.

Twenty seven
is a dangerous age, Vincent

Dave Hamill burns rubber on the winningest drag bike

Meet Ray Elger. He's a toolmaker by trade, 37 years old and a quiet, unassuming sort of guy, except when he's talking about his favourite mechanical topic, Vincent motorcycles. Oh yes; in between times he's probably won more sprint races than any other rider in Great Britain.

Meet Ray Elger's bike. It's 27 years old, an Egli Vincent. The engine's done about 140 000 miles and it hasn't had a major rebuild in six years. That's right, even the piston rings haven't been swapped since

1972. All of which hasn't stopped the bike taking Ray to every single win in that record breaking run, which must be some sort of record in itself. They're quite a pair Ray and his Vincent, a winning combination that's kept on winning despite all the odds.

So how did it all begin? "Well I bought this secondhand Vincent Rapide sidecar outfit way back in 1959. I used it on the road for years as a solo with the standard frame. Then in 1963 I went along to a

sprint meeting as a spectator and ended up entering the Vincent when another guy didn't turn up."

Ray came third on that initial competitive outing; not bad for a bog standard completely unprepared bike. From that day onwards he became a dedicated sprinter and by the following season he'd rebuilt the bike with advice and guidance from

151

Ted Hampshire, an ex-Vincent engineer. "It just started winning and winning." It ran consistent 12.1 and 12.2 second ets and "handled like a dream", although from personal experience with Philip Vincent's somewhat, uh, erratic rolling chassis, I'm inclined to take that last statement with a pinch of salt. Whatever, there's no doubting that Fritz Egli's renowned Vincent frames are a byeword for handling, and when the man himself raced and was beaten by Ray on one occasion he was so impressed that he insisted on making a frame for him. The result was that in 1969 Ray yanked the engine out of his Rapide (more of what happened to the frame anon) and dropped it into a brand spanking new Egli frame.

The new bike was some 50lb lighter, by Ray's admission more stable over bumps and more comfortable. It doesn't take a PhD in mathematics to figure out what this meant; faster ets. Like, the original Vinnie ran a best of 12.18 in 1966. In his first season with the Egli Ray dipped down into the 11s for the first time with an 11.97, and his best time to date is an 11.91 in 1976. Not bad for an engine that was built before I was born, huh?

So what makes the bike keep on going and going? Well it ain't a rubber band, that's for sure, so at this juncture a closer look at the engine is called for. If you think that you're about to read a long list of trick imported go-faster goodies and hyper-sophisticated, hyper-expensive tuning techniques, you're in for a disappointment. The amazing thing about Ray's engine is what *hasn't* been done to it. The Rapide wasn't even considered to be the "hottest" motor of the range, and when turbocharged multis are becoming the norm in dragging and sprinting today, it comes as something of a surprise to learn that so much power can be extracted from such a seemingly mild specification.

Bore and stroke are retained at a stock 84 x 90mm respectively, but high compression pistons raise the stock Rapide's 6.45:1 compression ratio to 9.8:1. Big carbs too; Amal 36mm Concentrics. Ray usually runs the Egli with a Vincent Mk2 cam, but lately he's been experimenting with an American Andrews cam obtained via George Emmrich. Apart from an Alpha Bearings oversize crank the bottom end's stock, while Ray ported and polished the heads with an electric drill and plenty of emery cloth. Valve springs come from BSA Gold Stars. "Trouble with standard Vincent springs is that they let go above 6000rpm. Well this engine will go above 7000 so we needed something a bit tougher." Ignition system is the Lucas TT magneto which was fitted to Vincent's potent road racer, the Series C Black Lightning many moons before the advent of solid state sparks.

That just about rounds off the engine modifications and though they mightn't seem very drastic, they account for a healthy power boost for a motor that wasn't exactly considered short on bhp in its heyday. The official factory figure is 45bhp at 5300rpm for the 1949 Series C Rapide. Well, this engine puts out a genuine 60bhp at 3500rpm (!) and 64bhp at 6500rpm measured at the rear wheel. Sceptical? Don't take my word for it or, for that matter, Ray's. Those figures were measured on a rolling road a couple of years back, and it's interesting to note that on the same day a Kwacker 1000 was peaking at 19bhp

less. Maybe a CBX could beat Ray's 27-year-old Vinnie, but there can't be many other bikes around capable of bettering that performance.

OK, you'd expect Britain's winningest sprint bike to be pampered, wrapped in cotton wool and never allowed out on public highways wouldn't you? Not so, it isn't used every day sure, but the Egli's com-

pletely street legal and Ray takes it out on the road pretty often. So wossit go like then? Aha thought you'd ask that, so we took a trip up to Ray's home near Oxford and he let us have a blast on the beast.

My first thought was of how small the bike was. I mean, when you're used to seeing 1000cc motors coming in large — some would say impossibly large — packages it comes as something of a shock to find a massive, monolithic Vincent twin nestling in a frame that wouldn't look out

of place on a 250. Talking about 250 with an all-up weight of approximate 370lb, the Egli must be in line for th slimmer of the year award. That puts it the same league as a Honda 250 Drea (392lb dry) or Yamaha XS250 (366lb) an makes the current crop of 1000cc Jap bike seem like obese behemoths in comparison

Unlike the big Japbikes though, the Vinnie isn't the easiest of bikes to start. 'Fac I chickened out, pleading injury from previous tumble as my excuse, and left Ra to do the hard work. "There's a knack t it", he said, "and once you master it yo don't have many problems". It helps you have leg muscles like the hind quarter of an ox, not that I'm comparing Ray wit that well known beast of burden y'unde stand. Course he *could* have retained Vi cent's valve lifter as fitted to the stock bik and saved himself hassles, but this iter tends to leak oil so he junked it and relie on good old fashioned leg power.

And so to the great moment when Ra flooded the carbs and took a swing on th kickstart which wouldn't have disgrace a first division footballer. Nothing. Anoth swing. Nothing. An even harder swing an beads of sweat on his face. Nothing. In th end it took a determined push start to fir the beast, and the sound which issue forth from its twin home made silence was memorable. Did I say silencers? P it this way; silent is about the *last* word I' use to describe the *basso profundo* bom bomp bomp sound of the engine idling To an engineer's ears — music. To a traff cop — a good excuse for getting the note book out.

Sat on the bike my initial impression compactness was reinforced considerabl Ray's a medium height wiry sort of ind vidual. Me? I'm medium sized (*what!* BM but I'm not admitting to anything else. Wi the bike in gear and rolling down the roa the time came for me to hike my legs u on the footrests. I did it with difficulty onl to find that what I thought were the rider rests were in fact the passenger peg Phew, it took a lot of contortions before squeezed myself into the proper ridin position which is, as Ray freely admit hardly comfortable.

I'd been warned that the power came brutally and the brakes weren't very won derful. I agree. Even with a triple disc se up a bike as potent as the Vinnie would b a handful to stop. With only a puny Norto drum brake up front (fitted with a Joh Tickle 2LS brake plate admittedly) stoppin from 100mph plus is a long drawn ou affair, and if you want to stop in a hurr engine braking is a better bet.

Power's the name of the game on Ray bike though, and what power. It comes at around 2200 revs and from then on th bike pulls like an express train. No tran mission of carburation lag; just powe great raw gobs of the stuff.

With a final drive ratio in top of 3.4:1 slightly higher than stock, but only slight — the ton equals 4400rpm, and there's sti a lot of power left at that juncture. couldn't find out exactly how much powe because the A40 in the middle of the even ing rush hour isn't the ideal place to tr these sort of things, so I contented myse with a "leisurely" 125mph and took Ray word for it that 150mph at the engine' 6600rpm power peak is a distinct pos sibility.

I've had the same feeling of exhilaratin almost limitless power on only a coupl

of bikes — the MV Monza and Laverda Jota spring to mind but I wouldn't have thought it possible on 27-year-old Vinnie until I had the pleasure of riding Ray's Egli. The bike's stable at those sort of speeds too; surprising considering how light it is, and some of the credit here must go to the Metal Profile front forks and Girling Manx Norton rear box.

Corners are where you've got to be *really* careful on the bike. As I've said the power comes in savagely, and if you don't open the throttle very gingerly out of a bend or roundabout, you could easily find yourself being carried away on a stretcher. For all that though the engine isn't a touchy narrow powerband racer. It can be as gentle as the next roadster, the difference being that when you twist the throttle on this un you're just going to keep on going.

Ray hasn't raced the bike regularly for a season, now, but like all lapsed drag racers I got the impression that it wouldn't take much to get him back into the fold. When the bike *was* racing, help and sponsorship came from Conway Motors in Shepherds Bush, John "Uncle Bunt" Reed who painted the tank and fairing and Matt Holder of Aerco Jig and Tool, the people who are all set to start building replica Vincent engines in the not-too-distant future. In the meantime he's sponsoring himself by making some of the most interesting and unusual jewellery I've seen in a long while and selling it at non-ripoff prices — interested wholesalers give us a

ring and we'll put you in touch.

Vincents seem to be a family business with the Elgers. Ray's brother races a 500 Comet on the circuits, and though they're not exactly family, Ray has close ties with Mathew and Margaret Mason, an Oxford couple who race a Vincent 1000 in Vintage races with great success. Remember I was going to tell you what happened to Ray's original Rapide frame? Well, it still lives on in the Mason's racer, the one you can see in the pix with the Egli, so it's certainly gone to a good home.

So if he suddenly rolled the big numbers on the sponsorship game would Ray stick to Vincents? "Yes certainly, although I think the next stage I'd go to would be a four valve head to give me more top end." One day Ray, one day.

Black Beauty

Peter Kelly meets a man who can transform a £100 heap of rubbish into a glittering classic — and is planning to give new birth to the V-twin Vincent.

THE word "perfection" has many different meanings to motor cyclists. It might describe anything from a Yamaha FS1E to a Honda six, depending on your point of view. But to many enthusiasts it still means a glittering Vincent V-twin.

Such is the aura surrounding these superb old machines — the last one left the Stevenage factory in the 1950s — that a whole new manufacturing capability has grown up around them with the one abject aim of keeping them on the road — at any price.

One man keeping himself busy seven days a week bringing these black beauties right back to their original gleaming specification — and in many ways even improving on it — is Tony Maugham, whose back-garden workshops in deepest Lincolnshire boasts over £50,000 worth of machining equipment. And far from being satisfied with renovation, he's planning to re-launch the Vincent and make it better than ever. With the means to produce some 300 individual Vincent items, it's no idle boast, either.

But what's so good about the Vincent anyway, when much more modern roadburners are available?

Tony puts it like this: "How many of your modern bikes do 100mph at a measly 4,600rpm, weigh less than 500lb and give

A Black Shadow nears completion in Tony Mangham's workshops.

Black Beauty

Reclamation is possible even with badly broken casings.

you such good fuel consumption figures as the Vincent? Even at 125mph they're revving at only 5,800, and at 50mph 2,300."

The Vincent, he says, sports many features that would still be considered advanced today, like the top frame member which acts as the oil tank, a remarkable back wheel that requires no tools to remove from the frame, a massive engine adding its strength to, rather than detracting from, the overall construction, and easy, sensible adjustment facilities everywhere you look. So convinced is Tony that the Vincent meets every modern need that he is already designing the first of a new batch, with a stronger, higher-revving 1100cc engine, Ceriani forks, a choice of disc or drum brakes, many more stainless steel items than the Vincent originally had, and the application of modern technology to actually improve the old V-twin's classic reputation for reliability and longevity.

Tony has been a Vincent fan for almost as long as he can remember. He moved to Lincolnshire after a long career in the Navy, and he's been a Vincent owner for 25 years. His own V-twin sidecar outfit, rebuilt and improved several times, has now covered a phenomenal 610,000 miles, and has won awards galore at Vincent rallies.

On a part-time basis, he's been doing work on Vincents for other people for 17 years, but for the past nine rebuilding and restoring the handsome black beauties has filled almost every hour of his life. Workshop sessions commonly go on until past midnight and right through weekends.

Recently the work has piled up to such an extent that he has taken on his son-in-law, Steve Hayward, on a full-time basis and his son Paul, 20, also gets deeply involved.

The whole crew are perfectionists, and their work includes full reclamation and renovation to as-new standard, including the manufacture of just about every component. Stainless steel is Tony's stock-in-trade; he had duplicated nearly every Vincent part in this, and they complement the pure black of the petrol tank perfectly.

Up until now, most of his work has been

restoration, and over the years he has built up his capacity so that he can manufacture the lot. Now, he's reached the stage where it is possible for him to actually build brand new Vincents from scratch, incorporating many of the improvements he has carefully tried out and perfected over the years. It has been a labour of love, and this can be amply seen in the shining machines when they finally emerge from Tony's workshop after months of labour.

But he can still transform a £100 heap of rubbish into a glittering classic — provided the owner is prepared to pay the price, and that might mean well over £3,000.

For investment purposes alone, it would be well worth it. But Tony despises the "investment" idea. "I want people who own these beautiful machines to keep them and enjoy them just like I do," he says. And he means it.

Patience

So what happens when you finally track down your (rapidly-diminishing) example in an old farmyard shed or somewhere and take it to Tony to restore?

"The first stage is to strip everything down and examine each part," says Tony. "Then I'll ask the customer back and tell him exactly what I think is required, what needs to be replaced or repaired, and what should be scrapped. This way he'll know exactly where he stands before I begin, right down to the price of the bits, the labour, even the stove-enamelling job."

A complete restoration can take months to carry out: Tony's customers have to have a lot of patience. "I always have a lot of jobs to do, and I work in batches of, say, 30 or 40 cylinder heads, or 30 or 40 flywheels. It's the logical way to go about it, but it takes time."

Reclamation as well as replacement is also a big part of his work. "A crankcase might be found on a rubbish tip with the top half broken," says Tony. "I can rebuild these and other components, like bearing housings, working to within ½ a thou. Sometimes it's even more accurate than the original."

A worn-out cylinder head might come in. Painstakingly, he'll clean it up, re-cut the threads and machine the valve seats until the finished article is almost like new.

He also works on new castings, which come exclusively from Matt Holder, who owns the Vincent name and keeps a large stock of basic components.

Tony has never been afraid to invest. His workshop — and the address is a closely-guarded secret for obvious reasons — has two brand new lathes, two milling machines, boring, drilling and honing machinery, jigs and tooling. He's even made a cam-grinder.

It's reached the stage where Tony has decided to look for a proper factory unit. It's not surprising, because his business has grown and grown, and he now makes more than 300 different items. Despite its expense, he prefers to work in stainless steel because of the quality of the final article — and this runs to all fork components, frame items and oil pipes.

Where the Vincent had limitations, Tony has brought them up to date. Six-volt electrics are out. He makes a special carrier for a 12-volt battery, and current from the standard six-volt dynamo is converted to 12 volts through a John Gardner unit. Miller,

The classic rearshock arrangement will be replaced by a single suspension unit.

Girdraulic fork on a restored Shadow. But Cerianis are on the way

who made the original electrical components, are no longer making them, so he uses a glass-fibre Lucas headlamp shell and a 12v quartz-halogen unit.

He is totally committed to attention to detail. Vincent bits like the little seat dampers are now made in stainless steel, the hub centres are skimmed and polished, the bolts are turned and all-new stainless nuts are used on his rebuilds. Crash bars, brake adjusters . . . even the tool tray beneath the seat are stainless.

He's even improved on the original Vincent seat. Keeping the same contours, replacements are in real hide. "All the rest crease your backside," he says, with all the authority of a much-travelled motor cyclist.

But now Tony is preparing for his biggest challenge yet — the all-new Vincents planned for 1979 and 1980.

The engines will look just like the old Vincents, but internally they'll be very much improved. All material specifications will be updated, cylinder liners will double in thickness and he will go over to stronger metric-size bearings. The mainshaft size will be increased from an inch to 30mm — about 1/16-in more, and 30mm bearings will be used. Although the metric components are cheaper, they will make the engine smoother and more robust — and will make it possible to increase the engine revs safely if necessary.

A Lucas alternator will be fitted — this

does away with the dynamo — and Rita transistorised ignition will be used. Amal 11 Concentrics will be fitted, and Tony is already fitting these to some of his rebuilds. He feels they work even better than the original carbs.

The engine will be increased in capacity to 1100cc. All timing gears will be precision-made to reduce noise, and he will redesign the cams. The clutch will be multi-plate instead of Vincent's rather special single-plate component. The new clutch will stand up to all the hammer the engine can give, because Tony has been using it himself for years — with a double-adult sidecar attached! The new clutch should also make for swifter gearchanges, because the Vincent item always gave a lag. The gearbox itself — a four-speeder — will remain the same. It is of a very good, very strong design.

The cylinder head shape will be slightly altered to give a shallower hemisphere and better gas-flow.

"I don't want to get away from a torquey vee-twin," said Tony. "I want a light machine giving 135 to 140mph losing none of its characteristics."

He also plans to produce a limited number of Series C Black Shadows as originally built, because he knows there is a demand for these.

For his own version, he believes Ceriani front forks will do the job adequately, but wants to give a choice of disc or drum brakes — some people will shudder at the prospect of discs on a Vincent!

A tank designer is working on a brand new fuel tank. It will keep much the same classic Vincent shape, but will be narrower at the back to give a more comfortable seating position.

The triangulated rear section of the frame will be kept, but using one large suspension unit instead of the two together favoured by the Vincent.

The top frame section will still be the oil tank, but Timken roller bearings will be used at the headstock.

Another classic touch; the five-inch diameter speedometer an/or rev-counter will still be used, renovated by the Auto Tempo Meter Company. Alloy wheels will go with the stainless steel and black of the rest of the machine. There will be hardly any chrome.

Perfection

A new bike, painstakingly made by Tony, might cost £3,500 to £4,000. But prices for Vincents have been climbing sharply in recent years. Three years ago, you could buy an old one for, say, £700 and you might spend £2,000 bringing it up to brand new specification. It used to be just the V-twins, but Tony has noticed recently that, as the "supplies" of old bikes dry up there is a renewed interest in the single-cylinder Comet, and his workshop had a whole row of these engines awaiting attention.

Meanwhile, Tony continues to build on perfection — he even plans a fully-enclosed chain on his new bikes — but basically the Vincent will lose nothing of its old glory in his hands, and will even pick up a few improvements. Nowadays, people who seek perfection are prepared to pay the price. In this sense, perhaps, Tony is more fortunate than the brilliant Vincent designers themselves. . .

Designing the Series B

PHIL IRVING

Chief Engineer,
the Vincent Engineering Co

AS the Second World War drew to a close the Vincent HRD company was in an awkward position, with a factory full of equipment for making munitions but only a few Government contracts to complete. In 1943, P C Vincent had arranged for me to be transferred from Associated Motor Cycles to Stevenage to develop an engine for the Air-Sea Rescue Service and a little later Matt Wright, the ex-New Imperial racing 'gaffer', was also enrolled to assist me. By the time the engine had been developed to meet the Air Ministry's tough specification the war was almost over. Thus no engines were required and therefore it was imperative to return to motorcycle manufacture with all speed.

Naturally, PCV, Matt Wright, the sales manager, J Pett, and I had frequently discussed the kind of machine we should make, bearing in mind certain factors which would not normally exist. One was that some materials, especially steel, were rigidly controlled and for some stupid reason the amount allocated to any firm was in proportion to the amount it had purchased pre-war. This led to the anomalous position whereby a firm like OK Supreme — if it had not been bombed out of existence — could have obtained all the steel it might have needed, whereas we could get very little.

On the other hand, aluminium was plentiful and relatively cheap. It was rumoured that the bulk of our output would have to be exported (eventually the figure turned out to be 80 per cent) in which case many machines would be used in right-hand-drive countries. We would have had no hope of competing on a price basis with factories such as AMC or BSA, which had maintained their motorcycle production during the war; neither did we have the right sort of machine tools or trained personnel to handle a large-scale output.

Conversely, the pre-war Rapide had achieved a remarkable reputation for two facets — its exceptional speed and its liability to clutch trouble. We decided that the best move would be to capitalise on the performance, eliminate the clutch trouble, and also overcome the steel shortage in one bold move by a major redesign of the Series A Rapide using aluminium wherever possible, manufacturing our own gearbox and clutch and retaining well-tried components like our duo-brake wheels and Brampton forks for which steel permits could be obtained without too much trouble.

At this point, it may be as well to dispel any misconceptions about my part in the proceedings. In 1943, PCV wrote to me regarding a transfer from AMC and stated that I would be regarded as co-designer with him and would be responsible for the preparation of drawings and the manufacture of experimental components, although I had no official title at first. Later on I became chief engineer. F E Walker, the

managing director, took little part in technical discussions except as regards the general policy of making an outstanding machine which would probably be expensive but would sell in a reasonable quantity without a huge initial outlay in new factory equipment.

As far as general layout was concerned, we wanted to reduce the wheelbase from the A's 58½in to the conventional 55in and tried various arrangements, one being to make the rear cylinder vertical and the front one almost horizontal (rather like the Ducati is now) but with the front downtube joined to the crankcases between the cylinder barrels. This scheme was rejected because it necessitated different castings for the heads and barrels and would have led to the lower cylinder fins rapidly becoming clogged with dirt on anything but sealed roads.

As we intended to make our own gearbox, preferably in unit with the engine, PCV propounded the idea of deleting the main frame almost entirely by utilising the power unit as the main structural member, to which a backbone carrying the steering column and the rear fork pivot bearing was to be attached. This provided the most compact arrangement possible and was of immense rigidity in all directions. Moreover, deflection of the rear wheel due to pull in the offset chain would be minimised by the force being transmitted directly to the rigid power unit instead of through some intermediate frame tubes which might (and do) give rise to flexure and rear wheel steering.

Phelon and Moore had used a somewhat similar idea for many years, making their inclined single-cylinder engine act as a frame member with a

Phil Irving pushes off the white-clad record breaker Rene Milhoux during a session in 1948. Vincents were used in many high speed record attempts.

The experimental staff at Stevenage. From left, chief mechanic Cliff Brown, Phil Irving, mechanic Malcolm Egginton, and tester George Brown.

The first Black Shadow, incorporating the huge design changes wrought by Phil Vincent and Phil Irving.

bracket attached to the cylinder head by four long bolts. We adopted this time-tested scheme in duplicate by fixing a bracket to the rear head, but were a bit worried about maintaining gas-tightness of the head joints under the action of violent frame stresses. Accordingly, each head was held down by four tubular bolts, through which passed four $\frac{3}{8}$in high-tensile bolts that retained the brackets. In theory, any stretch in the inner bolts would not reduce the tightness of the head joint, but it was an expensive construction which was soon superseded by more conventional one-piece bolts. The change was hastened by the discovery that ham-fisted private owners were liable to break the hollow bolts by overtightening the large nuts.

Another point to be considered was the thermal expansion of the engine which would be greater than that of the upper frame member, which was to be a welded sheet-steel component. To allow for this expansion and any cumulative dimensional errors, the rear fixing holes were slotted, any vertical load being carried on flat-sided dowels. The rear bolt was not fully tightened to permit 'creep' and while this construction has been criticised it has never given the slightest trouble even in heavy sidecar work. Being a rabid chair-man myself, I always bore this aspect in mind and provided sidecar attachment points on both sides of the machine — something which few other designers have ever bothered to do.

Brazed tubular construction was retained for the rear forks where rigidity combined with light unsprung weight was essential. In fact, the design differed very little from the pre-war version which had been trouble-free since it was introduced in 1931. The pivot-bearing consisted, as always, of two stout taper-roller bearings capable of covering 100,000 miles without requiring adjustment. It was attached to the rear of the gearbox and the end of the upper frame member by two through-bolts, which greatly assisted assembly.

As to the power unit, the flywheels, con-rods, big-ends and pistons were practically or actually unchanged from the Series A components, but the cylinder angle was altered from 47 to 50 degrees to suit available ignition equipment. We had hoped to use a BTH magneto, but the makers were reluctant to make a small modification to the HT brush positions and in any case BTH ceased to produce magnetos shortly after. Fortunately, Joe Lucas came to the rescue with the newly-designed KVF instrument which, being very compact, fitted neatly into the space available. However, we stuck to the Miller lighting set, using a 3½in diameter 50-watt generator which, we were informed, would remain in production. The crankcase was therefore designed with an integral cradle to suit this size. Despite

Turn to page 163

The joys of Vincent ownership

ROY HARPER

Author and editor of books on the Vincent marque

THIS is it, my first ride on a pre-war Rapide. This is a very special Rapide, however, no less than the works Show model displayed at Olympia in 1937.

The owner hesitates before relinquishing his glittering object of hero-worship. 'Do you know how to start it?' he asks anxiously.

'Yes,' I reply without conviction. The method of starting a pre-war Rapide is one of the secrets of the Series A sect of the Vincent brotherhood, and is handed down owner unto owner.

He is worried. I am worried. He is concerned about damage to the clutch, gearbox, chains, etc. I am concerned about my ankles, knees and neck (should the Beast kick back and propel me over the handlebars). I feel nervous — my life is about to depend on ancient bolts.

Although we are brothers, I am not of the sect, so he starts the monster for me. Raucous sounds rend the air and low-flying birds become high-flying birds. I straddle the bike and lean forward to grasp the handlebars. I ease the gear pedal into first and feed in the clutch. We're off! and the transmission joins in with a variety of sounds — another secret of the sect is knowing which noises are healthy and which are expensive.

I tweak the throttle. Wham! The Beast leaps forward like a startled stallion and hurtles into the seventies in eight seconds. Third gear whisks me into the nineties and wind pressure shoves me back, but I cling to the bars and click into top. The needle climbs to the ton and a gale flattens my cardboard peak against my helmet. My goggles are lifted and soon my eyes water and smart. I lift a hand from the bars but it's blown back. I grab the bars again to control the vibrating bike as it ploughs its way through the air. A dithering moped rider meanders into my path but I flick the bars and am out of danger. Into a right-hand bend now and the bike holds its line superbly. Straighten up, then into a roundabout. Due to the offset position of the engine in the frame, there is more weight on the right of the bike than the left, which makes right-hand bends easy and left-handers exciting. I wrestle my way around the traffic island and continue my wild dash as the engine purrs like a contented tiger. Meanwhile, oil is rushing round the system, lubricating cams, rockers, followers, pistons, big-ends, bearings and a considerable portion of my right leg. I return the Beast to its worried owner satisfied that the Vincent HRD has lived up to its legend.

The legend began in October 1936 when the prototype Vincent V-twin clocked 108mph on its first high-speed test run and became the world's fastest production vehicle on two, three or four wheels. *Motor Cycling*'s road tester later achieved 110mph but found the 1000cc engine nearly as thirsty as a 1979 200cc Japanese bike (Yamaha RD200DX), viz 45mpg. Braking was excellent — 26ft from 30mph.

Production of the Series A Rapide ended in 1939 when the BMW boys had to be sorted out. Then, in 1946, the Series B Rapide appeared and set new standards for reliability, speed and roadholding. Private owners eagerly tuned the Beast and times were continually up-dated as record after record fell to the thundering twins from Stevenage.

In the USA in 1948, Rollie Free became the first man to clock 150mph on an unsupercharged motorcycle when he rode a Black Shadow at Utah. In 1954, in New Zealand, Bob Burns tuned a second-hand Rapide and broke the world sidecar record. In 1955, he broke it again and Russ Wright took the world solo record on the same machine — all done on a wet road. In 1956, Russ clocked 198.3mph on a Black Lightning at Utah — a speed yet to be beaten by anyone riding an unsupercharged conventional motorcycle. During the past decade we have had the record-breaking exploits of Ron Vane (1000cc The Thing three-wheeler) and the nine-second drag racing achievements of Brian Chapman (500cc Mighty Mouse) to prove that the Vincent engine is still competitive.

Each racing or record success enhanced the legend of the Vincent, while on the open road riders of other machinery would try to blow Vincent owners off the road. Top gear gave me too great an advantage so I would drop into third, pull alongside and then, when the other bloke was flat on his tank on full throttle, I'd click into top and disappear.

Riders of the invincible Rapide inevitably formed themselves into a club (in 1948) and in 1949 the club journal *MPH* was published with the slogan 'Riders of the world's fastest standard motorcycle'. This was later dropped because it was thought to be 'putting on side'. It was, perhaps, a public relations exercise because the club had acquired a reputation for aloofness, especially among Triumph owners, as the following story shows.

In the fifties a pal of mine, Brian, used to court a girl in Newcastle and every weekend he left London and covered the 300 miles in six hours, a remarkable time considering the absence of motorways. A colleague of Brian disbelieved the time until one Friday he watched him ride off on his Rapide from London at 5pm and later rang Newcastle at 11pm to hear Brian answer!

During the cold winter months, Brian's ardour carried him through but one evening it was so cold he stopped the bike, got off and ran alongside to restore his circulation. A Triumph owner pulled up and, thinking that Brian was trying to bump-start his Vincent (Triumph owners always expect Vincents to break down), asked what the trouble was. Brian replied that he was 'just running alongside to keep warm'.

'Sarcastic blighter', growled the Triumph man, and rode off in a huff with another story of Vincent aloofness. (We always returned the wave of another motorcyclist but only if he was riding a Vincent, a tradition I maintain to this day.)

Sometimes, of course, Triumph riders happened to be policemen and the pace became rather hot. Like the occasion in New South Wales when a Vincent owner went so fast to get away from a patrolman that he overtook another policeman chasing another miscreant rider!

My own relations with the police have always been very cordial if stopped while riding a Vincent. One day, soon after acquiring a Series C Comet ('Bonka') I was riding through Hyde Park when I noticed a policeman on a Triumph proceeding in an easterly direction towards me. He wheeled round and tucked in behind me and I was apprehensive when we halted together at some traffic lights. However, we promptly hit it off like two Irishmen meeting in a pub and discovering they had both backed the Derby winner.

He liked Vincents. I liked Vincents. He wanted on. I owned one. He couldn't afford to run one. I couldn't afford to run one. He gazed sadly at the Comet with its bald tyres, flopping chain, trailing wires, rusty spokes and pipes, oil leaks and other flaws, and a wistful look appeared in his eyes as he envisaged an immaculate

Continued on page 163

If you owned a Series D Vincent Black Shadow like this example, wouldn't *you* feel aloof and elite?

Vincent ownership — a world-wide cult. Continental enthusiast (left) meets with a British rider at the Vincent International Rally in 1979.

Concours machines await judging at a VOC function. The club is one of the largest, best-run motorcycle organisations in the world.

Stevenage: a decade of delight

TED DAVIS
Chief Development Engineer, the Vincent Engineering Co

To work at one of the famous factories was the ambition of many motorcyclists after the Second World War. The factories were scattered from Kent to Yorkshire, and the choice was very largely yours. Names like Norton, AJS, Panther, Ariel, Vincent, Triumph, BSA, Velocette and Matchless were on the tanks of bikes and, in both road and off-road competition results, appeared worldwide. Every name conjured up a mystic magic in the minds of bike-starved returning servicemen, myself included.

Although Pa Norton's products loomed large in my thoughts, having raced a 350 Manx (or an International as the bike was known pre-war) at Donington and Cadwell, it was the Vincent HRD Company down in Stevenage that was to prove irresistible. Resumption of my racing activities in 1946 was with a 1938 Series A TT-replica Vincent, and no doubt this experience, coupled with my use at the time of one of the first Series B twins as a road bike, influenced my decision the following year to present myself for inspection by Jack Williams, who was manager at Stevenage at that time. Jack, who was to go on to greater things with AMC, had been a pre-war Vincent works rider and was a perfect gentleman at all times. He was only one of the great team of enthusiasts I met during my all-too-brief initial visit, all of whom were to become life-long friends. Money, or the company's lack of it, was slightly embarrassing for Jack, so such a distasteful topic was quickly disposed of and my first half an hour was spent discussing bikes and racing in particular. Then we went on a circular tour of the Old North Road factory, a section of which is still preserved under the Ancient Monuments Act.

So began a decade of delight; rarely did one have that Monday morning feeling, and never once was the word 'strike' even mentioned, although I must confess it passed through my mind when we made the Firefly, the bicycle with clip-on motor, especially when it came to the durability test programme. However, they say necessity is the mother of invention, and ways more amenable than riding them were found to test the wretched little things.

The V-twin that emerged in 1947 (of which 11,000 were eventually made) from such small beginnings nearly 20 years earlier was quite sensational for those days. Faster than most racing bikes on 'pool' (72 octane) petrol, it surely stole the Lucas slogan, 'King of the Road'. It was a different story from today's situation — in 1947 you got off your racer and on to a road bike if you wanted to go really quickly, and with deserted roads and no speed limits you could do, and did, just that! Averages on public roads equivalent to racing speeds were put up by Vincent testers with frequent monotony, but perhaps this was not so surprising when it is remembered that many of the riders were successful racers in their own right in Ireland, the Isle of Man and on mainland circuits. Yes, not only did Stevenage attract racers, it produced them and, regrettably, killed a few off.

But I'm rambling on too fast — this is a reminiscence of what it was really like to work behind that magic-sounding name (painted in gold, of course) on the end wall of the old factory, which today still butts onto the now-defunct Great North Road. Those walls which resounded to the off-beat exhaust throb of every Vincent ever made now imprison a class of reluctant schoolboys, two of whom are my own grandsons, both schoolboy scramblers. Working hours of eight till five, with overtime available most nights and on Saturday mornings, was not as dreary as it sounds. In fact for me and many others in the early days you only knew you had worked overtime when you got your pay packet.

Perhaps in retrospect I am seeing everything through rose-coloured specs, but then I was more fortunate than many, for after a relatively short spell in engine assembly and other sections, I was involved in test and development, with my own racing activities nicely filling in the weekends and holidays. (My wife is still putting up with something similar over 30 years later, albeit on a much milder note these days.)

The Vincent HRD Co existed primarily to make motorcycles for motorcyclists. And it wasn't too difficult a task when matters were guided by such people as Phil Irving, at 76 still happily and very actively with us, Ted Hampshire, George and Cliff Brown, Norman Brewster, Matt Wright, Dennis Minett, Jim Sugg, Paul Richardson and Jack Williams. Phil Vincent himself, who was to go down as one of the greats in motorcycling history, was not, as many

Series B Rapides awaiting despatch from the Stevenage factory. The writer is second from the left.

Seamy character of the Vincent factory is apparent in this shot of Ted Davis with the first of the enclosed Black Knight models to be made in 1954.

may imagine, an all-powerful, domineering figure who demanded total dedication from us all. Dedication seemed to, and seems still, to come from within each individual once he or she becomes involved with the Stevenage product. It was more of a family spirit. For example, in a recent letter to *MPH*, the club magazine, Elfrida Vincent described the scene very well when she wrote how much comfort Phil had received from the huge Vincent 'family' who gathered round during his long illness, and how the 'family' had comforted her after his death.

With such a team, making the bikes was easy — but making money was not. Had the acquisition of money been the prime motive behind all who worked at Vincent's, we would rapidly have given Stevenage a wide berth.

Just half a mile away from the Great North Road was the No 2 factory at Fishers Green where all the machining, plating and enamelling took place. Vincent's made or processed a very high percentage of their entire machine, including the hydraulic dampers and the stove enamelling ('any colour you like as long as it's black'). George Urlet, who still lives in Stevenage, was in control of the latter department, and was put in the enamelling shop 'temporarily' long before the war and left when he was 65. Using Pinching and Johnson paint, George did an unbeatable job unequalled anywhere today on a production basis.

With this conviction that eventually hundreds of Vincents would roll off the production lines weekly, Phil Vincent had tooled up the plant to do just that. The fact was that bike production ran at such low levels that we had the capacity to machine all of the Standard-Triumph car company's brake drums in addition to the bikes' requirements, as well as make or machine many other components for de Havilland, the Coal Board, and other concerns. These additional activities, plus the fuel injection Picador (a radio-controlled aircraft engine) and the airborne lifeboat engine (both Ministry contracts) helped keep the wolf from the door. Bike production ran at around 15 per week for the first year I was with the company, rising to a maximum of 60, by which time the quality was beginning to suffer and the cream of the initial assembly team had moved on to greener pastures, such as BRM, Jaguar, Rover, Rolls-Royce and Vauxhall, where many still work today. Among the apprentices was one J Surtees, who was to become world champion after making a brilliant showing early in his career with a home-built Grey Flash. They came from far and wide to work at Vincent's — Australia, the Continent, the USA —

and few failed to better themselves after they left, and even fewer would not admit to feeling just a little proud at having worked there.

In no way resembling the modern factories that exist today in Japan, the original Vincent works consisted of buildings, relatively ramshackle, that were not averse to admitting the odd downpour through the roof or even beneath the doors as the rain water ran down the sloping yard. Amenities were conspicuous by their absence — canteen tea had its uniquely distinctive flavour. The process of melting the resin out of the exhaust pipes after bending was suspected as the cause, as the welding and pipebending shop run by Bill Munsen was under the same roof as the tiny canteen! Out of these premises that outwardly — and inwardly for that matter — looked like a blacksmith's shop, came thousands of triangulated, cantilever, monoshock frames which were eventually to be copied some thirty years later on the super-automated, computer-controlled, Mig-welding Yamaha production lines. More corrugated roofing sheltered Dennis Minett's race shop, from which emerged such devices as the Burns and Wright world record-breaking Black Lightning, works Grey Flashes, and other projects.

At the top of the yard stood the substantial brick-built test and dynamometer house which was used predominantly in later years to develop the Picador engine, plus the odd blown twin as a 'twilighter'. Further tumbledown areas housed the drawing office, Archie Feast's stores, Ted Hampshire's engine and cycle assembly section, Jim Sugg's production road test department, and Norman Brewster's service department. It was all very homely and sufficiently disjointed to defy any form of efficiency, and yet it all ran like clockwork, due in no small measure to the people who controlled and operated it all, who were in turn prompted by their pride and faith in the product.

New models came and went — the Meteor, the Comet, Series Cs and Ds, a host of two-stroke power plants and the devices they drove, the three-wheeler and the infamous Firefly. Always Philip Vincent was in the picture, a brilliant mind fettered with mundane day-to-day business matters, until those very mundane matters were to call a halt to all that happiness at Stevenage and eventually close the doors for good.

Now, with the eighties upon us and a quarter of a century having passed since bike production stopped, Phil Vincent, Ted Hampshire, Jack Williams, Paul Richardson, Norman Brewster, Archie Feast, George Brown and many others are gone for ever. It is left to the Vincent Owners' Club and its members new and old to keep the flag flying — a task they do superbly with the same dedicated enthusiasm that started the whole story 50 years ago.

PHIL IRVING

From page 158

the assurance, Miller ended production of the big dynamo after a while and would only supply the 3in version, which necessitated making an awkward eccentric adaptor to bring the armature shaft to the correct centre height. As soon as possible, the integral cradle was deleted and replaced by a separate component which dispensed with the eccentric adaptor.

As a side-light on the electrics, Miller used to make a generator with built-in contact breaker points, and we actually toyed with the idea of using this generator plus a magneto to provide dual ignition. The idea was never carried out, although the heads were made so that two plugs could be fitted and at one time a small batch of two-plug heads was inadvertently produced.

For more reasons than just saving weight, the barrels consisted of finned aluminium jackets shrunk on to centrifugally-cast iron liners which were supplied by Clupet and finished to size after being fitted. The cylinder heads were made in either Y-alloy or RR53B, with aluminium bronze for the exhaust valve seats because of its high thermal conductivity, and austenitic cast iron for the inlets because of its work-hardening property which resists seal wear. The seats were made parallel and simply dropped into the recesses with the head heated to 200°C; we never had any

trouble with seats falling out except for a few which came loose after many years of racing, usually in cars where the cooling was inadequate. A pair of heads and barrels weighed almost the same as one pre-war head and barrel, resulting in a saving of 13lb in weight.

The timing gear was similar in principle to the Series A, with a large idler driving both camshafts. But the teeth were made of finer pitch and the idler gear spindle was made adjustable so that zero tooth backlash could be attained. The front camwheel drove a timed crankcase breather and this in turn drove the magneto, which was equipped with a Lucas automatic centrifugal advance, or ATD, which eliminated one handlebar lever and cable. The camshafts were carried on fixed spindles, Velocette style, and supported by a steady plate which was made of aluminium to maintain them parallel at varying temperatures; for the same reason the idler was made of phospor-bronze and later of the very special aluminium alloy, RR77.

The pre-war flat-faced lever cam-followers were retained, but the pivots were located below the camshafts instead of above as this eliminated the need for separate camshaft covers. With lever followers it is necessary to use non-symmetrical cam contours to obtain symmetrical valve-lift curves, and re-location of the follower pivots called for a redesign of the cams. As we had no cam-grinding equipment, I made the experimental cams by hand and production versions were entrusted to

Weyburnes who specialised in this work. A couple of years later I repeated the process to make the Mark 2 cams which started life by raising the American national speed record to over 150mph and went on to break numerous world records in the Black Lightning.

Initially, the aim was to make a fast but economical touring machine which would need about 45bhp with enough torque to pull a top gear so high that 100mph could be maintained at less than 5,000rpm. Lurking in the background was the thought that in time there might be 100bhp or more on tap, so the clutch and gearbox were designed to handle this sort of output. This brought up the difficulty that no contemporary clutch could transmit such power unless the spring pressure was far too great for the average rider, and impossible for the numerous ex-servicemen suffering from damaged left hands.

PCV had made several experimental clutches with spiral splines or with the pressure increased by a face-cam drive, but none was satisfactory until he hit on the idea of using a drum-type mechanism with internal shoes expanded by a single-plate primary clutch with very light springs. Most of the detail design work on this was done by a draughtsman named Ernie Welch, and the experimental model worked like a charm when fitted to a Series A Rapide. It was finger-light to operate and although running in oil showed no tendency to slip. The new chaincase was designed to incorporate this clutch, but to our consternation the

Continued on next page

ROY HARPER

From page 160

concours machine. 'Going to do it up, are you?' he enquired enviously.

'Yes, of course,' I replied.

The lights changed to green and, maintaining the cordiality of the meeting, I politely let him out-accelerate me.

This generous act didn't assuage his chagrin, however, for within 100 yards he had booked a long-haired youth (a learner) for some offence or other (I didn't loiter near the scene). The lad had made the mistake of riding a humble but immaculate BSA Bantam, which didn't interest the fuzz at all.

Sometimes the police were obliged to issue cautions of the 'move this vehicle or else' variety, like the time I lived in Eaton Square with my Rolls-Royce and Vincent keeping each other company outside the front door (ah, happy days — no parking meters or traffic wardens). Classic motorcycles may be *à la mode* in Belgravia now, but in those days they were strictly *de trop*, especially my Rapide after I'd removed its petrol tank

to do some deft work on the top end. Around me lived various cabinet ministers, judges, and other members of the establishment, and soon there were complaints that my motorcycle was lowering the tone of the neighbourhood. Pressure from high places was soon brought to bear on the chief constable and he duly arrived on my doorstep and politely asked me to remove the vehicle, or I could be charged with 'leaving litter'. I merely detached the front end and stowed the bike in the back of the Rolls-Royce, where, looking more repulsive than ever, it remained on view to the public more prominently than before.

And there was nothing anyone could do to banish it from sight.

This Rapide, a Series C model, was a great improvement over the pre-war Rapide, giving greater fuel economy (55-60mpg) and better roadholding. However, the Black Shadow, which first appeared in February 1948, was the ultimate roadster for looks and performance, and I once owned the 1952 works show model. This beautiful beast, its chromium-plated nuts and bolts sparkling against the black engine like diamonds dripping down a wealthy woman's velvet gown, was good for well over the ton in third gear (I never did find out the top speed in fourth gear) with

superb roadholding to match its performance. This Black Shadow was my first Vincent V-twin, and almost immediately after buying it I was to experience this excellent roadholding which was largely due to the new Girdraulics designed by Phil Irving. These were incredibly robust and resisted my many inadvertent attempts to bend them.

New to the Vincent thousand, I took the bike round to a veteran Vinnie enthusiast, Charlie, and said, 'Steering seems odd.' I expected him to examine the bike from front number plate to the rear light, but he merely said, 'Jump on', and away we went to our test track.

We lived in Middlesex and the test track was a stretch of de-restricted road alongside PCV's old school, Harrow. Halfway along the route was a sharp bend under a bridge. As we approached this bend I stood up on the rear footrests and noted the speed — 94mph. I'd just resumed my seat when the bike did a sudden heave-ho and lurched round the bend. Charlie wrestled with the plot, brought it under control, and stopped. Then other Vincent owners arrived and someone suggested we put a gauge on the front tyre. Phew! It registered 10lb.

Before buying the Shadow I'd been offered a Black Lightning in road trim, but didn't think I was ready for its

Continued on next page

Continued from previous page

clutch slipped hopelessly after a few miles of running on the prototype model, fortunately not misbehaving until the editors of *The Motor Cycle* and *Motor Cycling* had sampled and approved its characteristics. Nothing we could do would cure the slip except to isolate the clutch from oil which entailed a partial redesign of the case, adding several oil seals and making an unwelcome increase in width of half an inch. This clutch has often been harshly criticised and it does have some defects, but many examples have stood up to very hard work and are still running after 30 years' service.

Another criticised component is the engine-shaft shock-absorber with its 18 small duplex springs instead of the usual single large square-section spring. Again, there were cogent reasons for the choice. One was that the new design was appreciably narrower, but a more pressing one was the difficulty of obtaining heavy spring wire while small springs were readily available.

My vivid memories of trying to start a BMW with a sidecar mounted on the left side prompted the decision to design the starting mechanism so that a pedal could be fitted on either side of the machine. A left-side starter pedal could be fitted by the owner using ordinary tools but quite a number were supplied to solo riders with sub-standard or artificial right legs.

In an endeavour to escape from the 'plumber's nightmare' tag that had been fastened to the A Rapide, all the oilways in the new engine were drilled and there were no external pipes except those to and from the oil pump. In order to get oil to the overhead gear immediately on start-up, the return pipe was coupled to the rocker bearing housings by bolts with small oil holes feeding each rocker as the oil passed by on its way to the tank. This system has the disadvantage that the flow to the rockers is practically constant, irrespective of engine speed, and continuous running at the low speeds at which the engine is quite happy causes too much oil to be re-circulated instead of being returned to the tank.

Consequently, it was subsequently found advisable to place restricter wires in the rocker feeds for the running-in period, but they can with advantage be removed if the majority of the work is fast. The reciprocating-plunger worm-drive Pilgrim pump was adopted as the best method of avoiding oil running back into the crankcase overnight, which is always a possibility with gear pumps. The complete pump, including a bronze barrel, was beautifully made by Pilgrim and to obviate cutting the plunger teeth at an angle to suit the driving worm, the hole for the barrel was machined at an angle of 2°40'. If necessary the barrel could be extracted by using a long crankcase bolt screwed into the end-plug — in fact, almost everything which ever needed removal either had tapped extractor holes or a self-withdrawing taper to avoid the necessity for special tools. At first, the pump worms were phosphor bronze but some wore rather rapidly and the material was changed to case-hardened mild steel.

The upper frame member which embodies the steering head, the engine mounts and the saddle and rear frame-spring attachments also formed a six-pint oil tank and was originally designed as a sheet steel construction with a head-tube welded in place. However, it seemed to be impossible to avoid some distortion during the welding which in effect twisted the head out of line but the structure was so rigid that the error could not be corrected. For this and other reasons, the steering head was made as a separate component which was bolted to the front of the upper frame member — a construction which has never been known to fail in service even after years of sidecar racing.

The design was also affected by what we thought was a need to minimise the amount of damage caused by the inevitable spill or even a major crash by keeping all fragile components close in and making all projecting parts either able to fold up or to give way without breaking off. Consequently a Rapide can be thrown up the road without strewing the countryside with electrical gear.

Of course, this is only half the story about the genesis of a machine which is probably the most criticised design ever produced, but enough has been said to explain some of the things we did and why they were done during a very difficult trading period. Despite the critics, few, if any, other models have achieved success in so many fields of activity with nothing more than minor alterations to the original specification.

Continued from previous page

performance — it was capable of around 135-140mph so was nearly as slow as the Laverda Jota produced two decades later.

Phil Irving, the designer of the Black Lightning, left the works in 1949 to return to Australia and for the next five years P C Vincent produced his range of 1,000cc and 500cc motorcycles practically unaltered. He also catered for the public's demand for mopeds by distributing very successfully the 49cc NSU Quickly and producing the NSU-Vincent Fox (98cc and 125cc). Another venture was the Firefly, which consisted of a 49cc engine slung in a pedal-cycle frame. Its 18mph cruising speed stretched the patience of testers, but one boosted his test mileage by rigging up his mount on a set of rollers every night before switching on the rollers and going to bed. The Firefly was never popular with VOC members, but as One Track once pointed out, it was very useful as hardcore. The Firefly was originally made by Millers, who also admitted responsibility for the dynamo used on Series B and C models. The dynamos on my oil-spreading Vincents never lasted long, and I would complain about my electrics until a cynical pal suggested that the Miller was probably chosen because it could run in oil longer than any other.

Anyway, when PCV designed the Series D range in 1954 he used a Lucas dynamo and also coil ignition. As a result of this thoughtful act the Beast became easy to start and many owners are leading useful, energetic lives instead of sitting around nursing broken ankles, knees or hernias. The main alteration to the frame was the substitution of a single unit joining the rear frame member to a tube with a casting at each end in place of the Series C set-up: two spring boxes with a damper in between linked to the upper frame member (which doubled as an oil tank).

Unfortunately, PCV did not produce a bike that people wanted — he made a machine he thought they should have, i.e. one incorporating weather protection. As always, he insisted on quality — the black fibreglass enclosures were stove-enamelled! (and today it's impossible to get the same quality of finish). The public regarded the fairings as ugly appurtenances. Worse, they hid the famous V-twin engine and lopped 10mph off the top speed. Despite the world records by Burns and Wright in 1955 the Black Prince and Black Knight models were unpopular — only some 200 were made — and production ceased in December.

I've owned a Black Knight, 'Sir Nigel', for several years and although the windscreen is efficient, the pendulum effect of the front fairings doesn't help the steering; neither does the 3.50 x 19in front tyre instead of the proven 3.00 x 19in size used on the Series C Vincents. Nevertheless, the enclosed Series D provides a more comfortable ride than its predecessor and is therefore less fatiguing on a long trip, especially during inclement weather. Whenever I halt for a while members of the public, in their materialistic way, paw the bike and bore me with their bleats of 'wossiworf'.

Why so many of us keep our Vincents for several years is difficult to say. It's true that spares are plentiful, the bike is easy to service due to the accessibility of carburettors, tappets, bearings, etc., the seat, footrests and controls can be adjusted to suit the rider, the engine and gearbox will give 100,000 miles before replacements are necessary, and the faster one goes, the better the bike handles.

The answer, perhaps, is that the Vincent was designed by motorcyclists for enthusiasts and owed its progeny to two keen riders of the thirties — P C Vincent, an idealist of steely determination, who dreamed of producing a 125mph roadster, and P E Irving, a realist of immense practical ability, who enabled the dream to come true.

The first of the few

THE VINCENT V-twin is unquestionably the high point of the English motorcycle industry. Its reappearance in the late forties should have resulted in the immediate demise of the parallel twin and shown up the revered Norton Featherbed frame for the 'damn great trellis' that it is. That neither of these things happened is a further indictment of both the industry and the people who bought its products.

Both Vincent and the original HRD company were progressive; the Rapide had hydraulically damped suspension at both ends before most of the competition even had suspension at both ends. HRD were fitting the now common cantilever type rear suspension by 1928, although public objection to rear springing was the main reason for this choice of layout — it could be made to look like a rigid! Possibly more important was the fact that the creators of the machine were both riders as well as designers and manufacturers, a rare event in post-war corporations. Even the inevitable accountant seems to have been enthusiastic about the product.

The 1,000cc model tested is a 1947 Series B Rapide, updated to 1949 C specification principally by the addition of Girdraulic front forks and a rear damper. The Rapide could be considered as the equivalent of the T3 in the Guzzi range, or perhaps the Darmah of the Ducati stable. Although derived from the pre-war A series, the B is the result of a most thorough redesign and a degree of cost-no-object elaboration which is unlikely ever to be equalled in the realms of motorcycle manufacturing. This work was carried out with the single intention of making an already good machine work better for longer, and when introduced in 1946 the Rapide was the fastest produc-

Royce Creasey rides two Stevenage products to discover if reality matches the myth.

Classic Test

1,000cc Vincent Rapide and 500cc Comet

tion machine in the world. Well documented tests have seen 100,000 miles pass without major parts in the engine having to be replaced.

There is nothing like enough room in this test (or the entire magazine, for that matter) to permit consideration of this bike in full detail, but some idea of the degree of refinement that went into it can be gained by examining one of the simpler components — the rear wheel. Although not qd in the accepted sense, it can be removed in minutes using only a pair of pliers for the chain link. Torque arms for the twin brakes are retained by spring clips, and slackening the tommy bar on the axle allows the chain adjusters to be taken up by hand. Each click of the adjusters provides for about 300 miles of use. The wheel will fit either way round, has two sprockets to give alternative ratios and runs on adjustable rollers.

This kind of detailed thinking pervades the whole bike, and the adjustability extends to assembly settings. Half-time pinions come in .001in steps, over- and under-size. to get that timing gear backlash just right. Elaboration at this level can be criticised as extremely expensive, resulting in high prices, low sales — and eventual extinction. It is probable that if more thought had been devoted to the producton engineering side of the Vincent, costs could have been reduced without cheapening the bike, yet the Rapide justifies itself simply by still being here, thirty years later.

Apart from this detailing, which current fashion increasingly decries and is only of interest when the bike is not being ridden, there is the matter of the basic design. Messrs Vincent and Irving were more than progressive; they also had theories, and the chief among them was that wheel spindles should always stay in

Weighing less than 400lb, the Comet is agile and sure-footed in tight corners.

Bold tester uses up the ground clearance on Vincent's big one; the Rapide offers very stable handling characteristics.

line. The necessary stiffness to achieve this was the chief target of the post-war rethink. Frame flexing was dealt with at source by the removal of the frame; the headstock is fixed to a sheet-metal triangular oil tank which bolts to the cylinder heads and picks up the rear suspension struts. Words like 'neat' help one avoid becoming emotional when considering the elegance of this solution. The front forks are a similarly concinnate attempt to combine the rigidity of girders with the ride of telescopics, and include forged high-duty alloy blades. Modern thought indicates that keeping the wheels on the ground may be more useful than the benefits offered by the Vincent arrangement, and the Girdraulics on the Rapide are stuck with a high unsprung weight when compared with contemporary telescopic forks. In practice, the immense stiffness and stability of the Vincent design easily compensates for the slightly poorer ride, and the complete absence of dive under braking is an advantage that telescopics cannot match.

The suspension quality of the Girdraulics unfortunately relies on careful maintenance, although bearing life is around 20,000 miles, similar to that on the latest telescopics. It is very probable that the reputation the Vincent gained in the sixties for developing killer wobbles at speed was the result of unmaintained forks in what the VOC would probably call 'the wrong hands'. Anomalies in the design include mounting the headlight and speedo unsprung, and fitting cup 'n' cone head bearings when taper rollers appear everywhere else. Purpose-built Koni dampers are available for the Girdraulics, and indeed all the Vincent suspensions, and the level of performance is such that it would not be absurd for Ducati (for instance) to seriously consider an updated version of this fork for next year's model.

The rear suspension doesn't quite reach the standard of the front end, probably because when the cantilever layout was introduced it was so much better than anything else that no one noticed it wasn't perfect. Wheel control is fine, it's just a little flexible, and consideration of the rear fork reveals uncharacteristic lapses such as curved tubes and an absence of bracing. Carrying a passenger increases the flex considerably, as the rear seat supports act as levers on the fork, a defect that was cured on the later D model when the seat was mounted on a more conventional subframe. None of the passengers carried seemed to notice the unsprung nature of their end of the seat — numbed minds were more common than numbed backsides as a reaction to the Vincent experience.

The engine is undoubtedly the main visual attraction on the big Vincents. Its design is less than perfect; what can reasonably be described as over-elaboration causes its own problems in terms of fragility in some parts and very high rebuild costs. Technology has passed

by the hemispherical head, and in theory the Vincent's output and fuel and oil consumption do not meet modern standards. In practice it is a very pleasant device indeed, having the best match of bike, flywheel and reciprocating weights I've yet encountered. Flexibilty and response are exceptional, the transmission is snatch-free, and the degree of engine braking is just right. The rider can vary the output from just enough to keep the flywheels topped up whilst floating round town, to what has been justifiably described as 'constant and colossal' from nowhere to much too fast. The test Rapide is run regularly and was consequently in good adjustment. Starting in the morning was normally a one-kick affair and although its owner, Jack Barker (the social secretary of the VOC), told me it leaked oil, I never did find out where.

The gearchange suffers from the possibility of play between the positive stop and the selector cam, while a dragging clutch can make first impossible to engage even though the lever moves. At speed the change is delicate and a little slow, kidding you that it's better than it is until you relax and it rejects your selection. The clutch drag on Jack's machine was caused by new shoes, which improved considerably during the 600 miles of the test as they bedded in.

Shoes . . ? On a clutch . . ? Yes, well the Vincent clutch takes off where Hall Green gave up, and what's more it was all done on purpose. Deciding that 45bhp and a lot of torque were too much for the hand-operated clutches of the day, the design team settled on an all-power mechanical servo device as the solution. This component uses engine power to hold the friction surfaces together, while the lever connects and disconnects engine power. In extremely crude terms it works thus: engine power is fed into a simple single-plate clutch, and the output from this clutch can be considered as turning the actuating cam of a conventional drum brake. The 'brake shoes' are connected to the gearbox and the 'brake drum' to the engine. Simple, innit? Keen students will immediately spot that it can't be that easy and may rest assured that it isn't. In practice the primary clutch, which loads torque into the main clutch, will drive the bike up to around 50 mph, and centrifugal force assists marginally at the highest engine speeds. It's really worth reading up on the subject just to see how far out of hand clutch design can get.

Servo clutches traditionally suffer from various ills — they include sensitivity to weather conditions and a fairly random mode of operation. All these defects are detectable in the Vincent unit, but in entirely bearable moderation. The rest of the world would appear to have been better advised in either improving friction materials until they could take large power outputs or, more rarely, providing for servo actuation of a heavily sprung conventional clutch. This is the Velocette method, although it may have been an accident.

In engineering terms the Vincent clutch is unsupportable, but in practice it justifies its presence by providing a whole lot of fun. The Cosmic Supply Company must have had a hand in its origination, as the first touch of the primary clutch plates guarantees that anything may take place, from gradual, automatic take-up to 100 per cent connection between two firing pulses. An incidental advantage of all this uncertainty is that the evident concentration of the rider as a Vincent moves off the line acts as a complete deterrent to would-be racers. They invariably mistake the Vincent man's

Mighty 50-degree Vee is elaborate, powerful, flexible and smooth — the greatest of all the British engines?

Girdraulic fork — is arguably the best non-telescopic front end in motorcycling.

attempt to be gentle with expensive and ageing machinery for fear that wheelspin and wheelie will occur simultaneously! Incidentally, the engine, transmission and frame all seem to be quite capable of standing up to the vagaries of the clutch's performance.

Once the Vincent is rolling, however, these considerations of various oily bits of machinery become progressively irrelevant. With the bike at a standstill, the motor sounds like a worn-out tractor as it ticks over, as do Porsche and Coventry-Climax engines. But by the time the mid-eighties have been reached, all the rider is conscious of is a distant thunder, and the universe rippling past. Even moderate use of more throttle at this speed gives the impression that the bike is still while the horizon is being dragged helplessly closer. The noise levels produced by a stately but determined lift-off are of the sort commonly associated with the appearance of cracks in the road and collapsing buildings — Godzilla speaks when a Vincent moves! The heavy flywheels allow short bursts of throttle to carry the bike a considerable distance in almost complete silence, and the rider frequently arrives in the situation of overtaking other vehicles while the engine is on the over-run.

In terms of the riding experience, it is true of most of the English classics that they accomplish little that is not done better by other machines, but generally excel at managing everything rather well. This thirty-year-old Rapide does almost everything as well as the best moderns, and some things better. Fitted with Avon

Roadrunners and longer than standard Petteford springs to improve ride and ground clearance, the stability at extreme angles of lean is exceptional. Both ends begin to drift simultaneously, the high degree of stiffness permits easy control, and the bike leaves corners exactly on line. If a wrong line is chosen, correction can be carried out without the bike lapsing into weave or plunge, although the front forks can be confused by sudden movements. In particular, tight corners get the bike a little out of shape if taken by storm; the 'slow in, fast out' approach pays off, as the big Vincent needs to be poured rather than thrown into turns.

This excellent controlability and the engine's massive torque are matched by the plunge-free performance of the braking system which, although badly affected by water, is the match of the best double-disc units I've tried. It's true that these drums would fade first on the race track, but on the road the ease with which the front tyre can be just squealed right up to the point of slipping into a corner is virtually unique. At speed the steering needs pushing into turns, and although the Vincent front end is often accused of being heavy at low speed, the feel from the front tyre is very good. Tight corners in urban back streets require an application of the rear brakes to lighten the steering, but the lever pressure is high and more sensitivity would be useful. I am an enthusiastic supporter of this sort of handling, and the similarity of feel between the Velocette Venom and the Rapide is uncanny. In curves the two bikes follow exactly similar lines, the

Vincent drifting a little further out due to its slightly higher weight — which is far lower than any current production one-litre motorcycle.

In the period that the Vincent was being made the best roads in the country were of the type now considered lesser A roads. They were two-lane black-tops, with hills and curves and little villages. The A4155 from Sonning to Henley in Berkshire is an example, and running down it on the Rapide one evening at speeds I'm definitely not going to discuss qualifies as one of the year's great trips. The bike followed the road so easily that I had little to do but sit there, moving fingers and toes, mind blowing in the breeze. On more modern roads speeds are limited as usual by rider fatigue, and constant fast riding on these routes would require some sort of fairing such as the interesting bodywork fitted to the later D series Black Prince. There are certainly several bikes that can attain a higher speed sooner than the Rapide, but very few that could match it cross-country over long distances.

The little relative of the V-twins, the 500cc Comet, uses identical cycle parts. The minor difference in wheelbase is the result of detail alterations to the crankcase mountings, a cast bridge replacing the rear cylinder as a structural member. More importantly, the flywheels are essentially similar to those fitted to the larger engines, and this huge excess of weight overwhelms the single's output. The result feels like an Edwardian BSA B40, and the Comet is an example of how easy it is to spoil a good package by

The D Series centre stand in its folded position — the knack of hauling the bike onto it must be learnt.

For a 500, the Comet has big engine cases full of big flywheels, but its 28 bhp output is just not enough.

Single-cylinder engine looks slightly lost in the Comet. Cast bridge-piece takes the place of the bigger unit's rear cylinder.

Vincent ingenuity at the rear end produced a qd wheel with dual sprockets and chain adjustment at the twist of a knob.

changing a part of it. Naturally, the brakes and handling are very good, while the lower weight makes the Comet appreciably faster round tight corners than the Rapide. But the overall effect of the bike is still spoiled by its meagre power delivery. Until fairly high engine revs are reached throttle movement merely results in more noise being generated as the engine attempts to speed up the flywheels, and although the bike seems quite fast it lacks the balance of the better 500s from other manufacturers. The lack of that so-interesting servo clutch reduces the fun still further, and I have to say that I found the Comet a considerable disappointment.

It is traditional to provide some kind of summary of a bike under test, perhaps rating it against its contemporaries. But during the Vincent's period of manufacture there were no comparable machines, it was that far ahead of anything else being made. Turning to the designs produced in any period, we discover a few motorcycles that work so well that the rider can forget that a machine is involved. This is the end to which the best bikes have always aimed, the supply of an unequalled sensation with the minimum of interference from horrid machinery. These bikes can be counted on the fingers and come almost exclusively from Europe. They are regarded with what amounts to reverence by the riders who have experienced them, and are typically produced in rather smaller numbers than the 'superbikes' that flood the market. They are the few. The Vincent V-twin was the first of the few.

In Brief

	1947 VINCENT RAPIDE (modified to 1949 spec)	1950 VINCENT COMET
ENGINE		
Type	50 deg high cam V-twin	high cam single
Bore x stroke	84 x 90mm	84 x 90mm
Capacity	998cc	499cc
Compression ratio	7.5:1	6.8:1
Carburation	2 x 1⅛in Amal Monobloc	1⅛in Amal Monobloc
BHP @ rpm	45 @ 5,300	28 @ 5,800
Ignition	Lucas KVF GM1 magneto	Lucas K1F magneto
TRANSMISSION		
Primary drive	Triplex chain	single-row chain
Clutch	self-servo, single-plate	multi-plate
Gearbox	4 speed	4 speed
CYCLE PARTS		
Frame	engine used as main frame member	engine used as main frame member
Suspension	Girdraulic front forks; cantilever rear end	Girdraulic front forks, cantilever rear end
Tyres		
(front)	3.60 x 19 Avon Roadrunner	3.60 x 19 Avon Roadrunner
(rear)	4.10 x 19 Avon Roadrunner	4.10 x 19 Avon Roadrunner
Brakes		
(front)	2 x 7in sls drums	2 x 7in sls drums
(rear)	2 x 7in sls drums	2 x 7in sls drums
Wheelbase	56.5in	55.75in
Seat height	33in	33in
Ground clearance	6in	6in
Dry weight	468lb	390lb
Fuel capacity	3½gal	3½gal
PERFORMANCE		
Top speed	110mph (est)	90mph (est)
Standing ¼ mile	14.0secs (est)	18.0secs (est)
Fuel consumption	48mpg	70mpg
OWNER	Jack Barker, Gloucestershire.	

BEAST

It's now almost 25 years since the last Vincent V-twin rolled off the production line, but Ken Corkett discovered that it's not just the legend that lives on

THE legendary Vincent 1000 almost never happened; in fact, if on a certain day in 1936 design engineer Phil Irving had taken time off, we might have been cheated of one of the greatest motorcycles of all time. Irving had a drawing and a tracing of the Vincent 500cc single on his desk. For no particular reason, he inverted the tracing and laid it on top of the drawing, lining up the centres of the crankshaft pinion and timing gear idler wheel as he did so. Then it dawned on him — he had the ready made blueprint for a V-twin!

Phil Vincent, who had taken over the defunct HRD company, was called and soon became enthusiastic about building a big twin. In a short time the Series A Rapide was born.

The Rapide quickly won a reputation for high performance and exceptional flexibility. George Brown, among others, lapped Brooklands at over 100mph. Vincents had arrived!

However, it wasn't all plain sailing. The torque of the engine proved too much for the clutch, and the Burman gearbox failed regularly despite extensive modifications. The Series A, affectionately known as the 'Plumber's Nightmare' because of its profusion of external oil pipes, was coming to the end of its production life at the start of World War II in 1939.

After the war Irving and Vincent set about designing a new model — the Series B Rapide. All that remained of the Series A was the cantilever rear suspension and the engine's 84 x 90mm bore and stroke. The angle of the V was increased from 47 degrees to 50 to suit available magnetos.

Left: a Vincent Series C Rapide. Top left: alternative sprocket could be carried on opposite side of rear wheel. Cantilever frame was a consistent feature. Top right: note massive alloy castings and magneto cowling. Twin sidestands could be reversed to support front end. Above left: dual brakes front and rear were used up to Series D

The Series A had a wheelbase of 58.5 inches, due mainly to cramming the huge engine into a conventional frame, but the B's wheelbase was reduced to 56.5 inches by using the box-section oil tank as a top tube from which the engine / gearbox unit was suspended as a structural member. The new gearbox had none of the earlier unit's weaknesses and final ratios were determined by choice of rear sprocket.

The clutch was unique in that it had a single-plate pilot unit for pulling away; then, as power came in, a pair of shoes locked into contact with the drum — an all-power, mechanical servo device, in fact. It could be very fierce, and a pig to get used to, but once set up properly was no trouble. The primary chain was triplex with a massive slipper tensioner, but the poor old ⅝x ⅜-inch rear chain would not last long if you habitually used full performance.

WHEELS & SUSPENSION

Both wheels were more or less QD and secured by large wing-nuts and, apart from the need for a pair of pliers to remove the chain link, could be removed from the machine in minutes without using tools. Chain adjustment was by finger-operated knurled adjusters.

The Bs had a friction - damped Brampton girder front fork which many riders preferred to their successors, the Vincent Girdraulics. Girdraulics — an attempt to combine the best features of girder and telescopic forks — consisted of two light-alloy blades, two pairs of long springs and an hydraulic damper. Their handling characteristics took a little getting used to as there was no 'sinking at the head' as with telescopic forks.

Changing to sidecar trail was accomplished by turning the eccentric bushes round so that the long springs lay closer to the alloy blades. On Bs the rear suspension had two springs with no dampers, but Cs all had a central damper fitted.

The Vincent slogan was: 'The World's Fastest Standard Motorcycle', which it undoubtedly was. Record breakers were

The Shadow's handlebar layout is dominated by a massive 150 mph speedometer

quick to see its potential and in 1948 an American, Rollie Free, topped 150mph on a racing version of the 1000, called the Black Lightning, to capture the US solo record. New Zealanders Russell Wright and Robbie Burns took the world solo record to 185mph and sidecar record to 163mph, while George Brown, first on *Gunga Din* and then *Nero* and *Super Nero*, set enough sprint and hill-climb records to fill a book.

The standard Rapide was the tourer with its 110mph top speed and 7.5:1 compression ratio, while the sporting version was the Black Shadow with 8.5:1 compression ratio and a top speed of 125mph. This marvellous machine would cruise at 100mph, turning over at just 4300rpm, and rarely returned less than 50mpg — often a lot more.

At first glance, the main difference between the Shadow and the Rapide appears to be cosmetic. The Rapide was all silver except for the black tank. The Shadow had black anodised heads and barrels with stove-enamelled crankcases and covers. However, on closer inspection, you note that the Shadow's four brake drums are ribbed for better cooling, and the carbs are bigger. Naturally its cams are a little wilder, too. The massive, and extremely accurate, 150mph Shadow speedometer is another obvious feature.

FINAL YEARS

The last models made at the Vincent factory in Stevenage were the Series Ds; fully enclosed bikes which, although they had a lot going for them, were perhaps a little too revolutionary for the times. Gone was the brutish power appeal of the naked Vinnie and in its place was

a fully faired missile.

The Rapide equivalent was the Black Knight, while the Shadow became the Black Prince and the magneto gave way to coil ignition. Armstrong suspension units were used at the rear and a huge handle lay along the left hand side of the machine for lifting the bike on to its stand.

Alas, Vincent's last bid to boost sales failed and in 1955 production ceased. Reckoned a heavyweight in the 1950s, the Black Prince weighed about 460lb — light when compared to most of today's machinery.

Today, Vincent twins are more popular than they have ever been. In 1953 a brand new Black Shadow would have cost you £366, at a time when Triumph's high-performance 650 Tiger 110 was on offer at £240. A total of 11,000 Vincents — both singles and twins — were built, and perhaps half that number have survived. During the 1960s, in company with all old motorcycles, they became almost valueless and £50 might have bought you a reasonable example. Reflecting the recent massive growth of interest in classic motorcycles, you will be unable to secure a twin now for less than £3000.

Ironically, owning and maintaining a Vincent today is easier than it was when the bikes were still being manufactured. This is largely due to the foresight of the Vincent HRD Owners' Club, founded in 1948 and one of the largest and most efficient motorcycle organisations in the world.

Although the Vincent nam and what remained at the Stev nage factory was bought i 1974 by Matt Holder of the Bi mingham-based Aerco Jig an Tool Co — owner of the Scot Velocette and Royal Enfiel names — the club set up a sepa rate manufacturing company t produce Vincent spares in 197! The VOC Spares Co Ltd, limited company with £50,00 share capital, runs a thrivin wholesale and retail busines from premises at The Whar Burford Lane, Lymm, Cheshir (Lymm 3367). With parts avai able from Matt Holder through select band of dealers like Cor way Motors in London, VO Spares and other sources, th Vincent owner is well served.

READING MATTER

Likewise, there is an extensiv range of literature devoted to th history, care and exploits of Th Snarling Beast. The whole Vin cent saga is contained in *Th Vincent H.R.D. Story* by Ro Harper, *P.C.V. An Auto biography* by Philip Vincent, an *Fifty Years Of The Marque*. Als published by the Vincer Publishing Company is E.M.C Stevens' *Know Thy Beast*, th totally comprehensive an amazingly detailed Vincer owners' bible that's vital fo anyone contemplating restorin or running a post-war model. A four books are available fror Roy Harper & Co, 35 Gunte Grove, King's Road, Londo SW10 (01-352 4744).

So the legend of 'The World' Fastest Standard Motorcycle lives on into the 1980s. It' hardly surprising that it should for what other machine 25 year out of production can compar with modern superbikes on pe formance and remain more tha a match for them in terms o economy?